Lecture Notes in Computer Science 13590

More information about this series at https://www.springer.com/bookseries/558

Tomáš Skopal · Fabrizio Falchi · Jakub Lokoč ·
Maria Luisa Sapino · Ilaria Bartolini ·
Marco Patella (Eds.)

Similarity Search and Applications

15th International Conference, SISAP 2022
Bologna, Italy, October 5–7, 2022
Proceedings

Editors

Tomáš Skopal (ID)
Charles University
Prague, Czech Republic

Fabrizio Falchi (ID)
ISTI-CNR
Pisa, Italy

Jakub Lokoč (ID)
Charles University
Prague, Czech Republic

Maria Luisa Sapino (ID)
University of Torino
Torino, Italy

Ilaria Bartolini (ID)
University of Bologna
Bologna, Italy

Marco Patella (ID)
University of Bologna
Bologna, Italy

ISSN 0302-9743   ISSN 1611-3349 (electronic)
Lecture Notes in Computer Science
ISBN 978-3-031-17848-1   ISBN 978-3-031-17849-8 (eBook)
https://doi.org/10.1007/978-3-031-17849-8

This Springer imprint is published by the registered company Springer Nature Switzerland AG
The registered company address is: Gewerbestrasse 11, 6330 Cham, Switzerland

Preface

This volume contains the papers presented at the 15th International Conference on Similarity Search and Applications (SISAP 2022) held in Bologna during October 5–7, 2022. The conference was hosted by the University of Bologna and marked the return of SISAP as a hybrid event, after the two previous editions were held virtually due to the COVID-19 pandemic.

Classic domains like data mining, multimedia information retrieval, computer vision, pattern recognition, computational biology, geography, biometrics, machine learning, and many others still require novel similarity search modeling and data management approaches. Hence, SISAP has become a popular annual international conference for researchers focusing on similarity search challenges and related theoretical/practical problems, as well as the design of content-based similarity search applications. Many of the findings and projects have already been shared by the community in a gradually growing repository, allowing effective progress in many established challenges.

Traditionally, the call for papers welcomes full/short research papers, position papers, and demonstration papers, all presenting previously unpublished research contributions. SISAP 2022 also included the fourth edition of the SISAP Doctoral Symposium, allowing presentation of novel works of PhD students and productive interaction of young researchers with the international community.

This year, SISAP received 34 submissions from authors based in 18 different countries. The Program Committee (PC) was composed of 41 members from 16 countries. Each submission received three reviews, and the papers and reviews were thoroughly discussed by the chairs and PC members. Based on the reviews and discussions, the PC chairs accepted 15 full papers and eight short/demo papers, resulting in an acceptance rate of 48% for the full papers and a cumulative acceptance rate of 74% for full and short papers. After a separate review by the Doctoral Symposium Program Committee members, two Doctoral Symposium papers (out of three submitted manuscripts) were accepted for presentation and included in the program and proceedings.

The proceedings of SISAP are published by Springer in this volume in the Lecture Notes in Computer Science (LNCS) series. For SISAP 2022, as in previous years, there were also awards for the Best Paper, Best Student Paper, and Best Doctoral Symposium Paper, as judged by the PC chairs and the Steering Committee. The authors of selected excellent papers (based on reviews and presentation) were invited to submit more elaborate versions for publication in a special issue of the Information Systems (Elsevier) journal.

We would like to thank all members of the Program Committee for their effort and energy given to the conference. Next, we want to acknowledge our gratitude to the members of the organizing committee for the vast amount of work they have done, and to our sponsors and supporters for their generosity. Finally, we thank all the participants in the event who constitute the unique SISAP community.

August 2022   Tomáš Skopal
                                                                                  Fabrizio Falchi
                                                                                  Jakub Lokoč
                                                                                  Maria Luisa Sapino
                                                                                  Ilaria Bartolini
                                                                                  Marco Patella

Organization

General Chairs

Ilaria Bartolini   University of Bologna, Italy
Marco Patella   University of Bologna, Italy

Program Committee Chairs

Tomáš Skopal   Charles University, Czech Republic
Fabrizio Falchi   ISTI-CNR, Italy

Doctoral Symposium Chair

Maria Luisa Sapino   University of Turin, Italy

Publication Chair

Jakub Lokoč   Charles University, Czech Republic

Publicity Chair

Karina Figueroa   Universidad Michoacana de San Nicolás de Hidalgo, México

Steering Committee

Giuseppe Amato   ISTI-CNR, Italy
Edgar Chávez   CICESE, México
Stéphane Marchand-Maillet   University of Geneva, Switzerland
Pavel Zezula   Masaryk University, Czech Republic

Program Committee

Giuseppe Amato   ISTI-CNR, Italy
Laurent Amsaleg   CNRS-IRISA, France
Fabrizio Angiulli   University of Calabria, Italy
Ilaria Bartolini   University of Bologna, Italy
Panagiotis Bouros   Johannes Gutenberg University Mainz, Germany
K. Selcuk Candan   Arizona State University, USA

Contents

Doctoral Symposium

Applications

Numerical Data Imputation: Choose kNN over Deep Learning

Florian Lalande(✉) [ID] and Kenji Doya [ID]

Okinawa Institute of Science and Technology, 1919-1 Tancha, Onna-son,
Okinawa, Japan
`florian.lalande@oist.jp`

Abstract. Artificial neural networks (ANNs) are now ubiquitous in data science. In this respect, Deep-Learning (DL) methods have been developed to address missing data problems. The present study compares state-of-the-art DL Generative Adversarial Network (GAN) models with the well-established kNN algorithm (1951) for numerical data imputation. Using real-world and generated datasets in various missing data scenarios, we show that the good old kNN algorithm is still competitive with powerful DL algorithms for numerical data imputation. This review consolidates the emerging consensus that numerical data imputation does not necessarily require powerful or heavy DL tools.

Keywords: Data imputation · Deep learning · GAN · KNN

1 Introduction

Missing values is a serious issue in data science. Incomplete datasets result from uncollected, lost, censured or corrupted observations. Most machine learning (ML) algorithms cannot handle datasets with missing entries, and meticulous data preprocessing is therefore needed. The standard list-wise deletion (keeping only complete entries) has two main disadvantages: it greatly reduces the size of the dataset and induces a bias, which may lead to false positive claims [11][1].

Data imputation is an alternative preprocessing method involving estimation and replacement of the missing values. It allows to preserve the whole dataset for analysis but requires careful handling as it can also introduce a bias in the imputed dataset [6].

Many data imputation algorithms have been proposed: Mean-value substitution [10], C4.5 algorithm [15], CN2 induction algorithm [3], kNN (originally developed in 1951 [5], later adapted to data imputation [17]) or MissForest [16]. The kNN has shown best imputation quality among these various data imputation algorithms [1, 2, 8, 9, 14].

---

[1] Full code available at: https://github.com/DeltaFloflo/imputation_comparison.

Supplementary Information The online version contains supplementary material available at https://doi.org/10.1007/978-3-031-17849-8_1.

T. Skopal et al. (Eds.): SISAP 2022, LNCS 13590, pp. 3–10, 2022.
https://doi.org/10.1007/978-3-031-17849-8_1

But over the last decade, ANNs and DL have transformed the fields of statistics, computer science and data analysis. Notably, GANs have shown spectacular results at generating new observations from a given data distribution [7]. As such, GAN models have been developed to tackle the problem of missing values in data science. GAIN [18] and MisGAN [12] are two new GAN-based data imputation methods. While GAIN has been specifically developed for numerical data imputation, MisGAN is primarily designed to impute degraded images but can be adapted to work with tabular numerical data.

This work intends to compare data imputation performances of state-of-the-art GAN models (GAIN and MisGAN) with the standard and already established k-Nearest Neighbors algorithm (kNN). We evaluate the imputation quality in MCAR, MAR and MNAR scenarios (Sect. 2.1). This study is restricted to tabular numerical data, that is numerical data we can arrange into rows and columns in the form of a table with cells.

2 Data Imputation Setup

2.1 Missing Data Settings

Let x denote the complete vector of a given observation and m its missing value binary mask. Available data is the element-wise product $\widetilde{x} = x \odot m$. Data imputation methods seek to estimate the missing values of $\widetilde{x}$ by using patterns in the observed values. The probability distribution of m is referred to as the *missing data mechanism*.

Following the classification of Little and Rubin [13], missing data setups belong to one of the following three settings. **Missing Completely At Random (MCAR)**, where the missing data mechanism is assumed to be independent of the intrinsic probability distribution of x, and occurs completely at random, such that $p(m|x) = p(m)$. **Missing At Random (MAR)**, where the missing data mechanism can be fully explained by the observed data, i.e. $p(m|x) = p(m|\widetilde{x})$. Finally, **Missing Not At Random (MNAR)** which encompasses every other setting: the reason why data is missing depends on unobserved variables.

2.2 Data Imputation Algorithms

Generative Adversarial Imputation Nets (GAIN) have been proposed in 2018 as a GAN model specifically designed for numerical data imputation problems. GAIN generalizes the well-established architecture of GAN models by looking at individual cells rather than complete rows. The authors report state-of-the art imputation quality performances [18]. GAIN's parameters are updated to minimize the binary cross-entropy loss function for the discriminator on one hand, and a combination of the binary cross-entropy (for the generated cells) and the RMSE for the discriminator on the other.

MisGAN has been introduced in 2019 as another GAN model framework capable of handling complex datasets with missing values. Primarily developed for image completion, it can be adapted to handle numerical data. MisGAN claims state-of-the-art imputation quality for images [12]. MisGAN has three pairs of generator and discriminator. A first pair (G_x, D_x) attempts to model the probability distribution of the data, while another pair (G_m, D_m) tries to model the missing data mechanism. Both generators G_x and G_m are used in parallel to produce fake deteriorated observations. Finally, a third pair (G_i, D_i) is used to perform the imputation of missing values. When adapted to tabular data, the missing data mechanism has a multinomial distribution and does not require DL to be modeled. Instead, we choose to draw missing masks directly from the dataset distribution.

Finally, the **k-Nearest Neighbors (kNN)** algorithm is a non-parametric method, originally developed for classification in 1951 [5]. For data imputation tasks, the kNN algorithm selects the k nearest neighbors of a given incomplete observation, and uses available data from the selected neighbors to estimate missing values [17]. Despite its simplicity and its age, the kNN algorithm has been shown to outperform traditional data imputation algorithms [1,2,8,9,14]. The kNN imputes missing values using a weighted average of the selected neighbors. The most two common weighting systems are `uniform` and `distance`, respectively defined by $\frac{1}{k}$ (where k is the number of neighbors) and $\frac{1}{d_{ij}}$ (where d_{ij} is the distance between observations i and j. We respectively refer to these algorithms with the names kNN-uniform and kNN-distance.

2.3   Datasets

Seven real-world (from UCI ML Repository [4]) and two simulated datasets are used. For reproducibility, we use the same datasets used by authors of GAIN [18]. Two additional datasets have been selected: white wine and red wine datasets. We have also generated two Gaussian datasets, using random factors to create correlations. An extensive description of the datasets at play is provided in the Supplementary Materials. Table 1 shows the size of the nine datasets.

3   Methods

We begin by finding the appropriate hyperparameters for each method – the number of training epochs for GAIN and MisGAN, and the number of neighbors for the kNN. Then, we conduct several experiments with varying missing rates, missing data scenarios and datasets. Throughout the following experiments, we first inject missing values and immediately scale the datasets in the range $[0, 1]$ using min-max normalization. After imputation, the performances are computed using the normalized RMSE between ground truth and imputed missing values. Each experiment is repeated 20 times, and we report the mean and standard deviation of the RMSE.

3.1   Hyperparameters Tuning

We use the generated mixture of three Gaussians dataset (`mydata2` dataset) in MCAR scenario with 20% missing rate to select the optimal hyperparameters. Results are provided in Fig. 1.

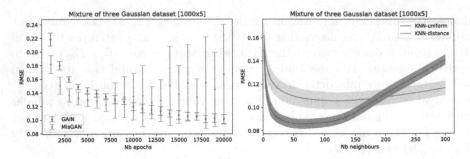

Fig. 1. Hyperparameter selection using the imputation RMSE on `mydata2` dataset in MCAR scenario with 20% missing rate. **(left)** For GAN models, we choose 5,000 epochs for MisGAN and 20,000 epochs for GAIN. **(right)** For the KNN algorithms, the optimal number of neighbors lies close to $N = 50$ neighbors.

For GAIN and MisGAN, we use from $1,000$ to $20,000$ epochs and choose the number of epochs that minimizes the imputation RMSE: approximately $20,000$ epochs for GAIN and $5,000$ epochs for MisGAN (see left panel of Fig. 1). MisGAN becomes unstable after $7,000$ epochs. As the RMSE of GAIN keeps decreasing, we train for more epochs (from $10,000$ to $100,000$ by steps of $10,000$ epochs) and found no improvement beyond $20,000$ epochs. We decide to fix the hyperparameter of GAIN at $20,000$ epochs.

For the kNN, we select $k = 50$ neighbors to minimize the imputation RMSE for both weight systems (see right panel of Fig. 1).

As these hyperparameters strongly depend on the dataset size and have been tuned on a dataset with $1,000$ observations, we apply a multiplicative factor to preserve similar proportions $f = \frac{n}{1000}$ for the following experiments, where n is the number of rows in the corresponding dataset. The number of training epochs accordingly becomes $\frac{5000}{f}$ for MisGAN and $\frac{20000}{f}$ for GAIN, and the number of neighbors is $50f$ for both kNN algorithms.

3.2   Imputation Experiment Designs

The following experiments are conducted 20. The mean and standard deviation of the imputation RMSE are provided in the next section.

1. Varying missing rate in MCAR setting from 10% to 80% (by steps of 10%) with the generated mixture of three Gaussians dataset
2. Real-world datasets in MCAR setting with 20% missing rate
3. All datasets in MAR setting, with overall 20% and 45% missing rates
4. All datasets in MNAR setting, with overall 20% and 45% missing rates

To generate MAR missing values, we subjectively select a column that we keep untouched throughout the full MAR experiment. We compute the quantiles of the selected column, scale the quantiles between 0 and 2μ (where μ is the overall missing rate) and interpret these values as common missing rates for all other columns. The selected variable for each dataset along with its meaning are reported in Table 1.

Table 1. List of the selected variables for MAR settings. Dataset sizes are also provided as well as the column number of the variable used to generate MAR missing data.

Dataset name	Size	MAR column	Meaning
breast	(569, 30)	0	Mean cell radius
credit	(30000, 14)	1	Customer age
letter	(20000, 16)	4	Total number of black pixels
news	(39644, 44)	0	Number of words in the title
spam	(4601, 57)	54	Average length of uppercase letter
wine_red	(1599, 12)	0	Fixed acidity
wine_white	(4898, 12)	0	Fixed acidity
mydata1	(1000, 5)	0	No meaning
mydata2	(1000, 5)	0	No meaning

To generate MNAR missing values, we compute the quantiles for every individual column (in the same way as MAR setting) which we scale in the interval $[0, 2\,\mu]$. We interpret these values as the missing probability for every corresponding cell. In MNAR settings, the higher the value of a cell relatively to its column, the more likely it will be missing.

4   Results and Interpretation

4.1   Varying Missing Rate in MCAR Setting

The imputation results are shown on the left panel of Fig. 2. As the RMSE for MisGAN is comparatively large, we only display the results of GAIN and kNN for clarity. We do not show the results of MisGAN for now on. Full results are available in the Supplementary Materials. Not surprisingly, the performances of GAIN and kNN deteriorate with increasing missing rates. GAIN and both kNN algorithms have comparable performances against varying missing rates.

4.2   Real-World Datasets in MCAR Setting

The right panel of Fig. 2 shows the imputation results, for this experiment. We see that both kNN algorithms perform better than GAIN over all available datasets. Note that we could not reproduce GAIN performances results.

From now, we also do not report the RMSE for the news dataset since the per formances have huge standard deviations regardless of the imputation method. This arises because of the nature of the news dataset: extremely sparse with few extreme outliers. The supplementary Materials provide full results.

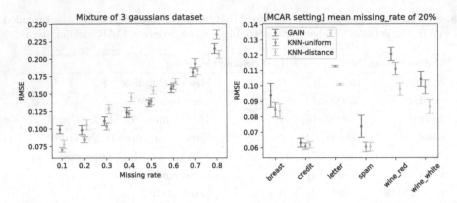

Fig. 2. MCAR scenario experiments. **(left)** Imputation RMSE for the mixture of 3 Gaussians dataset with varying missing rates. **(right)** Imputation RMSE for all real-world datasets (except the `news` dataset).

4.3 MAR Experiments

This paragraph refers to Fig. 3. With a missing rate of 20% in MAR setting, both kNN algorithms overall perform slightly better than GAIN. With a missing rate of 45%, the overall imputation quality deteriorates and the performances of GAIN, kNN-uniform and kNN-distance are now on par, with sometimes one method significantly performing better. Note that the trends and orders of magnitude do not change across datasets when the missing rate increases (from the left panel to the right).

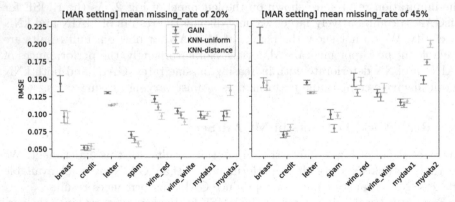

Fig. 3. MAR scenario experiments for all datasets. **(left)** MAR setting with average missing rate of 20%. **(right)** MAR setting with average missing rate of 45%.

4.4   MNAR Experiments

There is no clear best imputation method anymore in MNAR setting with a missing rate of 20%, c.f. Fig. 4. The RMSE is below 0.15 and close to the RMSE in MAR setting. With a missing rate of 45%, the RMSE becomes even larger than with the MAR experiments. GAIN now performs better than kNN.

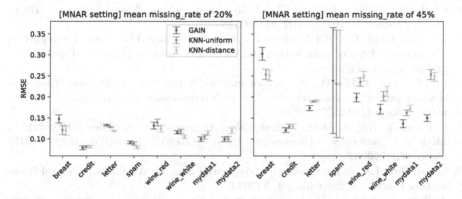

Fig. 4. MNAR scenario for all datasets. **(left)** MNAR setting with average missing rate of 20%. **(right)** MNAR setting with average missing rate of 45%.

5   Conclusion

The framework of MisGAN (initially designed to impute missing rectangular pixel blocs in images) do not adapt well for tabular data imputation, with large confidence intervals in its predictions. GAIN, which has been developed for tabular data imputation, shows good imputation quality especially in MNAR settings with high missing rates. DL architectures can learn complex relationships between variables, which can explain the good performances of GAIN in MAR and MNAR settings. But as a GAN model, training GAIN can be challenging and time consuming (see Supplementary Materials for quantitative results on training time).

The kNN shows competitive results in the face of DL models in spite of its simplicity and its age. This review reinforces previous results that massive DL algorithms do not necessary perform better for numerical data imputation [1,2,8,9,14]. It also appears that the imputation quality of an algorithm depends on the dataset itself rather than on the missing data mechanism per se: see the **breast** dataset where the kNN systematically performs better than GAIN, and **mydata2** (mixture of three Gaussian dataset) where GAIN performs better than kNN most of the time.

For its simplicity, its deterministic output (hence unambiguous reproducibility), and its low computational resources, we recommend to use the kNN for tabular data imputation when possible.

References

1. Batista, G.E., Monard, M.C.: A study of k-nearest neighbour as an imputation method. Front. Artif. Intell. Appl. **87** (2002)
2. Bertsimas, D., Pawlowski, C., Zhuo, Y.D.: From predictive methods to missing data imputation: an optimization approach. J. Mach. Learn. Res. **18**, 7133–7171 (2018)
3. Clark, P., Niblett, T.: The CN2 induction algorithm. Mach. Learn. **3** (1989). https://doi.org/10.1023/A:1022641700528
4. Dua, D., Graff, C.: UCI Machine Learning Repository: Data Sets. University of California, School of Information and Computer Science, Irvine (2019). https://archive.ics.uci.edu/ml
5. Fix, E., Hodges, J.L.: Discriminatory analysis. Nonparametric discrimination: consistency properties. Int. Stat. Rev./Revue Internationale de Statistique **57** (1989). https://doi.org/10.2307/1403797
6. Gelman, A., Hill, J.: Data Analysis Using Regression and Multilevel/Hierarchical Models. Cambridge University Press (2006). https://doi.org/10.1017/cbo9780511790942
7. Goodfellow, I.J., et al.: Generative adversarial nets. In: Advances in Neural Information Processing Systems, vol. 3 (2014)
8. Jadhav, A., Pramod, D., Ramanathan, K.: Comparison of performance of data imputation methods for numeric dataset. Appl. Artif. Intell. **33** (2019). https://doi.org/10.1080/08839514.2019.1637138
9. Jäger, S., Allhorn, A., Bießmann, F.: A benchmark for data imputation methods. Front. Big Data **4** (2021). https://doi.org/10.3389/fdata.2021.693674
10. Kalton, G., Kasprzyk, D.: The treatment of missing survey data. Surv. Methodol. **12** (1986)
11. Lall, R.: How multiple imputation makes a difference. Polit. Anal. **24** (2016). https://doi.org/10.1093/pan/mpw020
12. Li, S.C.X., Marlin, B.M., Jiang, B.: MisGAN: learning from incomplete data with generative adversarial networks. In: 7th International Conference on Learning Representations, ICLR 2019 (2019)
13. Little, R.J., Rubin, D.B.: Statistical analysis with missing data. Stat. Anal. Missing Data (2014). https://doi.org/10.1002/9781119013563
14. Poulos, J., Valle, R.: Missing data imputation for supervised learning. Appl. Artif. Intell. **32** (2018). https://doi.org/10.1080/08839514.2018.1448143
15. Salzberg, S.L.: C4.5: programs for machine learning by J. Ross Quinlan. Morgan Kaufmann Publishers, Inc., 1993. Mach. Learn. **16**, 235–240 (1994). https://doi.org/10.1007/bf00993309
16. Stekhoven, D.J., Bühlmann, P.: MissForest-non-parametric missing value imputation for mixed-type data. Bioinformatics **28** (2012). https://doi.org/10.1093/bioinformatics/btr597
17. Troyanskaya, O., et al.: Missing value estimation methods for DNA microarrays. Bioinformatics **17** (2001). https://doi.org/10.1093/bioinformatics/17.6.520
18. Yoon, J., Jordon, J., Schaar, M.V.D.: Gain: missing data imputation using generative adversarial nets. In: 35th International Conference on Machine Learning, ICML 2018, vol. 13, pp. 9042–9051 (2018)

COSINER: COntext SImilarity data augmentation for Named Entity Recognition

Ilaria Bartolini[1], Vincenzo Moscato[2], Marco Postiglione[2], Giancarlo Sperlì[2(✉)], and Andrea Vignali[2]

[1] Alma Mater Studiorum, University of Bologna, Bologna, Italy
ilaria.bartolini@unibo.it
[2] University of Naples Federico II, Naples, Italy
{vincenzo.moscato,marco.postiglione,giancarlo.sperli,
andrea.vignali}@unina.it

Abstract. To alleviate the scarcity of manually annotated data in Named Entity Recognition (NER) tasks, data augmentation methods can be applied to automatically generate labeled data and improve performance of existing methods. However, based on manipulations of the input text, current techniques may generate too many noisy and mislabeled samples. In this paper we propose *COntext SImilarity-based data augmentation for NER (COSINER)*, a method for NER data augmentation based on context similarity, i.e. we replace entity mentions with the most plausible ones based on the available training data and the contexts in which entities usually appear. We conduct experiments on popular benchmark datasets, showing that our method outperforms current baselines in various few-shot scenarios, where training data is assumed to be strongly limited. Experimental results show that not only does COSINER overcome baselines in terms of NER performances in highly-limited scenarios (2%, 5%), but also its computing times are comparable to simplest augmentation methods.

Keywords: Named Entity Recognition · Data augmentation · Similarity learning · Few shot learning

1 Introduction

Named Entity Recognition (NER) aims to identify and extract entities of interest—e.g. diseases, chemical agents and genes in medicine—from unstructured text data. It is the first and fundamental step of many downstream applications, such as Q/A agents and knowledge graphs building.

Training NER models usually requires large amounts of manually annotated data to be used as the ground truth reference, but a high-quality annotation process is time-consuming and expensive, particularly in specialized domains such as legal, historical, or biomedical where domain knowledge is needed.

© The Author(s), under exclusive license to Springer Nature Switzerland AG 2022
T. Skopal et al. (Eds.): SISAP 2022, LNCS 13590, pp. 11–24, 2022.
https://doi.org/10.1007/978-3-031-17849-8_2

As a consequence, it is rare that the budget required to make domain experts annotate large quantities of data is available. Furthermore, domain experts in specialized areas are often not readily available due to the specialization required for their work and the important commitments that keep them busy. For these reasons, current literature has and continues to explore *few-shot learning*, which consists in novel ways to deal with data and models to work in scenarios with limited training datasets.

One common way to deal with the lack of data is *data augmentation*, which consists in increasing the size of the available dataset with new samples generated by means of heuristics or external data sources. Augmentation methods explored in current literature for natural language processing (NLP) tasks usually manipulate words in the original sentence by word replacement [1], random deletion [2], word position swap [3] and generative models [4]. Applying these transformations to NER input samples is not possible due to the token-level classification implied by this task (each manipulation impacts labels). Thus, data augmentation techniques for NER are comparatively less studied [5].

Despite the promising results of data augmentation, currently proposed data manipulation methods may often generate too many noisy and mislabeled samples, since new data may be syntactically and/or semantically incorrect.

To alleviate this issue, we propose a *COntext SImilarity-based data augmentation for NER (COSINER)* approach which exploits similarity metrics for the generation of augmented examples so as to create sentences which are as plausible as possible in a real context. Specifically, we define a *context-based mention replacement* augmentation technique which replaces mentions appearing in the input data with mentions in an *Entity Lexicon* which are likely to appear in the same context. In Fig. 1 we show an augmentation example for an input sentence.

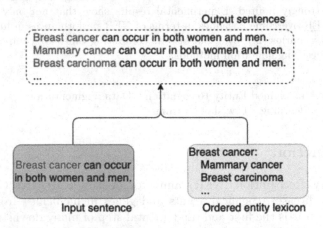

Fig. 1. Example of NER data augmentation for an input sample. The mention *"Breast cancer"* is replaced with mentions from the Entity Lexicon, which is ordered based on a context-based similarity metric

We run extensive experiments on three benchmark datasets popular in the biomedical field to assess the performance of our methods. Specifically, we compare COSINER with a set of baselines from current literature and show that exploiting similarity to perform data augmentation leads to higher performance. The chosen domain (i.e., biomedical) is one in which usually there are few data, however our methodology is general and can be applied to any application concerning NER. We also show that the performance obtained with COSINER is due to the first-ranked samples, and thus we do not need huge augmented datasets to improve results, which is a benefit in terms of computing time.

2 Related Work and Theoretical Background

In this section, we examine related work and provide the theoretical background needed to properly understand the key concepts of our methodology. In particular, in Sect. 2.1 an overview of the Named Entity Recognition (NER) task is first given, then an in-depth examination of few-shot learning methods is reported in Sect. 2.2. Finally in Sect. 2.3 we focus on data augmentation and its applications on NER.

2.1 Named Entity Recognition

Named Entity Recognition (NER) task falls in the area of Natural Language Processing (NLP), which is a branch of Artificial Intelligence (AI) focusing on the understanding and processing of natural language with the aim to complete a wide variety of tasks, such as sentiment analysis, text classification, machine translation, and so on.

NER is the first and fundamental task of many applications, such as knowledge graph construction [6], scientific discovery [7], machine translation [8] and question answering [9]. It is the task of identifying mentions of entities from unstructured text and classifying their type (e.g. person, organization, disease, drug).

Formally, the input to a NER model is a sequence of tokens $\mathbf{x} = [x_1, x_2, \ldots, x_T]$ of length T, while the output is a paired sequence of categorical values $\mathbf{y} = [y_1, y_2, \ldots, y_T]$, $y_i \in \mathcal{Y}$ indicating the entity type of each token. NER datasets are collections of pair-wise data $\mathcal{D} = \{(\mathbf{x}_n, \mathbf{y}_n)\}_{n=1}^N$, N being the number of examples.

Several annotation schemes exist to associate labels to input tokens so as to individuate entity mentions [10]. Since it is the most widespread in few-shot NER applications, in this work we will refer to the IOB2 scheme, i.e. we map each token to its corresponding label which may refer to the *beginning*, *inside* or *outside* of an entity mention. An example is shown in Fig. 2.

2.2 Few-Shot Learning

Real-world applications often require large amounts of annotated data to reach comparable results to the current literature. Unfortunately, the annotation process is time-consuming and highly expensive, especially in specific fields where

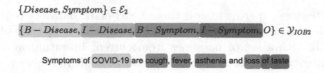

Fig. 2. Example of NER. Tagging with IOB2 format with 2 entity types (Disease and Symptom)

domain knowledge is required to produce high-quality datasets. Furthermore, merging together different datasets has revealed to be unfruitful due to inconsistencies between the different annotation criteria between datasets, even if they refer to the same context [11]. It is thus necessary to deal with *few-shot* learning scenarios, where training data are extremely limited.

Meta learning [12] and *transfer learning* [13] are training paradigms allowing model parameters to easily adapt to new tasks, domain or languages. *Active learning* [14] aims to select the most informative examples from an unsupervised data source to be annotated, so as to get the best possible results from model training. *Distant supervision* [15] and *self learning* [16] leverage unsupervised data sources to increase the size of the training set by using heuristics or the model itself to annotate examples.

In this work, differently from other approaches, we will increment the size of the training corpus by relying just on the available data, by performing text manipulation on input samples.

2.3   Text Data Augmentation

Data augmentation methods based on manipulation of the available corpus have been deeply explored in tasks for sentence-level classification [2,3], but they are still understudied for token-level classification tasks, where NER lies. Recent work shows that data augmentation for NER is a promising research field [5, 17]. Techniques described as follows and exemplified in Table 1 are available in current literature [5]:

- *Mention Replacement (MR)*: one entity mention from an input sample is randomly replaced with another mention from the original training set.
- *Label-wise token replacement (LwTR)*: each token from an input sample is randomly replaced (with a certain probability) with any other word with the same label within the training dataset.
- *Synonym replacement (SR)*: each word from the input sample is randomly replaced with a synonym, which could be retrieved by using WordNet [18].

However, the improvements brought by data augmentation techniques drastically decrease in few-shot scenarios [19]. This is due to the fact that these methods may produce a high quantity of noisy data since text manipulation could generate grammatically and semantically incorrect samples, and the problem is exacerbated when the size of augmented data prevails the original corpus.

Table 1. NER data augmentation examples. Disease entity mentions are in *italic*, while manipulated tokens are **bolded** (they may overlap).

Method	Example
Input example	*Breast cancer* can occur in both women and men
MR	***Diabetes*** can occur in both women and men
LwTR	*Breast cancer* can **complain** in both women and men
SR	*Breast **tumor*** can occur in both women and men

To handle this issue, the pillar idea behind our framework is to generate plausible augmented samples by employing a similarity-based approach.

To the best of our knowledge, this is the first work to analyze *context-based similarity* for data augmentation. Specifically, we manipulate input samples by replacing entity mentions with similar mentions both syntactically and semantically, i.e. the mentions are likely to appear in the same contexts.

3   COSINER Methodology

In a nutshell, COSINER exploits *mention replacement* to augment the original training set. Proposed and studied by Dai et al. [5], this technique consists in selecting with a binomial distribution the entities of interest within the sentences of the dataset to replace with another randomly-selected entity of the same dataset. However, the randomness of this approach leads to the generation of many noisy or even mislabeled samples which could negatively affect model performance. Hence, we employ a similarity-based methodological flow to replace the entity mention with its most similar entities in terms of syntax, semantic and context. An overview of the proposed methodological flow is shown in Fig. 3 and all the steps are described in the following.

Lexicon Generation. In order to replace mentions, each *concept* (entity mention) involved in the training set must be collected. A *concept* may be composed of a single or multiple words and the number of its occurrences in the training set $C_{concept}$ is also stored. Lexicon will include a variable amount of entities depending on the number of mentions within the dataset. Note that the execution time of the similarity values between entity pairs is heavily affected by the size of the Lexicon. However, in this work we ignore this problem since we run our experiments in few-shot scenarios, where the available corpus is limited, thus resulting in small Lexicons.

Embeddings Extraction. To compute similarity between entities of our dataset we need a numerical representation $V_{concept}$ of all the concepts within the Lexicon. To accomplish this objective, we use a pre-trained language model [20,21] as a feature extractor. For each mention in the Lexicon, the feature

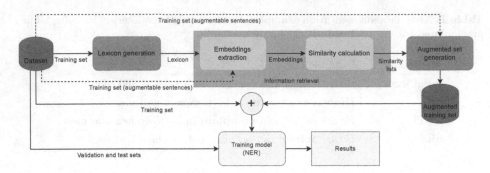

Fig. 3. COSINER methodological flow (rounded boxes represent steps). (1) Given the original training set, a Lexicon with all the entities is generated, (2) then all entities are mapped to an embedded space extracted from sentences with at least one mention. (3) Similarity values among embedding pairs are computed so as to link each entity to a ranked list of its most (least) similar entities. (4) The augmented training set is thus generated. (5) Finally, a model is trained by exploiting both the original and augmented training sets.

extractor receives as input each sentence in which that mention appears and maps every token onto its word embedding $V_{context}$, i.e. an array of numerical features that represents the token in the context where it appears. If mentions are composed of more than one token, $V_{context}$ is retrieved by averaging word embeddings of all the tokens. After retrieving a $V_{context}$ for an input sentence, the overall numerical representation of the concept $V_{concept}$ is updated as follows:

$$V_{concept} = V_{concept} + lr \cdot (1 - sim) \cdot V_{context},\qquad(1)$$

where lr is a regularization term defined by the reciprocal of the number of times a mention appears in the whole dataset and sim is the cosine similarity between $V_{concept}$ and $V_{context}$:

$$lr = \frac{1}{C_{concept}}\qquad(2)$$

$$sim(V_{concept}, V_{context}) = \max(0, \frac{V_{concept}}{||V_{concept}||} \cdot \frac{V_{context}}{||V_{context}||})\qquad(3)$$

It is worth to note that $V_{concept}$ is initialized to the $V_{context}$ value of the first sentence in which the mention appears.

Similarity Computation. The cosine similarity between the embeddings $V_{concept}$ of every pair of entities in the Lexicon is thus computed. Therefore, a ranked-list of similarity scores $z_{ij} = sim(V_{concept}^i, V_{concept}^j)$ is linked to each Lexicon entry. We define two ranking criteria:

- Maximum (descending order): the most similar concepts are in the first positions. In this way, we can generate plausible augmented samples to retain

the consistence of the context provided by the sentence, thus increasing the number of data, but remaining as close as possible to the training distribution;
– Minimum (ascending order): the least similar entities are used to go as far as possible from the knowledge boundary in order to recognize and correctly classify extreme cases.

Augmented Set Generation. The augmented set is generated by taking into consideration all the sentences with at least one mention. Then, to each sentence will be associated its own similarity value s_m computed as the average of the entity similarity scores z_{ij} of the new entities within the phrase. We define two strategies:

– Local Augmentation: for each sentence, k new samples are generated. The advantage of this approach is that we generate new samples for each sentence in the original training set.
– Global Augmentation: for each sentence, k new samples are generated just like the previous strategy. Then we rank all the new generated sentences in a single list by their similarity value s_m and select the first h element to be used in the augmented training set. In this way, we focus on samples which are nearer to the original training distribution, but we may prefer augmenting some sentences w.r.t. others.

In Fig. 4 we highlight the differences between the two strategies.

NER Model Training. We refer to the IOB2 scheme [22] for NER token-classification task, each token being thus associated to the B (beginning of an entity mention), I (inside) or O (outside) label. The original training dataset and the augmented samples are fed to a Transformer network backbone [20,21] to extract the contextualized representation of each token x_j in an input sample $\mathbf{x}$, $\mathbf{z} = f_{\theta_{PLM}}(x_j)$, θ_{PLM} being the set of PLM parameters. Thereafter, a linear layer (a.k.a. *classification head*) with parameters $\theta_L = \{\mathbf{W}, \mathbf{b}\}$ projects the Transformer-based representation $\mathbf{z}$ into the label space, $f_{\theta_L}(\mathbf{z}) = Softmax(\mathbf{Wz} + \mathbf{b})$. The model parameters are then optimized by minimizing cross-entropy.

4   Experiments

In this section, we evaluate the effectiveness and the efficiency of our method on three popular benchmark datasets from the biomedical field. Results show that our method surpasses selected baselines from current literature in most of the datasets and few-shot scenarios, while guaranteeing computing times comparable to simplest augmentation methods.

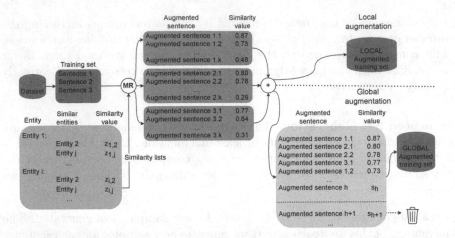

Fig. 4. COSINER Augmentation strategies. The initial steps of the local and global strategies are shared. First of all, k augmented sentences for each phrase with at least one mention are generated starting from similarity lists and the training set via Mention Replacement (MR), then the sentence similarity value s_m is calculated and assigned to each augmented example. For **local strategy** all the augmented examples are used in the new training set. For the **global strategy** instead, a new list is created with all the examples ordered by their s_m and the first h sentences are selected for the augmented training set.

4.1   Experimental Setup

Datasets and Few-Shot Scenarios. We train and evaluate our method on three popular benchmark datasets annotated from biomedical articles. Details are provided as follows:

- NCBI-Disease [23]: consists of 793 PubMed abstracts, including 6,881 *disease* entity mentions;
- BC5CDR [24] consists of 1,500 PubMed articles, including 15,935 *chemical* and 12,852 *disease* mentions. We consider only *chemical* mentions in our experiments to add variety to entities, since diseases have already been used in NCBI. Therefore our approach has been developed to be applied only to one entity type.
- BC2GM [25] consists of 20,000 sentences from PubMed abstracts, including 20,702 *gene* entities.

We have established three few-shot scenarios based on the percentage of samples from the available corpora used to apply our methods: 2%, 5% and 10%, respectively. We report all our experimental results in these three few-shot scenarios. Statistics of the datasets and few-shot scenarios are shown in Table 2. The experiments were carried out using a Kaggle notebook that provides a NVIDIA Tesla P100 GPU with 16 GB of memory and 2-core of Intel Xeon CPU with 13 GB of RAM in the configuration used.

Table 2. Statistics of the benchmark datasets used in our experiments.

Dataset	Entity type	N. annotations	Dataset splits			Few-shot size		
			Train	Dev	Test	2%	5%	10%
NCBI-disease	Disease	6881	5425	924	941	108	271	542
BC5CDR	Chemical	15411	4561	4582	4798	91	228	456
BC2GM	Gene	20703	12575	2520	5039	251	628	1257

Training Details. Based on previous work on few-shot learning [26], we assume to operate in scenarios where data to tune hyperparameters are not available. Hence, we choose hyperparameters based on previous work and practical considerations. Specifically, we use a pre-trained biomedical Transformer network [27] and train all our models for 5 epochs with a learning rate of $5 \cdot 10^{-5}$, an AdamW optimizer [28], a batch size of 8 and a maximum sequence length of 512. We train each model with five different seeds and report average results and 95% confidence intervals. We evaluate the quality of methods $F1$ scores computed with the seqeval[1] Python framework.

4.2   Results

Comparison with Baselines. We compare our best results[2] with baselines from the current literature [5] described as follows:

- No Augmentation: we report results obtained with the original training set.
- Mention replacement (MR): we randomly select a mention from the original training set with the same entity type for each mention in the instance.
- Label-wise token replacement (LwTR): for each word within a sentence we randomly chose whether or not to replace it with any other word within the dataset which has the same label.
- Synonym replacement (SR): for each word within a sentence a binomial distribution chooses whether or not to replace it with a synonym from WordNet [18].

Examples of generated samples per baseline are shown in Table 1. For each baseline, we generated one augmented sample per sentence (whenever possible), thus resulting in training datasets at most twice as large as the original.

Table 3 compares F1 scores of the different baselines with our method. Results indicate that COSINER, thanks to its effective use of context-based similarities, surpasses baselines in most of the scenarios and datasets. The high scores of the SR baseline prove the importance of generating plausible augmented samples

---

[1] https://github.com/chakki-works/seqeval.
[2] Our best results are obtained with the *maximum similarity* and *local augmentation* methods for similarity and augmentation set computation, respectively. In Sect. 4.2 we compare all the different approaches.

when transforming input sentences. Random replacements of MR and LwTR baselines result in too many noisy samples which, in some cases, may even decrease the performance obtained without applying any augmentation method.

Table 3. Comparative results between the local augmentation strategy with maximum similarity technique and baselines.

Dataset size	Method	NCBI-disease	BC5CDR	BC2GM
2%	No augmentation	0.651 ± 0.122	0.792 ± 0.067	0.644 ± 0.031
	MR	0.666 ± 0.084	0.813 ± 0.032	0.64 ± 0.02
	LwTR	0.677 ± 0.101	0.828 ± 0.019	0.642 ± 0.037
	SR	0.692 ± 0.103	0.813 ± 0.032	0.662 ± 0.033
	COSINER (ours)	$\mathbf{0.692 \pm 0.081}$	$\mathbf{0.832 \pm 0.022}$	$\mathbf{0.665 \pm 0.038}$
5%	No augmentation	0.735 ± 0.041	0.85 ± 0.02	0.711 ± 0.012
	MR	0.743 ± 0.048	0.849 ± 0.021	0.713 ± 0.006
	LwTR	0.743 ± 0.072	0.86 ± 0.039	0.699 ± 0.012
	SR	0.758 ± 0.044	0.858 ± 0.03	0.719 ± 0.011
	COSINER (ours)	$\mathbf{0.765 \pm 0.035}$	$\mathbf{0.863 \pm 0.042}$	$\mathbf{0.726 \pm 0.022}$
10%	No augmentation	0.791 ± 0.028	0.875 ± 0.013	0.759 ± 0.017
	MR	0.794 ± 0.018	0.874 ± 0.034	0.754 ± 0.01
	LwTR	0.789 ± 0.023	0.882 ± 0.017	0.741 ± 0.012
	SR	0.803 ± 0.033	$\mathbf{0.883 \pm 0.018}$	0.763 ± 0.012
	COSINER (ours)	$\mathbf{0.816 \pm 0.066}$	0.882 ± 0.007	$\mathbf{0.767 \pm 0.023}$

Effects of Increasing the Augmented Set Size. When generating an augmented dataset, the number of augmented samples is generally an important parameter to consider. Hence, we experimented our method with three different *budgets* for the augmented set: small (100 samples), medium (300 samples) and large (500 samples).

Figure 5 shows the results obtained on the three benchmark datasets. As expected, since—thanks to the similarity-based approach—the most informative examples are in the first ranked positions, there is no big difference in using higher budgets.

Effects of Parameters for Similarity Computation and Augmented Set Generation. Table 4 shows results obtained with different configurations of parameters for similarity computation (Maximum vs Minimum) and augmented set generation (Local vs Global) discussed in Sect. 3. As expected, the use of Maximum similarity computation leads to higher performance, since augmented samples are plausible and thus nearer to the test distribution. However, the high results obtained with the Minimum configuration show that sometimes it may be beneficial to consider "distant" entities to expand the scope of action of the

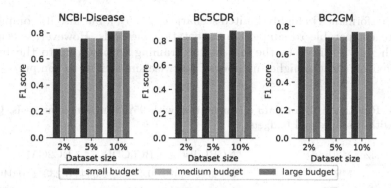

Fig. 5. Comparative results between the small, medium and large budget of local augmentation strategy with maximum similarity technique

NER model, especially in strongly limited few-shot settings. With regards to the augmentated set generation, Local criterion is generally better thanks to the augmentation of *all* the sentences in the original dataset.

Table 4. Comparative results between COSINER techniques with their best budget.

Dataset size	Similarity	Strategy	NCBI disease	BC5CDR	BC2GM
2%	Maximum	Global	0.688 ± 0.077	0.83 ± 0.023	0.658 ± 0.036
	Minimum	Global	0.683 ± 0.086	0.823 ± 0.032	0.652 ± 0.027
	Maximum	Local	0.689 ± 0.088	$\mathbf{0.832 \pm 0.022}$	$\mathbf{0.665 \pm 0.038}$
	Minimum	Local	$\mathbf{0.692 \pm 0.081}$	0.824 ± 0.015	0.659 ± 0.049
5%	Maximum	Global	$\mathbf{0.765 \pm 0.035}$	0.858 ± 0.023	0.717 ± 0.007
	Minimum	Global	0.756 ± 0.028	0.853 ± 0.029	0.713 ± 0.009
	Maximum	Local	0.76 ± 0.031	$\mathbf{0.863 \pm 0.042}$	$\mathbf{0.726 \pm 0.022}$
	Minimum	Local	0.764 ± 0.041	0.86 ± 0.031	0.714 ± 0.007
10%	Maximum	Global	0.807 ± 0.038	0.88 ± 0.018	0.76 ± 0.02
	Minimum	Global	0.807 ± 0.029	0.873 ± 0.016	0.761 ± 0.012
	Maximum	Local	$\mathbf{0.816 \pm 0.066}$	$\mathbf{0.882 \pm 0.007}$	$\mathbf{0.767 \pm 0.023}$
	Minimum	Local	0.807 ± 0.038	0.876 ± 0.016	0.76 ± 0.009

Efficiency of Data Augmentation. We compared the execution time required to perform data augmentation[3] with the different baselines and budgets. Results listed in Table 5 show that not only does COSINER overcome baselines in terms

---

[3] We have not considered the execution time required to generate Lexicon and embeddings, since they are one-time operations that can be performed off-line.

of NER performance in highly-limited scenarios (2%, 5%), but also its computing times are comparable to simplest augmentation methods. However, execution time is highly sensitive to the size of the training corpus, due to the bigger entity Lexicon and the higher number of pairwise similarities to compute.

Table 5. Run times (s) for data augmentation with 95% confidence intervals. Comparison with baselines and budgets.

Dataset size	Method	NCBI disease	BC5CDR	BC2GM
2%	MR	0.123 ± 0.020	0.117 ± 0.044	0.233 ± 0.040
	LwTR	0.149 ± 0.067	0.141 ± 0.066	0.288 ± 0.171
	SR	3.271 ± 0.670	3.322 ± 0.293	4.374 ± 0.643
	COSINER (small)	0.389 ± 0.218	0.445 ± 0.192	2.859 ± 0.975
	COSINER (medium)	0.44 ± 0.472	0.428 ± 0.272	2.975 ± 1.3539
	COSINER (big)	0.529 ± 0.491	0.586 ± 0.202	3.415 ± 1.765
5%	MR	0.212 ± 0.065	0.198 ± 0.091	0.436 ± 0.204
	LwTR	0.287 ± 0.171	0.264 ± 0.111	0.656 ± 0.251
	SR	3.703 ± 1.493	4.016 ± 0.893	4.494 ± 1.137
	COSINER (small)	1.541 ± 1.002	1.578 ± 0.936	15.555 ± 5.233
	COSINER (medium)	1.678 ± 0.811	1.601 ± 1.134	17.257 ± 7.973
	COSINER (big)	1.705 ± 0.628	1.717 ± 0.496	16.711 ± 9.581
10%	MR	0.329 ± 0.139	0.342 ± 0.054	0.846 ± 0.316
	LwTR	0.591 ± 0.264	0.502 ± 0.145	1.206 ± 0.528
	SR	4.238 ± 1.362	4.233 ± 1.174	6.069 ± 2.463
	COSINER (small)	4.286 ± 1.305	4.367 ± 1.087	60.416 ± 19.012
	COSINER (medium)	4.689 ± 1.601	4.553 ± 1.276	60.508 ± 31.661
	COSINER (big)	4.864 ± 0.916	4.961 ± 1.841	62.386 ± 22.487

5   Conclusions

In this work, we have applied a *context similarity*-based methodology to generate plausible augmented data to boost performance of NER tasks, thus reducing the deleterious effects of noisy and mislabeled data which are often generated with current techniques. Our experiments have revealed the appropriateness of our method, which outperforms several baselines with comparable execution times. In the future, this approach could be used in combination with other techniques than Mention Replacement. Further experimentation will be done on different application contexts and with multiple entity types.

References

1. Cai, H., Chen, H., Song, Y., Zhang, C., Zhao, X., Yin, D.: Data manipulation: towards effective instance learning for neural dialogue generation via learning to augment and reweight. In: Proceedings of the 58th Annual Meeting of the Association for Computational Linguistics, pp. 6334–6343. Association for Computational Linguistics (2020)
2. Wei, J., Zou, K.: EDA: easy data augmentation techniques for boosting performance on text classification tasks. In: Proceedings of the 2019 Conference on Empirical Methods in Natural Language Processing and the 9th International Joint Conference on Natural Language Processing (EMNLP-IJCNLP), Hong Kong, China, pp. 6382–6388. Association for Computational Linguistics (2019)
3. Min, J., McCoy, R.T., Das, D., Pitler, E., Linzen, T.: Syntactic data augmentation increases robustness to inference heuristics. In: Proceedings of the 58th Annual Meeting of the Association for Computational Linguistics, pp. 2339–2352. Association for Computational Linguistics (2020)
4. Yoo, K.M., Shin, Y., Lee, S.G.: Data augmentation for spoken language understanding via joint variational generation. In: Proceedings of the AAAI Conference on Artificial Intelligence, vol. 33, pp. 7402–7409 (2019)
5. Dai, X., Adel, H.: An analysis of simple data augmentation for named entity recognition. In: Proceedings of the 28th International Conference on Computational Linguistics, Barcelona, Spain, pp. 3861–3867. International Committee on Computational Linguistics (2020)
6. Postiglione, M.: Towards an Italian healthcare knowledge graph. In: Reyes, N., et al. (eds.) SISAP 2021. LNCS, vol. 13058, pp. 387–394. Springer, Cham (2021). https://doi.org/10.1007/978-3-030-89657-7_29
7. Wang, X., Hu, V., Song, X., Garg, S., Xiao, J., Han, J.: ChemNER: fine-grained chemistry named entity recognition with ontology-guided distant supervision. In: Proceedings of the 2021 Conference on Empirical Methods in Natural Language Processing, Punta Cana, Dominican Republic, pp. 5227–5240. Association for Computational Linguistics (2021)
8. Gekhman, Z., Aharoni, R., Beryozkin, G., Freitag, M., Macherey, W.: KoBE: knowledge-based machine translation evaluation. In: Findings of the Association for Computational Linguistics: EMNLP 2020, pp. 3200–3207. Association for Computational Linguistics (2020)
9. Li, B.Z., Min, S., Iyer, S., Mehdad, Y., Yih, W.T.: Efficient one-pass end-to-end entity linking for questions. In: Proceedings of the 2020 Conference on Empirical Methods in Natural Language Processing (EMNLP), pp. 6433–6441. Association for Computational Linguistics (2020)
10. Alshammari, N., Alanazi, S.: The impact of using different annotation schemes on named entity recognition. Egypt. Inform. J. **22**(3), 295–302 (2021). https://doi.org/10.1016/j.eij.2020.10.004
11. Li, J., Sun, A., Han, J., Li, C.: A survey on deep learning for named entity recognition. IEEE Trans. Knowl. Data Eng. 1 (2020). https://doi.org/10.1109/TKDE.2020.2981314
12. Schmidhuber, J.: On learning how to learn learning strategies (1995)
13. Henderson, M., Vulić, I.: ConVEx: data-efficient and few-shot slot labeling. arXiv:2010.11791 [cs] (2020)
14. Shen, Y., Yun, H., Lipton, Z.C., Kronrod, Y., Anandkumar, A.: Deep active learning for named entity recognition. arXiv:1707.05928 [cs] (2018)

15. Lou, Y., Qian, T., Li, F., Ji, D.: A graph attention model for dictionary-guided named entity recognition. IEEE Access **8**, 71584–71592 (2020). https://doi.org/10.1109/ACCESS.2020.2987399
16. Huang, J., et al.: Few-shot named entity recognition: a comprehensive study. arXiv:2012.14978 [cs] (2020)
17. Ding, B., et al.: DAGA: data augmentation with a generation approach for low-resource tagging tasks. In: Proceedings of the 2020 Conference on Empirical Methods in Natural Language Processing (EMNLP), pp. 6045–6057. Association for Computational Linguistics (2020)
18. Miller, G.A.: WordNet: a lexical database for English. Commun. ACM. **38**(11), 39–41 (1995). https://doi.org/10.1145/219717.219748
19. Chen, S., Aguilar, G., Neves, L., Solorio, T.: Data augmentation for cross-domain named entity recognition. In: Proceedings of the 2021 Conference on Empirical Methods in Natural Language Processing, Punta Cana, Dominican Republic, pp. 5346–5356. Association for Computational Linguistics (2021)
20. Devlin, J., Chang, M.W., Lee, K., Toutanova, K.: BERT: pre-training of deep bidirectional transformers for language understanding. In: Proceedings of the 2019 Conference of the North American Chapter of the Association for Computational Linguistics: Human Language Technologies, Minneapolis, Minnesota, vol. 1, pp. 4171–4186. Association for Computational Linguistics (2019)
21. Brown, T., et al.: Language models are few-shot learners. In: Larochelle, H., Ranzato, M., Hadsell, R., Balcan, M.F., Lin, H. (eds.) Advances in Neural Information Processing Systems, vol. 33, pp. 1877–1901. Curran Associates Inc. (2020)
22. Ramshaw, L.A., Marcus, M.P.: Text chunking using transformation-based learning. In: Armstrong, S., Church, K., Isabelle, P., Manzi, S., Tzoukermann, E., Yarowsky, D. (eds.) Natural Language Processing Using Very Large Corpora, pp. 157–176. Springer, Cham (1999). https://doi.org/10.1007/978-94-017-2390-9_10
23. Doğan, R., Leaman, R., Lu, Z.: NCBI disease corpus: a resource for disease name recognition and concept normalization. https://pubmed.ncbi.nlm.nih.gov/24393765/
24. Li, J., et al.: BioCreative V CDR task corpus: a resource for chemical disease relation extraction. www.ncbi.nlm.nih.gov/pmc/articles/PMC4860626/
25. Smith, L., Tanabe, L.K., nee Ando, R.J., et al.: The BioCreative II - critical assessment for information extraction in biology challenge. https://doi.org/10.1186/gb-2008-9-s2-s2
26. Schick, T., Schütze, H.: Exploiting cloze-questions for few-shot text classification and natural language inference. In: Proceedings of the 16th Conference of the European Chapter of the Association for Computational Linguistics: Main Volume, pp. 255–269. Association for Computational Linguistics (2021)
27. Lee, J., Yoon, W., Kim, S., Kim, D., Kim, S., So, C.H., et al.: BioBERT: a pre-trained biomedical language representation model for biomedical text mining. Bioinformatics **36**(4), 1234–1240 (2020)
28. Loshchilov, I., Hutter, F.: Decoupled weight decay regularization. In: ICLR (2019)

An Application of Learned Multi-modal Product Similarity to E-Commerce

My Hong Le[1,2] and Alexander Hinneburg[2(✉)] (iD)

[1] Relaxdays, Halle/Saale, Germany
myhong.le@relaxdays.de
[2] Martin-Luther-University Halle-Wittenberg, Halle (Saale), Germany
hinneburg@informatik.uni-halle.de

Abstract. Product similarity search is an important tool for e-commerce companies to manage their portfolios of products and to find competitive prices on large electronic market places. The specific requirements for this similarity search application are (i) the similar products should be competitive products with respect to a given query product, (ii) related and just generally similar products should be treated as not similar products. Thus, the similarity between products should be learned from data. We propose to use classification models for entity matching and image classification to learn a multi-modal model for similarity search. Further, we propose a way to construct a meaningful training data set to learn the relevant similarities between product pairs. Extensive experiments show that a transformer based language model combined with Siamese convolutional neural networks outperform competitive baseline models.

Keywords: Learned similarity · Multi-modal similarity · Transformer

1 Introduction

The burgeoning e-commerce industries purvey millions of products on the dominating e-commerce platforms such as Amazon and eBay. Before introducing a potential new product, these prospering industries carry out a competitive market analysis to address the following questions:

1. Analyse whether the own company offers similar products.
2. Determine the similar products that are offered by the competitors.

One cannot rely on a simplistic approach: using a search engine of the market place may turn up some similar products but would fail to provide a thorough analysis of these products in the marketplace. Collaborative filtering [8,20] is not applicable as the imperative user-purchase data is inadequate for the e-commerce companies competing commercially. Hence, employing a content-based similarity approach would help to gain better insights.

T. Skopal et al. (Eds.): SISAP 2022, LNCS 13590, pp. 25–39, 2022.
https://doi.org/10.1007/978-3-031-17849-8_3

Product 1 M. Graham Artist Oil Paint Phthalo Green 1.25oz/37ml Tube: Artist
quality oil paint made with walnut oil, solvent free / Increased pigment
loads for stronger more vibrant colors / Colors retain their clarity and
are free from the discoloration associated with drying oils / Lightfast
rating I Excellent; Slow drying time; Transparent / Made in the USA

Product 2 Winsor & Newton Winton Oil Color Paint, 37-ml Tube, Sap Green:
Winsor & Newton Winton Oil Colours are high quality yet affordable,
delivering trusted performance. / Series: 1/Color Code: 599 / Perma-
nence Rating: A - Permanent / Transparency / Opacity: T / Lightfast-
ness Rating: ASTM I - Excellent

Product 3 Uchida Marvy Deco Color Fine Point Paint Marker Art Supplies, Violet: This fine point paint marker is great for writing and detail drawings
on glass, paper, wood, clay, porcelain, stone, metal and mirrors. / The
paint is opaque and xylem based. / Its oil based formula allows for a
gloss finish to any project. / It is acid free, lead free, lightfast, weather-
proof and pigmented. / Great for crafting, home and office use; available
in violet color

Fig. 1. Textual descriptions of three products: product 1 and 2 are quite similar products, namely spice racks, while product 3 is multi-functional turntable.

We propose to compute product similarities by first filtering unrelated products using general descriptions like categories. Later, the remaining set of products is filtered by a combination of trained classifiers. These classifiers determine
the probability of whether a particular product bears similarity to a query product. We use a multi-modal approach consisting of two kinds of classifiers: (i)
a pretrained transformer language model that is finetuned to recognize similar
products based on textual descriptions and (ii) a Siamese neural network trained
to judge product similarity based on product images.

Product entity matching, a problem which is closely related to product similarity search, has been experimentally shown to benefit from the language understanding capabilities of transformers to distinguish between relevant and non-
relevant parts in the textual descriptions of products [12,13]. Textual descriptions of similar products often describe their identical properties using diverse
words. On the other hand, the textual descriptions of two unrelated products
share a similar narrative style with minute discrepancies. Figure 1 shows three
example products. The first two products are different brands of green oil paints
for artists. Despite the different wording in the descriptions, our used language
model classifies this pair as similar. In contrast, the third product is a pen that
can also be used by artists but has different applications. The baselines classify product pairs (1, 2) and (1, 3) as similar, while the language model classifies
those pairs as not similar. This is more meaningful in our application as product
1 and 2 are competing while product 3 has related but different use cases. These
example products demonstrate that a certain degree of language understanding is required to construct a meaningful similarity measure for the analysis of
similar e-commerce products.

In some cases, text descriptions do not fully capture the product, for instance there is a large variety of oil paints. Images may provide an additional meaningful mode of discrimination between those very similar and just remotely similar products. In this paper, we demonstrate that images can also be employed as a useful tool to distinguish products with misleadingly similar text descriptions, e.g. oil paint, related products like pens or other kinds of paint. In these cases, high text similarities could be corrected by a second model that measures similarity based on the images of the products.

The two models we use for similarity calculation take pairs of product descriptions as input. Given such pair of product descriptions, both models are trained to classify the input as cases of similar and not similar pairs. We derived suitable training data from a public collection of product descriptions crawled from the Amazon market place. In many cases, a product page includes beside the textual description and images of the product a table with similar products that is compiled by Amazon. These tables are different from other recommendations on a product page that show related but potentially non-similar products. For instance products that are brought frequently together with the product on the current product page and recommendations based on browsing history. However, not every Amazon product page contains a table of similar products. The product pairs for training and testing data are derived from those tables of similar products.

The model architectures we used for the classifiers are the Ditto model [12,13] that is originally used for product entity matching based on textual descriptions. Ditto extends a pretrained transformer language model like BERT [3,14,19] and is trained to classify pairs of textual product descriptions. For images, we propose to use a convolutional neural network [9] as building block in a Siamese network [1,2]. The contributions of our paper include

- We provide a training data set for learning similarities between pairs of products with modern neural network architectures.
- We propose a multi-modal approach to learn similarities between commercial products based on textual descriptions and images.
- We conduct extensive experiments and compare our approach to realistic baselines. The experiments show that our learned similarity approach based on language models and images outperforms competitive baselines.
- We present use case scenarios that demonstrate the applicability of our approach in a setting of an e-commerce company.

The remainder of the paper is organized as follows: next, we discuss related work in Sect. 2. In Sect. 3, we present our approach for learned similarity. Section 4 details the construction of the training data and baselines and explains the extensive experiments and use cases. Section 5 concludes the paper.

2 Related Work

Similarity search for e-commerce products has been studied for the case that products are described by structural data [7]. This approach employs a different but straight forward similarity function for each different kind of attribute like (multi)-categorical, dimensional and numerical.

More recent research investigates entity matching, which can be seen as a special case of product similarity search. Entity matching aims at finding all pairs of product entities from possibly multiple sources that represent the same product. A machine learning pipeline approach [17] works as follows: first, embeddings for product images and text features are learned. Second, features from product descriptions are extracted and then for each pair of products, a vector containing similarity values is constructed by computing similarity for each feature attribute in an analogous way as in [7]. Last, a classifier (for e.g. random forest, SVM, naive Bayes, logistic regression) is trained using the similarity vectors of these product pairs to identify matching products.

Different neural architectures are evaluated for product matching that have been proposed for other matching problems in natural language processing [15]. The investigated neural network architectures include RNN, Smooth Inverse Frequency (SIF) sentence embeddings and early attention-based approaches. Those neural architectures already show advantages over traditional learning approaches, especially with respect to robustness on noisy data. The best approach is named DeepMatcher.

In general, entity matching is considered as a classification problem. A product pair is input to a neural network. Standard loss functions measure model performance on given training data and help optimize the model parameters such that the loss function is minimized. Another option is to train a Siamese neural network with a triplet loss function using contrastive learning. This loss function also learns good embeddings that are comparable to those learned by the pairwise classification approach.

Deep learning approaches such as the deep entity matching model Ditto [12, 13] use blocking and pre-trained transformers like BERT [3] or its variants [14, 19]. The blocking step efficiently filters all pairs that will not match using implicit comparison. The remaining pairs are candidate matching pairs. Each pair is transformed into an input sequence that is classified by a transformer neural network as matching or not matching. This approach treats both structured and unstructured input data as textual data and outperforms other SOTA entity matching systems like DeepMatcher and DeepER [5]. In this paper, we utilize Ditto model as a part of our product similarity search application.

Recently, Ditto was compared to another entity matcher called GTA [4] that also uses transformers to compute embeddings. However, GTA is designed for structured data and it employs a relational transformers, which is not pre-trained for language understanding. Therefore, GTA shows better performance than Ditto only for structured data. In our application, Ditto is preferred over GTA, since structured data is usually not available in real-life use cases of product similarity.

Several approaches use image data in combination with other sources to improve product similarity search. Embeddings derived by a convolutional neural network (CNN) could improve the performance of a model based on sentence embeddings for entity matching [17]. In this paper, we also investigate options to use image data to improve product similarity search.

3 Learning Similarities for Products

The key observation for our use case of product similarity search is that similarities between products may depend on subtle differences in the descriptions. Therefore, it seems not plausible to define a similarity function without using any data like in [7]. Instead, our approach applies binary classification models to product pairs that proved already successful for product entity matching. But in contrast to entity matching, we train these models on pairs of similar but non-matching products. After training, we can use the classification probability as a similarity score. This similarity function for ranking products is learned from the product data.

Since the used classification models in our approach are expensive to apply to all products in a collection, we use a blocking step first on all possible product pairs of an e-commerce catalog. Given a query product, the blocking step filters out all products that are not in the same category or sub-category. The remaining products are ranked by the learned similarity function. In the following subsections, we briefly review the applied models and describe a way to combine the results from models for textual descriptions of products and for product images to a multi-modal similarity score.

3.1 Similarity of Textual Product Descriptions

A product description consists of three parts, namely the product title, a list of product features and a short product description in form of free text. We use the Ditto model [12,13] to compute similarities on these textual informations of the products. Given a query product q and a product p from the collection of products, first, the textual parts are concatenated to a single sequence of tokens. The sequence contains the CLS-, SEP- and END-tokens that are introduced by the general transformer model, which in turn is the main part of the Ditto model. Following the Ditto approach, the textual parts of the products are prefixed with strings that name the particular parts like title, features and description. Names and values are separated by additional special tokens [COL] and [VAL] that are introduced by Ditto.

$$\text{sim}_{\text{text}}(q,p) = \text{ditto}(\text{seq}(q,p)) \text{ with} \tag{1}$$
$$\text{seq}(q,p) = [\text{CLS}] +$$
$$[\text{COL}] + \text{`title'} + [\text{VAL}] + q.\text{title} +$$
$$[\text{COL}] + \text{`feature'} + [\text{VAL}] + q.\text{features} +$$
$$[\text{COL}] + \text{`description'} + [\text{VAL}] + q.\text{description} +$$
$$[\text{SEP}] +$$
$$[\text{COL}] + \text{`title'} + [\text{VAL}] + p.\text{title} +$$
$$[\text{COL}] + \text{`feature'} + [\text{VAL}] + p.\text{features} +$$
$$[\text{COL}] + \text{`description'} + [\text{VAL}] + p.\text{description} +$$
$$[\text{END}]$$

The respective, textual parts of the query product and the product from the collection are represented by $x.\text{title}$, $x.\text{features}$ and $x.\text{description}$ with $x \in \{p,q\}$. The sequence is then tokenized in the appropriate way for the used transformer model and is then input into the transformer. The output of the transformer is an embedding vector for each token of the input sequence. The Ditto model extends the transformer model by adding a fully connected linear layer with dropout that takes the embedding of the CLS-token as input and has two outputs for the two classes *similar* and *not similar*. On top of the linear layer comes a softmax-function that normalizes the output to probabilities. The probability for class *similar* is returned as the similarity score for the pair of textual product descriptions.

The used transformer is a pre-trained neural network that is finetuned to classify pairs of products. The finetuning is done by minimizing the cross entropy loss function using stochastic gradient. During the pre-training step, popular transformers like BERT use the special token CLS for classification tasks. Hence, the embedding of CLS-token is also used for the classification of similar products in our approach.

Following the Ditto approach, we apply data augmentation and summarization heuristics during the training (finetuning) of the model. Data augmentation slightly modifies given training data and as a result, the amount as well as diversity of the training set is increased. The modification operations include randomly deleting single tokens or whole column-value pairs from the sequences. Another modification is to swap the order of the two products in a sequence.

Summarization computes term frequency (TF) and inverse document frequency (IDF) scores for each token in the training data. Tokens (except the special tokens) with low TF-IDF scores are dropped. This step eliminates stop words and other tokens with low information value. Both heuristics helped to improve the performance of Ditto for product entity matching. Thus, we also applied these methods in our application scenario.

3.2   Similarity of Product Images

Product images are another valuable source to compute a meaningful similarity score. After converting the images to the same size, each image is transformed into an embedding vector. Similarity between two images is then measured as cosine similarity between the respective embedding vectors.

We use a Siamese neural network approach [1], which is very suitable to learn how to compare multidimensional vectors [2]. A Siamese neural network which utilizes triplet loss consists of three identical feed forward subnetworks. That implies that all subnetworks share the same configuration with the same weight. Hence, the total number of parameters is effectively that of a single one. The particular Siamese network model we use [9] stacks several convolutional layers and possesses a fully connected normalization layer at the end that computes the output embedding vector.

Siamese networks that are trained by minimizing a triplet loss function take three input images called anchor, positive example and negative example. The triplet loss forces the network to learn how to embed input images such that the distance between anchor and positive is minimized and at the same time the distance between anchor and negative is maximized [10]. Hence, triplet loss can be defined in terms of a distance function d

$$L(A, P, N) = \max\big(d(A, P) - d(A, N) + \alpha, 0\big) \tag{2}$$

with A is the anchor, P the positive and N the negative example. Thus, the training data for a Siamese network consists of such triplets (A, P, N). During training, the three networks with shared weights compute the embedding vectors of the three images. The network weights are adjusted using a back-propagation process that starts from the triplet loss function. The parameter $\alpha > 0$ of the loss function, which is called margin, helps to push not similar image embeddings farther away and to bring similar image embeddings closer to each other.

3.3   Multi-modal Model

The similarity scores that are output by the (trained) models for pairs of textual product descriptions and product images are linearly combined to a multi-modal similarity score. Thus, the score p_t from the text model and the score p_i from the image model are weighted and combined to a multi-modal score p_m as follows:

$$p_m = \beta \cdot p_t + (1 - \beta) \cdot p_i \text{ with } 0 \le \beta \le 1 \tag{3}$$

When the similarity score exceeds a threshold the product pair is considered similar. The parameters α, β and the classification threshold are estimated by evaluating the F1 values on training data. The parameter settings with the highest F1-score on the training data are used.

4   Experiments

In this section, we first explain how the training data set is constructed and how the models for the learned product similarity function are trained and tested. Second, we give details about the baselines that we compare with our approach. Then, we present the result of the main experiments that show how our multi-modal approach performs with respect to the baselines. In the following ablation studies, we experimentally verify and discuss the impact and contribution of each main building block. Last, we show an use case of how to apply the newly learned similarity measure in an e-commerce application scenario.

4.1   Datasets and Model Training

We constructed the training data using the *Amazon review data 2018* [16]. This data set consists of millions of product metadata and reviews in about 25 different product categories. For our experiments, we concentrated on seven particular categories that are also included in the product catalog of Relaxdays: *arts, home, garden, pet supplies, sports, tools* and *toys*. The product metadata schema includes 18 product attributes. From those, we used the ASIN (an Amazon product identifier), *categories* and *similar* (an HTML table of similar products) for filtering and generation of class labels (*similar* and *not similar*). For the training of the textual similarity models, we used the attributes *title, feature* and *description*. The training data for the image similarity model was extracted from the *image* attribute, which contains a list of URLs pointing to product images. We used the first working image URL in each list to retrieve one image for each product.

Blocking: Similarity functions like Ditto are expensive. Thus, given a query q, the similarity function should not be executed for every pair (q, p) with p is a product from the collection. Therefore, blocking is an established pre-filtering heuristic [12,21]. Products that are not similar are efficiently filtered out. We use a simple but meaningful heuristic that uses the subcategories as filter. Each product in the Amazon dataset belongs to a main category and to one or several subcategories. After the blocking step, products of only the same subcategory are compared with the expensive learned similarity function. This kind of blocking step is also applicable to the application data at Relaxdays.

Definition of Labels: Labeled product pairs with class labels *similar* and *not similar* are necessary to train networks like Ditto and the Siamese networks. The generated labeled data is in line with the used blocking method that means no similar product pair has products that belong to different product subcategories. As the first step, for each subcategory, a product graph is created, the nodes of which correspond to the respective products. Two nodes are connected with an undirected edge, if and only if one corresponding product appears in the table of similar products of the other product. In general, those graphs consists of several connected components. Manual inspection revealed that products in the same connected component are similar with respect to product images and descriptions, while products from different connected components are dissimilar. Thus, we labeled product pairs that are directly connected with an edge as *similar* and product pairs with products in the same subcategory but in different connected components as *not similar*.

To improve the quality of the training data, products without title, description or image are removed. Further, connected components with fewer than 15 products are also removed. Product pairs are randomly selected from all remaining connected components to be included in the training data for a given subcategory.

The triplets for training with the triplet loss function are generated by first randomly selecting the anchor product from a given subcategory. Second, a product from the same connected component in the subcategory that is directly connected by an edge with the anchor product is selected as positive example. Third, another product from a different connected component in the subcategory is selected as negative example. The triplet anchors are uniformly selected from all categories and connected components.

Training, Validation and Testdata: From each of the seven main categories, 1200 pairs of similar and 3000 pairs of not similar products are randomly selected. Thus, the union of these data sets consists of 29400 pairs in total. For the training of the image similarity models, from each main category, 2000 triplets are randomly selected. The models are trained on a random but fixed subset of 60% of the data, 20% are used for validation and the remaining 20% are used for testing. The Data is available at: https://github.com/myle93/similar_product.

Parameter Estimation: We used grid search to estimate the best settings for the parameters α, β and the classification threshold of the different models. The grid search uses the F1 measure on training data to evaluate the settings of particular values. For each main product category, a separate grid search is done and specific values for α, β and the classification threshold are estimated.

4.2   Baselines

We describe competitive baselines for textual similarity search and for image similarity search. The baseline for textual similarity search is then combined with the Siamese CNN model to a multi-modal baseline model as described in Sect. 3.3. The parameter and the threshold of the multi-modal baseline are estimated in the same way as for the proposed multi-modal model.

Text retrieval and similarity search map documents, which are product descriptions in our application, to vectors that are compared using cosine similarity. We use cosine similarity in combination with a weighting scheme that multiplies term frequency (TF) with the inverse document frequency (IDF). The tokenization is based on words, which is in contrast to the Ditto model that uses subword tokenization. As preprocessing step, stop words and punctuations are removed. A threshold determines up to which similarity score, product pairs are considered as similar. The threshold is estimated experimentally from the given data.

ResNet [6] is a popular pretrained neural model for image classification. It takes images with a resolution of 32 by 32 pixels [18]. The resolutions of product images vary between 28 by 28 and 40 by 40 pixels. Thus, all images are converted to a resolution of 32 by 32. We use ResNet with pretrained weights and without any fine-tuning to compute embeddings for the images. Analogous to the baseline for textual similarity search, we use a threshold to classify images as *similar* and *not similar*.

4.3   Multi-modal Similarity

We compare our proposed multi-modal similarity model with a multi-modal baseline as well as with the individual parts of the multi-modal models. The language models are trained on the union of all training data from all seven main categories we worked with. The rationale behind this decision is that large pre-trained transformer models like BERT benefit from more training data. However, for the image data, we train a separate Siamese CNN model for each category. Thus, the Siamese CNN models could specialize on properties that are specific for each category. In the ablation studies, we experimentally analyze various alternatives to these decisions.

Table 1. Left: F1-Score as metric to evaluate the performance of each model on test data of each category. Columns from left to right: product categories, text baseline, image baseline, transformer-based Ditto model for textual product data, multi-modal baseline tf-idf + Siamese CNN, our proposed model Ditto + Siamese CNN. Right: weights of the proposed multi-modal model consisting of the Ditto and Siamese CNN model. Note that the shown weights are not used for the multi-modal baseline model. For this model, the weights are separately estimated.

Category	tf-idf	Siamese CNN	Ditto	multi-modal baseline	multi-modal model	weights	
						β	$1 - \beta$
	(text)	(image)	(text)	(text+image)	(text+image)	(text)	(image)
art	0.880	0.885	0.948	0.965	**0.980**	0.47	0.53
pet supplies	0.641	0.583	0.744	0.680	**0.755**	0.84	0.16
home	0.657	0.589	0.841	0.692	**0.864**	0.66	0.34
garden	0.708	0.586	0.829	0.743	**0.825**	0.72	0.28
sport	0.795	0.636	0.836	0.830	**0.873**	0.65	0.35
toys	0.654	0.572	0.809	0.698	**0.823**	0.67	0.33
tools	0.653	0.536	0.831	0.644	**0.841**	0.63	0.37

Table 1 (left) shows that our proposed multi-modal model consistently out-performs all other models with respect to F1 values on test data over all product categories. Our proposed multi-modal model has significant gains over the

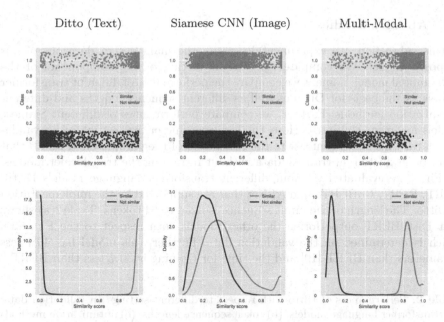

Fig. 2. The figures in the columns from left to right show the similarity scores for pairs of the classes *similar* and *not similar* computed by the Ditto model (left), the Siamese CNN image model (middle) and the combined multi-modal model (right). The top plots shows the scores for class labels plus a random Gaussian values on the y-axis to avoid over plotting. The bottom plots show class-specific densities.

multi-modal baseline model that uses the simple td-idf-model for textual product descriptions. The gains are much less pronounced with respect to the Ditto model that uses textual product descriptions as the sole data source. This shows that the pretrained transformer model that powers the Ditto model contributes the main part to the performance of the multi-modal model.

The Siamese CNN models for product images are on their own not that powerful. However, the language model and the Siamese CNN model are not redundant as there are cases where the image model successfully corrects the language model. Figure 2 shows that the Ditto model returns similarity scores that are close to the binary class labels. In most cases, the Ditto model is right but not in all cases. The Siamese CNN image model returns a distribution of similarity scores that uses the full range from zero to one. While this blurs the similarity scores of the combined multi-modal model, the combination is more helpful than harming the classification rates and the F1 scores.

Last, we looked at the weights of the proposed multi-modal model that are presented in Table 1 (right) for each product category. Except the *art* category, the weights for the language model are consistently higher than the weights for the image models. This is expected, because the language model has consistently better F1-Scores in all categories than the image model. However, the weights for the image model are not close to zero but approximately 0.3 on average. This shows that the image model contributes a significant part to the overall result.

4.4   Ablation Studies

In this subsection, we experimentally verify the main design decisions of our proposed model. We compare the various setting of the components of the multi-modal model, namely, we compare the performance of different transformer models as the basis for Ditto as well as different sequence lengths and different optimization methods. Further, we compare performances of different Siamese models for image similarity. Here, the hyperparameters are estimated on validation data, which is in contrast to the estimation of the parameters α and β that could be evaluated on training data without retraining the transformer models.

First, we evaluated the four different transformer language models Distil-BERT, BERT, RoBERTa und XLNet that are supported by the implementation of Ditto. The length of the input sequence is fixed to 64 tokens. Table 2(a) shows that DistilBERT outperforms the other models with respect to the F1 score, which is determined on the validation data. Further, this model has 40% less parameters than BERT [19] and the time for training is 50% less than BERT.

Table 2. Performances of Ditto with respect to different settings on validation data: (a) transformer language models, (b) token sequence lengths, (c) optimization methods for Ditto.

(a)

Model	Time Training	F1
DistillBERT	30 min	**87.1**
BERT	60 min	82.3
RoBERTa	50 min	74.0
XLNet	75 min	78.1

(b)

Seq. len.	F1
32	67.8
64	**87.1**
128	86.3
256	79.8
512	77.4

(c)

Model	F1
Ditto(plain)	49.1
Ditto(S)	86.8
Ditto(S+DA)	86.9
Ditto(S+KD)	85.1
Ditto(S+DA+KD)	**87.1**

Next, we checked the impact of the length of the token sequence of the input for the DistilBERT model. Table 2(b) shows that a length of 64 tokens has the best F1 score. Larger token sequences have better recall but precision gets worse.

Last, we evaluated the impact of the different optimization methods of Ditto, namely summarization (S), data augmentation (DA) and domain knowledge (KD). Table 2(c) shows the results of several combinations of the methods. The combination of all three methods gives the best performance. Summarization seems to have the largest impact, while data augmentation and domain knowledge have little additional impact. We used Ditto(S+DA+KD) in all the other experiments and referred as Ditto to this methods.

We also analyzed the pretrained image model ResNet50 as alternative building block to the CNN network that we used in the Siamese network for image similarity. In this experiments, both models are trained with the union of the data from all categories. The margin α is set to 0.2. Contrary to our expectations, the popular ResNet50 [11] performs less well that the simpler CNN network, as shown in Table 3(a). In order to increase the performance of image similarity models, we trained Siamese CNN models on the data of separate categories. Due to worse performance and high training costs, we did not further investigate the ResNet50. Table 3(b) shows the F1 performances for different settings for α and different categories. This modification increased the performance, however, the image models still perform less well than the Ditto model on textual product descriptions. We also investigated data augmentation to improve the image model, however, no improvement was found.

Table 3. Comparison of image models on validation data: (a) F1-Score of ResNet50 and the CNN model as building blocks in a Siamese network for image similarity, (b) F1-Score of Siamese CNN models for different settings for α and different categories.

(a)

Model	F1
ResNet50	52.7
CNN	**68.1**

(b)

Category	$\alpha = 0.2$	$\alpha = 0.6$	$\alpha = 0.8$	$\alpha = 0.9$
art	78.4	**87.4**	84.3	85.9
pet supplies	55.3	58.7	**60.8**	58.5
home	52.6	54.4	55.6	**58.4**
garden	50.0	56.0	**57.1**	54.7
sport	58.8	**64.3**	63.7	61.3
toys	54.1	57.3	58.3	**60.4**
tools	48.2	53.6	**56.2**	54.7

4.5   Use Case

Suppose an employee in the sales department wants to analyze the competing products of – for example – a steel engineer ruler[1], which is in the product subcategory *Tool/Home Improvement, Measuring/Layout Tools, Linear Measurement* in order to decide if the product should be included into the companies portfolio and what a fair product price could be. The similarity search with our proposed multi-modal approach returns for the given query exclusively other steel engineer rulers as the top 10 similar products[2], which are all directly competing products. In contrast, the multi-modal baseline returns also similar products like tape measures for construction workers and dress makers as well as feeler gauges[3] that are classified as *not similar* by our approach. The results of the

---

[1] We specify the Amazon ASIN and embed the full link in the PDF file: B00AG7XYF0.

[2] We give the ASINs of the top 5 results: B004490010, B004490TNQ, B000065CEB, B0015AQMSS, B0017JW7I6.

[3] Generally similar but unrelated products returned by the multi-modal baseline: B00A6W2AOQ, B00Y73TB1A, B001737NYU, B01AO2KO3Q.

baseline could be explained by terms like steel and measure that appear in the description of the query as well as in those of the returned results. Relevant for the application use case are only the steel engineer rulers, because the other products are not directly competing products with respect to the query.

5   Conclusions

We proposed an effective product similarity search application based on an entity matching approach that uses transformer language models. This shows that entity matching technology can be effectively reused to be part of similarity search methods. Further, we demonstrated that combining a language model with an image model to a multi-modal improves the performance. The proposed model can learn the specific needs of our similarity search application. Last, we published our training data set, which can be used to learn improved models for product similarity search applications. Future work includes the development of models that integrate language and text and can learn joint pattern of product descriptions and product images.

References

1. Bromley, J., Guyon, I., LeCun, Y., Säckinger, E., Shah, R.: Signature verification using a Siamese time delay neural network, pp. 737–744 (1993)
2. Chicco, D.: Siamese neural networks: an overview. **2190**, 73–94 (2021)
3. Devlin, J., Chang, M.W., Lee, K., Toutanova, K.: BERT: pre-training of deep bidirectional transformers for language understanding. CoRR abs/1810.04805 (2018)
4. Dou, W., et al.: Empowering transformer with hybrid matching knowledge for entity matching. In: Bhattacharya, A., et al. (eds.) Database Systems for Advanced Applications, pp. 52–67. Springer, Cham (2022). https://doi.org/10.1007/978-3-031-00129-1_4
5. Ebraheem, M., Thirumuruganathan, S., Joty, S.R., Ouzzani, M., Tang, N.: Distributed representations of tuples for entity resolution. Proc. VLDB Endow. **11**(11), 1454–1467 (2018)
6. He, K., Zhang, X., Ren, S., Sun, J.: Deep residual learning for image recognition. In: 2016 IEEE Conference on Computer Vision and Pattern Recognition, CVPR, pp. 770–778. IEEE Computer Society (2016)
7. Hoffmann, U., da Silva, A.S., de Carvalho, M.G.: Finding similar products in e-commerce sites based on attributes. In: Calì, A., Vidal, M.E. (eds.) Proceedings of the 9th Alberto Mendelzon International Workshop on Foundations of Data Management. CEUR Workshop Proceedings, vol. 1378 (2015)
8. Huang, Z., Zeng, D., Chen, H.: A comparison of collaborative-filtering recommendation algorithms for e-commerce. IEEE Intell. Syst. **22**(5), 68–78 (2007)
9. Koch, G., Zemel, R., Salakhutdinov, R., et al.: Siamese neural networks for one-shot image recognition. In: ICML Deep Learning Workshop, vol. 2 (2015)
10. Kumar, V., Carneiro, G., Reid, I.D.: Learning local image descriptors with deep Siamese and triplet convolutional networks by minimizing global loss functions. In: IEEE Conference on Computer Vision and Pattern Recognition, CVPR, pp. 5385–5394. IEEE Computer Society (2016)

11. Kuwahara, T., et al.: Current status of artificial intelligence analysis for endoscopic ultrasonography. Dig. Endosc. **33**(2), 298–305 (2021)
12. Li, Y., Li, J., Suhara, Y., Doan, A., Tan, W.C.: Deep entity matching with pre-trained language models. Proc. VLDB Endow. **14**(1), 50–60 (2020)
13. Li, Y., Li, J., Suhara, Y., Wang, J., Hirota, W., Tan, W.C.: Deep entity matching: challenges and opportunities. ACM J. Data Inf. Qual. **13**(1), 1:1–1:17 (2021)
14. Liu, Y., et al.: Roberta: a robustly optimized BERT pretraining approach. CoRR abs/1907.11692 (2019)
15. Mudgal, S., et al.: Deep learning for entity matching: a design space exploration. In: Proceedings of the 2018 International Conference on Management of Data, SIGMOD, pp. 19–34. ACM (2018)
16. Ni, J., Li, J., McAuley, J.: Justifying recommendations using distantly-labeled reviews and fine-grained aspects. In: Proceedings of the 2019 Conference on Empirical Methods in Natural Language Processing and the 9th International Joint Conference on Natural Language Processing (EMNLP-IJCNLP), pp. 188–197 (2019)
17. Ristoski, P., Petrovski, P., Mika, P., Paulheim, H.: A machine learning approach for product matching and categorization. Semant. Web **9**(5), 707–728 (2018)
18. Sachan, A.: Detailed guide to understand and implement ResNets (2019). https://cv-tricks.com/keras/understand-implement-resnets/
19. Sanh, V., Debut, L., Chaumond, J., Wolf, T.: DistilBERT, a distilled version of BERT: smaller, faster, cheaper and lighter. CoRR abs/1910.01108 (2019)
20. Sarwar, B.M., Karypis, G., Konstan, J.A., Riedl, J.: Item-based collaborative filtering recommendation algorithms. In: Proceedings of the Tenth International World Wide Web Conference, WWW 10, pp. 285–295. ACM (2001)
21. Thirumuruganathan, S., et al.: Deep learning for blocking in entity matching: a design space exploration. Proc. VLDB Endow. **14**(11), 2459–2472 (2021)

Deep Vision-Language Model for Efficient Multi-modal Similarity Search in Fashion Retrieval

Gianluca Moro(iD) and Stefano Salvatori(✉)(iD)

Department of Computer Science and Engineering - DISI, University of Bologna, Cesena, Italy
{gianluca.moro,s.salvatori}@unibo.it

Abstract. Fashion multi-modal retrieval has been recently addressed using vision-and-language transformers. However, these models cannot scale in training time and memory requirements due to the quadratic attention mechanism. Moreover, they design the retrieval as a classification task, assigning a similarity score to pairs of text and images in input. Each query is thus resolved inefficiently by pairing it, at runtime, with every text or image in the entire dataset, precluding the scalability to large-scale datasets. We propose a novel approach for efficient multi-modal retrieval in the fashion domain that combines self-supervised pre-training with linear attention and deep metric learning to create a latent space where spatial proximity among instances translates into a semantic similarity score. Unlike existing contributions, our approach separately embeds text and images, decoupling them and allowing to collocate and search in the space, after training, even for new images with missing text and vice versa. Experiments show that with a single 12 GB GPU, our solution outperforms, both in efficacy and efficiency, existing state-of-the-art contributions on the FashionGen dataset. Our architecture also enables the adoption of multidimensional indices, with which retrieval scales in logarithmic time up to millions, and potentially billions, of text and images.

Keywords: Fashion multi-modal retrieval · Text and images · Metric learning · Linear attention · Deep learning

1 Introduction

A growing number of deep neural networks have been proposed in information retrieval to address the problem of multi-modal retrieval, which involves matching queries and documents across different modalities. Much studied in this context are Text-to-Image and Image-to-Text retrieval. These are not trivial tasks, especially if addressed in the fashion domain, where queries can refer to fine-grained details of clothes and garments (e.g., *"Low sneakers in black polished leather. Round toe. Closure with tone-on-tone laces..."*). The precision

© The Author(s), under exclusive license to Springer Nature Switzerland AG 2022
T. Skopal et al. (Eds.): SISAP 2022, LNCS 13590, pp. 40–53, 2022.
https://doi.org/10.1007/978-3-031-17849-8_4

required is higher than in general domain retrieval, where the focus is instead on coarse-grained objects (e.g., *"A yellow fire hydrant in front of a blue wall"*).

Recently, state-of-the-art (SOTA) results in fashion multi-modal retrieval have been obtained by FashionBERT [14] and KaleidoBERT [43] using Vision-and-Language (V+L) transformers, which are transformers [37] able to process both text and images in a single architecture. These models are trained with multiple self-supervised tasks and perform retrieval by assigning a similarity score to text-image pairs fed to the model as a single, coupled input. Despite their efficacy, the solutions proposed in [14] and [43] suffer from two main drawbacks: (i) they are inefficient on large-scale datasets since they perform retrieval by coupling a query with every document in the dataset at runtime; (ii) the attention mechanism has a quadratic space-time complexity which precludes self-supervised pretraining and inference on limited computational resources without overly reducing the input length.

In this paper, we address both the above limitations and propose a solution for fashion multi-modal retrieval that is more efficient and effective than previous approaches. Our contribution is two-fold: (i) we introduce a linear complexity V+L transformer that can be trained on low-resource regimes and can handle longer inputs and larger batch sizes with reduced inference and training times; (ii) we propose a two-stage training that combines self-supervised pretraining and deep metric learning to generate a joint latent space where, in the end, text and images can be separately embedded. Our trained model can be used to output individual latent representations for both texts and images without having them interact with each other in the inner layers at runtime. This strategy significantly increases retrieval performance since embeddings can be computed offline, and multidimensional indices can be used to run a nearest neighbor search in logarithmic time. We achieve new SOTA Rank@K accuracies for Text-to-Image and Image-to-Text retrieval on the FashionGen [32] dataset, proving the efficacy of our approach. Furthermore, we demonstrate the efficiency of our linear V+L transformer, showing that we can perform self-supervised pretraining on a single GPU with 12 GB of RAM, unlike previous SOTA solutions that are trained with a higher number of more powerful computational resources.

2   Related Work

Fashion Retrieval and V+L Transformers. Early solutions toward fashion multi-modal retrieval with deep learning were proposed in [44] and [21]. Using probabilistic and algebraic methods, the authors combined a bag-of-word model with convolutional and recurrent neural networks to address the text-image retrieval task. Despite the effectiveness of recurrent neural networks [10] however, improvements in fashion multi-modal retrieval have been recently obtained mainly through the transformer architecture. Many solutions have already been proposed [23–25,31,34,38] for retrieval with V+L transformers on general-domain datasets. These rely on pretrained convolutional neural networks (CNN) to extract Regions of Interest (RoIs) from images and treat them as tokens to be fed to the transformer model together with text tokens. Some authors [14,43], however, claimed that RoIs are not suitable for retrieving fashion products since they tend to ignore fine-grained details. Instead, they improved retrieval results by subdividing images into square patches and feeding them to a V+L transformer as dense vectors extracted with a pretrained image model (i.e., ResNet [17]). However, one downside of these transformer-based approaches is that they cannot be easily adopted on low resource regimes since their self-attention mechanism has a quadratic space-time complexity. Indeed, many "X-former" [36] models have been studied to reduce the computational complexity of the attention layers [2,20,42], but their application on V+L transformers has not yet been explored. In this work, we propose a linear-complexity V+L transformer based on the *Fast Attention Via Positive Orthogonal Random Features* (FAVOR+) algorithm [2] that provides a scalable, low-variance and unbiased estimation of the attention matrix. Our model is thus efficient and lightweight compared to previously proposed architectures [14,15,43] for Image-to-Text and Text-to-Image retrieval in the fashion domain.

Representation vs Interaction. Representation learning and deep metric learning have been applied in many natural language processing tasks [7,8,28]. Some works regarding multi-modal retrieval [11,13,39] proposed to learn a joint latent space where text and images representations are embedded and the distance between vectors represents a measure of similarity. These models can be referred to as *Representation-Focused* and are usually trained with ranking losses such as Contrastive Loss [16] or Triplet Loss [18]. Nevertheless, SOTA results have been recently obtained by V+L transformers [14,23–25,31,43] trained with multiple self-supervised tasks to assign a similarity score to text-image pairs. This strategy has the advantage that texts and images can freely interact in the attention layers, thus allowing the model to learn deeper relationships between the two modalities. We refer to these models as *Interaction-Focused*. One disadvantage of Interaction-Focused architectures is that they are not trained to generate a latent representation of images and texts, thus excluding the possibility of using efficient indexing strategies on embeddings [3,19,29]. As also addressed in [26], this fact limits the application of these solutions to large-scale datasets, in which, instead, efficient access methods are essential. Our work aims to keep the advantages of both Interaction and Representation approaches by combining a self-supervised pretraining phase and a metric learning fine-tuning for efficient multi-modal retrieval in the fashion domain.

3   Methodology

3.1   FAVOR+ Linear Attention

Many solutions have been proposed to reduce the computational complexity of the attention layer. We decided to adopt FAVOR+ since it is one of the most efficient ones in terms of speed and memory requirements [35].

Denoting the input length with L and hidden dimensions with d, FAVOR+ reduces time complexity from $O(L^2 d)$ to $O(Lrd)$ and space complexity from $O(L^2 + Ld)$ to $O(Lr + Ld + rd)$ with r hyperparameter such that $r \ll L$.

It starts by formulating classical attention in the following way:

$$Att(\mathbf{Q}, \mathbf{K}, \mathbf{V}) = \mathbf{D}^{-1}\mathbf{A}\mathbf{V} \quad \mathbf{A} = \exp(\frac{\mathbf{Q}\mathbf{K}^\top}{\sqrt{d}}) \quad \mathbf{D} = \mathrm{diag}(\mathbf{A}\mathbf{1}_L) \qquad (1)$$

where $\mathrm{diag}(.)$ is the diagonal matrix with the input vector as the diagonal and $\mathbf{1}_L$ is the all-ones vector. $\mathbf{Q}, \mathbf{K}$, and $\mathbf{V}$ are intermediate projections of the input obtained with matrices of learnable weights. Their dimension is $L \times d$, therefore the overall cost of computing A in Eq. 1 is quadratic with respect to L.

The core idea behind FAVOR+ is to define a function $\phi : \mathbb{R}^d \to \mathbb{R}_+^r$ such that, given two vectors $\mathbf{x}, \mathbf{y}$, the product $\phi(\mathbf{x})^\top \phi(\mathbf{y})$ approximates $\exp(\mathbf{x}^\top \mathbf{y})$. Equation 1 can be now transformed as follows:

$$Att(\mathbf{Q}, \mathbf{K}, \mathbf{V}) = \hat{\mathbf{D}}^{-1}(\mathbf{Q}'((\mathbf{K}')^\top \mathbf{V})) \quad \hat{\mathbf{D}} = diag(\mathbf{Q}'((\mathbf{K}')^\top \mathbf{1}_L)) \qquad (2)$$

where $\mathbf{Q}', \mathbf{K}' \in \mathbb{R}^{L \times r}$ are matrices with rows given as $\phi(q_i^\top)^\top$ and $\phi(k_i^\top)^\top$, with q_i, k_i being the i-th row-vector of $\mathbf{Q}$ and $\mathbf{K}$ respectively.

Ordering computation in Eq. 2 according to the parentheses avoids explicitly computing the L^2 matrix, hence providing a linear approximation of the attention mechanism. It can be shown that ϕ must be of the form: $\phi(\mathbf{x}) = \frac{h(\mathbf{x})}{\sqrt{r}} f(\mathbf{W}\mathbf{x})^\top$ where h and f are carefully chosen functions and $\mathbf{W} \in \mathbb{R}^{r \times d}$ is a matrix of r random orthogonal vectors[1]. The higher r the better the approximation.

3.2 Pretraining

The model architecture used in this first training phase is shown in Fig. 1. It is a transformer model where the attention layer is approximated using the FAVOR+ algorithm, and a paired input of the form *(text, image)* is used to allow multimodal semantics.

Each text is split up into tokens using the BERT tokenizer [4]. Two special tokens ([CLS] and [SEP]) are added at the beginning and the end of the sentence. Each token is transformed through a text embedding layer into a dense vector $t \in \mathbb{R}^{768}$. Positional embeddings are added to the representation obtained and segmentation embeddings are employed to differentiate it from visual input: we use an array of zeroes for texts and an array of ones for images. We do not extract RoIs from images, as they have already proven ineffective in fashion retrieval [14]. Each image is split instead into a fixed number of square patches (64 in our experiments), transformed into 2048 dimensional vectors using ResNet50 [17]. Patches are then processed through image, positional, and segmentation embedding layers to get a representation $p \in \mathbb{R}^{768}$. Text and image vectors are then

---

[1] The reader can refer to [2] for further technical details and a rigorous proof of why this approximation works.

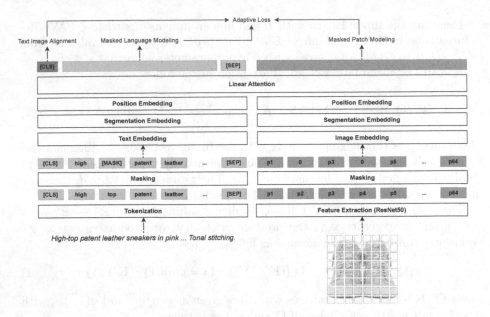

Fig. 1. Pretraining architecture. Texts are tokenized, masked with a certain probability and given in input to the embedding layers to extract an intermediate latent representation; images are split into patches, transformed into dense vectors, masked, and, as for texts, processed through image embedding layers. The representations obtained are then concatenated and fed as input to the linear attention layers. The model is trained on 3 tasks: Text-Image Alignment, Masked Language Modeling and Masked Patch Modeling. The three losses are combined using the Adaptive Loss strategy.

concatenated and interact with each other through the linear attention layers[2]. The model is trained on three tasks.

Text-Image Alignment (TIA). The output of the [CLS] token is used to predict whether the input text is describing the given image. Given a text-image pair (t, p) sampled from the dataset D, and called $s(t, p)$ the score returned by the classifier, the loss is a binary cross entropy defined as follows

$$L_1(\theta) = -E_{(t,p) \sim D}[y \log s_\theta(t, p) + (1 - y) \log (1 - s_\theta(t, p))]$$

where y is the true label of the input and θ denotes the weights of the model.

Masked Language Modeling (MLM). We randomly mask 15% of input text tokens: 80% of the time they get replaced with a special [MASK] token, 10% with a random word, and 10% of the time they stay unchanged. Denoting with $t_{\backslash i} = \{t_1, ..., [MASK]_i, ..., t_n\}$ the input sentence in which the i-th token has been masked, the following loss is minimized for all masked tokens t_i

$$L_2(\theta) = -E_{(t,p) \sim D}[log P_\theta(t_i | t_{\backslash i}, p)]$$

---

[2] The total input length L is therefore the sum of both text tokens and image patches.

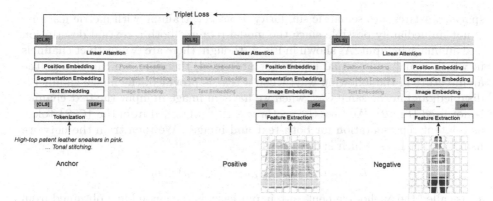

Fig. 2. Architecture for Triplet Loss training. The product description is used as the anchor element, and the corresponding image and a random image are used as positive and negative elements, respectively. When a text is given in input, the image processing channel is disabled, and, in the same way, if an image is given, the text processing channel is not used. In both cases the final representation is given by the output vector relative to the CLS token.

where $P_\theta(t_i|t_{\backslash i}, p)$ denotes the probability assigned by the model to the masked-out token t_i given its surrounding text $t_{\backslash i}$ and image patches p.

Masked Patch Modeling (MPP). For this task, image patches are masked instead of text tokens. Given input patches $p = \{p_1, \ldots, p_m\}$, we denote with $p_{\backslash i} = \{p_1, \ldots, \mathbf{0}_i, \ldots, p_m\}$ the sequence in which the i-th patch has been masked and replaced with a zero vector (we mask five patches per image). The model must reconstruct the image by learning a continuous distribution over the values of the masked patches. If $Distr(p_i)$ is the real distribution and $Distr_\theta(p_i|p_{\backslash i}, t)$ is the one predicted by the network given its surrounding patches and the text t, we want to minimize their Kullback-Leibler divergence

$$L_3(\theta) = E_{(t,p)\sim D}[KL(Distr_\theta(p_i|p_{\backslash i}, t)||Distr(p_i))]$$

The final loss is the weighted sum of the three losses with optimal weights computed dynamically during training according to the Adaptive loss algorithm [14]:

$$L(\theta) = \sum_{i=1}^{3} w_i L_i(\theta) \quad w_i = \frac{(L - \nabla L_i^2)^{-1}}{\sum_{i=1}^{3}(L - \nabla L_i^2)^{-1}}$$

3.3   Metric Learning

After the first self-supervised training phase, the model has learned semantic relationships between text and images. Starting from the weights obtained, we can perform a second training with metric learning to generate a latent space where texts and images can be separately embedded and their distance in this space translates into semantic similarity. However, training with metric learning is not immediately possible since the model requires both a textual description and an image in input. As shown in Fig. 1, though, there are two distinct channels in which visual and textual inputs get processed; therefore, we can change the architecture in the following way: when a text is provided, the image channel is disabled, and in the same way, when we have an image in input the text channel is not used (Fig. 2). We take the vector $x \in \mathbb{R}^{768}$ obtained from the [CLS] token as a latent representation for both text and images. We then train the network using Triplet Loss, which is defined as:

$$L = max(0, d(x_a, x_p) - d(x_a, x_n) + m)$$

x_a is called the anchor element and, in our case, is the embedding obtained from the description of a product in the dataset. x_p and x_n are called positive and negative samples. x_p is the embedding of the photo associated with the given description and x_n is the embedding of a random image from the dataset. d is the euclidean distance and m is an hyperparameter called *margin*.

After this training phase terminates, we can efficiently perform multi-modal retrieval using the nearest neighbor search (k-NN) strategy: we compute the distances between the query embedding and the text or image embeddings extracted with our model and use them to sort the results from closest to farthest.

4 Experiments

4.1 Dataset

We run experiments on the FashionGen dataset [32], which contains 293,008 images (256×256 size) of fashion products, subdivided in categories and subcategories, paired with textual descriptions provided by professional stylists. It includes 67,666 products that appear in the dataset photographed several times at different angles up to a maximum of 6. The dataset is split up into 260,480 records for training and 32,528 for validation.

For pretraining, we extracted two records for each product: one positive *(text, image)* pair, in which the description of the product is paired with its corresponding image, and one negative *(text, image)* pair in which the same description is paired with a random image taken from the same subcategory. We set the maximum description length to 512 and split images into 64 (8×8) patches.

For metric learning, we considered each product description as an anchor element. Positive elements are selected among the images of that product taken at different angles, and negative elements are images selected from other random products in the dataset.

4.2 Implementation and Training Details

We implemented our model in pytorch with the HuggingFace's Transformers library [41]. The Transformer architecture consists of 12 layers with 768 hidden size, 12 self-attention heads, and 3072 intermediate size. We used `gelu`

Table 1. Results obtained by our model compared to previous solutions proposed in literature tested on the FashionGen dataset.

Tasks		VSE	VSE++	SCAN	PFAN	ViLBERT	VLBERT	Image Bert	OSCAR	Fashion Bert	Kaleido Bert	Our
ITR	R@1	4.01%	4.59%	4.59%	4.29%	20.97%	19.26%	22.76%	23.39%	23.96%	27.99%	**34.70%**
	R@5	11.03%	14.99%	16.50%	14.90%	40.49%	39.90%	41.89%	44.67%	46.31%	60.09%	**70.50%**
	R@10	22.14%	24.10%	26.60%	24.20%	48.21%	46.05%	50.77%	52.55%	52.12%	68.37%	**83.70%**
TIR	R@1	4.35%	4.60%	4.30%	6.20%	21.12%	22.63%	24.78%	25.10%	26.75%	33.88%	**35.80%**
	R@5	12.76%	16.89%	13.00%	20.79%	37.23%	36.48%	45.20%	49.14%	46.48%	60.60%	**70.20%**
	R@10	20.91%	28.99%	22.30%	31.52%	50.11%	48.52%	55.90%	56.68%	55.74%	68.59%	**83.30%**

as activation function and a 0.1 dropout factor. We loaded pretrained weights from *bert-base-uncased*. The Masked Patch Modeling head and the image processing layers, which are not available in the classic BERT architecture, were randomly initialized from a 0 mean, 0.2 standard deviation normal distribution. For the FAVOR+ algorithm we used the following hyperparameters: $r = 64$, orthogonal_features=True and redraw_features=True. The model was trained using a single Titan XP GPU with 12 GB of available RAM. Adam optimizer was used, with parameters $\beta_1 = 0.95, \beta_2 = 0.999$, and weight decay $1e^{-4}$. Pre-training run for 20 epochs with a base learning rate of $2e^{-5}$ warmed up for the first 5000 steps and then reduced with cosine scheduling strategy. We used a batch size of 16 records, the largest size available in our GPU. For Triplet Loss training, we reduced to 10 the number of epochs and changed the learning rate to a constant value of $5e^{-6}$. We used the *hard mining* technique to train on triplets that satisfied the condition $d(x_a, x_n) < d(x_a, x_p)$ (more experiments on triplet mining are reported in Sect. 6). We set the margin hyperparameter $m = 1.0^3$.

4.3 Results

We evaluated our model on two multi-modal retrieval tasks in the fashion domain: Text-to-Image and Image-to-Text retrieval. For a fair comparison, we adopted the same evaluation methods used in [14] and [43]:

- **Text-to-Image Retrieval (TIR):** Given a description of a product, the model must find the corresponding image among 100 other random images of products from the same subcategory.
- **Image-to-Text Retrieval (ITR):** Given an image of a product, the model must find the corresponding description among 100 other random descriptions of products from the same subcategory.

Model performances are evaluated using the Rank@K metric (with $K = \{1, 5, 10\}$), that measures how many times the correct image or text appears in the first K retrieved documents. We report the results in Table 1 compared with other models proposed in the literature that employ different approaches, in particular: VSE [13] and VSE++ [11] do not use any attention mechanism and directly

---

[3] In some of our preliminary experiments we also tested $m = 0.1$ but we found no substantial differences (the results were slightly worse in that case).

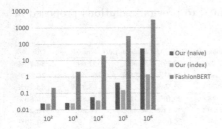

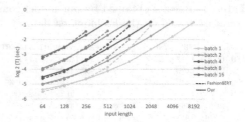

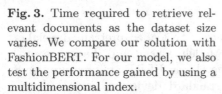

Fig. 3. Time required to retrieve relevant documents as the dataset size varies. We compare our solution with FashionBERT. For our model, we also test the performance gained by using a multidimensional index.

Fig. 4. Comparison between our model and FashionBERT in terms of backward pass speed and maximum input length allowed. Plots are shown up to when each model produces an out-of-memory error.

projects text and images into a joint latent space using an LSTM and a CNN model trained with metric learning; SCAN [22] and PFAN [40] combine RoIs with some attention mechanisms but without employing a complete transformer architecture; ImageBERT [31], ViLBERT [25], VLBERT [34], and OSCAR [24] are all Interaction-Focused V+L transformers that jointly process RoIs and text tokens; FashionBERT [14] and KaleidoBERT [43] are patch-based V+L transformer models that represent the current SOTA for multi-modal retrieval in the fashion domain. As shown in Table 1, our model outperforms previous solutions improving all Rank@K accuracies. We believe that the main reason for this improvement lies in using the two training phases to generate a latent space that better encodes text and image similarities. Our solution is thus effective and efficient since multidimensional indexing strategies can be employed on pre-computed embeddings to improve performance. We further examine this claim in the next section, where we also show the advantages of our linear V+L transformer.

5   Efficiency and Scalability

Retrieval Efficiency. We generated sample databases of different sizes and collected, for each of them, the time required to find the top 100 results for a given query. We compared our model with FashionBERT to show the advantages of our solution compared to the SOTA ones (note that the results we obtained for FashionBERT would be equal for KaleidoBERT since they share an equivalent architecture). We tested two retrieval strategies for our model: (i) naïve k-NN search and (ii) indexed k-NN search using a Ball-Tree [30] index. For Fashion-BERT, all the text-image alignment scores are computed on the GPU, and the results are ordered on the CPU. For our model, the query embedding is generated using a GPU while the k-NN is performed on the CPU. Figure 3 shows that FashionBERT requires more than a second to perform retrieval on 1000 documents. Our model, instead, using a multidimensional index, manages to perform better even on a dataset containing 10^6 products. Tests up to a million records are, in this case, sufficient to prove the advantages of our solution compared to the SOTA ones. However, if one is willing to trade off accuracy for higher efficiency, our solution enables the use of approximate k-NN strategies to scale up to datasets with billions of products.

Training Efficiency. To test the advantages of our linear V+L transformer, we compared the time required for a backward pass with our model and Fashion-BERT, which uses quadratic attention. As we can see from Fig. 4, our model can handle bigger batch sizes for each input length, and if we fix the batch size, it can process longer sequences. Using bigger batch sizes also reduces the overall training time since it allows to process more records on each iteration[4]. Furthermore, we could train the model with bigger images, splitting them into more patches or with longer descriptions even with limited computation resources. This allows our model to be used in much broader real-world applications.

6   Ablation Studies

Contributions of the Training Phases. To test the effectiveness of our training procedure and study the contribution of each training phase, we conducted the following ablations studies: (i) we performed retrieval using the Text-Image Alignment score returned by our pretrained model, as in [14,43], and (ii) we trained the model starting directly from metric learning, skipping the self-supervised pretraining phase. The results obtained are reported in Table 2. We can see that our model, trained with both pretraining and metric learning, obtains better results then the ones that use only one of the two training phases. This confirms that both pretraining and metric learning are required to obtain SOTA accuracies. Moreover, this proves that the semantic relationships between texts and images learned during the self-supervised pretraining are used in the second phase to generate a better latent semantic space.

Selecting Triplets. Triplet mining involves selecting a specific subset of triplets with certain characteristics during training. One of the most effective techniques studied in literature is *hard negative mining* [1,11], which selects only hard instances for which $d(x_a, x_n) < d(x_a, x_p)$. To test the effect of this strategy in our solution, we conducted two experiments: one with hard mining and one using all triplets. As shown in Table 3, the model obtains better results with hard negative mining than with the naïve approach, which uses all triplets during training. We believe that this way of exploiting informative triplets, combined with more sophisticated ranking losses, could be a promising line of research for future works.

---

[4] Pretraining with our linear attention model took $\sim$72 h to complete, and metric learning required $\sim$15 h. Using a quadratic Transformer, pretraining would have ended in $\sim$100 h and metric learning in $\sim$24 h.

Table 2. Contribution of each training phase to downstream results. ML = model trained with metric learning only; P = pretrained model using the TIA score.

Tasks		ML	P	Our
ITR	R@1	22.00%	27.80%	**34.70%**
	R@5	54.80%	60.40%	**70.50%**
	R@10	71.30%	76.60%	**83.70%**
TIR	R@1	25.30%	26.70%	**35.80%**
	R@5	58.20%	59.10%	**70.20%**
	R@10	73.30%	76.00%	**83.30%**

Table 3. Results obtained with and without the hard triplet mining technique during the metric learning phase.

Tasks		All triplets	Hard triplets
ITR	R@1	22.00%	**34.70%**
	R@5	48.80%	**70.50%**
	R@10	65.50%	**83.70%**
TIR	R@1	20.70%	**35.80%**
	R@5	51.60%	**70.20%**
	R@10	67.90%	**83.30%**

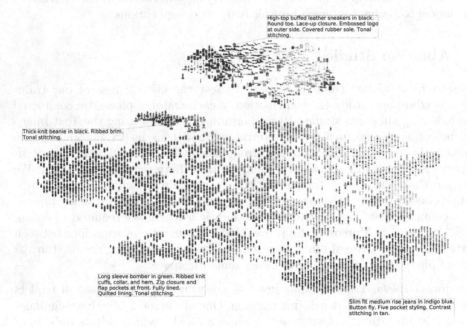

Fig. 5. t-SNE visualization of the FashionGen validation set using image embeddings extracted with our model. 4 sample captions are also embedded to show that they are placed near images they describe. Best viewed in color at high resolution. (Color figure online)

7   Visualization

In Fig. 5 we provide a low-dimensional representation of the latent space learned by our model. We projected the 768-dimensional image embeddings into a 2-dimensional space using t-SNE. We also embedded 4 sample captions to show that semantic relationships between text and images are preserved and each text is indeed placed near images that it describes.

8   Conclusions

Current SOTA solutions for fashion multi-modal retrieval use V+L transformers that model an image and its textual caption as a coupled representation, providing poor performance on large-scale datasets. We presented a novel approach for retrieval in the fashion domain that decouples the image and its caption with separated embeddings. Our solution combines self-supervised pretraining and deep metric learning to generate a multi-modal latent space where the spatial proximity among text and images corresponds to their semantic similarity. We improved all Rank@K metrics on the FashionGen dataset and showed that our solution could efficiently scale up to millions of records thanks to multidimensional indices. We also incorporated a kernelized linear attention method (i.e., FAVOR+) to approximate the quadratic attention matrices and reduce the memory and time required to train our model. Our linear V+L transformer is promising to be extended to other domains and datasets as it allows for longer descriptions and higher resolution images in input. Since we do not use RoIs in the architecture, we believe the proposed solution is suitable for applications in which fine-grained details are more important than coarse-grained objects (e.g., medical and biomedical domain [5,6,9]). Further improvements could be made by also introducing structured information to the input such as visual segmentation graphs [33] or semantic parsing graphs [12]. Retrieval from external knowledge [27] could also be used to further improve model accuracies.

References

1. Cerroni, W., Moro, G., Pirini, T., Ramilli, M.: Peer-to-peer data mining classifiers for decentralized detection of network attacks, vol. 137, pp. 101–107, January 2013
2. Choromanski, K.M., et al.: Rethinking attention with performers. In: ICLR. OpenReview.net (2021)
3. Datar, M., Immorlica, N., Indyk, P., Mirrokni, V.S.: Locality-sensitive hashing scheme based on p-stable distributions. In: SCG, pp. 253–262. ACM (2004)
4. Devlin, J., Chang, M., Lee, K., Toutanova, K.: BERT: pre-training of deep bidirectional transformers for language understanding. In: NAACL-HLT (1), pp. 4171–4186. Association for Computational Linguistics (2019)
5. Domeniconi, G., Masseroli, M., Moro, G., Pinoli, P.: Discovering new gene functionalities from random perturbations of known gene ontological annotations. In: KDIR, pp. 107–116. SciTePress (2014)
6. Domeniconi, G., Masseroli, M., Moro, G., Pinoli, P.: Cross-organism learning method to discover new gene functionalities. Comput. Methods Programs Biomed. **126**, 20–34 (2016)
7. Domeniconi, G., Moro, G., Pasolini, R., Sartori, C.: Cross-domain text classification through iterative refining of target categories representations. In: KDIR, pp. 31–42. SciTePress (2014)

8. Domeniconi, G., Semertzidis, K., López, V., Daly, E.M., Kotoulas, S., Moro, G.: A novel method for unsupervised and supervised conversational message thread detection. In: DATA, pp. 43–54. SciTePress (2016)
9. Endo, M., Krishnan, R., Krishna, V., Ng, A.Y., Rajpurkar, P.: Retrieval-based chest X-ray report generation using a pre-trained contrastive language-image model. In: ML4H@NeurIPS. Proceedings of Machine Learning Research, vol. 158, pp. 209–219. PMLR (2021)
10. Fabbri, M., Moro, G.: Dow jones trading with deep learning: the unreasonable effectiveness of recurrent neural networks. In: DATA, pp. 142–153. SciTePress (2018)
11. Faghri, F., Fleet, D.J., Kiros, J.R., Fidler, S.: VSE++: improving visual-semantic embeddings with hard negatives. In: BMVC, p. 12. BMVA Press (2018)
12. Frisoni, G., Moro, G., Carlassare, G., Carbonaro, A.: Unsupervised event graph representation and similarity learning on biomedical literature. Sensors 22(1), 3 (2022)
13. Frome, A., et al.: Devise: a deep visual-semantic embedding model. In: NIPS, pp. 2121–2129 (2013)
14. Gao, D., et al.: FashionBERT: text and image matching with adaptive loss for cross-modal retrieval. In: SIGIR, pp. 2251–2260. ACM (2020)
15. Goenka, S., et al.: FashionVLP: vision language transformer for fashion retrieval with feedback. In: Proceedings of the IEEE/CVF Conference on Computer Vision and Pattern Recognition, pp. 14105–14115 (2022)
16. Hadsell, R., Chopra, S., LeCun, Y.: Dimensionality reduction by learning an invariant mapping. In: CVPR (2), pp. 1735–1742. IEEE Computer Society (2006)
17. He, K., Zhang, X., Ren, S., Sun, J.: Deep residual learning for image recognition. In: CVPR, pp. 770–778. IEEE Computer Society (2016)
18. Hoffer, E., Ailon, N.: Deep metric learning using triplet network. In: Feragen, A., Pelillo, M., Loog, M. (eds.) SIMBAD 2015. LNCS, vol. 9370, pp. 84–92. Springer, Cham (2015). https://doi.org/10.1007/978-3-319-24261-3_7
19. Jégou, H., Douze, M., Schmid, C.: Product quantization for nearest neighbor search. IEEE Trans. Pattern Anal. Mach. Intell. 33(1), 117–128 (2011)
20. Kitaev, N., Kaiser, L., Levskaya, A.: Reformer: the efficient transformer. In: ICLR. OpenReview.net (2020)
21. Laenen, K., Zoghbi, S., Moens, M.F.: Cross-modal search for fashion attributes. In: KDD 2017 (2017)
22. Lee, K.-H., Chen, X., Hua, G., Hu, H., He, X.: Stacked cross attention for image-text matching. In: Ferrari, V., Hebert, M., Sminchisescu, C., Weiss, Y. (eds.) ECCV 2018. LNCS, vol. 11208, pp. 212–228. Springer, Cham (2018). https://doi.org/10.1007/978-3-030-01225-0_13
23. Li, G., Duan, N., Fang, Y., Gong, M., Jiang, D.: Unicoder-VL: a universal encoder for vision and language by cross-modal pre-training. In: AAAI, pp. 11336–11344. AAAI Press (2020)
24. Li, X., et al.: OSCAR: object-semantics aligned pre-training for vision-language tasks. In: Vedaldi, A., Bischof, H., Brox, T., Frahm, J.-M. (eds.) ECCV 2020. LNCS, vol. 12375, pp. 121–137. Springer, Cham (2020). https://doi.org/10.1007/978-3-030-58577-8_8
25. Lu, J., Batra, D., Parikh, D., Lee, S.: ViLBERT: pretraining task-agnostic visiolinguistic representations for vision-and-language tasks. In: NeurIPS, pp. 13–23 (2019)
26. Miech, A., Alayrac, J., Laptev, I., Sivic, J., Zisserman, A.: Thinking fast and slow: efficient text-to-visual retrieval with transformers. In: CVPR, pp. 9826–9836. Computer Vision Foundation/IEEE (2021)

27. Moro, G., Pagliarani, A., Pasolini, R., Sartori, C.: Cross-domain & in-domain sentiment analysis with memory-based deep neural networks. In: KDIR, pp. 125–136. SciTePress (2018)

28. Moro, G., Valgimigli, L.: Efficient self-supervised metric information retrieval: a bibliography based method applied to COVID literature. Sensors **21**(19), 6430 (2021)

29. Muja, M., Lowe, D.G.: Fast approximate nearest neighbors with automatic algorithm configuration. In: VISAPP (1), pp. 331–340. INSTICC Press (2009)

30. Omohundro, S.M.: Five Balltree Construction Algorithms. International Computer Science Institute, Berkeley (1989)

31. Qi, D., Su, L., Song, J., Cui, E., Bharti, T., Sacheti, A.: ImageBERT: cross-modal pre-training with large-scale weak-supervised image-text data. CoRR abs/2001.07966 (2020)

32. Rostamzadeh, N.: Fashion-Gen: the generative fashion dataset and challenge. CoRR abs/1806.08317 (2018)

33. Sadegharmaki, S., Kastner, M.A., Satoh, S.: FashionGraph: understanding fashion data using scene graph generation. In: 2020 25th International Conference On Pattern Recognition (ICPR), pp. 7923–7929. IEEE (2021)

34. Su, W., et al.: VL-BERT: pre-training of generic visual-linguistic representations. In: ICLR. OpenReview.net (2020)

35. Tay, Y., et al.: Long range arena: a benchmark for efficient transformers. CoRR abs/2011.04006 (2020)

36. Tay, Y., Dehghani, M., Bahri, D., Metzler, D.: Efficient transformers: a survey. CoRR:2009.06732 (2020)

37. Vaswani, A., et al.: Attention is all you need. In: NIPS, pp. 5998–6008 (2017)

38. Wang, J., et al.: GIT: a generative image-to-text transformer for vision and language. arXiv preprint arXiv:2205.14100 (2022)

39. Wang, L., Li, Y., Lazebnik, S.: Learning two-branch neural networks for image-text matching tasks. CoRR:1704.03470 (2017)

40. Wang, Y., et al.: Position focused attention network for image-text matching. In: IJCAI, pp. 3792–3798 (2019). ijcai.org

41. Wolf, T., et al.: Transformers: state-of-the-art natural language processing. In: Proceedings of the 2020 Conference on Empirical Methods in Natural Language Processing: System Demonstrations, pp. 38–45 (2020)

42. Zaheer, M., et al.: Big bird: transformers for longer sequences. In: NeurIPS (2020)

43. Zhuge, M., et al.: Kaleido-BERT: vision-language pre-training on fashion domain. In: CVPR, pp. 12647–12657. Computer Vision Foundation/IEEE (2021)

44. Zoghbi, S., Heyman, G., Gomez, J.C., Moens, M.F.: Fashion meets computer vision and NLP at e-commerce search. Int. J. Comput. Electr. Eng. (IJCEE) **8**, 31–43 (2016). https://doi.org/10.17706/IJCEE.2016.8.1.31-43

Stable Anchors for Matching Unlabelled Point Clouds

Ubaldo Ruiz[1,2], Stephane Marchand-Maillet[3], and Edgar Chavez[1(✉)]

[1] Centro de Investigación Científica y de Educación Superior de Ensenada (CICESE), Ensenada, Baja California, Mexico
{uruiz,elchavez}@cicese.edu.mx
[2] Consejo Nacional de Ciencia y Tecnología (CONACYT), Mexico City, Mexico
[3] Viper IR & ML Group, University of Geneva, Geneva, Switzerland

Abstract. We define an anchor as a small sample representing a point cloud. Weighted or labeled point clouds are amenable for a stable anchor extraction, a sampling method ensuring a consistent selection of points across realizations of the same point cloud. In this work, we present a heuristic to extract a stable anchor from *unlabeled* point clouds when the points have no weights and are indistinguishable. This problem arises when we need to query an extensive collection of point clouds and want to avoid a sequential comparison with all members of the collection. Our method consists in assigning as weight a centrality measure. We show that our approach preserves several times the bare minimum required to identify point clouds under similarity transformations.

Keywords: Point clouds · Stable anchors · Centrality measures

1 Introduction

A *point cloud* is a collection of points in $\mathbb{R}^d$. They come from a variety of sources such as stars in a sensor [9], invariants in images [5], high energy in selected bands of audio [8], LIDAR readings [6], fingerprints, iris scans and other biometrics [1,3]. Acquisition of points is subject to noise and artifacts. Noise comes from sensor outputs, and artifacts create insertions and deletions to the point cloud. The main problem is determining if two are readings of the same object. We call each reading a *realization* of an object. This work will consider points in the plane or $\mathbb{R}^2$. Two-dimensional point clouds cover many applications, from audio matching to star navigation or fingerprint recognition, and are interesting enough to be studied by themselves.

The core problem regarding point clouds is matching. There are two versions of the matching problem, the *online* version where two point clouds P and Q and a parametric transformation f are given simultaneously, and the objective is

---

This work was supported in part by Catedras-CONACYT project 1850 and in part by CONACYT grant A1-S-21934.

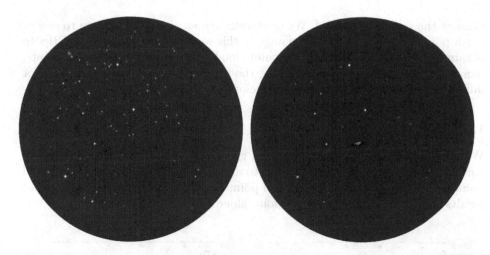

Fig. 1. Robust constellation extracted from a FOV, by selecting the stars with higher apparent brightness

to find the transformation parameters, which in turn gives the correspondence. There are two canonical algorithms to solve the online problem, namely RAndom SAmpling Consensus (RANSAC) [4] and Iterative Closest Point (ICP) [7]. Vanilla RANSAC, and countless variations with heuristic improvements, are the gold standard for the general problem. In contrast, ICP and its variations are more restrictive, applying only to congruences in dense 3D point clouds.

We are interested in the *offline* point cloud matching version. That is, given $\{P_1, P_2, \ldots, P_M\}$ point clouds, determine if Q matches $f(P_i)$ with f a congruence or similarity transformation. One example is matching an audio excerpt of a few seconds against every track ever recorded, as in the popular Shazam application [8]. Another example is autonomous star identification, matching the image captured in a sensor against every star in the sky [9].

In the Shazam approach, the spectrograms of audio tracks are processed by extracting unique high-energy spots at a certain time/frequency combination [8]. For the star identification, something similar is performed. All the stars within the FOV are filtered by apparent brightness, luminosity, or color to identify the central star; only those stars passing the filter will be compared with the corresponding patterns in a star catalog. In Fig. 1 we illustrate this process in a simulated FOV in a starfield.

Both examples described share a common characteristic; points have a label, the energy at a time/frequency in the Shazam algorithm, and the apparent brightness in the autonomous star identification. This motivates our definition of a *stable anchor*. In both cases, the idea is to obtain a robust sample of points with a high probability of being selected across object representations. Low energy points or dim stars will be subject to noise more easily.

When points are indistinguishable, selecting a robust constellation is not straightforward. Randomly selecting a sample is not reproducible across realizations of the same point cloud. We must resort to an external measure to distinguish points for unlabeled point clouds. In this work, we investigate heuristics to obtain stable anchors for unlabeled point clouds; we want to select stable points, increasing the probability of obtaining the same points in the constellation for different realizations of the same point cloud.

1.1 Using Geometric Graphs

We will consider the point cloud as a geometric graph. Nodes of the graph corresponds to points and edge weights to distances. We hypothesize that central points are robust across realizations of point clouds. Our objective is to produce results similar to that of a labeled point cloud.

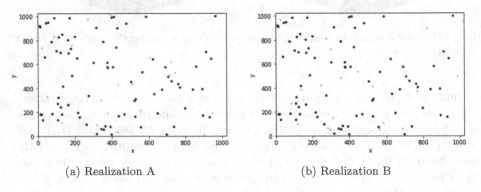

(a) Realization A   (b) Realization B

Fig. 2. Two realizations of the same point cloud. Black points are common in both realizations. Gray points appear only in one of the realizations. (Color figure online)

Figure 2 illustrates the problem. We have two realizations of the same point cloud: the points match up to a certain amount of noise, and gray points illustrate insertions and deletions. The objective is to obtain a stable anchor from the point cloud by only inputting the point configuration. Notice that without labels, e.g., energy levels, we cannot use the same technique as in Shazam.

The proposed solution is illustrated in Fig. 3. The point cloud is enriched by assigning each point a centrality measure. In the example, we used Betweenness centrality, discussed below in the manuscript. Heaviness represents centrality; heavier points are more central. Notice that heavy points could be gray or black. Gray heavy points will not be reproducible because they are artifacts from the realization. We believe this procedure will produce enough robust or stable points to identify a point cloud correctly. We will analyze this in the experimental section.

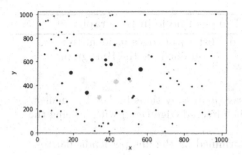 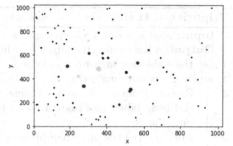

(a) Betweenness centrality in Realization A

(b) Betweenness centrality in Realization B

Fig. 3. Centrality in two realizations of the same point cloud. Black points are common in both realizations. Gray points appear only in one of the realizations. (Color figure online)

2 Measures of Centrality

In this section, we describe the centrality measures studied in this work. In particular, we focused our attention on the Tukey depth, the Betweenness centrality, and three approaches based on the Half-Space Proximal Graph (HSP).

2.1 Tukey Depth

Let $S \subset \mathbb{R}^d$ be a finite set of n points. The Tukey depth of a point $p \in S$ is defined as the minimum number of points of S contained in any closed half-space containing p. Notice that points in the boundary of S will have smaller depth values compared to those in the inner regions.

2.2 Betweenness Centrality

Betweenness centrality is a general measure of centrality in a graph based on shortest paths. There is at least one shortest path between every pair of nodes in a connected graph. For unweighted graphs, the shortest path minimizes the number of edges in the path, and for weighted graphs, it minimizes the sum of the weights of the edges. The betweenness centrality of a node is defined as the number of shortest paths that pass through that node, and the following expression gives it

$$y(u) = \sum_{s \neq u \neq t} \frac{\sigma_{st}(u)}{\sigma_{st}} \qquad (1)$$

where σ_{st} is the total number of shortest paths from s to t and $\sigma_{st}(u)$ the number of those paths passing through u (the ones having u as end-node are not considered).

Algorithm 1: HSP Test (to be applied to each node in the graph)

    Input: a node u of a geometric graph and a list L_1 of edges incident to u

    Output: a list of directed edges L_2 which are retained for the HSP graph

1 Set the forbidden area F(u) to be $\emptyset$

2 **while** L_1 *is not empty* **do**

3   Remove from L_1 the shortest edge, say (u,v) (any tie is broken by smaller end-node label) and insert into L_2 the directed edge (u,v) with u being the initial node

4   Add to $F(u)$ the open half-plane determined by the line perpendicular to the edge (u,v) in the middle of the edge and containing the vertex v

5   Scan the list L_1 and remove from it any edge whose end-node is in $F(u)$

2.3 Half-Space Proximal Graph

Chavez et al. proposed the Half-Space Proximal (HSP) graph in [2]. This graph has many desirable properties for network applications. In particular, ad-hoc networks are represented by Unit Disk Graphs (UDG), where the nodes represent network hosts. An edge connects two nodes if the Euclidean distance between them is less than a given unit, where the unit represents the common transmission range of the hosts. The HSP test determines the neighbors retained within each node's range for constructing a geometric sub-graph of the UDG. That sub-graph is referred to as the HSP graph, and it is a sparse directed or undirected sub-graph of the UDG. Using a sub-graph of the UDG is useful in many network tasks like power optimization or routing.

The HSP is conjectured to be t-spanner with a finite stretch factor; it is invariant under similarity transformations, the max out-degree of the HSP elements depends on the intrinsic dimensionality of the data, and it corresponds to the kissing number of that dimension. For dimensions 1, 2, 3, and 4 it is known that the max out-degree is 2, 6, 12 and 24, respectively. For higher dimensions, only lower and upper bounds are known. In this work, we will make use of those results.

Let S be a point set in the Euclidean plane. The HSP test is performed at each point $p_i \in S$, and it partitions S using a set of representative points based on the neighbors of p_i. Those representative points are connected to p_i in the HSP graph. For constructing the HSP graph, in this work, we assume we have a geometric graph $G = (V, E)$ with coordinates (u_x, u_y) for each node u in the Euclidean plane. Each vertex has a unique integer label. The method for selecting the neighbors for each node in the HSP graph is described in Algorithm 1 and an example is shown in Fig. 4. That figure illustrates the process of discarding elements in the forbidden half-space represented by a shaded area. An edge (u,w) is forbidden by an edge (u,v) if the Euclidean distance between w and v is smaller than the one between w and u. An important feature of the HSP test is that there is no explicit use of the nodes' coordinates, and each node chooses its neighbors without setting parameters.

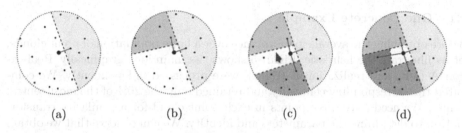

Fig. 4. An illustration of the HSP test for a point in the Euclidean plane.

The HSP degree is a good centrality estimation of each element in a point set. One can observe that nodes in the HSP graph with higher out-degree, for example, ≥ 4 in the Euclidean plane, are located in the central regions. With the above, we can compute a candidate solution to our problem.

2.4 HSP Depth

The HSP test can be used to compute an approximation of the Tukey depth of a point p. Each point of that set and p define a half-space in this work. Thus, we count the number of points in each of those half-spaces containing p, and the minimum value is used to approximate the Tukey depth. We denote this approach as HSP Depth.

2.5 HSP* Degree

Notice that HSP is defined for any metric space. In particular in the above definitions we used the euclidean distance between two dimensional points. Changing the metric will produce a different graph for the same set of vertices. If we can assign a set to each point in the cloud, then we can use a distance between sets as a metric. There are several candidates to set distances, one of them is the Dice coefficient defined as $\mathbf{D}(X,Y) = \frac{2|X \cap Y|}{|X \cup Y|}$. We can still use the HSP test Algorithm 1 to build the graph, just changing the appropriate line. In the HSP* we first compute the reverse k-nearest neighbors of each point in the cloud. This set will be used as a proxy for the point and the distance between vertices will be now the Dice coefficient between the corresponding sets. Essentially we are counting the number of common reverse k-nearest neighbors, for a large k, for any given pair of points. We denote this variant as HSP*.

3 Experiments

This section presents an experimental evaluation of the previous approaches to compute a candidate set of points that are more likely to be identified again if the original cloud is subject to perturbations.

3.1 One Concrete Example

Before obtaining the average performance over a large population of point clouds, let us illustrate the heuristic. Figure 5 shows the main idea graphically. Realization A (left) and realization B (right), were processed independently. We computed the corresponding centrality and retained only the 20% of the most central points. We need only three points in each point cloud for a similarity transformation to determine the parameters and identity. We can observe that we obtain more than the bare minimum with this procedure. Notice also that realization A and realization B are noisy versions of each other, plus insertions and deletions.

3.2 Experimental Setup

We created a database of 1000 point clouds in $\mathbf{R}^2$. Each point cloud P_i has 100 points randomly generated in $[0, 1024] \times [0, 1024]$. We studied the performance of each approach under two types of perturbations: noise and insert/delete operations. The goal of each experiment was to quantify how many candidates obtained in the original clouds persist in the perturbed versions of the clouds.

Note that the Betweenness centrality requires a graph; thus, in our case, the k-nearest neighbor graph of each P_i with $k = 50$ is used. Additionally, the HSP* requires the reverse nearest neighbors of each point. In that case, we computed them employing the k-nearest graph of each P_i with $k = 20$.

For both experiments, first, we computed the cardinality of the set of points in P_i having an out-degree ≥ 4, using the HSP test. We denote that value as c_i, and it is the number of points retrieved after each approach is executed. We ranked the points according to the corresponding criteria for each centrality test. For example, when the Tukey depth is considered, we sort the results in descending order; thus, the most central points are the top. Then, we selected a set of cardinality c_i containing the points with the highest rank; those points are used for the comparisons. The sets obtained for each centrality measure in the original clouds correspond to the baseline.

In the experiments, we report both the precision and the average cardinality of the intersection between the baseline and the results obtained under perturbations. Note that in some applications, like computing an affine transformation between point clouds, retrieving a minimum number of stable points is more important than achieving perfect precision.

3.3 Noise

For this experiment, we perturbed a subset of points in each P_i with random uniform noise in $[0, 100]$ before applying the centrality tests. Some results of the experiment are shown in Fig. 6b. That figure reports the precision of each approach vs. the fraction of points perturbed with noise. Support of 1.0 indicates that none of the points in the original cloud were perturbed, and a value of 0.7 than 70% of the points remain clean, and 30% of them were perturbed with noise. Figure 6d shows the average cardinality of the intersection vs. the fraction

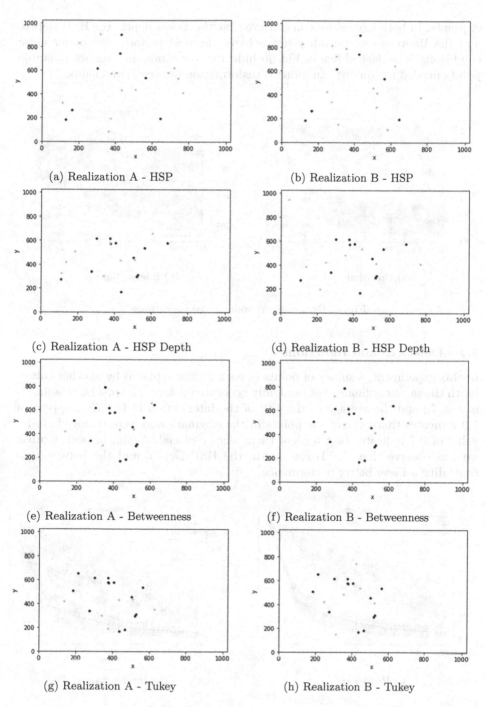

(a) Realization A - HSP

(b) Realization B - HSP

(c) Realization A - HSP Depth

(d) Realization B - HSP Depth

(e) Realization A - Betweenness

(f) Realization B - Betweenness

(g) Realization A - Tukey

(h) Realization B - Tukey

Fig. 5. For a fixed point cloud and two realizations (A and B), we show the preserved points after applying several centrality tests. We selected the 20 most central points, black points correspond to the points preserved across realizations. (Color figure online)

of points. In both figures, we can observe that the Tukey depth, the HSP Depth, and the Betweenness centrality test achieve the best performance under noise conditions. The dashed line in Fig. 6b indicates the minimum number of stable points needed to compute an affine transformation between two clouds.

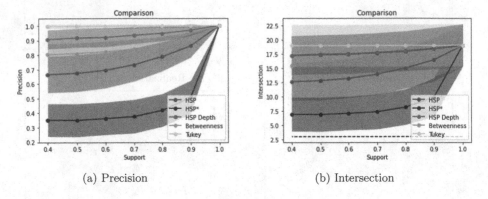

(a) Precision   (b) Intersection

Fig. 6. Performance under noise conditions

3.4   Deletions and Insertions

In this experiment, a subset of points in each P_i was replaced by another subset (with the same cardinality) of randomly generated points. The precision is shown in Fig. 7a and the average cardinality of the intersection in Fig. 7b. Support of 1.0 indicates that none of the points in the original cloud were removed, and a value of 0.7 indicates that 30% of them were replaced. Again, in both figures, we can observe that the Tukey depth, the HSP Depth, and the betweenness centrality achieve better performance.

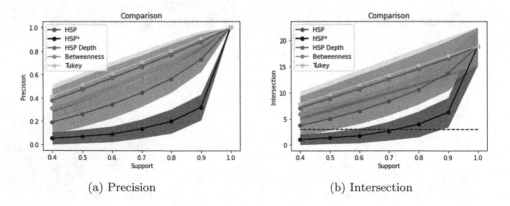

(a) Precision   (b) Intersection

Fig. 7. Performance under insert/delete operations

4 Conclusions and Future Work

We showed experimentally that it is possible to extract a robust constellation from unlabeled point clouds using the notion of centrality. The upper bound of Tukey centrality we propose is the most stable centrality for constellation extraction.

The method shown can be easily generalized to higher dimensions, given that we used only the distance between points to compute the centralities.

References

1. Agarwal, D., Bansal, A.: A utility of pores as level 3 features in latent fingerprint identification. Multimed. Tools Appl. **80**(15), 23605–23624 (2021)
2. Chavez, E., et al.: Half-space proximal: a new local test for extracting a bounded dilation spanner of a unit disk graph. In: Anderson, J.H., Prencipe, G., Wattenhofer, R. (eds.) OPODIS 2005. LNCS, vol. 3974, pp. 235–245. Springer, Heidelberg (2006). https://doi.org/10.1007/11795490_19
3. Daugman, J.: New methods in iris recognition. IEEE Trans. Syst. Man Cybern. Part B (Cybern.) **37**(5), 1167–1175 (2007)
4. Derpanis, K.G.: Overview of the RANSAC algorithm. Image Rochester NY **4**(1), 2–3 (2010)
5. Lowe, G.: Sift-the scale invariant feature transform. Int. J. **2**(91–110), 2 (2004)
6. Raj, T., Hashim, F.H., Huddin, A.B., Ibrahim, M.F., Hussain, A.: A survey on lidar scanning mechanisms. Electronics **9**(5), 741 (2020)
7. Rusinkiewicz, S., Levoy, M.: Efficient variants of the ICP algorithm. In: Proceedings third International Conference on 3-D Digital Imaging and Modeling, pp. 145–152. IEEE (2001)
8. Wang, A.: An industrial strength audio search algorithm. In: Proceedings of the 4th International Conference on Music Information Retrieval, ISMIR 2003, Baltimore, Maryland, USA, 27–30 October 2003 (2003)
9. Zhang, G., Wei, X., Jiang, J.: Full-sky autonomous star identification based on radial and cyclic features of star pattern. Image Vis. Comput. **26**(7), 891–897 (2008)

Visual Exploration of Human Motion Data

Petra Budikova[✉][ID], Daniel Klepac, David Rusnak, and Milan Slovak

Faculty of Informatics, Masaryk University, Brno, Czech Republic
budikova@fi.muni.cz

Abstract. Human motion data are beginning to appear in many application domains, which brings a need to develop user-friendly motion processing applications. One of important open challenges is the presentation of high-dimensional spatio-temporal motion data to end users in a way that is easy to understand and allows fast browsing and exploration of the motion datasets. For many applications such as computer-assisted rehabilitation or motion learning, it is also very desirable to visualize the differences between two motion sequences. In this paper, we present a publicly available software tool that provides the visualization functionality for individual motion sequences, comparison of two motions, and exploration of large motion datasets.

Keywords: Human motion data · Skeleton sequences · Visualization · Multimedia exploration · Explainability of similarity

1 Motivation

Human motion can be described by a sequence of skeleton poses, where each pose keeps 2D/3D coordinates of important body joints in a specific time moment. Such spatio-temporal skeleton data can be utilized in a number of application domains, ranging from gaming and sports to healthcare and security [12]. With the recent advances in human pose estimation from ordinary videos [4], a huge explosion of motion processing application can be expected in the near future. Consequently, efficient and effective tools are needed for different phases of motion data processing.

In this paper, we study the problem of motion data understanding from the user point of view. Motion data are a rich source of information, but in their raw form they are represented by long vectors of float numbers, which are completely uninteligible to humans. This is typically solved by displaying the source video recordings, when available, or creating animations of the skeleton data [13]. However, viewing the videos or animations is time-consuming and therefore not suitable for situations where users desire to quickly grasp the content of multiple motion sequences, e.g., when browsing or querying collections of motion data. Therefore, we propose to represent each motion by a single static image that captures the most significant poses and can be read at a glance. We focus especially on the visualization of so-called *motion actions*, which are short motions

© The Author(s), under exclusive license to Springer Nature Switzerland AG 2022
T. Skopal et al. (Eds.): SISAP 2022, LNCS 13590, pp. 64–71, 2022.
https://doi.org/10.1007/978-3-031-17849-8_6

with a clear semantic meaning, e.g. a jump, throw, or a cartwheel. While the motion data can be captured as a long unsegmented sequence, users are typically interested in retrieving and viewing only the short segments that contain some activity of interest. If needed, the longer motions can be represented as sequences of images for individual segments.

Apart from the motion data itself, it is also difficult to understand, and explain, how the similarity between two motion actions is measured. The concept of similarity is instrumental to all motion processing tasks, ranging from query-by-example searching to action classification, event detection, or computer-aided rehabilitation [12]. Although the similarity is often hidden in complex machine learning models such as neural networks, we need to understand it to be able to interpret, analyze, and optimize the machine learning techniques, and to improve our own movements in computer-assisted motion learning. Therefore, evaluations of motion similarity are another area that calls for easy-to-understand visualizations.

Yet another set of challenges appears when we extend our focus to large collections motion data. Let us consider some popular motion datasets, such as HDM05 [10], PKU-MMD [5], or NTU [6]. These contain thousands or tens of thousands of motion actions, accompanied by metadata that determine their semantic categories. After downloading such dataset, it is possible to find out the number of categories, their frequencies, and view the videos of some random samples. However, there is no efficient way to gain insight into what really happens in the individual motion sequences, how diverse the categories are, if there are any natural clusters, etc. Yet all this information is essential for designing the motion processing applications.

To answer all these challenges, we have created a new JavaScript library for motion data visualization and exploration. The MocapViz library[1] offers three mutually cooperating modules: visualization of individual short motions, visual explanation of differences between two motion sequences, and effective exploration of large motion data collections. The first two modules can be integrated within an arbitrary web presentation that utilizes motion data. The exploration module produces a complete web presentation of a given motion dataset, which allows interactive data browsing as well as detailed inspection of selected motions and their relationships. The functionality of all modules is demonstrated in two public web interfaces for the exploration of HDM05 and PKU-MMD datasets.

2 Preliminaries: Processing of Human Motion Data

Human motion is recorded as sequence $S = (P_1, \ldots, P_l)$ of skeleton poses P_i $(1 < i \leq l)$, where each pose $P_i \in \mathbb{R}^{j \cdot dim}$ represents the skeleton configuration estimated in time moment i and consists of $dim \in \{2, 3\}$ coordinates of j tracked *joints*. The number and position of the body joints and the dimensionality dim depends on the hardware or software tools used to acquire the data. We denote this as the *body model* and take it as one of the visualization inputs.

---

[1] http://disa.fi.muni.cz/research-directions/motion-data/mocapviz/.

The raw skeleton sequences are spatio-temporal data, which can be compared by sequence alignment methods. In particular, the Dynamic Time Warping (DTW) algorithm [9] is usually applied, since it takes into account the possible differences in speed of the compared movements. The algorithm finds optimal matching between the poses of the two compared motions, and computes the overall distance as the sum of distances of the mapped poses. However, the processing of raw skeleton sequences with DTW is rather expensive due to the high dimensionality of the skeleton data and the quadratic computation time of the DTW. Moreover, some complex relationships between motions may not be discovered by the DTW. Therefore, state-of-the-art motion processing techniques often represent motions by some derived features and learn complex similarity models by machine learning techniques, especially the neural networks [12]. These approaches provide very good application results, but the similarity computation is embedded in the learned model and cannot be easily explained.

The objective of our work is to visualize motion data and explain their similarity in a way that is easily understandable to humans. For the visualization of individual movements, the raw skeleton data representation is the most suitable, since it is the most detailed and semantically clear. For the comparison of two motion sequences, we utilize sequence alignment methods that can be intuitively explained over visualizations of the skeleton sequences.

3   Visualization of Single Motion Sequence

As discussed earlier, motion data are usually surveyed by watching the source video, if available, or watching the animated skeleton sequences. Sequences of stick figures are routinely used to represent motions in research papers, but these are created manually. In [3], the technique of *MotionCues* is proposed, which creates a single 3D figure representing the whole motion, with arrows expressing the movement of individual body parts. This visualization is compact and well understandable, but only suitable for very simple actions. The *Motion Belts* technique [15] is the most similar to ours: it draws selected key-poses on a timeline and uses pose coloring to express their orientation. However, the poses are sometimes clumped together, making it difficult to determine what is happening, and the use of moving viewpoint is not very intuitive.

The MocapViz motion visualization module represents each action by a single static image, which contains the most representative poses placed on a timeline (Fig. 1). The keyposes are selected by a curve simplification algorithm and rendered as 2D stick figures. A few poses preceding each keypose are also drawn with a low opacity, which provides a better feeling of the movement. For each motion, a static camera position is chosen so that maximum information is shown; the camera is typically placed orthogonally to the motion direction. To make the poses easier to read, we use different colors for left/right body parts, and add artificial "nose" line that expresses the direction where the skeleton is looking. Furthermore, we also provide a bird-eye view of the motion in space, to allow better understanding of the spatial dimension that is lost in the 2D image.

Fig. 1. Cartwheel motion from the HDM05 dataset visualized in a single image. The bird-eye view map on the left shows how much the person moved in space.

The MocapViz library can visualize any type of skeleton-based human motion data, provided that the appropriate body model is supplied. The most popular Vicon and Kinect body models are already included in the library. Noticeably, the visualizations are only able to display the movement of a single person. Interactions between several people are more difficult to depict because of the spatial relationships between the skeletons, and would require a different approach.

4   Understanding Motion Similarity

The evaluation of similarity between two motion sequences is the core concept of all motion processing tasks, and its explanation is vital for both researchers and common users who work with motion processing applications. A superficial understanding of motion similarity can be obtained by visually comparing the motion images presented in the previous section, but much more insight can be gained from a detailed analysis of the sequence mapping found by the sequence alignment methods.

The visualization of the DTW mapping over skeleton sequences is studied in several existing research works. Malmstrom et al. [7] focus on angles of the joints making up individual body parts and visualize their differences in several graphs, which are detailed but difficult to understand for common users. In [2], color-coded bars are used to depict the development of motion in time. Urribarri et al. [14] focus on the visualization of time differences between the two compared motions. However, none of these techniques combines the visualizations of mapping with visualization of individual skeleton sequences, nor do they provide a combination of multiple views on the sequence differences.

In MocapViz, on the other hand, we strive to provide a comprehensive view on the dissimilarity of two movements. Therefore, we have designed several new visualizations that focus on different aspects of the motion data. The first two are shown in Fig. 2, the other two examples are not included due to space restrictions but can be found on the web-page of the MocapViz library.

- *Overall similarity of motion sequences* (Fig. 2-A): To visualize the complete pose-to-pose mapping of the compared sequences, we first represent each motion by the motion image presented earlier. To be able to draw the mapping among all poses and not just the key-poses depicted in the motion image, we add a time-line of dots representing all the poses. The dots are connected by

A: pose mapping and the differences of complete mapped poses

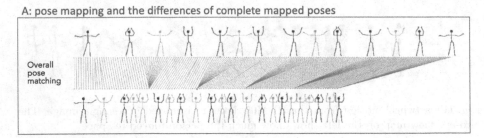

B: differences of matched poses in individual body parts

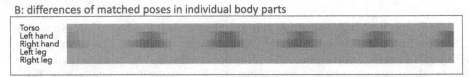

Fig. 2. Two views on the differences between two clapping motions from the HDM05 dataset. We can observe that the main differences occur when the actors move their hands apart – one of them claps faster and doesn't move hands far apart, the other one spreads his hands more.

lines that express the optimal pose-to-pose mapping, colored on the red-green scale to express the closeness of individual mapped poses. Depending on user settings, the closeness of pose matching can be evaluated in the context of the specific two actions (thus highlighting even small differences in two similar motions) or in the context of the whole dataset (to better distinguish between minor and major differences).

- *Differences of matched poses in individual body parts* (Fig. 2-B): Some pairs of motions may only differ e.g. in the movement of hands, while the legs are static or move in the same way. To highlight such situations, we visualize the closeness of pose mapping for individual body parts.
- *Detailed view on the matched poses*: For any two mapped poses, it is possible to view the detailed drawing of the poses and the computed differences between individual body parts.
- *Visualization of time alignment*: In this view, we detect and visualize the changes of speed in the compared motions, using the algorithm of [14].

In the current implementation, the optimal mapping between two skeleton sequences is determined by the DTW algorithm. However, the implementation is extensible, so the DTW distance can be seamlessly replaced by other sequence alignment algorithms. The only input required by the MocapViz module for visualization of movement differences are the two motion sequences to be compared, normalized according to user preferences. Data normalization is not part of the visualization procedure, since different approaches to position or orientation normalization may be suitable for individual use cases.

5 Exploration of Human Motion Datasets

The aim of multimedia exploration is to reveal the content of a whole multimedia collection, often totally unknown to the users who access the data. The exploration principles are mostly studied in the domain of image retrieval [8, 11]. To the best of our knowledge, only one similar technique exist for motion data [2]. However, this approach focuses on the level of individual poses, which is useful for understanding detailed variations of a small collection of movements (e.g. for gaming and animation applications) but not for the browsing of large collections. Therefore, we took inspiration from the image exploration interfaces and combined them with our methods for motion data visualization.

The construction of exploration systems for large datasets usually comprises two steps. First, the large input collection has to be organized into a hierarchical tree structure, so that individual nodes of the tree can be visualized on a single screen. Next, the actual visualization needs to be designed, allowing intuitive browsing through the hierarchy and presenting each node in a way that conveys the maximum information about the relationships between individual objects within the node. For collections of motion sequences, we further find it important to incorporate the information about semantic categories of individual motions into the exploration interface. Let us recall that motion collections such as the HDM05, PKU-MMD, or NTU datasets contain short motion sequences sorted into semantic categories that determine the type of the motion (jump, run, etc.). For people who want to familiarize themselves with the dataset, it is also very relevant to see to what extent the semantic categories agree with the natural clustering of data as provided by the content-based distance measures (e.g., the DTW algorithm). Therefore, the additional objective of our exploration interface is to allow browsing by both the semantic categories and the content-based clusters, and to provide information about the semantic diversity of the content-based clusters.

Preparation of the Hierarchical Structure. We process the input dataset in a top-down manner, gradually breaking the collection into smaller clusters of mutually similar objects. Sufficiently small clusters become the leaf nodes of the tree hierarchy, larger clusters give rise to subtrees. In particular, we utilize the hierarchical k-medoid clustering, which allows us to limit the number of subtrees for each internal node of the hierarchy. The parameter k was set to 10, with the maximum size of the leaf nodes being 20. During the construction of the hierarchical tree, we also collect some interesting statistics, such as the sizes of individual subtrees or the number of different semantic categories contained in each subtree. A separate hierarchy is also computed for each semantic category that contains more than 20 objects.

The computation of the hierarchical structures is performed off-line, using the MESSIF library for content-based data management [1], and the results are saved as a JSON file. If preferred, users can employ their own tools to produce the hierarchies in the defined format and submit them to the exploration interface.

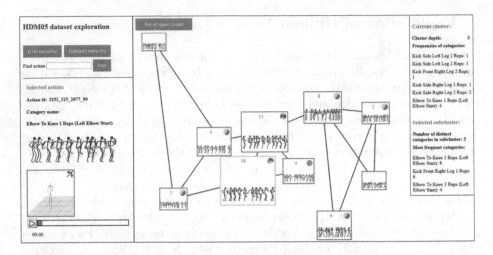

Fig. 3. Visual exploration of the HDM05 dataset.

Exploration Interface. The exploration interface is the third module of the MocapViz library. It was designed to allow easy orientation and browsing in the collection, and to provide rich information about individual motion objects and their relationships. The interface consists of three main parts (see Fig. 3).

In the central part, users can browse the hierarchical tree structure (either complete or for a selected semantic category) and display individual nodes. In case of leaf nodes, all objects in the node are shown, whereas for inner nodes of the hierarchical tree, we show the medoids of the subtrees. The next level of the hierarchy is accessed by double-clicking on the subtree representative. The nodes are displayed using the force-based layout [8], which places the objects on the screen in such way that the more similar ones are close to each other and the more distant objects are placed further apart. Individual objects are represented by the motion images, edges between them are color-coded to express the level of similarity and upon clicking reveal the full visualization of the similarity between the two connected motions. The motion images representing subtrees of the hierarchy also contain information about the size of the respective subtree and a pictogram that expresses the subtree diversity in terms of semantic categories.

The left and right panels of the exploration interface contain additional details about the selected action and cluster, respectively. The action details include a full motion image of the given action, its animation, and information about related actions. For clusters, we provide more detailed information about the distribution of semantic categories within the cluster.

6   Conclusions

Visualization of human motion data is an important part of creating insightful and user-friendly motion processing applications. The MocapViz library presented in this paper provides a unique set of techniques for visualizing human motion data, explaining their relationships, and exploration of large motion datasets. Its functionality is demonstrated in two public interfaces for the exploration of the HDM05 and PKU-MMD datasets. The exploration interfaces as well as the MocapViz library are available at http://disa.fi.muni.cz/research-directions/motion-data/mocapviz/.

References

1. Batko, M., Novak, D., Zezula, P.: MESSIF: metric similarity search implementation framework. In: Thanos, C., Borri, F., Candela, L. (eds.) DELOS 2007. LNCS, vol. 4877, pp. 1–10. Springer, Heidelberg (2007). https://doi.org/10.1007/978-3-540-77088-6_1
2. Bernard, J., Wilhelm, N., Krüger, B., May, T., Schreck, T., Kohlhammer, J.: Motionexplorer: exploratory search in human motion capture data based on hierarchical aggregation. IEEE Trans. Vis. Comput. Graph. **19**(12), 2257–2266 (2013)
3. Bouvier-Zappa, S., Ostromoukhov, V., Poulin, P.: Motion cues for illustration of skeletal motion capture data. In: 5th International Symposium on Non-Photorealistic Animation and Rendering (NPAR), pp. 133–140. ACM (2007)
4. Chang, S., et al.: Towards accurate human pose estimation in videos of crowded scenes. In: 28th ACM International Conference on Multimedia (MM), pp. 4630–4634. ACM (2020)
5. Liu, C., Hu, Y., Li, Y., Song, S., Liu, J.: PKU-MMD: a large scale benchmark for skeleton-based human action understanding. In: Workshop on Visual Analysis in Smart and Connected Communities (VSCC@MM 2017), pp. 1–8. ACM (2017)
6. Liu, J., Shahroudy, A., Perez, M., Wang, G., Duan, L., Kot, A.C.: NTU RGB+D 120: a large-scale benchmark for 3D human activity understanding. IEEE Trans. Pattern Anal. Mach. Intell. **42**(10), 2684–2701 (2020)
7. Malmstrom, C., Zhang, Y., Pasquier, P., Schiphorst, T., Bartram, L.: Mocomp: a tool for comparative visualization between takes of motion capture data. In: 3rd International Symposium on Movement and Computing (MOCO), pp. 11:1–11:8. ACM (2016)
8. Moško, J., Lokoč, J., Grošup, T., Čech, P., Skopal, T., Lánský, J.: Evaluating multilayer multimedia exploration. In: Amato, G., Connor, R., Falchi, F., Gennaro, C. (eds.) SISAP 2015. LNCS, vol. 9371, pp. 162–169. Springer, Cham (2015). https://doi.org/10.1007/978-3-319-25087-8_15
9. Müller, M.: Information Retrieval for Music and Motion. Springer, Cham (2007)
10. Müller, M., Röder, T., Clausen, M., Eberhardt, B., Krüger, B., Weber, A.: Documentation Mocap Database HDM05. Technical Report CG-2007-2, Universität Bonn (2007)
11. Nguyen, G.P., Worring, M.: Interactive access to large image collections using similarity-based visualization. J. Vis. Lang. Comput. **19**(2), 203–224 (2008)
12. Sedmidubsky, J., Elias, P., Budikova, P., Zezula, P.: Content-based management of human motion data: survey and challenges. IEEE Access **9**, 64241–64255 (2021)
13. Sedmidubsky, J., Zezula, P.: Recognizing user-defined subsequences in human motion data. In: International Conference on Multimedia Retrieval (ICMR), pp. 395–398. ACM (2019)
14. Urribarri, D.K., Larrea, M.L., Castro, S.M., Puppo, E.: Overview+detail visual comparison of karate motion captures. In: Pesado, P., Arroyo, M. (eds.) CACIC 2019. CCIS, vol. 1184, pp. 139–154. Springer, Cham (2020). https://doi.org/10.1007/978-3-030-48325-8_10
15. Yasuda, H., Kaihara, R., Saito, S., Nakajima, M.: Motion belts: visualization of human motion data on a timeline. IEICE Trans. Inf. Syst. **91**(4), 1159–1167 (2008)

Foundations

On Projections to Linear Subspaces

Erik Thordsen$^{(\boxtimes)}$ and Erich Schubert

TU Dortmund University, Otto-Hahn-Straße 14, 44227 Dortmund, Germany
{erik.thordsen,erich.schubert}@tu-dortmund.de

Abstract. The merit of projecting data onto linear subspaces is well known from, e.g., dimension reduction. One key aspect of subspace projections, the maximum preservation of variance (principal component analysis), has been thoroughly researched and the effect of random linear projections on measures such as intrinsic dimensionality still is an ongoing effort. In this paper, we investigate the less explored depths of linear projections onto explicit subspaces of varying dimensionality and the expectations of variance that ensue. The result is a new family of bounds for Euclidean distances and inner products. We showcase the quality of these bounds as well as investigate the intimate relation to intrinsic dimensionality estimation.

1 Introduction

The probably most important research on linear subspace projections was written by Pearson in his 1901 paper on Principal Component Analysis (PCA). The concept of PCA explains how the variance of a data set can be decomposed into orthogonal components, each of which covers the maximum amount of variance. This fundamental result has been employed in many fields including dimensionality reduction, clustering [1], intrinsic dimensionality estimation [5], and many more. The decomposition also implies linear projections that preserve the least amount of variance. Yet, it yields little information on the less tangible middle ground of random projections. The Johnson-Lindenstrauss lemma shows that random projections can preserve distances well, and the effect of random projections on, e.g., intrinsic dimensionality [6] has also been explored in the past. But we could not find literature on the effect of random projections on the variance itself. In this paper, we investigate the effect on a projected point's squared norm which entails effects on the variance of the data set. The arising bounds for the Euclidean distance as well as for inner products are explored in Sect. 2. The projections required for these bounds rely on the normal vectors of the linear subspace on which we project, which are drawn from the data set itself. Using measures based on points from the data set to assess boundaries on norms is a concept already employed in, e.g., spatial indexing. Methods like LAESA [7] use so-called pivot/reference/prototype points and the triangle inequality to prune

Part of the work on this paper has been supported by Deutsche Forschungsgemeinschaft (DFG), project number 124020371, within the Collaborative Research Center SFB 876 "Providing Information by Resource-Constrained Analysis", project A2.

T. Skopal et al. (Eds.): SISAP 2022, LNCS 13590, pp. 75–88, 2022.
https://doi.org/10.1007/978-3-031-17849-8_7

the data set during spatial queries. Tree-based methods like the Balltree [8] use the triangle inequality to exclude entire subtrees, while permutation based indexing [3,14] uses the relative closeness to reference points to partition the data. The central points in these approaches fulfill a role equivalent to pivots. Using pivots for random projections, however, yields fundamentally stronger pruning capabilities, as discussed in Sect. 2. In Sect. 3, we analyze the expected values of variance preserved by random projections. These expectations are closely related to PCA, yet costly to compute exactly. To compensate for the computational cost and fathom the relation to eigenvalues we propose an approximation of the expected values in terms of eigenvalues. The expected values are related to the Angle-Based Intrinsic Dimensionality (ABID) estimator [13]. We explore the relationship in Sect. 4, which leads to a tangible link between indexing complexity and intrinsic dimensionality. To highlight the practical implications as well as showcase the efficacy of the introduced bounds we propose a very simple index and our empirical results in Sect. 5. Lastly, we close with a summary of this paper and a short outlook on future research in Sect. 6.

In this paper, we denote the i-th eigenvalue of some matrix M with $\lambda_i^{(M)}$. We do not care about the specific order of eigenvalues but assume that corresponding eigenvalues of matrices that admit the same eigenvectors are in the same order. We write M^c as an abbreviation for $V\Lambda^c V^T$ where V is the matrix containing the eigenvectors of M as columns and Λ^c is the diagonal matrix containing $(\lambda_i^{(M)})^c$ on the diagonal. We write $C(X)$ for the covariance matrix of data sets X where we assume X to be origin-centered unless otherwise specified. We denote the normalizations of vectors x and data sets X with $\tilde{x}$ and $\tilde{X}$, respectively. Whenever Euclidean spaces and distances are discussed, the dot product is implied by the inner product.

2   Pivotal Bounds in Euclidean Spaces

We consider linear subspace projections of *query points* onto the linear subspace spanned by (not necessarily orthogonal) *pivots* or *reference points* $\{r_1, \ldots, r_k\}$, $k \leq d$ drawn from the same distribution as the analyzed data set, e.g., by choosing them from the data set itself. In the case of affine subspace projections, both the query and reference points are shifted by a *center* point c. We assume all (shifted) reference points to be linearly independent. Otherwise, we discard reference points until linear independence holds. The projection $\pi(x-c; r_1-c, \ldots, r_k-c)$ of some shifted query point $x-c$ onto the affine subspace (shortened to $\pi(x-c)$ whenever the choice of reference points is clear) is then given by

$$\pi(x - c) = \sum_{i=1}^{k} \langle x - c, \hat{r}_i \rangle \hat{r}_i \tag{1}$$

where the $\hat{r}_i$ are the normalized orthogonal vectors obtained from the Gram-Schmidt process applied to the $r_i - c$. These can be recursively computed from

$$\hat{r}_1 = \frac{r_1 - c}{\|r_1 - c\|} \qquad \hat{r}_i = \frac{(r_i - c) - \sum_{j=1}^{i-1} \langle r_i - c, \hat{r}_j \rangle \hat{r}_j}{\left\| (r_i - c) - \sum_{j=1}^{i-1} \langle r_i - c, \hat{r}_j \rangle \hat{r}_j \right\|} \tag{2}$$

where $\|x\|$ is shorthand for $\langle x, x \rangle^{1/2}$. In the following, we will repeatedly require the evaluation of $\langle \cdot, \hat{r}_i \rangle$ and $\|\pi(\cdot; \cdot)\|$. Although (1) and (2) can be evaluated explicitly every time, it can be more convenient to represent the (squared) norm after projection in terms of inner products (especially in kernel spaces):

$$\|\pi(x - c)\|^2 = \sum_{i=1}^{k} \langle x - c, \hat{r}_i \rangle^2 \tag{3}$$

since all $\hat{r}_i$ are normalized and pairwise orthogonal. We can reduce $\langle \cdot, \hat{r}_i \rangle$ to

$$\langle x - c, \hat{r}_i \rangle = \frac{\langle c,c \rangle - \langle c,x \rangle - \langle c,r_i \rangle + \langle x,r_i \rangle - \sum_{j=1}^{i-1} \langle x-c, \hat{r}_j \rangle \langle r_i-c, \hat{r}_j \rangle}{\left(\langle c,c \rangle - 2\langle c,r_i \rangle + \langle r_i,r_i \rangle - \sum_{j=1}^{i-1} \langle r_i-c, \hat{r}_j \rangle^2 \right)^{1/2}} \tag{4}$$

which can also be used recursively to compute the $\langle r_i - c, \hat{r}_j \rangle$ in (4). In the non-affine case, $c = \mathbf{0}$, (4) simplifies to

$$\langle x, \hat{r}_i \rangle = \frac{\langle x,r_i \rangle - \sum_{j=1}^{i-1} \langle x, \hat{r}_j \rangle \langle r_i, \hat{r}_j \rangle}{\left(\langle r_i,r_i \rangle - \sum_{j=1}^{i-1} \langle r_i, \hat{r}_j \rangle^2 \right)^{1/2}} \tag{5}$$

Note that the denominator and parts of the nominator need to be computed just once. Further, we omit the explicit computation of any $\hat{r}_i$ which would be infeasible in, e.g., RBF kernel and general inner product spaces. With dynamic programming, $\|\pi(x - c)\|^2$ can be computed in $\Theta(pk^2)$ time, where p is the effort required to compute an inner product.

In spatial indexing, pivots have been successfully used to bound distances via the triangle inequality [7,8]. We propose to bound distances in terms of a decomposition of the squared Euclidean norm into dot products given by

$$d_{Euc}(x, y)^2 = \|x - y\|^2 = \langle x - y, x - y \rangle = \langle x, x \rangle + \langle y, y \rangle - 2 \langle x, y \rangle \tag{6}$$

From this we can derive bounds for the Euclidean distance between two points given a bound on the dot product $\langle x, y \rangle$, assuming $\langle x, x \rangle$ and $\langle y, y \rangle$ are known. Let $\hat{r}_1, \ldots, \hat{r}_k$ be pivot points previously orthogonalized by the Gram-Schmidt process as defined in Sect. 3. We can decompose $x - c$ and $y - c$ into k components aligned along the $\hat{r}_i$ and one orthogonal remainder. We will call this $(k + 1)$-th component $x_\perp$ and $y_\perp$, respectively. It then follows that

$$\langle x - c, y - c \rangle = \langle x_\perp, y_\perp \rangle + \sum_{i=1}^{k} \langle \langle x - c, \hat{r}_i \rangle \hat{r}_i, \langle y - c, \hat{r}_i \rangle \hat{r}_i \rangle \tag{7}$$

Because the $\hat{r}_i$ are pairwise orthogonal, this decomposition is uniquely defined. Since all $\hat{r}_i$ have a unit norm, we can rewrite this equation to

$$\langle x, y \rangle = \langle x_\perp, y_\perp \rangle + \langle c, x \rangle + \langle c, y \rangle - \langle c, c \rangle + \sum_{i=1}^{k} \langle x - c, \hat{r}_i \rangle \langle y - c, \hat{r}_i \rangle \tag{8}$$

All of the terms on the right-hand side then either depend on x or y, but not on both, except for $\langle x_\perp, y_\perp \rangle$. In the semantics of Euclidean spaces, both $x_\perp$ and $y_\perp$ lie in the same $(d-k)$-dimensional linear subspace. We can compute both as $x_\perp = (x - c) - \pi(x - c)$ and $y_\perp = (y - c) - \pi(y - c)$, respectively, but do not

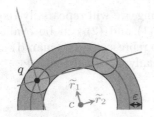

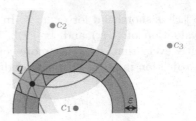

(a) Combined center and pivot   (b) Intersection of triangle inequality

Fig. 1. Eligible search spaces around a query point q after filtering with the lower bounds obtained from one, two, or three centers and/or pivots.

know their relative orientation. Yet, we can bound their inner product using the Cauchy-Schwarz inequality resulting in the bounds $\pm(\langle x_\perp, x_\perp \rangle \cdot \langle y_\perp, y_\perp \rangle)^{1/2}$. By orthogonality of $x_\perp$ and $\pi(x - c)$ we know $\|x_\perp\|^2 = \|x - c\|^2 - \|\pi(x - c)\|^2$. The bounds for the inner product $\langle x - c, y - c \rangle$ then follow as

$$\langle c, x \rangle + \langle c, y \rangle - \langle c, c \rangle + \sum_{i=1}^{k} \langle x - c, \hat{r}_i \rangle \langle y - c, \hat{r}_i \rangle \tag{9}$$

$$\pm \left(\begin{pmatrix} \langle x, x \rangle + \langle c, c \rangle - 2 \langle c, x \rangle - \sum_{i=1}^{k} \langle x - c, \hat{r}_i \rangle^2 \end{pmatrix} \right)^{1/2}$$
$$\cdot \left(\langle y, y \rangle + \langle c, c \rangle - 2 \langle c, y \rangle - \sum_{i=1}^{k} \langle y - c, \hat{r}_i \rangle^2 \right)$$

which in the non-affine case, $c = \mathbf{0}$, becomes

$$\sum_{i=1}^{k} \langle x, \hat{r}_i \rangle \langle y, \hat{r}_i \rangle \pm \left(\left(\langle x, x \rangle - \sum_{i=1}^{k} \langle x, \hat{r}_i \rangle^2 \right) \cdot \left(\langle y, y \rangle - \sum_{i=1}^{k} \langle y, \hat{r}_i \rangle^2 \right) \right)^{1/2} \tag{10}$$

Inserting both of these values into (6) gives bounds on the squared Euclidean distance and, consequentially, on the Euclidean distance. These bounds are a generalization of at least two bounds known from the literature. When we assume the affine case and $k = 0$ pivots, the bounds derived from (6) and (10) reduce to

$$\langle x, x \rangle + \langle y, y \rangle - 2 \langle c, x \rangle - 2 \langle c, y \rangle + 2 \langle c, c \rangle \pm 2 \|x - c\| \|y - c\| \tag{11}$$

$$= (\|x - c\| \pm \|y - c\|)^2 \tag{12}$$

which are the bounds easily derivable from the triangle inequality. For the non-affine case with $k = 1$ pivots and normalized x and y, the inner product bounds (10) reduce to

$$\langle x, \hat{r}_1 \rangle \langle y, \hat{r}_1 \rangle \pm \left(\left(1 - \langle x, \hat{r}_1 \rangle^2 \right) \left(1 - \langle y, \hat{r}_1 \rangle^2 \right) \right)^{1/2} \tag{13}$$

which is the triangle inequality for cosines introduced in [10]. Triangle-inequality-based bounds have been used in spatial indexing in methods like, e.g., LAESA [7]. For multiple pivots, these approaches take the minimum or maximum of the bounds obtained separately for each pivot. In our terminology, we refer to such pivots as centers c. Those are fundamentally different from the term pivots introduced here: When performing an ε-range query for a query point y, the eligible search space for vectors x according to the upper bound in (12) is a hyperspherical shell centered at c. This geometric shape can be described as the sumset (the set of all sums of pairs in the cartesian product) of a $(d-1)$-sphere of radius $\|y-c\|$ centered at c and a d-ball of radius ε. When using pivots as per our definition, each pivot induces a hyperplane orthogonal to the $\hat{r}_i$ which intersects with the hypersphere. Consequentially, the resulting eligible search space is the sumset of a $(d-1-k)$-sphere of radius $(\|y-c\|^2 - \|\pi(y-c)\|^2)^{1/2}$ and a d-ball of radius ε. This is illustrated in two dimensions in Fig. 1. Each of the pivots eliminates an entire dimension from the sphere-part of the search space whereas the minimum lower bounds obtained from multiple centers produce an intersection of multiple hyperspherical shells. While $d-1$ pivots can reduce the search space to the sumset of at most 2 points and an ε-ball, the intersection of even d hyperspherical shells in the best case produces a volume that can be roughly described as a distorted hypercube with an "edge length" of about 2ε. The resulting volume can be exponentially larger in d than the search volume using $d-1$ pivots. As the volumes of regular shapes in Euclidean space expand exponentially in dimensions, one would expect an approximately exponential reduction in search space over an increasing number of pivots, whereas using the minimum upper bound over multiple centers does not induce such a reduction in search space volume. It is, therefore, of little surprise that the cosine bounds introduced in [10] ($k=1$), produced tighter bounds empirically than the triangle inequality ($k=0$), and were successfully applied to improve the performance of spherical k-means clustering [11]. Qualitatively, there is a clear argument for using a larger amount of pivots. However, the reduction in search space comes at the price of increased computational cost as the evaluation of $\langle y, \hat{r}_i \rangle$ is quadratic and the evaluation of the bounds is linear in k. Blindly increasing k is not universally advantageous for the computational cost of spatial indexing queries. But how many pivots tighten the bounds enough to counterweigh the overhead? More precisely, how much more of a point's squared norm does the k-th randomly drawn pivot drawn cover on average? Although the answer does not refer to an optimal pivot choice, by arguing over expectations of underlying distributions, this conservative argument likely holds for previously unknown query points.

3 Expected Variance of Random Projections

The analysis of squared norms after projection is closely related to spectral analysis. If we chose any normalized vector v, $\mathbb{E}_{x \in X}\left[\|\pi(x - \mathbb{E}_{y \in X}[y]; v)\|^2\right]$ is simply the variance of X in direction v. Consequentially, for any pair of a normalized eigenvector e_i and the corresponding eigenvalue $\lambda_i^{(C(X))}$, we know that $\mathbb{E}_{x \in X}\left[\|\pi(x; e_i)\|^2\right] = \lambda_i^{(C(X))}$ for any origin-centered X. By orthogonality of the eigenvectors, this argument can be extended to any number of eigenvectors $e_1, \ldots, e_n$ as

$$\mathop{\mathbb{E}}_{x \in X} \left[\| \pi(x; e_1, \ldots, e_n) \|^2 \right] = \sum_{i=1}^{n} \lambda_i^{(C(X))} \tag{14}$$

Pearson [9] showed that the eigenvectors of the covariance matrix are precisely the maximizers of this term, i.e. they are the solution to

$$\mathop{\arg\max}_{e_1, \ldots, e_n} \mathop{\mathbb{E}}_{x \in X} \left[\| \pi(x; e_1, \ldots, e_n) \|^2 \right] \tag{15}$$

If one intended to evaluate how much of the squared norm of any point is remaining after the projection onto k directions maximally, the answer immediately follows from the sum of the k largest eigenvalues. Employing the corresponding eigenvectors as $\hat{r}_i$ would then be a reasonable approach. Yet, both eigenvectors and eigenvalues can be sensitive to noise in limited data sets [4]. They may not be an optimal choice when new and unknown data arises. We, hence, focus on the expectation of these values for a random set of reference points drawn from the data. More precisely we inspect

$$E_k^{\Sigma}(X) := \mathop{\mathbb{E}}_{\substack{r_1, \ldots, r_k \in X \\ \forall i \neq j : r_i \neq r_j}} \left[\mathop{\mathbb{E}}_{x \in X} \left[\| \pi(x - c; r_1 - c, \ldots, r_n - c) \|^2 \right] \right] \tag{16}$$

As with the eigenvectors and eigenvalues of the covariance matrix, this expected value is the sum of components introduced by each additional reference point taken into consideration. This naturally sums up the total variance of the data set for $k = d$. Through varying k we can obtain a cumulative description of how much variance an arbitrary linear projection within the data set can explain and the difference of neighboring values gives the amount of variance explained at random by the k-th component. We will write this difference as $E_k(X) := E_k^{\Sigma}(X) - E_{k-1}^{\Sigma}(X)$ where $E_0^{\Sigma}(X) = 0$. It follows that $E_k^{\Sigma}(X) = \sum_{i=1}^{k} E_k(X)$. Practically evaluating the expected value from any data set X for any $k \gg 1$ is infeasible, as it involves $\binom{|X|}{k}$ possible sets of reference points. It is much easier to estimate the value by the Monte Carlo method (i.e. choosing a fixed number of random sets of reference points) or to approximate it from the covariance matrix if it well describes the data set's distribution.

We will only consider the non-affine case of $c = \mathbf{0}$, as the affine case is analogous and introduces numerous subtractions hindering readability. We will also omit the constraint that the reference points must not be linearly dependent to improve readability. Starting from (16) we can deduce

$$E_k(X) = E_k^{\Sigma}(X) - E_{k-1}^{\Sigma}(X) = \mathop{\mathbb{E}}_{\substack{x \in X, \\ r_1, \ldots, r_k \in \tilde{X}}} \left[\left\langle x, \frac{r_k - \pi(r_k; r_1, \ldots, r_{k-1})}{\| r_k - \pi(r_k; r_1, \ldots, r_{k-1}) \|} \right\rangle^2 \right] \tag{17}$$

Here the term $r_k - \pi(r_k; r_1, \ldots, r_{k-1})$ is the projection of r_k onto the linear subspace orthogonal to all $r_1, \ldots, r_{k-1}$. We can represent this projection by a matrix multiplication with a matrix, which we will call A_{k-1}.

$$= \mathop{\mathbb{E}}_{\substack{x \in X, \\ r_1, \ldots, r_k \in \tilde{X}}} \left[\frac{\langle x, A_{k-1} r_k \rangle^2}{\langle A_{k-1} r_k, A_{k-1} r_k \rangle} \right] = \mathop{\mathbb{E}}_{\substack{x \in X, \\ r_1, \ldots, r_k \in \tilde{X}}} \left[x^T \frac{A_{k-1} r_k r_k^T A_{k-1}^T}{\mathrm{tr}\left(A_{k-1} r_k r_k^T A_{k-1}^T \right)} x \right] \tag{18}$$

By rewriting $r_i r_i^T$ as R_i this further simplifies to

$$= \mathbb{E}_{\substack{x \in X, \\ r_1,\dots,r_k \in \widetilde{X}}} \left[x^T \frac{A_{k-1} R_k A_{k-1}^T}{\mathrm{tr}\left(A_{k-1} R_k A_{k-1}^T\right)} x \right] \tag{19}$$

$$= \mathrm{tr} \left(\mathbb{E}_{r_1,\dots,r_{k-1} \in \widetilde{X}} \left[\mathbb{E}_{r_k \in X} \left[\frac{A_{k-1} R_k A_{k-1}^T}{\mathrm{tr}\left(A_{k-1} R_k A_{k-1}^T\right)} \right] \right] \mathbb{E}_{x \in X} \left[x x^T \right] \right) \tag{20}$$

By replacing $\mathbb{E}_{x \in X} \left[x x^T \right]$ with the covariance matrix $C(X)$ and renaming the innermost expected value to $C_k(X)$ we then obtain

$$= \mathbb{E}_{r_1,\dots,r_{k-1} \in \widetilde{X}} \left[\mathrm{tr}\left(C_k(X) C(X) \right) \right] \tag{21}$$

A_0 is the identity matrix I_d, as the linear subspace orthogonal to an empty set of vectors is the entire space. Consequentially, we can define A_k recursively as

$$A_k = A_{k-1} - \frac{A_{k-1} R_k A_{k-1}^T}{\mathrm{tr}\left(A_{k-1} R_k A_{k-1}^T\right)} = A_{k-1} - \frac{A_{k-1} R_k A_{k-1}}{\mathrm{tr}(A_{k-1} R_k A_{k-1})} \tag{22}$$

As all R_i are symmetric, all A_i are symmetric as well. The expected value over r_k of $\frac{A_{k-1} R_k A_{k-1}}{\mathrm{tr}(A_{k-1} R_k A_{k-1})}$ now (approximately) equals the covariance matrix of X after being projected to the linear subspace orthogonal to $r_1,\dots,r_{k-1}$ and normalized. It follows immediately that $C_1(X) = C(\widetilde{X})$ and thereby $E_1(X) = \mathrm{tr}\left(C(\widetilde{X}) C(X)\right)$. However, $E_k(X)$ for $k > 1$ is much less easily defined because the A_i are dependent on the effective values of all r_j, $j \leq i$, and not only on r_i. To circumvent the problem we assume that all A_i are aggregate matrices just like $C(X)$ and sufficiently independent of each other to evaluate the $C_k(X)$ recursively. To highlight this assumption we will denote the approximated A_i as a function of X as $A_i(X)$. We further assume that all $A_i(X)$, $C_i(X)$, and $C(X)$ admit the same eigenvectors, whereby

$$E_k(X) = \mathbb{E}_{r_1,\dots,r_{k-1} \in \widetilde{X}} \left[\mathrm{tr}\left(C_k(X) C(X) \right) \right] = \sum_{i=1}^{d} \lambda_i^{(C_k(X))} \lambda_i^{(C(X))} \tag{23}$$

We will hereafter omit the (X) in superscripts of eigenvalues for readability. Although the resulting values are no longer exact due to these two assumptions, they allow us to approximate the expected value by deriving the value of $\lambda_i^{(C_k)}$. Assuming that X is multivariate normally distributed, we can extract this value from the definition of $C_k(X)$ using the corresponding eigenvector e_i:

$$\lambda_i^{(C_k)} = e_i^T C_k(X) e_i = \mathrm{tr}\left(e_i e_i^T C_k(X) \right) \tag{24}$$

$$= \mathbb{E}_{r_k \in X} \left[\frac{r_k^T A_{k-1}(X) e_i e_i^T A_{k-1}(X) r_k}{r_k^T A_{k-1}(X)^2 r_k} \right] \tag{25}$$

$$= \mathbb{E}_{r_k \in \mathcal{N}_{0_d, I_d}} \left[\frac{r_k^T C(X)^{1/2} A_{k-1}(X) e_i e_i^T A_{k-1}(X) C(X)^{1/2} r_k}{r_k^T C(X)^{1/2} A_{k-1}(X)^2 C(X)^{1/2} r_k} \right] \tag{26}$$

$$= \mathbb{E}_{r_k \in \mathcal{N}_{0_d, I_d}} \left[\frac{r_k^T e_i e_i^T C(X) A_{k-1}(X)^2 r_k}{r_k^T C(X) A_{k-1}(X)^2 r_k} \right] \tag{27}$$

We now substitute $C(X)A_{k-1}(X)^2$ with $D_{k-1}(X)$ which entails $\lambda_j^{(C)}\left(\lambda_j^{(A_{k-1})}\right)^2$ is equal to $\lambda_j^{(D_{k-1})}$. In favor of brevity we will omit the exponent (D_{k-1}) from here on. As per Proposition 2 in Kan and Bao [2], $\lambda_i^{(C_k)}$ then equals

$$= \int_0^\infty \frac{\operatorname{tr}\left(e_i e_i^T D_{k-1}(X)(I_d + 2tD_{k-1}(X))^{-1}\right)}{|I_d + 2tD_{k-1}(X)|^{1/2}}\, dt \tag{28}$$

$$= \int_0^\infty \frac{\lambda_i}{(1+2t\lambda_i)^{1/2}\prod_{j=1}^d (1+2t\lambda_j)^{1/2}}\, dt \tag{29}$$

This integral is closely related to elliptic integrals and we do not provide a simple and closed-form solution. Solving the integral numerically would again involve too much computational effort. We instead propose to substitute the λ_j in the denominator with $(\lambda_i^2 \prod_{j=1}^d \lambda_j)^{1/(d+2)}$ whereby the integral takes the form of a scaled beta prime distribution:

$$\lambda_i^{(C_k)} \approx \lambda_i B(\alpha,\beta)\int_0^\infty \frac{t^{\alpha-1}\left(1+2(\lambda_i^2\prod_{j=1}^d\lambda_j)^{\frac{1}{d+2}}t\right)^{-\alpha-\beta}}{B(\alpha,\beta)}\, dt \tag{30}$$

where $\alpha = 1$, $\beta = \frac{d}{2}$, and $B(\alpha,\beta)$ is the beta function. The integral over the scaled beta distribution is known to equal the scaling factor, whereby

$$\lambda_i^{(C_k)} \approx \frac{\lambda_i B(\alpha,\beta)}{2(\lambda_i^2\prod_{j=1}^d\lambda_j)^{\frac{1}{d+2}}} \propto \lambda_i^{\frac{d}{d+2}} \tag{31}$$

As the $\lambda_i^{(C_k)}$ are eigenvalues of a normalized distribution, their sum must equal 1. Using this constraint, we can drop all factors independent of λ_i and derive

$$\lambda_i^{(C_k)} \approx \lambda_i^{\frac{d}{d+2}}\Big/ \sum_{j=1}^d \lambda_j^{\frac{d}{d+2}} \tag{32}$$

As the λ_j are dependent on $\lambda_j^{(C)}$ and $\lambda_j^{(A_{k-1})}$, this leads to the recursive definition

$$\lambda_i^{(C_k)} \approx \frac{\left(\lambda_i^{(C)}\left(\lambda_i^{(A_{k-1})}\right)^2\right)^{\frac{d}{d+2}}}{\sum_{j=1}^d \left(\lambda_j^{(C)}\left(\lambda_j^{(A_{k-1})}\right)^2\right)^{\frac{d}{d+2}}} \qquad \lambda_i^{(A_k)} \approx \lambda_i^{(A_{k-1})} - \lambda_i^{(C_{k-1})} \tag{33}$$

This recursion terminates at $\lambda_i^{(A_0)} = 1$ and $\lambda_i^{(C_0)} = 0$. These approximations can be computed efficiently in $\Theta(dk)$ and inserted in (23) to give an approximation of $E_k(X)$. Since the approximations are based on the assumption that X is distributed according to some multivariate normal distribution they need not be accurate. Since all occurrences of any r_k in the formulae involve some sort of normalization, this approximation extends to any distribution of X for which $\{C(X)^{-1/2}x \mid x \in X\}$ is spherically symmetrically distributed, which includes cases like, e.g., d-balls. We also did not compensate for the requirement that all r_k must be pairwise different, as these arguments are based on distributions rather than point sets. In empirical tests the sample size, however, did not contribute to approximation quality. The biggest issue with this approximation is the fact, that while the A_i as variables in r_1 through r_i must have eigenvalues in

$\{0,1\}$, the approximated eigenvalues $\lambda_i^{(A_k)}$ can become negative whereby latter E_k can be vastly overestimated. As we know that the $E_k^\Sigma(X)$ must sum to the total variance of X, we propose to cut off any excess in $E_k^\Sigma(X)$ and determine the $E_k(X)$ based on these cut values. To summarize, the approximation proceeds as follows: For all $1 \le k \le d$ compute the $\lambda_i^{(C_k)}$ values using the recursive formulations (33). Use these values to compute $E_i(X)$ values and reduce $E_i(X)$ values for larger k to not have their sum exceed the total variance of X, which compensates for negative $\lambda_i^{(A_k)}$. Even though this approximation from a theoretical point makes the wrong assumptions that the r_k are pairwise different and that the $C_i(X)$ are statistically independent, the approximation in our experiments gave close enough results to have it worth considering, especially as the exact computation of values has an enormous computational cost. The approximation via the Monte Carlo method is known to converge on the exact values, yet, might require enormous samples.

While (23) requires the covariance matrix of a mean-centered data set, the approach via Monte Carlo sampling applies directly to inner product values and, hence, to kernel spaces. The approximation in (23) can then be used in black-box optimization to obtain an approximate spectral analysis of the kernel space. The obtained spectrum is neglecting the scale of the eigenvalues of the covariance matrix as the $E_i(X)$ are invariant under the scaling of these values. In this manner, we can perform approximate spectral analysis even in spaces that do not allow for a direct approach, such as the RBF kernel space which has infinitely many dimensions. Naturally, the method must be applied in a truncated fashion for infinite dimensions, for which we here propose two solutions: Firstly, one can estimate $E_1(X)$ through $E_k(X)$ for some fixed k using the Monte Carlo method and rescale these values to sum to 1. This implies neglecting the remaining $d-k$ dimensions and assuming the data to have 0 variance along with these directions. The $d-k$ smallest eigenvalues of the covariance of such a data set must then be 0, too. Finding any set of k eigenvalues that leads to these $E_1(X)$ through $E_k(X)$ values then solves the truncated case. Secondly, one can assume that the remaining variance not explained by $E_k^\Sigma(X)$ is distributed over the remaining $d-k$ values according to some user-defined distribution. Assuming a uniform distribution, for example, would explain the remaining variance as noise in the embedding space which might be a reasonable assumption.

A special case can further be made on the evaluation of $E_k(X)$ values on normalized data. When working on $\widetilde{X}$ instead of X, which can be achieved in kernel space by dividing the occurrences of x in the formulae by $\langle x, x \rangle^{1/2}$, we immediately obtain that $E_1(\widetilde{X})$ equals the sum of squared eigenvalues of $C(\widetilde{X})$. While this equality does not hold for the approximation via eigenvalues of $C(\widetilde{X})$, it is approximately obtained from the Monte Carlo method or precisely for an exhaustive evaluation of $E_1(\widetilde{X})$. Just as the constraint of the sum of eigenvalues of $C(\widetilde{X})$ equalling 1, this additional constraint can be used in the black-box optimization for retrieving the original eigenvalues from $E_k(\widetilde{X})$ values. Using (31), these eigenvalues can be approximately translated into the relative eigenvalues of the non-normalized data whenever the data can be assumed to obey the distributional constraints of the approximation.

4   Random Projections and ID Estimation

As stated in the previous section, $E_1(\widetilde{X})$ equals the sum of squared eigenvalues of $C(\widetilde{X})$. The reciprocal of this specific value has been introduced as an estimator for intrinsic dimensionality named ABID [13], that is

$$\mathrm{ID}_{ABID}(X) = E_1(\widetilde{X})^{-1} = E_1^{\Sigma}(\widetilde{X})^{-1} \tag{34}$$

For one, this observation adds additional semantics to the meaning of ABID as the number of basis vectors of a random projection to fully explain the variance in a data set. Yet, it also implies the applicability of the E_k values in the realm of ID estimation. Although E_1 gives the part of total variance a random projection based on in-distribution basis vectors can explain, not all E_k values are necessarily equal. That is, the projection onto two random directions does not necessarily cover twice the variance covered by projecting onto one random direction. This linearity is exclusively true for spherically symmetrical distributions such as d-balls and for all other distributions we would certainly expect $E_2^{\Sigma}(X) < 2E_1^{\Sigma}(X)$. Ultimately, we are looking for the smallest k such that $E_k^{\Sigma}(X) \geq \mathrm{tr}\,(C(X))$, that is, the number of random projections required to explain the entire variance of X. Unfortunately, we only have formulae for integer k but we can generalize the approach of ABID in the sense of extrapolating from a fixed E_k which results in a parameterized ID estimator which we name the Thresholded Random In-distribution Projections (TRIP) Estimator:

$$\mathrm{ID}_{TRIP}(X, k, \eta) = k + \frac{(1 - \eta)\,\mathrm{tr}\,(C(X)) - E_k^{\Sigma}(X)}{E_k(X)} \tag{35}$$

where k is the number of considered projections and $\eta \in [0, 1]$ is a fraction describing how much of the variance we attribute to noise. Semantically this answers the question *"How many random projections are required to explain $(1-\eta)$ of the total variance if every further projection covers as much variance as the last one?"*. In the linear case of spherically symmetrical distributions as above, this estimator is ideally constant for $\eta = 0$ and all $1 \leq k \leq d$. On other distributions with $\eta = 0$, we would expect a curve that starts at (approximately, dependent on implementation) $\mathrm{ID}_{ABID}(X)$ for $k = 1$ and approaches k for increasing k as the $E_i(X)$ are monotonically falling. Equality is likely only reached for $k = d$, as this requires zero variance after k projections, which is unlikely in presence of high-dimensional noise. The factor η is intended to compensate for this. For $\eta > 0$, the curve again starts at approximately $\mathrm{ID}_{ABID}(X)$, approaches k, and after some k drops below it. As for parameter choice, η is application dependent whereas k can either be chosen empirically, or we can inspect values $1 \leq k \leq d$ to find the k at which $\mathrm{ID}_{TRIP}(X, k, \eta)$ is closest to k. The latter is likely not feasible in a local ID fashion when using the Monte Carlo or exhaustive methods but can be done when using the approximation introduced in Sect. 3. When using a fixed k, obtaining an ID below this k is a strong indicator of having chosen k too large. In addition, the curve of $\mathrm{ID}_{TRIP}(X, k, \eta)$ over varying k, just like the curve of $E_i(X)$, gives insights into the local distribution characteristics of the data set that goes beyond ID estimation. These curves can theoretically help distinguish different subspaces, even when they share similar local ID.

Referring back to the discussions of indexing with linear projections in Sect. 2, we can now state a clear connection between indexing with random in-distribution pivots and intrinsic dimensionality measures. The $E_k^\Sigma(X)$ values answer how much variance on average is covered by a set of k random pivots. The expected covered variance is – in an idealized case of, e.g., uniformly distributed hyperballs – reciprocally related to intrinsic dimensionality. This is most explicitly stated in the relation to ABID and gives rise to the TRIP estimator above. Using this geometric concept of ID estimation, we can argue on an on-average appropriate number of pivots in spatial indexing. In Sect. 2 we observed that the eligible search space for range queries when using k pivots is the sumset of a $(d - 1 - k)$-sphere and an ε-ball. The radius of the hypersphere is equal to the norm of the component orthogonal to all pivots, and roughly describes how close the bounds derived in Sect. 2 are to the true distances. But there is a clear limit as to how much precision one needs in a finite data set. If this radius drops below the distance between nearest points, removing this slack from the distance estimates does not improve the discriminability. By choosing $\eta = \delta^2 / \operatorname{tr}(C(X))$ where δ is the, e.g., mean/median/p-percentile of nearest neighbor distances, we can use the TRIP estimator to evaluate just how many random projections exhaust the discriminative potential of pivoted indexing on average.

5   Pivot Filtering Linear Scan

For quality evaluation of the bounds as well as to validate the theoretical claims, we embed the bounds in a simple and easy-to-implement index. During the initialization, we choose k random pivots. As mentioned in Sect. 2, we pre-compute all parts of the equations that are independent of query points such as $\langle x, \hat{r}_i \rangle$ or the denominators in (4). Range and n-nearest neighbor queries were implemented according to Algorithms 1 and 2. The algorithms are quite similar to LAESA [7] but do not require aggregation of multiple bounds as discussed in Sect. 2. Both algorithms are at least linear in $|X|$, which should be accounted for when comparing the performance with tree-based indices. Integrating the bounds into a tree-based index is a nearby extension but out of the scope of this paper. Both Algorithms 1 and 2 are trivially adaptable to search for the largest instead of the smallest distances. This index is also trivially adaptable to work on inner products instead of distances by exchanging the bounds. For our experiments, we implemented the index in the Rust language and called the functions from a Python wrapper to compare them to the cKDTree and BallTree implementations of SciPy [15]. The source code is publicly available at https://github.com/eth42/pfls. Using this very simple index we investigated the theoretical claims and the quality of the bounds. Figure 2 displays the results of applying the index to the MNIST training data set. All queries were 100-nearest-neighbor queries for 1000 query points drawn from the same data set. We performed 100 queries for each set of parameters and instantiated a new index for each query. As seen

---

Algorithm 1 n-nearest neighbor query for distances

---

function QUERY($y \in \mathbb{R}^d, n \geq 1$)
    $ls \leftarrow$ lower bounds of $d(x,y)$ for all $x \in X$ as per (6) and (10)
    $h \leftarrow$ empty max heap
    sort X by ascending $ls[x]$
    for $x \in X$ **do**
        if $|h| < n$ **or** ($ls[x] < h.max.key$ **and** $d(x,y) < h.max.key$) **then**
            push x onto h with key $d(x,y)$
            if $|h| > n$ **then** remove entry with largest key from h
        else if $ls[x] \geq h.max.key$ **then break**
    return h as array/list

Algorithm 2 range query for distances

---

function QUERY-RANGE($y \in \mathbb{R}^d, \varepsilon \in \mathbb{R}$)
    $ls, hs \leftarrow$ lower and upper bounds of $d(x,y)$ for all $x \in X$ as per (6) and (10)
    $v \leftarrow$ empty list
    for $x \in X$ **do**
        if $ls[x] < \varepsilon$ **and** ($hs[x] < \varepsilon$ **or** $d(x,y) < \varepsilon$) **then** Push x into v
    return v

---

in Fig. 2a, the number of distance computations initially drops exponentially as we increase the number of pivots, which supports the theoretical claim that each pivot effectively eliminates one dimension from the data set and reduces the remaining search space exponentially. For increasing k, the descent in distance computations diminishes as the bounds become tight enough to sufficiently discriminate on neighboring points, and the query time eventually increases due to the cost of computing the bounds. In Sect. 4, we argued that the bounds only need to be as tight as to differentiate between nearest neighbors. To validate this claim, we investigated the ID$_{TRIP}$ values using an η equal to the 10-percentile of squared 1-nearest-neighbor distances divided by the total variance of the distribution. The smallest k for which ID$_{TRIP}(X, k, \eta) \leq k$ is around 150 as can be seen in Fig. 2c. The minimum computation time in Fig. 2b is around 100 but the query time at $k = 150$ is not that much larger than at $k = 100$. The exact percentile is an educated guess and could be supported by inspecting the histogram of nearest-neighbor distances. Yet, the region of k that provides low query times is wide enough that rough estimates and educated guesses are likely to give good results. We conclude that ID$_{TRIP}$ can be used to estimate a proper value for k by deriving η from a percentile of 1-nearest neighbor distances. To estimate a proper k efficiently, the approximation introduced in Sect. 3 can be used, which practically is sufficiently similar to the values obtained from Monte Carlo sampling as displayed in Fig. 2c. Lastly, we compared query times on HSV color histograms of the ALOI data set with varying numbers of dimensions [12]. The considered variants consist of 110250 instances with 27, 126, and 350 dimensions, respectively. As can be seen in Fig. 3 the query performance of our index is

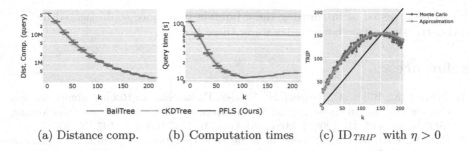

(a) Distance comp.   (b) Computation times   (c) ID_{TRIP} with $\eta > 0$

Fig. 2. Experimental results on varying numbers of pivots. Additional pivots exponentially reduce the distance computations, but the query time stagnates once the average discriminative power of the bounds has been exploited. A suitable number of pivots is suggested at the crossing point of ID_{TRIP} with the diagonal. Lines are average values, shaded area indicates the minimum and maximum.

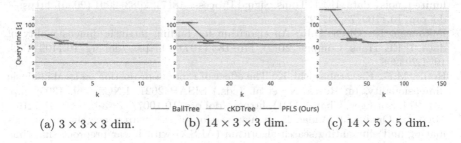

(a) $3 \times 3 \times 3$ dim.   (b) $14 \times 3 \times 3$ dim.   (c) $14 \times 5 \times 5$ dim.

Fig. 3. Query times for ALOI color histograms with varying dimensionality.

mostly unaffected by increasing dimensionality. Due to our index using a linear scan, the tree-based reference implementations were faster on low dimensionality. For sufficiently high dimensional or small enough data sets, our index can outperform these reference implementations. For larger data sets, extending the approach to a tree-based structure appears promising.

6 Conclusion

In this paper, we introduced new bounds for Euclidean distances and inner products using a pivot-based approach. We showed that these bounds generalize the well-known bounds based on the triangle inequality. We argued why an increased number of pivots exponentially reduces the eligible search space of certain queries and derived an approach to estimate a reasonable number of pivots for practical purposes. We further showed how this number of pivots is intimately related to intrinsic dimensionality estimation. Lastly, we implemented the bounds in a simple and easily reproducible index that operates on both inner products and their induced distances and allows queries for the smallest and largest values. The empirical data presented aligns with the theoretical considerations and highlights the qualitative performance of implementing the bounds. Further research should be invested in integrating these bounds into more sophisticated indices or constructing a tree-based index using these bounds.

References

1. Achtert, E., Böhm, C., Kriegel, H., Kröger, P., Zimek, A.: Robust, complete, and efficient correlation clustering. In: SIAM International Conference on Data Mining (SDM), pp. 413–418 (2007). https://doi.org/10.1137/1.9781611972771.37
2. Bao, Y., Kan, R.: On the moments of ratios of quadratic forms in normal random variables. J. Multivar. Anal. **117**, 229–245 (2013). https://doi.org/10.1016/j.jmva.2013.03.002
3. Chávez, E., Figueroa, K., Navarro, G.: Effective proximity retrieval by ordering permutations. IEEE Trans. Pattern Anal. Mach. Intell. **30**(9), 1647–1658 (2008). https://doi.org/10.1109/TPAMI.2007.70815
4. Everson, R.M., Roberts, S.J.: Inferring the eigenvalues of covariance matrices from limited, noisy data. IEEE Trans. Signal Process. **48**(7), 2083–2091 (2000). https://doi.org/10.1109/78.847792
5. Fukunaga, K., Olsen, D.R.: An algorithm for finding intrinsic dimensionality of data. IEEE Trans. Comput. **20**(2), 176–183 (1971). https://doi.org/10.1109/T-C.1971.223208
6. Houle, M.E., Kawarabayashi, K.: The effect of random projection on local intrinsic dimensionality. In: Reyes, N., et al. (eds.) SISAP 2021. LNCS, vol. 13058, pp. 201–214. Springer, Cham (2021). https://doi.org/10.1007/978-3-030-89657-7_16
7. Micó, L., Oncina, J., Vidal, E.: A new version of the nearest-neighbour approximating and eliminating search algorithm (AESA) with linear preprocessing time and memory requirements. Pattern Recognit. Lett. **15**(1), 9–17 (1994). https://doi.org/10.1016/0167-8655(94)90095-7
8. Omohundro, S.M.: Five Balltree Construction Algorithms. International Computer Science Institute Berkeley, Berkeley (1989)
9. Pearson, K.: On lines and planes of closest fit to systems of points in space. London, Edinb. Dublin Philos. Mag. J. Sci. **2**(11), 559–572 (1901)
10. Schubert, E.: A triangle inequality for cosine similarity. In: Reyes, N., et al. (eds.) SISAP 2021. LNCS, vol. 13058, pp. 32–44. Springer, Cham (2021). https://doi.org/10.1007/978-3-030-89657-7_3
11. Schubert, E., Lang, A., Feher, G.: Accelerating spherical k-means. In: Reyes, N., et al. (eds.) SISAP 2021. LNCS, vol. 13058, pp. 217–231. Springer, Cham (2021). https://doi.org/10.1007/978-3-030-89657-7_17
12. Schubert, E., Zimek, A.: ELKI multi-view clustering data sets based on the Amsterdam library of object images (ALOI). Zenodo (2010). https://doi.org/10.5281/zenodo.6355684
13. Thordsen, E., Schubert, E.: ABID: angle based intrinsic dimensionality. In: Satoh, S., et al. (eds.) SISAP 2020. LNCS, vol. 12440, pp. 218–232. Springer, Cham (2020). https://doi.org/10.1007/978-3-030-60936-8_17
14. Vadicamo, L., Gennaro, C., Amato, G.: On generalizing permutation-based representations for approximate search. In: Reyes, N., et al. (eds.) SISAP 2021. LNCS, vol. 13058, pp. 66–80. Springer, Cham (2021). https://doi.org/10.1007/978-3-030-89657-7_6
15. Virtanen, P., et al.: SciPy 1.0: Fundamental Algorithms for Scientific Computing in Python. Nat. Methods, **17**, 261–272 (2020). https://doi.org/10.1038/s41592-019-0686-2

Concept of Relational Similarity Search

Vladimir Mic$^{(\boxtimes)}$ and Pavel Zezula

Masaryk University, Brno, Czech Republic
xmic@fi.muni.cz

Abstract. For decades, the success of the similarity search has been based on a detailed quantification of pairwise similarity of objects. Currently, the search features have become much more precise but also bulkier, and the similarity computations more time-consuming. While the k nearest neighbours (kNN) search dominates the real-life applications, we claim that it is principally free of a need for precise similarity quantifications. Based on the well-known fact that a selection of the most similar alternative out of several options is a much easier task than deciding the absolute similarity scores, we propose the search based on an epistemologically simpler concept of relational similarity. Having arbitrary objects q, o_1, o_2 from the search domain, the kNN search is solvable just by the ability to choose the more similar object to q out of o_1, o_2 – the decision can also contain a neutral option. We formalise such searching and discuss its advantages concerning similarity quantifications, namely its efficiency and robustness. We also propose a pioneering implementation of the relational similarity search for the Euclidean spaces and report its extreme filtering power in comparison with 3 contemporary techniques.

Keywords: Efficient similarity search · Relational similarity · Similarity comparisons · Effective similarity search

1 Introduction and Preliminaries

Efficient similarity search in complex objects, actions, and events is a central problem of many data processing tasks [1,13,15]. Geometric models of similarity are established as a basic and practically the only approach to an efficient similarity search [17]. They assume a domain of the searched objects D and a distance function $d : D \times D \mapsto \mathbf{R}_0^+$ that quantifies the dissimilarity of two objects. Two basic types of similarity queries are the kNN(q) and $range(q,r)$ queries, where $q \in D, k \in \mathbf{N}, r \in \mathbf{R}_0^+$. Having a searched dataset $X \subseteq D$ and a query object $q \in D$, kNN(q) queries search for k most similar objects $o \in X$ to q, and $range(q,r)$ queries search for objects $o \in X$ within distance $d(q,o) \leq r$. In

---

This research was supported by ERDF "CyberSecurity, CyberCrime and Critical Information Infrastructures Center of Excellence" (No. CZ.02.1.01/0.0/0.0/16_019/0000822).

T. Skopal et al. (Eds.): SISAP 2022, LNCS 13590, pp. 89–103, 2022.
https://doi.org/10.1007/978-3-031-17849-8_8

this article, we focus on kNN(q) queries which are more user friendly since setting the k value is intuitive and does not require any knowledge of the searched space.

Most of the approaches to kNN(q) query executions maintain k distances $d(q, o)$ between q and k closest objects o found during the query evaluation. Typically, they require plenty of expensive distance computations [7,10,11]. We claim that kNN(q) queries do not require most of the dissimilarity quantifications since they ask just for the ordered list of k objects $o \in X$.

We propose to replace most of the *precise dissimilarity quantifications* with possibly much simpler decisions on which of the objects $o_1, o_2 \in X$ is more similar to $q \in D$. These decisions can use several independent and domain-specific views. The similarity/relevance comparisons of 2 objects with respect to the referent are widely used, e.g., in active learning, and they are well discussed theoretically [3]. Yet, they are not directly used to speed up the similarity search, according to our best knowledge. We discuss advantages of this *relational similarity search* considering the evaluation efficiency, effectiveness, and robustness while preserving the applicability. We formalise the relational kNN similarity search and propose the implementation for high dimensional Euclidean spaces.

The rest of the article is organised as follows. Sect. 2 presents the concept of relational similarity, Sect. 3 describes the implementation of relational similarity for Euclidean spaces and the experiments, and Sect. 4 concludes the paper.

2   Similarity Quantifications vs. Relational Similarity

This article focuses on kNN(q) similarity queries, and we start with the simplest case of the 1NN(q) search for the most similar object $o \in X$ to q.

2.1   One Nearest Neighbour Search

Consider an intermediate state of the 1NN(q) query execution, i.e., the objects:

- q: the query object
- $o_{top} \in X$: the most similar object to q found so far
- $o \in X$: object that is checked whether forms a better answer than o_{top}

In this situation, search techniques based on similarity quantifications usually know the distance $d(q, o_{top})$ and evaluate $d(q, o)$ to decide the more similar object to q out of o_{top} and o. Evaluation of $d(q, o)$ is generally expensive [4,14,17], and the only optimisation related to this paper is applicable to distance functions which do not decrease during $d(q, o)$ evaluation: Since $d(q, o_{top})$ is known, object o is relevant just until $d(q, o)$ is known to be bigger than $d(q, o_{top})$. Therefore, $d(q, o)$ evaluation can be interrupted when $d(q, o) > d(q, o_{top})$ is guaranteed.

Nevertheless, the question whether o provides a better query answer than o_{top} is often much simpler than $d(q, o)$ evaluation, as illustrated by Fig. 1. Here, we consider the image similarity search, though our ideas are applicable to various

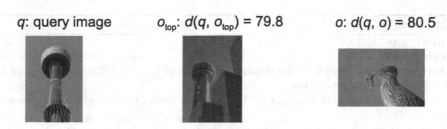

Fig. 1. Three images during the 1NN(q) search: query image q, the answer candidate o_{top}, and image o from the dataset. Despite distances $d(q, o_{top}) \approx d(q, o)$, approaches to efficiently discard o as irrelevant to q exist and are used by humans. In this case, it is checking the contours of q, o_{top}, o, for instance.

domains. Distances $d(q, o_{top}) = 79.8$ and $d(q, o) = 80.5$ provided in Fig. 1 are the actual distances of corresponding image visual descriptors *DeCAF* described in Sect. 3.1. The distances suggest that $d(q, o)$ evaluation cannot be cut much before its end since the difference $d(q, o) - d(q, o_{top})$ is small. At the same time, image o with the bird is *obviously* irrelevant to the query image q, and this is quickly realised by humans. By an analogy, an efficient formal approach to choose the 1NN(q) query answer from o_{top} and o should exist.

We inspire our thoughts by humans, who typically give a quick glimpse at each of the images q, o_{top}, o, trying to make a *quick* decision on which of o_{top}, o is more similar to q. If the first glimpse is insufficient to decide, the human gives another glimpse at images q, o_{top}, o trying to choose the more similar image to q, and then continues (if necessary) in this iterative process until making the decision. The conclusion can also be *"I do not know"* or *"the similarities of o_{top} and o to q are (almost) the same"*.

To illustrate this iterative approach, we again consider Fig. 1 and a human who first focuses on the colours in the images, for instance. Colours of images q, o_{top}, o in Fig. 1 cannot efficiently distinguish the suitability of o_{top} and o as the 1NN(q) answer, so after no success with the first glimpse, the considered human gives another glimpse at all objects q, o_{top}, o. Let us assume that the humans' second glimpse reveals o displaying a different object than q and o_{top} since he/she focuses on the image contours. Therefore, he/she decides that o_{top} forms a better 1NN(q) answer than o.

The *iterative* process of the human deciding on which of o_{top}, o forms a better 1NN(q) answer is in a principal contrast with the similarity quantifications performed by contemporary similarity search techniques. Most of the data domains are nowadays associated with an expensive similarity function d, and both distances $d(q, o)$ and $d(q, o_{top})$ are evaluated (with the possible early termination of $d(q, o)$ evaluation) whenever the relevance of $o \in X$ and o_{top} with respect to q must be decided. Different approaches of humans and contemporary search engines motivate us to formalise the concept of the relational similarity search that follows the humans' attitude.

Algorithm 1. Approach to the $simRel(q, o_1, o_2)$ evaluation

---

Input: $q, o_1, o_2 \in D$
Input: $maxIt \in \mathbf{N}$ ▷ max number of iterations
Output: 0, 1 or 2 describing the similarity relation of q, o_1, o_2 defined by Equation 1
for $i = 0; i < maxIt; inc(i)$ **do**
    Give a quick glimpse at q, o_1, o_2 (*)   ▷ (efficiently) extract additional (small)

                                                      piece of information from q, o_1, o_2
    if *similarity of* q, o_1 *is bigger than the similarity of* q, o_2, *for sure* **then**
        return 1
    if *similarity of* q, o_1 *is lower than the similarity of* q, o_2, *for sure* **then**
        return 2
return 0
(*) Information extracted from q and o_1 must be cached, otherwise it is extracted
many times during the $kNN(q)$ search.

2.2 Relational Similarity Search

Beside of the pairwise similarity quantification $d : D \times D \mapsto \mathbf{R}_0^+$, we define
function (*the similarity relation*) $simRel : D \times D \times D \mapsto \{0, 1, 2\}$:

$$simRel(q, o_1, o_2) = \begin{cases} 1 & \text{similarity of } q, o_1 \text{ is bigger than the similarity of } q, o_2 \\ 2 & \text{similarity of } q, o_1 \text{ is lower than the similarity of } q, o_2 \\ 0 & \text{similarity of } q, o_1 \text{ is the same as the similarity of } q, o_2, \\ & \text{or the difference in the similarities is as small as its} \\ & \text{proper investigation does not pay-off, and similarities} \\ & \text{can be treated arbitrarily} \end{cases}$$

(1)

    We propose the $simRel$ evaluations according to the informal concept
sketched by Algorithm 1. The actual $simRel$ implementations should be dependent on the data domain as well as on the application, which is well captured
by the doubled semantic of the equality $0 = simRel(q, o_1, o_2)$. The applications
preferring the search efficiency should implement the $simRel$ in an approximate
manner and return 0 in more cases than the applications requiring high search
effectiveness. We have shown that the $simRel$ captures the core of the $1NN(q)$
search. In the following, we propose an algorithm for the $kNN(q)$ search.

2.3 The k Nearest Neighbour Search with the Relational Similarity

To achieve the best search efficiency, we assume an abstract $simRel$ implementation and discuss the kNN search algorithm, first. Let us consider $q \in D$, and
$o_1, o_2, o_3 \in X$ such that $0 = simRel(q, o_1, o_2) = simRel(q, o_2, o_3)$. In other words,
o_1 and o_2 are interchangeable in their similarity to q, and so do objects o_2 and
o_3. Notation suggests the transitivity of these equations, i.e., the deduction of
the equality $simRel(q, o_1, o_3) = 0$. Still, it does not hold, in general, so the kNN
search algorithms have to deal with this *non-transitivity*.

Algorithm 2. The $kNN(q)$ search with the $simRel$ function

Input: *query object* $q \in D$
Input: $k \in \mathbf{N}$ ▷ the minimum size of the answer
Input: the searched dataset $X \subseteq D$
Output: $candSet(q)$ ▷ at least k objects $candSet(q) \subseteq X$ likely to be similar to q
$ans \leftarrow X.first$
$objUnknownRelation \leftarrow \emptyset$
for each $o \in X \setminus X.first$ **do**
    ADDOTOANSWER($q, o, k, ans, objUnknownRelation$)   ▷ procedure defined below
return $ans \cup objUnknownRelation$ ▷ optionally return ans for extreme efficiency
procedure ADDOTOANSWER($q, o, k, ans, objUnknownRelation$)
    $idxWhereAdd \leftarrow \infty$ ▷ position in ans where add o
    $indexesToRemove \leftarrow \emptyset$ ▷ positions of objects in ans to remove
    for $i = ans.size - 1; i >= 0; decrement(i)$ **do**
        $sim \leftarrow simRel(q, ans[i], o)$
        if $sim = 1$ **then**   ▷ $ans[i]$ is more similar object to q than o
            if $i < k - 1$ **then**
                for each $i \in indexesToRemove$ **do**
                    if $ans.size < k$ **then break**
                    $ans.remove(i)$
                $ans.add(i + 1, o)$ ▷ add o to ans just after $ans[i]$
            return
        if $sim = 2$ **then**   ▷ o is more similar object to q than $ans[i]$
            $idxWhereAdd \leftarrow i$
            $indexesToRemove.add(i)$
    if $idxWhereAdd \neq \infty$ **then**   ▷ the lowest position where to add o
        for each $i \in indexesToRemove$ **do**
            if $ans.size < k$ **then break**
            $ans.remove(i)$
        $ans.add(idxWhereAdd, o)$
        return
    $objUnknownRelation.add(o)$ ▷ $simRel(q, ans[i], o)$ is 0 for all $ans[i] \in ans$
end procedure

We propose the search algorithm which starts to build the query answer $ans(kNN(q))$ as a list of the most similar objects $o \in X$ found during the query execution. When $o \in X$ is asked whether it is one the k nearest neighbours of q, the *non-transitivity* of the equalities $0 = simRel(q, o_1, o_2)$ motivates us to focus on objects $o_a \in ans(kNN(q))$ such that $simRel(q, o_a, o) \neq 0$. We start to check $ans(kNN(q))$ from its end:

- If we find $o_1 \in ans(kNN(q))$ such that $simRel(q, o_1, o) = 2$, i.e., o matches the query object q better than o_1, we mark o_1 to be removed from $ans(kNN(q))$.
- We remember the lowest position i of $o_1 \in ans(kNN(q)) : simRel(q, o_1, o) = 2$. If $ans(kNN(q))$ does not contain $o_2 : simRel(q, o_2, o) = 1$, i.e., o_2 matches q better than o, then o is inserted to $ans(kNN(q))$ at position i.

- If $ans(kNN(q))$ contains o_2 such that $simRel(q, o_2, o) = 1$ and o_2 is at the position $i < k-1$ (numbering from 0) of $ans(kNN(q))$, we add o into $ans(kNN(q))$ just after o_2.
- Finally, we delete as many of marked objects o_1 from the answer $ans(kNN(q))$ as the answer size does not decrease below k.

An important case remains: If $ans(kNN(q))$ contains just objects o_a such that $simRel(q, o_a, o) = 0$, we add o into list $objsUnknown(q)$ of objects with an unknown relation to q. The way of $objsUnknown(q)$ processing is application dependent, and we consider two variants. The search algorithm returns either $candSet(q) = ans(kNN(q)) \cup objsUnknown(q)$, or $candSet(q) = ans(kNN(q))$. The second option which ignores list $objsUnknown(q)$ is suitable for the applications oriented on a high *efficiency* and just the *relevance* of query answers. In both cases, $candSet(q)$ is processed sequentially, i.e., distances $d(q, o), o \in candSet(q)$ are evaluated to return k most similar objects from $candSet(q)$ as a query answer. It can be just an approximation of the precise answer. The whole relational kNN search is formalised by Algorithm 2.

3 Proof of Concept for Euclidean Spaces

The only goal of the *simRel* implementations is to algorithmize Eq. 1 for a specific application and domain D to provide a suitable trade-off between the evaluation efficiency, correctness, and the number of equalities $simRel(q, o_1, o_2) = 0$. We assume that the *simRel* implementations should follow the humans' behaviour, i.e., the smaller the difference in the similarities of q, o_1 and q, o_2, the longer time to decide the $simRel(q, o_1, o_2)$ correctly, or return 0 to save time.

The concept of relational similarity has potential to improve various aspects of the similarity search. We present a *simRel* implementation to efficiently search high-dimensional Euclidean spaces with a low memory consumption and just a small decrease in the search effectiveness.

No ambition to improve the search effectiveness enables us to implement the *simRel* which *approximates* the search space $(\mathbf{R}^\lambda, \ell_2)$ – here ℓ_2 is the Euclidean distance function and λ is the length of vectors. Motivated by the humans' abilities, we want to implement $simRel(q, o_1, o_2)$ in a way that the bigger the difference $|\ell_2(q, o_1) - \ell_2(q, o_2)|$, the more efficient $simRel(q, o_1, o_2)$ evaluation. Consequently, we want to capture as much information about each $o \in X$ in one number, then capture as much of the remaining information in the second number, etc. This informal description sufficiently fits the *Principal component analysis* (PCA) [12,16], i.e., the transformation of vectors $o \in X$ of length λ to the vectors $o^{PCA(L)} \in \mathbf{R}^L$ of length $L < \lambda$ such that the variance of values in coordinates of $o^{PCA(L)}$ decreases with the coordinates' index, and the shortened vector $o^{PCA(L)}$ preserves as much of the information about o as possible. First coordinates of vectors $q^{PCA(L)}$, $o_1^{PCA(L)}$, $o_2^{PCA(L)}$ thus often contain sufficient information to decide $simRel(q, o_1, o_2)$).

Our $simRel(q, o_1, o_2)$ implementation starts to evaluate $\ell_2(q^{PCA(L)}, o_1^{PCA(L)})$ and $\ell_2(q^{PCA(L)}, o_2^{PCA(L)})$ distances in parallel. During the evaluation, it checks

Algorithm 3. Concept of $simRel(q, o_1, o_2) = simRel(q^{PCA(L)}, o_1^{PCA(L)}, o_2^{PCA(L)})$ implementation for a high dimensional Euclidean space

---

Input: $q^{PCA(L)}, o_1^{PCA(L)}, o_2^{PCA(L)}$ ▷ vectors q, o_1, o_2 shortened by the PCA
Input: thresholds $t(\Omega)$ defined for each $0 \le \Omega < L$ ▷ learned by Algs. 2 and 4
Output: 0, 1, or 2   ▷ result of $simRel(q, o_1, o_2)$ – see Eq. 1
for $\Omega = 0; \Omega < L; inc(i)$ do
     $diff \leftarrow difSqPref(q^{PCA(L)}, o_1^{PCA(L)}, o_2^{PCA(L)}, \Omega)$ ▷ function defined by Eq. 2
     if $diff > t(\Omega)$ then
         return 2
     if $diff < -t(\Omega)$ then
         return 1
return 0

---

which of the vectors $o_1^{PCA(L)}$ and $o_2^{PCA(L)}$ is currently closer to $q^{PCA(L)}$ and how much. If one of the vectors $o_1^{PCA(L)}, o_2^{PCA(L)}$ is *sufficiently* closer to $q^{PCA(L)}$ than the second one, we claim the result of $simRel(q^{PCA(L)}, o_1^{PCA(L)}, o_2^{PCA(L)})$. We use this result as the estimation of $simRel(q, o_1, o_2)$.

Formally, we denote $o^{PCA(L)}[i]$ the value in the ith coordinate of $o^{PCA(L)}$, and define:

$$difSqPref(q^{PCA(L)}, o_1^{PCA(L)}, o_2^{PCA(L)}, \Omega) = $$
$$\sum_{i=0}^{\Omega} \left(q^{PCA(L)}[i] - o_1^{PCA(L)}[i] \right)^2 - \sum_{i=0}^{\Omega} \left(q^{PCA(L)}[i] - o_2^{PCA(L)}[i] \right)^2 \quad (2)$$

We evaluate this function for each integer $\Omega : 0 \le \Omega < L$, and consider thresholds $t(\Omega) \in \mathbf{R}_0^+$ which determine the stop conditions for the $simRel(q, o_1, o_2)$ evaluation: we start with $\Omega = 0$ and use Eq. 2 as follows:

- If $difSqPref(q^{PCA(L)}, o_1^{PCA(L)}, o_2^{PCA(L)}, \Omega) > t(\Omega)$, then $simRel(q, o_1, o_2) - 2$
- If $difSqPref(q^{PCA(L)}, o_1^{PCA(L)}, o_2^{PCA(L)}, \Omega) < -t(\Omega)$, then $simRel(q, o_1, o_2) = 1$
- If $\Omega = L - 1$, then $simRel(q, o_1, o_2) = 0$, else increment Ω

The (non-optimised) $simRel$ implementation which takes $t(\Omega)$ thresholds as an input is formalised by Algorithm 3.

We learn thresholds $t(\Omega)$ using Algorithm 2 which evaluates $kNN(q)$ queries with random query objects on a sample of the dataset X and use the $simRel$ implementation formalised by Algorithm 4. This $simRel$ implementation does not use the thresholds $t(\Omega)$ but learns them instead. First, it evaluates distances $\ell_2(q^{PCA(L)}, o_1^{PCA(L)})$ and $\ell_2(q^{PCA(L)}, o_2^{PCA(L)})$. Let us assume inequality $\ell_2(q^{PCA(L)}, o_1^{PCA(L)}) \le \ell_2(q^{PCA(L)}, o_2^{PCA(L)})$ – if it does not hold, the notation of o_1 and o_2 is swapped. For each $\Omega : 0 \le \Omega < L$, the $simRel$ algorithm stores a list $wit[\Omega]$ of observed positive values $difSqPref(q^{PCA(L)}, o_1^{PCA(L)}, o_2^{PCA(L)}, \Omega)$. These values $wit[\Omega]$ are witnesses of the insufficiency of prefix of length Ω: while

---

Algorithm 4. *simRel* implementation to learn thresholds $t(\Omega), 0 \leq \Omega < L$

Input: $q^{PCA(L)}, o_1^{PCA(L)}, o_2^{PCA(L)}$ ▷ vectors q, o_1, o_2 shortened by the PCA

Input: *perc* ▷ Percentile $0 < perc < 1$

Output: thresholds $t(\Omega)$ defined for each $0 \leq \Omega < L$

Output: 0, 1, or 2 ▷ the result of $simRel(q, o_1, o_2)$ – see Equation 1

$d1 \leftarrow \ell_2(q^{PCA(L)}, o_1^{PCA(L)})$

$d2 \leftarrow \ell_2(q^{PCA(L)}, o_2^{PCA(L)})$

$diffQO1 \leftarrow 0;\ diffQO2 \leftarrow 0$

$order \leftarrow d1 < d2$

wit ▷ static array of length L

for $i = 0; i < L; inc(i)$ **do**

    $diffQO1\ +=\ (q^{PCA(L)}[i] - o_1^{PCA(L)}[i])^2$

    $diffQO2\ +=\ (q^{PCA(L)}[i] - o_2^{PCA(L)}[i])^2$

    $orderCurr \leftarrow diffQO1 < diffQO2$

    if $order \neq orderCurr$ **then**

        $wit[i].add(|diffQO1 - diffQO2|)$ ▷ the absolute values of the difference

if $diffQO1 = diffQO2$ **then**

    return 0

$diffQO1 < diffQO2$? **return** 1 : **return** 2

define $t[\Omega]$ as percentile *perc* of $wit[\Omega]$ ▷ when sample queries evaluated by Alg. 2

---

first Ω coordinates of vectors (i.e. function *difSqPref*) suggests the inequality $\ell_2(q^{PCA(L)}, o_1^{PCA(L)}) > \ell_2(q^{PCA(L)}, o_2^{PCA(L)})$, the last coordinates $i : \Omega < i < L$ of vectors change the relation to the final inequality $\ell_2(q^{PCA(L)}, o_1^{PCA(L)}) \leq \ell_2(q^{PCA(L)}, o_2^{PCA(L)})$. When all the queries are evaluated, each $wit[\Omega]$ is sorted and $t(\Omega)$ is defined as a given percentile *perc* of $wit[\Omega]$. The percentile defines the trade-off between the *simRel* correctness, evaluation times and the number of the equalities $0 = simRel(q, o_1, o_2)$: the bigger the *perc*, the longer and the more precise the *simRel* decisions with possibly more neutral assessments $0 = simRel(q, o_1, o_2)$. In the experiments, we use the *perc* $= 0.85$. The whole approach to determine thresholds $t(\Omega)$ is formalised by Algorithm 4, and a Java implementation of this article is provided upon request.

3.1 Test Data

We examine the *DeCAF* image visual descriptors [5] extracted from the *Profiset image collection*[1] to verify the *simRel* implementation. We use a subset of 1 million descriptors that are derived from the Alexnet convolutional neural network [6] as the data from the second-last fully connected layer (FC7). Each descriptor consists of a 4,096-dimensional vector of floating-point values that describes characteristic image features, so there is a correspondence 1 to 1 between images and descriptors. Pairwise similarities of the DeCAF descriptors are expressed by Euclidean distances.

---

[1] http://disa.fi.muni.cz/profiset/.

Table 1. Median accuracy of the 30NN(q) search in DeCAF descriptors shortened by the PCA to length L: k' vectors are pre-selected in a shrunk space and refined

Length L	Size k'							
	30	50	100	1,000	5,000	10,000	15,000	20,000
8	3.3%				73.3 %	86.7 %	93.3 %	96.7 %
10	3.3 %					86.7 %	96.7 %	100 %
12	6.7 %			60.0 %	93.3 %	98.3 %	100%	
24	23.3 %	33.3 %	46.7 %	93.3 %	100%			
68	53.3 %	66.6 %	86.7 %	100 %				
256	70 %	86.7 %	100 %					
670	80 %	96.7 %	100 %					
1,540	86.7%	100%						

3.2 PCA and Relational Similarity Search Implementation

The PCA defines vectors with the most of information in their first coordinates. The relational similarity $simRel(q, o_1, o_2)$ is thus decided just by a short prefix of vectors $q^{PCA(L)}$, $o_1^{PCA(L)}$, $o_2^{PCA(L)}$ in most of the cases, and we propose to store just prefixes of $o^{PCA(L)}, o \in X$ in the main memory while the long descriptors o can be in the secondary storage. If the prefixes are insufficient to decide $simRel(q, o_1, o_2)$, zero is returned. The proposed $simRel$ implementation contains several sources of approximation errors, and we address the setting of parameters one by one to mitigate them. We consider 30NN(q) queries on 4,096-dimensional DeCAF descriptors. Reported statistics are the medians over 1,000 query evaluations with different query objects q selected in random. The *ground-truth* consists of 30 closest objects $o_{NN} \in X$ to q as defined by ℓ_2 distance function.

The first parameter to be fixed is length L of vectors shortened by the PCA, and we set it experimentally using the *filter & refine* paradigm: Having an object $q \in D$, we select k' closest vectors $o^{PCA(L)}$ to $q^{PCA(L)}$ using the ℓ_2 distances, find the corresponding vectors $o \in X$ to form $c(q) \subseteq X$, and re-rank these o according to $\ell_2(q, o)$. Finally, we consider just 30 closest objects $o \in c(q)$ and check how many of them are the true nearest neighbours from the ground-truth.

Table 1 provides the median search[2] accuracy for various L and k'. For instance, vectors shortened to just 24 dimensions are of a quality that the set $c(q)$ of size 1,000 vectors (0.1 % of the dataset) contains 28 out of 30 (93.3 %) true nearest neighbours per median query object q. Since the proposed $simRel$ implementation speeds up the search by efficient and quite accurate similarity comparisons, we use the $simRel$ together with a high-quality approximation of DeCAF descriptors given by $L = 256$. Having $L = 256$, the $candSet(q)$ of 100

---

[2] Diploma thesis [2] provides a rich experimental analysis of the PCA applied to the same dataset of the DeCAF descriptors.

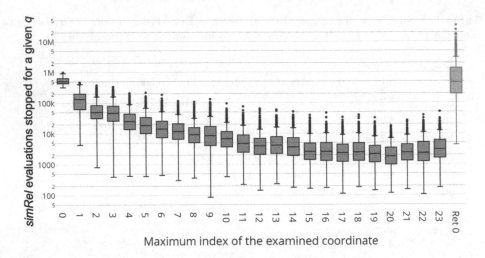

Fig. 2. Early terminations of *simRel* evaluations. The first coordinate of vectors shortened by the PCA decides 511,850 *simRel* evaluations per median query (Color figure online)

vectors contains all 30 true nearest neighbours per median query, so in the following, we address 100NN(q) search in vectors $o^{PCA(L)}, o \in X, L = 256$.

3.3 Experimental Verification of the Relation Similarity Search

The *simRel* evaluations must be efficient to pay-off. We use just first 24 coordinates of vectors $o^{PCA(L)}, o \in X$ with 4B precision per coordinate stored in the main memory. The memory occupation is thus $24 \cdot 4B = 96B$ plus ID per $o \in X$. We learn thresholds $t[\Omega]$ by Algorithms 2 and 4 evaluating a hundred 30NN(q) queries with different q than 1,000 tested and a sample of 100K objects $o \in X$.

Number of *simRel* evaluations during kNN(q) execution by Algorithm 2 can be almost $k \cdot |X|$, but this happens just if $simRel(q, o_1, o_2) = 0$ for nearly all examined triplets. Figure 4a reports numbers of *simRel* evaluations during 100NN($q^{PCA(L)}$) search in the prefixes of 1M vectors $o^{PCA(L)}$. All box plots in this paper depict the distribution of values over 1,000 randomly selected query objects. The *simRel* evaluation counts are from 1.027M to 35.23M with the quartiles 1.2M, 1.47M and 2.37M, respectively. The results are thus much better than the theoretical worst case of almost $100 \cdot 1M = 100M$ *simRel* evaluations.

The *simRel* implementation given by Algorithm 3 adaptively decides how many out of 24 coordinates to use for an efficient *simRel* decision. Figure 2 presents numbers of *simRel* terminations just after checking the ith coordinate of vectors $q^{PCA(L)}, o_1^{PCA(L)}, o_2^{PCA(L)}$. Indexes i are on the x-axis, and y-axis depicts the number of *simRel* terminations. The only exception is the last grey box plot which represents the last stored coordinate of $o^{PCA(L)}$: Since we are interested in the *simRel* result, we use two box plots here. The red right-most box

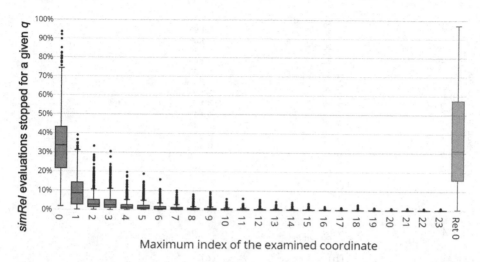

Maximum index of the examined coordinate

Fig. 3. Relative numbers early terminations of the *simRel* evaluations during the query execution after checking the ith coordinate of vectors (Color figure online)

plot, as well as the last grey box plot depict the numbers of *simRel* evaluations which use all 24 coordinates – the red box plot depicts the zero results of *simRel* computations, and the last grey box plot depicts non-zero results. The first coordinate of $q^{PCA(L)}$, $o_1^{PCA(L)}$, $o_2^{PCA(L)}$ is sufficient to decide 513,133 *simRel* comparisons per median query – see the first box plot in Fig. 2. The first and third quartiles are 439,776 and 645,781, respectively, the minimum is 324,425 and the maximum is 999,756. Value $simRel = 0$ is returned in 456,929 evaluations per median query, as depicted by the red box plot. This statistic has a large variance over q: the first and third quartiles are 192,897 and 1.35M, respectively, the minimum is 4,272, and the maximum is 34.2M.

Figure 3 also reports the *simRel* terminations after checking the ith coordinate of vectors, but expressed relatively with respect to the number of *simRel* evaluations during the query execution. The first box plot depicts that 33.68 % of *simRel* evaluations performed during the median query execution are terminated just after the check of the first coordinate of $q^{PCA(L)}$, $o_1^{PCA(L)}$, $o_2^{PCA(L)}$. This statistic also have a large variance, and ranges from 1.91 % to 93.74 % with the quartiles 21.65 %, 33.64 %, and 43.08 %. The relative number of equalities $0 = simRel(q, o_1, o_2)$ during the query execution ranges from 0.42 % to 97.18 % with the quartiles 15.94 %, 31.04 %, and 57.30 % – see the red box plot in Fig. 3. We suppose that query objects with a large number of $simRel = 0$ are probably outlying objects, and we postpone their investigation for the future work. We emphasise that the prevalent early termination of *simRel* evaluations leading to flexible evaluation times figure the key advantage of the *simRel* in comparison with most of the traditional search techniques based on, for example, dimensionality reduction or hashing.

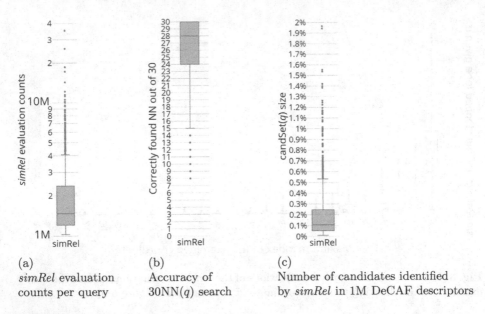

(a)
simRel evaluation
counts per query

(b)
Accuracy of
30NN(*q*) search

(c)
Number of candidates identified
by *simRel* in 1M DeCAF descriptors

Fig. 4. Statistics gathered during 100NN search in 1M dataset, distributions over 1,000 query objects *q*

Table 2. Comparison of the filtering power

	simRel	GHP_50_256 [8]	GHP 80_256 [9]	PPP-Codes [11]
candSet(*q*) size	1,076 (0.11 %)	3,214 (0.32 %)	3,368 (0.37 %)	10,546 (1.05 %)
Memory per $o \in X$	96 B	32 B	32 B	96 B

Finally, we chain all steps and report results of Algorithm 2 evaluating 30NN queries in the original space of 4,096-dimensional DeCAF descriptors. The *simRel* implementation uses the first 24 coordinates of $o^{PCA(L)}$, $L = 256$. First, we evaluate Algorithm 2 to return $candSet(q) = ans(kNN(q)) \cup objsUnknown(q)$, i.e., we also refine the objects with an unknown relation to *q*. Figure 4b illustrates that Algorithm 2 correctly finds 28 out of 30 true nearest neighbours per median query. Figure 4c reports $candSet(q)$ sizes which express the only number of 4,096-dimensional descriptors from *X* that we access during the query execution and evaluate their ℓ_2 distances to *q*. It ranges from 101 to 19,643, i.e., from 0.01 % to 1.96 % of the dataset, with the quartiles 524; 1,076; and 2,477. The median thus expresses that the *simRel* filters out 99.89 % of the 1M dataset, 1,076 objects remains, and 28 out of them are in the set of 30 true nearest neighbours – all for a median query object *q*.

Table 2 compares[3] the filtering power of the *simRel* with 3 most powerful filtering techniques we have ever tried. The *GHP_50_256* [8] and *GHP_80_256* [9]

---

[3] This data are adopted from Table 4.3 in the thesis [7]. The experiments in the thesis are conducted on the same data as this paper, including the query objects *q*.

techniques transform DeCAF descriptors to the bit-strings of length 256 bits in the Hamming space. In this space, they identify the $candSet(q)$ which they re-rank to return 30 most similar objects $o \in candSet(q)$. The *pivot permutation based* index *PPP-codes* [11] stores distances to 24 reference objects (*pivots*) which is the only information used to identify the $candSet(q)$ before its refinement. We set parameters of all examined techniques to produce $candSet(q)$ with the median accuracy 28/30. However, the results of all techniques except of the *simRel* are *simulations* describing the *minimum* $candSet(q)$ size implying this accuracy. The $candSet(q)$ size must be set in advance in case of GHP_50_256, GHP_80_256, and *PPP-codes*, and no support for an estimation of a suitable $candSet(q)$ size is provided. The numbers presented for these 3 techniques thus form just a theoretical optimum. On the contrary, the result of the *simRel* describes a real usage which requires no hidden knowledge. Having the same memory overhead as the PPP-codes and 3 times bigger overhead than the bit-strings, the filtering with the *simRel* is 3 times, 3.1 times, and 9.8 times more powerful than the filtering with GHP_50_256, GHP_80_256, and *PPP-codes*, respectively.

Proposed *simRel* implementation has an advantage of automatic adapting to particular query objects q, which causes a significant variance in the *simRel* evaluation times and numbers of *simRel* evaluations during the query execution. Conversely, plenty of search techniques execute the similarity queries with fixed parameters and no adaptation to particular query objects. It leads to wasting computational sources in case of easy-to-evaluate query objects, or a low-quality evaluation of difficult queries [10].

Finally, we examine the 30NN search with Algorithm 2 ignoring objects $objsUnknown(q)$ with an unknown relation to q. The search accuracy of such search has median 10/30 and the third quartile 14/30, but the $candSet(q)$ is pretty small with just 252 objects (0.0252 % of X) per median q. We visualise online[4] the answer of typical quality to one 30NN query evaluated in this way. Its accuracy is 12/30 and it requires just 250 $\ell_2(q, o)$ evaluations to re-rank the $candSet(q)$. We emphasise that the order of the images is given by full ℓ_2 distances of the DeCAF descriptors depicted below each image. All answer images are relevant to q.

4   Conclusions

The content preserving features of contemporary digital data objects become more precise but also more voluminous and their similarity quantifications more computationally demanding. The partitioning techniques are not able to constrain the query response set sufficiently, and many distance computations are needed to get the result. We have proposed the relational similarity search to reduce the number of distance computations. In general, a large number of not necessary distance computations is eliminated by an efficient selection of a more similar data object out of two to the referent. We exemplify the approach by the search in a challenging high-dimensional Euclidean space and demonstrate

---

[4] https://disa.fi.muni.cz/~xmic/2022SISAP/SimRelJustKnown.png.

the savings of 99.89 % distance computations per median query when finding 28 out of 30 nearest neighbours. The search algorithm can also be set to prefer the search efficiency at the cost of accuracy. In that case, we have observed the filtering of 99.9748 % of the dataset with the search accuracy of 33.3 % per median query, but still achieving a good answer relevance. In the future, we plan to implement the *simRel* in other domains, and combine the approach with the similarity indexes to efficiently search large datasets.

References

1. Amato, G., Falchi, F., Vadicamo, L.: Visual recognition of ancient inscriptions using convolutional neural network and fisher vector. ACM J. Comput. Cultural Heritage **9**(4), 21:1–21:24 (2016)
2. Brázdil, J.: Dimensionality reduction methods for vector spaces. Master's thesis, Masaryk University, Faculty of Informatics, Brno (2016). https://is.muni.cz/th/v9xlg/. Supervisor Pavel Zezula
3. Chang, R.: Are Hard Cases Vague Cases? Value Incommensurability: Ethics, Risk, and Decision-Making, pp. 50–70. Routledge, New York (2021)
4. Deza, M.M., Deza, E.: Encyclopedia of Distances, pp. 1–583. Springer, Heidelberg (2009). https://doi.org/10.1007/978-3-642-00234-2
5. Donahue, J., et al.: DeCAF: a deep convolutional activation feature for generic visual recognition. In: Proceedings of the 31th International Conference on Machine Learning, ICML, China, pp. 647–655 (2014)
6. Krizhevsky, A., Sutskever, I., Hinton, G.E.: ImageNet classification with deep convolutional neural networks. In: Advances in Neural Information Processing Systems 25, pp. 1097–1105. Curran Associates, Inc. (2012)
7. Mariachkina, I.: Experimental verification of a synergy of techniques for efficient similarity search in metric spaces (2022). https://is.muni.cz/th/m14as/. Bachelor's thesis, Masaryk University, Faculty of Informatics, Brno, supervisor Vladimir Mic
8. Mic, V., Novak, D., Zezula, P.: Designing sketches for similarity filtering. In: 2016 IEEE 16th International Conference on Data Mining Workshops (ICDMW), pp. 655–662 (2016)
9. Mic, V., Novak, D., Zezula, P.: Sketches with unbalanced bits for similarity search. In: Beecks, C., Borutta, F., Kröger, P., Seidl, T. (eds.) SISAP 2017. LNCS, pp. 53–63. Springer, Heidelberg (2017). https://doi.org/10.1007/978-3-319-68474-1_4
10. Mic, V., Novak, D., Zezula, P.: Binary sketches for secondary filtering. ACM Trans. Inf. Syst. **37**(1), 1:1–1:28 (2018)
11. Novak, D., Zezula, P.: PPP-codes for large-scale similarity searching. Trans. Large-Scale Data- and Knowl.-Centered Syst. **24**, 61–87 (2016)
12. Pearson, K.: On lines and planes of closest fit to systems of points in space. Philos. Mag. Series 6 **2**(11), 559–572 (1901)
13. Sedmidubský, J., Elias, P., Zezula, P.: Effective and efficient similarity searching in motion capture data. Multimed. Tools Appl. **77**(10), 12073–12094 (2018)
14. Skopal, T., Bustos, B.: On nonmetric similarity search problems in complex domains. ACM Comput. Surv. **43**(4), 34:1–34:50 (2011)
15. Skopal, T., Durisková, D., Pechman, P., Dobranský, M., Khachaturian, V.: Videolytics: system for data analytics of video streams. In: ACM International Conference on Information and Knowledge Management (CIKM), Australia, pp. 4794–4798. ACM (2021)

16. Wall, M.E., Rechtsteiner, A., Rocha, L.M.: Singular value decomposition and principal component analysis. In: Berrar, D.P., Dubitzky, W., Granzow, M. (eds.) A Practical Approach to Microarray Data Analysis, pp. 91–109. Springer, Heidelberg (2003). https://doi.org/10.1007/0-306-47815-3_5

17. Zezula, P., Amato, G., Dohnal, V., Batko, M.: Similarity Search - The Metric Space Approach, vol. 32 (2006). https://doi.org/10.1007/0-387-29151-2

On the Expected Exclusion Power of Binary Partitions for Metric Search

Lucia Vadicamo[1]([⊠])[iD], Alan Dearle[2][iD], and Richard Connor[2][iD]

[1] Institute of Information Science and Technologies (ISTI), CNR, Pisa, Italy
lucia.vadicamo@isti.cnr.it
[2] University of St Andrews, St Andrews, Scotland, UK
{al,rchc}@st-andrews.ac.uk

Abstract. The entire history and, we dare say, future of similarity search is governed by the underlying notion of partition. A partition is an equivalence relation defined over the space, therefore each element of the space is contained within precisely one of the equivalence classes of the partition. All attempts to search a finite space efficiently, whether exactly or approximately, rely on some set of principles which imply that if the query is within one equivalence class, then one or more other classes either cannot, or probably do not, contain any of its solutions.

In most early research, partitions relied only on the metric postulates, and logarithmic search time could be obtained on low dimensional spaces. In these cases, it was straightforward to identify multiple partitions, each of which gave a relatively high probability of identifying subsets of the space which could not contain solutions. Over time the datasets being searched have become more complex, leading to higher dimensional spaces. It is now understood that even an approximate search in a very high-dimensional space is destined to require $\mathcal{O}(n)$ time and space.

Almost entirely missing from the research literature however is any analysis of exactly when this effect takes over. In this paper, we make a start on tackling this important issue. Using a quantitative approach, we aim to shed some light on the notion of the exclusion power of partitions, in an attempt to better understand their nature with respect to increasing dimensionality.

Keywords: Metric search · Binary partitioning · Exclusion power · Curse of dimensionality

1 Introduction

We are interested in similarity search spaces of the form (U, d) where U is some universe of objects and d is a distance function $d : U \times U \to \mathbb{R}^+$ satisfying the metric postulates [16]. The function d is typically the only meaningful defined operation over U. The task is normally to search a finite (but typically very large) set $S \subset U$ for a small set of objects which are similar to a query object $q \in U$, i.e. to find some small subset $\mathcal{Q}(q, t) = \{s \in S \mid d(q, s) \leq t\}$ for some

© The Author(s), under exclusive license to Springer Nature Switzerland AG 2022
T. Skopal et al. (Eds.): SISAP 2022, LNCS 13590, pp. 104–117, 2022.
https://doi.org/10.1007/978-3-031-17849-8_9

appropriate t. We refer to t as the query threshold. In this paper this definition suffices to encompass both range and nearest neighbour queries and we do not distinguish between them[1].

We use the term *partition* to refer to an equivalence relation defined over U, such that each element is contained in precisely one of the equivalence classes defined by the relation. In the domain of metric search, since d is the only operation available over elements of U, such partitions must be defined in terms of distances to objects identified within the set. For example, for a distinguished value $p \in U$, a simple ball partition may be defined as $\mathcal{F} = \{F_0, F_1\}$

$$F_0 = \{u \in U \mid d(p, u) > \tau\}$$
$$F_1 = \{u \in U \mid d(p, u) \leq \tau \} \tag{1}$$

for some constant value τ.

The processing of similarity queries normally takes place in two distinct phases. In a first *pre-processing* phase, a set of partitions is defined over U. Each element of S is analysed with respect to a number of these, and information about the inclusion of each element within the defined equivalence classes is noted.

In the second *query* phase, the query is analysed with respect to the same set of partitions, at which point deductions may be made about whether solutions to the query are likely to be present in the defined equivalence classes. With reference to the previous example, if $q \in F_1$, it may be possible to reason that any solution to q is more likely to be in F_1 than F_0. The more similar q is to p, the higher the likelihood that this is true. If the space in question is a metric space, and $d(q, p) \leq \tau - t$, then it is impossible for F_0 to contain any values within distance t of the query.

In general, the set of partitions identified at pre-processing time contains the only information which can be used in order to avoid a full scan of the database. In all cases, the choice of partitions is thus critical to the efficacy of the mechanism.

1.1   Binary Partitions

To simplify the domain, we restrict our analysis to binary partitions used in a simplified *exact* search mechanism. To avoid committing the discussion to a particular search mechanism, we consider a notional metric search framework with the following properties:

– A finite set of n binary partitions $\{\mathcal{F}^j\}_{j=1}^n$, where $\mathcal{F}_j = \{F_0^j, F_1^j\}$ is made of two classes, is established at pre-processing time, with respect to a fixed set of m reference objects $p_1, \ldots, p_m \in U$

---

[1] A nearest neighbour query can be formulated as a range query where the query threshold is not known in advance but it is set iteratively as the distance to the current k-th nearest neighbour [16].

- At query time, the distances from the query q to all reference objects are calculated
- A set of classes which cannot contain any solution to the query is thus established
- All objects which cannot be thus excluded comprise a *candidate result set* whose objects must be tested individually against the query.

Note that many different indexing and filtering mechanisms fall within this general description. In the most general sense, the success of search for solutions to an individual query is related to the following properties of the set of partitions used during the process:

1. the number of available partitions;
2. for each partition, the probability of the distances between the query and the reference objects allowing exclusion of one of the classes of the partition;
3. for any such partition and query, the size of the class which can be thus excluded, and
4. the independence of the set of classes which can be excluded for a given query. For example if all the excluded classes have a common intersection, the value of each one is diminished.

In this article, we address only properties (2) and (3). They are clearly in tension with each other: for example, a partition class which defines only a very small volume of the infinite space is likely to have a high probability of exclusion for an arbitrary query, but is likely to contain only a small number of objects from the finite set. Similarly, a class defining a relatively large volume of the space, thus likely to contain many objects, is less likely to be excluded.

The main contribution of this article is a quantified study of this effect in various metric spaces of different dimensionality.

2   Related Work

Chávez et al. [2] proposed a unifying model to analyse existing indexing algorithms for proximity search by observing that all indexing algorithms for proximity searching consist of building a set of equivalence classes. They remark that every partition of a space induces an equivalence relation, and conversely, every equivalence relation induces a data partitioning. At query time some classes are discarded and the others form a candidate results set that should be exhaustively searched for query solutions. Therefore, the most important tradeoff when designing the data partitioning is to balance the cost of finding the candidate results set (*internal complexity*) and the cost of refining it (*external complexity*). The internal complexity is evaluated as the number of distance calculations d needed to compute the candidate result set C and the external complexity is $|C|$ distance computations. They defined the *discriminative power* of a search algorithm as the ratio of internal complexity to external complexity, which serves as an indicator of the performance fitness of the equivalence relation. Moreover, they observed that two classes of techniques exist based on equivalence relations, namely, pivoting and compact partitions.

Pivoting based techniques rely on building a relation based on the distances between an element and a number of preselected pivots (also called reference points, vantage points, keys). The distances between elements and pivots and between the query q and the pivots are used together with the triangle inequality to filter out elements of the database without actually measuring their distance to q. For example, using ball pivoting the equivalence classes correspond to a family of "rings" or "sphere shells" centered on a pivot. Points within the same sphere shell (i.e., at the same distance from a pivot) are in the same equivalence class. In [3] Chávez points out that in this class of algorithms generally improve as more pivots are added.

Compact partitions are based on the class of the points that have some preselected object as their closest center. Thus the partitions induced using this technique correspond to a Delaunay tessellation over the space. Thus using this approach, the universe is divided into a set of spatial zones and complete zones may be discarded by performing a few distance evaluations. Chávez demonstrates that compact partitioning algorithms deal better with high dimensional metric spaces.

In [8,9] Hetland describes the problem of metric indexing as storing the points from a dataset in some data structure which is later traversed to efficiently extract those points relevant to some query. This data structure is described as a bipartite digraph of points and regions which he defines as a *sprawl*. Each region is defined with respect to a set of source points, called foci or pivots $p_1, .., p_m$. Region membership is defined in terms of distances $x = [d(u, p_1), \ldots, d(u, p_m)]$. Hetland also defines an *ambit* to be a function $f(x)$ (remoteness map) and a threshold or radius r, that describe a partition region (i.e., a partition class). Such ambits are equivalent to the partition functions described in this paper, which also correspond to the *certification functions* introduced by Pestov and Stojmirović [11]. In [8] Hetland describes a number of different bifocal linear ambits which include ball and hyperboloid remoteness. Using Hetland's classification the 4-point hyperplane partitioning (defined below) is a nonlinear ambit based on a non-metric-preserving power transform. In [8] he gives other examples of nonlinear ambits including those based on a Hamacher product and a Cantor function.

3   Quantifying the Value of a Partition Set

3.1   Unifying Partition Functions

To unify the quantitative treatment of different kinds of binary partition with their associated distance constraints, we recently introduced [6] the concept of a binary partition $\mathcal{F} = \{F_0, F_1\}$ characterised by a *partition function* $f : U \to \mathbb{R}$ and a *balancing factor* $\tau \in \mathbb{R}$ with the following properties:

1. $F_0 = \{s \in U \mid f(s) > \tau\}$ and $F_1 = \{s \in U \mid f(s) \leq \tau\}$
2. $d(s_1, s_2) \geq |f(s_1) - f(s_2)|$ for all $s_1, s_2 \in U$ (*distance lower-bound* property)

Note that if $f(s) = \tau$, then s is on the partition boundary and by convention we include the partition boundary in F_1. Moreover f should be defined in a way so that it both determines the classes F_0, F_1 and provides a rule to estimate a lower-bound of the actual distance between two data points. The lower-bound is used to derive the exclusion rules used at query time. Specifically, given a query q and a query threshold t, then we have that

- if $f(q) \leq \tau - t$ then F_0 can be excluded
- if $f(q) > \tau + t$ then F_1 can be excluded

This characterisation provides us with a unified framework to describe the most common metric binary partitioning principles, namely *ball partitioning* [13,16], *generalised hyperplane partitioning* [13,16], and *4-point hyperplane partitioning* [4,7], together with their exclusion rules. Specifically, as proved in [6], we have that

- a *ball partitioning* given a pivot p and a radius r is characterised by the function

$$f_{\text{Ball}}(s) = d(s, p), \qquad \forall s \in U$$

and the balancing factor $\tau = r$;
- a *generalised hyperplane partitioning* of the form

$$\begin{aligned} F_0 &= \{s \in U \mid d(s, p_1) - d(s, p_0) > \alpha\} \\ F_1 &= \{s \in U \mid d(s, p_1) - d(s, p_0) \leq \alpha\} \end{aligned} \tag{2}$$

for two given pivots p_0 and p_1 and offset α, is characterised by the function

$$f_{\text{Hyp}}(s) = \frac{d(s, p_1) - d(s, p_0)}{2}, \qquad \forall s \in U \tag{3}$$

and balancing factor $\tau = \alpha/2$;
- a *4-point hyperplane partitioning*

$$\begin{aligned} F_0 &= \{s \in U \mid d(s, p_1)^2 - d(s, p_0)^2 > \alpha\} \\ F_1 &= \{s \in U \mid d(s, p_1)^2 - d(s, p_0)^2 \leq \alpha\} \end{aligned} \tag{4}$$

that can be characterised by the function

$$f_{\text{4pHyp}}(s) = \frac{d(s, p_1)^2 - d(s, p_0)^2}{2d(p_0, p_1)}, \qquad \forall s \in U \tag{5}$$

and balancing factor $\tau = \alpha/2d(p_0, p_1)$. This kind of partition is valid only on the large class of Supermetric Spaces meeting the 4-point property [7]. The partition boundary can be visualised as a hyperplane in a 2D Euclidean space obtained using the nSimplex projection [5] to transform the data; with the hyperplane being orthogonal to the line containing the two pivots in the 2D Euclidean space. Moreover, if $\tau = \alpha = 0$ then the classes F_0 and F_1 are exactly the same as the generalised hyperplane partitioning above, but the 4-point property [4,7], rather than the triangle inequality, is used for estimating the distance lower-bound.

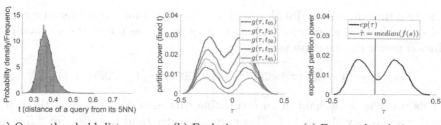

(a) Query threshold distances   (b) Exclusion power   (c) Expected exclusion power

Fig. 1. *8-dimensional Euclidean dataset*: Example of typical query threshold distances (a), power graphs for a 8-dimensional Euclidean dataset (b), and expected exclusion power (c). The left-hand figure shows the distribution of the fifth nearest neighbour distances for a set of 5000 queries. The middle figure show the exclusion power graphs over τ for five representative t values (0.05, 0.25, 0.5, 0.75, 0.95-th percentiles of the query threshold distribution) in the case of a generalised hyperplane partitioning. The right-hand figure shows the Expected exclusion power over τ (Color figure online)

We define the *balance ratio* of a binary partition $\{F_0, F_1\}$ of the finite search set S as the ratio of the smaller of $|F_0|$ or $|F_1|$ to $|S|$, giving a value in the range $[0, 0.5]$ where a higher value means a more even balance ratio. Note that when changing the balancing factor τ, the partition boundary moves and thus its balance ratio changes as well.

This unification (f, τ) allows the characterisation of the *balance ratio* and *power* of a partition as the value of τ is altered, as shown in the next Section.

3.2 Partition Exclusion Power

We introduce the notion of partition *exclusion power* to represent the amount of exclusion possible for a partition characterised by some given value of τ and a function f. In essence, the power of a partition is an estimate of the probability of being able to deduce that $d(q, s) > t$, for some distance t, for arbitrarily selected $q \in U$ and $s \in S$.

For the remainder of this article, we use the assumption that the distribution of query and data within the sampled spaces are equivalent. This is probably a reasonable assumption in most metric query scenarios, although there are likely to be specialist examples where it is not the case. The same analysis may be performed whenever the distribution of both query and data can be characterised, whether they are equivalent or not.

In [6], for a range query $\mathcal{Q}(q, t)$, we defined the exclusion power of the partition $\mathcal{F} = \{F_0, F_1\}$ as the probability of excluding one element s on the basis of the data partition to which it belongs:

$$P(s \in F_0) \cdot P(\mathcal{Q}(q, t) \subset F_1) + P(s \in F_1) \cdot P(\mathcal{Q}(q, t) \subset F_0) \qquad (6)$$

which can be rewritten in terms of f and τ as

$$P(f(s) > \tau) \cdot P(f(q) \leq \tau - t) + P(f(s) \leq \tau) \cdot P(f(q) > \tau + t) \qquad (7)$$

If $\mathrm{CDF}(x)$ is the cumulative distribution function of $f(s)$ for $s \in S$ (assuming that the distribution is the same for data and query points, as noted above) then the exclusion power can be expressed as

$$g(\tau, t) = (1 - \mathrm{CDF}(\tau)) \cdot \mathrm{CDF}(\tau - t) + \mathrm{CDF}(\tau) \cdot (1 - \mathrm{CDF}(\tau + t)) \qquad (8)$$

This provides a mechanism for estimating exclusion power of a partition for a fixed τ and query threshold t. Therefore, to understand the effect of different values of τ an *exclusion power graph* may be constructed which is plotted across the range of τ for a fixed value of t. This allows the optimum value of τ to be deduced for a range query with threshold t. The exclusion power graph is dependent on the query threshold. Thus queries with different thresholds will result in different power graphs. Figure 1b shows the resultant power graphs for various thresholds over eight dimensional euclidean data as described in the caption.

To define a *general exclusion power measure* independent from the specific query threshold, in this paper we propose to use the *expected partition power*:

$$ep(\tau) = \int g(\tau, t) h(t) dt \qquad (9)$$

where $h(t)$ is the probability density function associated with the query threshold distribution (e.g., the red curve in Fig. 1a). In Fig. 1c, we show the expected partition power graph for the same 8-dimensional Euclidean data used above.

The exclusion power defined here is closely related to the concept of *discriminative power* (i.e., the ratio of internal complexity to external complexity) defined by Chávez in [2]. Adjusting the τ values thus changes the discriminative power. In this paper we show how exclusion power may be used to optimise τ so that for the same internal complexity we minimise the external complexity i.e. we find the τ that optimises the discriminative power.

4   Power Analysis in High(er) Dimensional Data

It is clear that if a partition has a balance ratio of 0 (i.e., all the data objects are in the same partition class) then it is of no value in terms of exclusion, whereas a value of 0.5 is unlikely to be optimal in a high dimensional space. In fact, it has long been known, if only as a rule of thumb, that balanced tree-structured indexes lose their performance as dimensionality increases, and unbalanced structures perform better. For example, the List of Clusters [1,12] is known to perform better than a Balanced Vantage Point Tree [15] in *higher* dimensions, although we lack a formal definition of the meaning of *higher* in this context. Here, we investigate this phenomenon from a new point of view by using the expected exclusion power estimation.

For a partition $\{F_0, F_1\}$, defined by a pair (f, τ), a set of *witness* data values may be used to calculate approximations of the different values of balance ratio and expected partition power (Eq. 9) varying τ. Note that if τ is selected as the

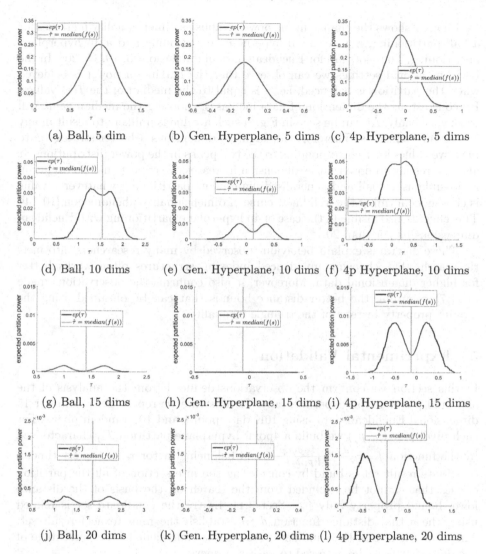

Fig. 2. Expected powers for Euclidean data at dimensions 5, 10, 15, 20, for ball partitioning (left), generalised hyperplane partitioning (middle), 4p hyperplane partitioning (right). The expected power was evaluated using 100 queries over 10K witness data points. Two pivots p_1, p_2 were randomly selected for each dataset; p_1 is used to build the ball partition, both p_1 and p_2 are used for the hyperplane partitions.

median of $\{f(s), s \in S\}$ then the partition classes are balanced (i.e., the balance ratio is 0.5). Therefore, if an exclusion occurs, half of the dataset will be excluded. Moving τ from the median value will produce partitions with a different balance ratio. To understand the effect of different values of τ the expected exclusion power graph may be constructed and optimum value(s) of τ can be deduced.

Figure 2 shows the change in the power graphs as dimensionality increases for a ball partitioning, a generalised hyperplane partitioning and a 4p hyperplane partitioning. The plots are for Euclidean data of dimensions 5, 10, 15, 20^2. In the low dimensional settings we can observe that the maximum power is achieved when the partition is balanced, i.e. τ is equal to the median of the $f(s)$ values. By contrast, as the dimension of data increases, choosing the median value will work very badly. As can be seen in Fig. 2l such a value is unlikely to result in any successful exclusions. Therefore, for high(er) dimensions a better strategy is to pick two values for τ corresponding to the two peaks in the power distributions. It also interesting to note that as dimension increases, we expect that no exclusion is possible using ball and generalised hyperplane partitioning whatever τ value is chosen, confirming the well know curse of dimensionality phenomenon [10,14]. This effect is also visible in the case of 4p hyperplane partitioning with Euclidean dimensions bigger than 20.

These diagrams explain behaviour observed by many researchers into metric search, that choosing unbalanced indexing structures often works better for higher dimensional data. Moreover, it also confirms the observations made in [4,7] regarding the better distance bounds that can be obtained using the 4-point property instead of the triangle inequality.

5　Experimental Validation

In this section we confirm the observations deduced from the analysis of the expected power graph experimentally. To illustrate we report the results for 15 dimensional Euclidean data using 10K data points and 100 random pivots. For each pivot pair (p_i, p_j) we build a 4point hyperplane partition $\mathcal{F}_{ij}$ characterised by the function $f_{ij} = \frac{d(s,p_j)^2 - d(s,p_i)^2}{2d(p_i,p_j)}$ and balancing factor τ_{ij}. At query time, a candidate result set is build by considering the intersection of all the partition classes that cannot be excluded from the search on the basis of the distance lower-bound property only (see Sect. 3.1). Lastly the candidate set is refined using the actual distance function d to establish the final (exact) result set. Therefore the size of the candidate result set is equivalent to the percentage of the data that must be accessed to answer a query.

Figure 3a plots the size of the candidate set as a proportion of the entire dataset using different approaches to select the τ_{ij} values. The top (blue) curve shows the performance when all the partitions are balanced, i.e., for each partition defined by the pair (f_{ij}, τ_{ij}) the τ_{ij} is set to be the median of $f_{ij}(s)$ values. The bottom (orange) curve shows τ_{ij} set to maximise the expected power (see Eq. 9) estimated on a small set of 2,000 witness points using 100 random queries (different from those used at test time). The x-axis shows all the $\binom{100}{2}$ partitions $\mathcal{F}_{ij}$ even although a small subset of these take part in the exclusions. In

---

[2] All results in this article are derived using randomly generated uniformly distributed Euclidean data in different dimensions as stated. All code is available on request from the authors.

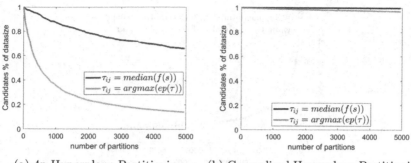

(a) 4p Hyperplane Partitioning   (b) Generalised Hyperplane Partitioning

Fig. 3. Size of candidate set as proportion of whole for τ_{ij} set to the median of $f_{ij}(s)$ values and the τ_{ij} values that maximises the expected partition powers (15D Euclidean data). (Color figure online)

both cases 500 test queries were considered and the average percentage of data accessed to answer a single query was computed and plotted in the y-axis. From this plot a clear difference can be seen in the exclusion power with τ_{ij} set to have balanced partitions and that with the τ_{ij} values set to maximise the partition powers. The balanced version manages to exclude very little data whereas the powered version excludes more than the 85% of the data. For completeness, in Fig. 3b we shows the results also for generalised hyperplane partitioning, i.e. using $f_{ij} = (d(s, p_j) - d(s, p_i))/2$. Note that it does not result in any exclusions - i.e. the candidate set size is about 100% of the dataset being queried, as predicted by the expected power graph in Fig. 2h.

Figure 3a only shows the exclusion for a single maximum power for each pivot pair. However, as shown in Fig. 2h, the expected power graph for 15 dimensional data results in two power peaks (and consequently two different optimal τ_{ij} can be selected). In practice this results in two partitions being created for each pivot pair in the case of hyperplane partitioning. The plot shows the exclusions possible when a single optimal value and both optimal values are used. With 100 pivots and using one or two optimal τ_{ij} values for each pivot pair results in 4,950 and 9,900 partitions respectively. Figure 4 shows the size of the candidate set as proportion of whole when partitions derived from a single and both the optimal τ_{ij} values are used. In this plot the exclusions derived from the common partitions are in plotted corresponding to the leftmost part of the x-axis resulting in a common exclusion curve. As can be seen, the 4,950 extra partitions available when two peaks are used result in (some) more exclusion. The size of the candidate set as a fraction of the total data when the partitions derived from both power peaks are used is 10.37%, in other words 89.63% exclusion is achieved.

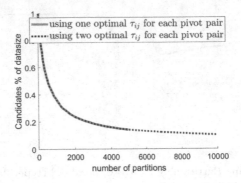

Fig. 4. Size of candidate set as proportion of whole when one optimal τ or two optimal τ values for each pivot pair are selected to maximise the expected partition powers (15D Euclidean data).

Table 1. Average percentage of partitions activated and candidate set size for 5, 10, 15 and 20 dimensional Euclidean data, 100 pivots and 500 queries over 10,000 data points

Dims	Balanced Partitions		Maxpower Partitions	
	Part. Activated	*Candidates*	*Part. Activated*	*Candidates*
5	44.62%	1.43%	44.63%	1.25%
10	3.11%	6.53%	13.76%	2.37%
15	0.05%	65.80%	6.57%	14.15%
20	0.0002%	99.60%	3.00%	49.63%

5.1   The Relationship Between Activated Partitions and Exclusions

We say that a partition is "activated" for a query if using the distance lower-bound property is possible to exclude one of the classes of the partition.

Table 1 shows the percentage of partitions that are activated for queries over 5, 10, 15 and 20 dimensional data. In each experiment 500 queries are executed with 100 pivots (4,950 partitions) over 10,000 data points. As before, the two columns correspond to the cases when all τ_{ij} have been set to have balanced partitions (left) and that with the τ_{ij} values set to maximise the expected power (right). The data shown is the average over the queries. Two numbers are presented for each experiment: the percentage of partitions that are activated and the size of the candidate set as a proportion of the dataset being queried.

As can be seen in the table, the number of partitions that are activated at query time are considerably different both in terms of the dimension of the data and the techniques used to select all the τ values.

In general, balanced partitions perform noticeably worse than the powered partitions and the number of partitions that are activated drops dramatically as the Euclidean dimension increases. Whilst the number of partitions activated also drops when the power is maximised, enough partitions are activated to

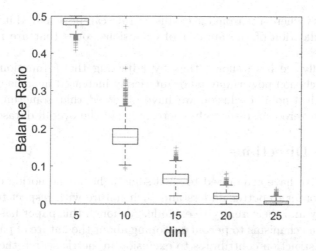

Fig. 5. Balance ratio for increasing dimensions using τ_{ij} values that maximise the expected power

permit approximately 50% of the data to be excluded in the case of 20 dimension and the partitions set to maximise the expected power even when a single power peak is employed.

We also observed, as shown in Fig. 5, that choosing the best τ values results in increasingly un-balanced partitions. Moreover, adding more partitions often does not serve to substantially increase the number of exclusions. We believe that this effect is caused by a lack of *independence* of the objects in the activated partition classes.

6   Conclusions

In this paper we have presented a generalised treatment of exclusion power for binary partitions. The model abstracts over the partition type and we have shown its application to ball partitions, generalised hyperplane partitions and 4-point partitions.

Exclusion power explains the well known differences in the number of exclusions that are possible with respect to both the dimensionality of the data and partition balance ratio.

In addition understanding how to maximise the possibility of exclusion, power diagrams also serve to indicate the probability of exclusions occurring. The understanding the probability of exclusion power determines if a dataset can be usefully queried at all using an exact metric search, i.e. if the size of candidate set is a small fraction of the size of the total dataset. This is useful in its own right since it may be applied independently of any particular algorithm to establish the amount of exclusion that is potentially possible.

In the cases where a reasonable exclusion rate can be achieved it can be used to give an indication of the number of exclusions zones that are necessary to achieve exclusion.

Additionally we have shown that by adjusting the f function and the τ values, the exclusion power may be dramatically increased in some cases. When combined with 4-point exclusion we have observed that sometimes exclusion rates rise from zero to a respectable percentage of the overall dataset.

7   Future Directions

In this paper we have attempted to shed some light on the notion of partitions in general in order to better understand their nature with respect to increasing dimensionality and their ability to exclude. Although this paper has established some general mechanisms to permit reasoning about the nature of partitions and how their construction contributes to exclusion in metric search there is clearly much more work to be done. In particular, we have only touched on the nature of the independence of partitions. Clearly the amount of exclusion that is possible, the independence of the partitions and their power are linked. We are currently investigating this issue but the work is at an early stage.

Acknowledgments. This work was partially funded by AI4Media - A European Excellence Centre for Media, Society, and Democracy (EC, H2020 n. 951911) and by Economic & Social Research Council, ADR UK Programme ES/W010321/1.

References

1. Chávez, E., Navarro, G.: A compact space decomposition for effective metric indexing. Pattern Recogn. Lett. **26**(9), 1363–1376 (2005). https://doi.org/10.1016/j.patrec.2004.11.014
2. Chávez, E., Navarro, G., Baeza-Yates, R., Marroquín, J.L.: Searching in metric spaces. ACM Comput. Surv. **33**(3), 273–321 (2001). https://doi.org/10.1145/502807.502808
3. Cháivez, E., Navarro, G.: A compact space decomposition for effective metric indexing. Pattern Recogn. Lett. **26**(9), 1363–1376 (2005). https://doi.org/10.1016/j.patrec.2004.11.014. https://linkinghub.elsevier.com/retrieve/pii/S0167865504003733
4. Connor, R., Cardillo, F.A., Vadicamo, L., Rabitti, F.: Hilbert exclusion: improved metric search through finite isometric embeddings. ACM Trans. Inf. Syst.(TOIS) **35**(3), 17:1–17:27 (2016). https://doi.org/10.1145/3001583
5. Connor, R., Vadicamo, L., Rabitti, F.: High-dimensional simplexes for supermetric search. In: Beecks, C., Borutta, F., Kröger, P., Seidl, T. (eds.) SISAP 2017. LNCS, vol. 10609, pp. 96–109. Springer, Cham (2017). https://doi.org/10.1007/978-3-319-68474-1_7
6. Connor, R., Dearle, A., Vadicamo, L.: Investigating binary partition power in metric query. In: Proceedings of the 30th Italian Symposium on Advanced Database Systems, SEBD 2022, CEUR Workshop Proceedings, vol. 3194, pp. 415–426. Tirrenia (PI), Italy, 19–22 June 2022. http://ceur-ws.org/Vol-3194/paper49.pdf, http://CEUR-WS.org

7. Connor, R., Vadicamo, L., Cardillo, F.A., Rabitti, F.: Supermetric search. Inf. Syst. **80**, 108–123 (2019). https://doi.org/10.1016/j.is.2018.01.002
8. Hetland, M.L.: Comparison-based indexing from first principles. http://arxiv.org/abs/1908.06318
9. Hetland, M.L.: Metrics and ambits and sprawls, oh my. In: Satoh, S., et al. (eds.) SISAP 2020. LNCS, vol. 12440, pp. 126–139. Springer, Cham (2020). https://doi.org/10.1007/978-3-030-60936-8_10. http://arxiv.org/abs/2008.09654
10. Naidan, B., Boytsov, L., Nyberg, E.: Permutation search methods are efficient, yet faster search is possible. Proc. Int. Conf. Very Large Data Bases **8**(12), 1618–1629 (2015)
11. Pestov, V., Stojmirović, A.: Indexing schemes for similarity search: an illustrated paradigm. Fund. Inform. **70**(4), 367–385 (2006)
12. Sadit Tellez, E., Chávez, E.: The list of clusters revisited. In: Carrasco-Ochoa, J.A., Martínez-Trinidad, J.F., Olvera López, J.A., Boyer, K.L. (eds.) MCPR 2012. LNCS, vol. 7329, pp. 187–196. Springer, Heidelberg (2012). https://doi.org/10.1007/978-3-642-31149-9_19
13. Uhlmann, J.K.: Satisfying general proximity/similarity queries with metric trees. Inf. Process. Lett. **40**(4), 175–179 (1991)
14. Weber, R., Schek, H.J., Blott, S.: A quantitative analysis and performance study for similarity-search methods in high-dimensional spaces. In: Proceedings International Conference on Very Large Data Bases, vol. 98, pp. 194–205 (1998)
15. Yianilos, P.N.: Data structures and algorithms for nearest neighbor search in general metric spaces. In: Proceedings of the Fourth Annual ACM-SIAM Symposium on Discrete Algorithms, SODA 1993, pp. 311–321. Society for Industrial and Applied Mathematics (1993)
16. Zezula, P., Amato, G., Dohnal, V., Batko, M.: Similarity Search: The Metric Space Approach, vol. 32. Springer, New York (2006). https://doi.org/10.1007/0-387-29151-2

Similarity Search with the Distance Density Model

Markéta Křenková$^{(\boxtimes)}$, Vladimir Mic, and Pavel Zezula

Masaryk University Brno, Brno, Czech Republic
`krenkova.m@mail.muni.cz`

Abstract. The metric space model of similarity has become a standard formal paradigm of generic similarity search engine implementations. However, the constraints of identity and symmetry prevent from expressing the subjectivity and dependence on the context perceived by humans. In this paper, we study the suitability of the Distance density model of similarity for searching. First, we use the Local Outlier Factor (LOF) to estimate a data density in search collections and evaluate plenty of queries using the standard geometric model and its extension respecting the densities. We let 200 people assess the search effectiveness of the two alternatives using the web interface. Encouraged by the positive effects of the Distance density model, we propose an alternative way to estimate the data densities to avoid the quadratic LOF computation complexity with respect to the dataset size. The sketches with unbalanced bits are clarified to be in correlation with LOFs, which opens a possibility for an efficient implementation of large-scale similarity search systems based on the Distance density model.

Keywords: Metric space similarity model · Perceived similarity · Data-dependent similarity · Distance density model · Effective and efficient similarity search

1 Introduction

Similarity search in complex domains such as multimedia relies on formal models of similarity perceived by humans. Current search is dominated by geometric models, mostly by *metric spaces*. Metric space (D, d) is given by a domain D of searched objects and the distance function $d : D \times D \mapsto \mathbf{R}_0^+$ which quantifies the dissimilarity of objects. While the domain D can be an arbitrary set, function d must meet the metric postulates: *non-negativity*, *identity*, *symmetry*, and *triangle inequality* [17]. The goal of the similarity search is to efficiently find the most similar objects o from a given dataset $X \subseteq D$ to an arbitrary query object $q \in D$.

While the metric postulates facilitate the efficient searching, their veracity with respect to the *perceived similarity* $sim(.,.)$ has been disputed [10,15]. Please

This research was supported by ERDF "CyberSecurity, CyberCrime and Critical Information Infrastructures Center of Excellence" (No. CZ.02.1.01/0.0/0.0/16_019/0000822).

notice that while we introduce a notation $sim(o_1, o_2)$ to denote the *perceived* similarity of $o_1, o_2 \in D$, this $sim(o_1, o_2)$ cannot be formalised by a function and it is just approximated by similarity models.

The identity and non-negativity of function d assume that the similarity $sim(o, o)$ is the same for all $o \in D$. This is sort of inconsistent [15] with real-life experiments, according to which some objects o – typically those with less significant features – are confused with others more often than objects with strong features. The experience also reveal [14,15] that the perceived similarity $sim(o_1, o_2)$ is not always symmetric. Due to the *prototypicality* or the *centrality* property, the statement "o_1 is similar to o_2" can be perceived differently than its inverse "o_2 is similar to o_1". For instance, more tourists in Bologna are likely to say "*the tower in Bologna is similar to the Leaning tower in Pisa*" than tourists in Pisa who say "*the Leaning tower in Pisa is similar to the tower in Bologna*".

This paper extends the thesis [8] and elaborates on discrepancies between the perceived similarity and its geometric approximation. Specifically, we focus on the influence of a *context* in which the similarity is assessed. Such problem has been formalised in [10] as a matter of a density around objects $o \in X$. We refer to the models of $sim(o_1, o_2)$ which respect the local density of objects $o \in X$ around o_1, o_2 as the "*data-dependent similarity models*". On the contrary, the similarity models (D, d) that do not take the local densities of $o \in X$ into account are denoted as "*the geometric similarity models*", and corresponding d is the "*geometric distance function*". The notation used throughout the article is summarised in Table 1.

The influence of local densities around $o_1, o_2 \in D$ on $sim(o_1, o_2)$ was pointed out by Krumhansl [10], who proposed to enhance geometric distance functions d with these densities. Her proposal from the late 70s could not be experimentally verified for decades due to a lack of the data amount and their insufficient descriptive quality. Current situation is the opposite one: the *scalability* of the search in data-dependent similarity models is crucial.

Aryal et al. [1,2] propose the *Mp-Dissimilarity*. Having solid analytical foundations that well follow the Krumhansl's proposal, the *Mp-Dissimilarity* is expensive to evaluate in current high dimensional data and big datasets. Effectiveness of several data-dependent models is compared in [3], where *Mp-Dissimilarity* is illustrated to provide better classification accuracy and retrieval results than the Euclidean and Cosine distance functions.

In this article, we focus on both, the effectiveness and efficiency of the similarity search in data-dependent similarity models.

– We verify the veracity of 2 implementations of the Krumhansl's similarity model with respect to $sim(., .)$. First, we use the Local Outlier Factor (LOF) to estimate the object density. Then, we let people to assess which of two images is more similar to the query image q, and compare these assessments of various triplets of images q, o_1, o_2 with both implementations.
– Second, we propose a scalable implementation of the Krumhansl's similarity model. We use binary sketches of objects $o \in X$ to estimate the local densities. The sketches are not only effective but also efficient to create and use.

Table 1. Notation used throughout this paper

(D, d)	The metric space similarity model: domain D and distance function d
$sim(o_1, o_2)$	Perceived similarity of objects $o_1, o_2 \in D$ (as perceived by people)
$q \in D$	Query object
$X \subseteq D$	The searched dataset
o, o_1, o_2	Objects from the domain D or the searched dataset X (always specified)
$k\text{-NN}(q)$	k nearest neighbours to query object q
$\bar{d}(o_1, o_2)$	Data-dependent distance of $o_1, o_2 \in D$
$\delta(o)$	Spatial density of $o \in D$
$LOF(o)$	The local outlier factor of $o \in D$
$\bar{d}_{LOF}(o_1, o_2)$	Data-dependent distance of $o_1, o_2 \in D$ using $LOF(o_1)$ and $LOF(o_2)$ to compute objects o_1 and o_2 densities
$sk(o),$	Binary sketch of $o \in D$
λ	The length of sketches $sk(o)$ in bits
$card(sk(o))$	Cardinality of sketch $sk(o)$, i.e., number of bits set to 1
$\bar{d}_{sk}(o_1, o_2)$	Data-dependent distance of $o_1, o_2 \in D$ using $card(sk(o_1))$ and $card(sk(o_2))$ to compute objects o_1 and o_2 densities
$d(q^{10})$	The ranking of 10NN to q from X defined by the distance function d
$\bar{d}_{LOF}(q^{10})$	The ranking of 10NN to q from X defined by the distance function $\bar{d}_{LOF}$
$\bar{d}_{sk}(q^{10})$	The ranking of 10NN to q from X defined by the distance function $\bar{d}_{sk}$

The rest of the paper is organised as follows. Section 2 introduces the Distance density model and the LOF function. Section 3 describes the gathering of information about the similarities of images using the crowd-sourcing. Section 4 provides results of searching with the data-dependent distance function based on $LOF(o)$ values. Section 5 describes the Distance density model implementation that uses the binary sketches of objects, and Sect. 6 provides the results of searching with this implementation. Section 7 concludes the paper.

2   Data-Dependent Similarity Search

Figure 1 illustrates that the perceived similarity $sim(o_1, o_2)$ is also inferred by other objects $o \in X$. Specifically, Fig. 1a suggests that "Church 1" and "Church 2" are likely to be perceived as *quite similar* when we search the dataset X of generic buildings. On the other hand, the same churches do not seem to be so similar when searching the dataset X of only churches, as illustrated by Fig. 1b, since "Church 1" is more similar to "Church 3" than to "Church 2", and "Church 2" is more similar to "Church 4" than to "Church 1". The perceived similarity $sim(o_1, o_2)$ of "Church 1" and "Church 2" is thus inferred by other objects $o \in X$, but the geometric distance $d(o_1, o_2)$ that quantifies the similarity of the churches does not reflect this. Conversely, it is always the same.

(a) Dataset of generic buildings

(b) Dataset of churches

Fig. 1. Example of the data-dependent perception of similarity: Churches 1 and 2 are likely perceived as similar when compared with general buildings (Fig. (a)), but they are rather dissimilar when searching the dataset of churches (Fig. (b))

Krumhansl [10] defines her data-dependent similarity model called *the Distance density model*. She formalises the similarity of $o_1, o_2 \in D$ using the metric space (D, d) and densities of objects $o \in X$ around o_1, o_2. Her central observation is that objects o_1, o_2 located in a relatively dense region are perceived less similar than other objects o_3, o_4 within the same geometric distance $d(o_3, o_4) = d(o_1, o_2)$ but in less dense regions of space (D, d).

Formally, the Krumhansl's model uses the data-dependent distance function:

$$\bar{d}(o_1, o_2) = d(o_1, o_2) + \alpha \cdot \delta(o_1) + \beta \cdot \delta(o_2) \tag{1}$$

where $\delta(o_i) \in \mathbf{R}^+$ is a density of objects $o \in X$ around $o_i \in D$, and $\alpha, \beta \in \mathbf{R}_0^+$ are constants to adjust the range of δ. In general, function $\bar{d}(.,.)$ can violate the axioms of the identity and the symmetry due to the influence of $\delta(o_1)$ and $\delta(o_2)$, but it always satisfies the triangle inequality rule [10].

There are several approaches to computing the spatial density $\delta(o)$ [3,10]. We first use the *Local outlier factor* (*LOF*) [5], similarly as Aryal et al. in [4].

2.1 Local Outlier Factor Expressing the Local Density

Breunig et al. [5] define the Local outlier factor (LOF) of $o \in D$ to express how much o is an outlier in the searched space according to the density of its neighbourhood. The larger the LOF(o), the more outlier the object o within the dataset X. LOF(o) is evaluated by comparing the density of $o_1 \in X$ around o with the densities of $o_1 \in X$ around the k nearest neighbours of o from X. For details, please see [5].

We define the spatial density $\delta(o)$ of $o \in D$ as an inverse of $LOF(o)$, similarly as Aryal et al. in [4]:

$$\delta(o) = 1/\text{LOF}(o) \tag{2}$$

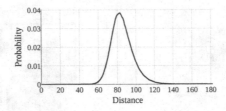

Fig. 2. Euclidean distance distribution for the DeCAF descriptors

We denote $\bar{d}_{LOF}$ the data-dependent distance function made by the substitution of Eq. 2 to Eq. 1. Evaluation of LOF(o) values for all $o \in X$ has the time complexity $\mathcal{O}(|X|^2)$ [5] which makes it infeasible for most of the contemporary datasets. In the following, we set reasonable environment to verify the veracity of $\bar{d}_{LOF}$ with respect to $sim(.,.)$.

We collect information about the perceived similarities $sim(q, o_1)$, $sim(q, o_2)$ for selected triplets $q, o_1, o_2 \in D$ using the crowd-sourcing. We then compare the perceived similarities with the geometric distances $d(q, o_1), d(q, o_2)$, and the data dependent distances $\bar{d}_{LOF}(q, o_1), \bar{d}_{LOF}(q, o_2)$, respectively, to discuss the contribution of LOF(o) values to the similarity search effectiveness.

2.2   Test Data

The data examined in this article are the *DeCAF* image visual descriptors [7] extracted from the *Profiset image collection*[1] which consists of 20 million images. The DeCAF descriptors are derived from the Alexnet convolutional neural network [9] as the data from the second-last fully connected layer (FC7). Each descriptor consist of a 4,096-dimensional vector of floating-point values that describes characteristic image features, so there is a correspondence 1 to 1 between images and their descriptors. Pairwise similarities of descriptors are expressed by the Euclidean distances and their distribution over the searched dataset is depicted in Fig. 2.

2.3   Setting Experiments with $\bar{d}_{LOF}$ Function

Setting α and β for the Data-dependent Distance Function. To be able to evaluate $\bar{d}_{LOF}$, Eq. 1 requires to set values α and β. Having a query object q, the effect of $\alpha \cdot \delta(q)$ is the same for all distances $\bar{d}(q, o), o \in X$, and thus α does not matter and can be 0 for the evaluation simplicity. Suitable value of β depends on a range and distribution of the distances $d(o_1, o_2), o_1, o_2 \in X$, and we perform a simple experiment to find a suitable β for our dataset.

We select 10 query images q in random, and find 10 nearest neighbours in the dataset X for each q using the Euclidean function d and the data-dependent function $\bar{d}_{LOF}$ with various β values. If $\beta = 0$, the nearest neighbours given by d

---

[1] http://disa.fi.muni.cz/profiset/.

and $\bar{d}_{LOF}$ for each q are the same. The differences increase with increasing β, and we assume a global optimum β_{opt} such that the influence of local densities $\beta \cdot \delta(o)$ in the function $\bar{d}_{LOF}$ is counter-productive for $\beta > \beta_{opt}$. We have visualised and inspected all query answers for $\beta : 2 \leq \beta \leq 10 \wedge \beta$ divisible by 0.25. We have observed the expected results: the global optimum $\beta_{opt} \approx 7$, and if $\beta \gg 7$, irrelevant images dissimilar to q qualifies to the 10NN answers. Therefore, we use $\beta = 7$ for $\bar{d}_{LOF}$ searching our dataset.

Dataset to Test $\bar{d}_{LOF}$. Due to the $LOF(o)$ evaluation complexity, we select a subset of 10,000 descriptors and 150 query objects q in random from all 20 million descriptors for the experiments with $\bar{d}_{LOF}$. Moreover, we have to ensure a presence of descriptors similar to query descriptors q in the tested dataset. Therefore, we found 100 nearest neighbours o_{NN} for each q in a set of 20 million DeCAF descriptors using the Euclidean distances, and added these near neighbours to the tested dataset of 10,000 descriptors. The overall size of the dataset is thus $|X| \approx 10{,}000 + |Q| \cdot 100$, i.e., almost 25,000 descriptors: In fact, 7 nearest neighbours are present in 10,000 random descriptors, so we have $|X| = 24{,}993$ descriptors. The distance distribution of the DeCAF descriptors (see Fig. 2) suggests that the separation of the clusters in X is limited, i.e., it is meaningful to search for semantically better near neighbours to q than those artificially added. We have also verified this assumption manually.

$\bar{d}_{LOF}(q^{10})$ and $d(q^{10})$ Rankings. Having the dataset X of 24,993 descriptors, we have found 10 nearest neighbours for all 150 query objects q using $\bar{d}_{LOF}$ and d, respectively, to get:

1. *the $\bar{d}_{LOF}(q^{10})$ rankings*, and
2. *the $d(q^{10})$ rankings*, respectively.

Since our goal is to verify the contribution of $\bar{d}_{LOF}$ to the searching effectiveness in comparison with the Euclidean function d, we further select 45 query objects q out of all 150 with maximum differences in $\bar{d}_{LOF}(q^{10})$ and $d(q^{10})$ rankings.

3   Crowd-Sourcing to Examine the Perceived Similarity

We use the crowd-sourcing to collect the information about the perceived similarities of images. We have implemented a web application in which respondents select a more similar image out of o_1, o_2 to a given query image q.

We prepared triplets q, o_1, o_2 to emphasise differences between $\bar{d}_{LOF}(q^{10})$ and $d(q^{10})$ rankings. Specifically, we made all triplets $(q, \bar{o}_i, o_i)$ such that image $\bar{o}_i$ is in the ith position of the $\bar{d}_{LOF}(q^{10})$ ranking, o_i is the image in the ith position of $d(q^{10})$ ranking and $\bar{o}_i \neq o_i$. In total, we used 150 triplets of images $(q, \bar{o}_i, o_i)$ in the crowd-sourcing.

The triplets of images are visualised in the web application as illustrated in Fig. 3. Respondents are asked to select a value on the slider to assess which of images $\bar{o}_i, o_i$ is more similar to a query image q above them and how much. The slider offers all integer values from 0 to 100 with an implicit neutral value 50.

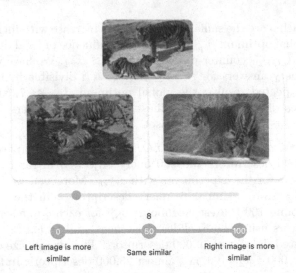

Fig. 3. A screenshot from the web application to collect information about the perceived similarities

Users are provided with no information about any of the distances nor rankings. In total, we have collected approximately 4,000 answers from 200 respondents, so we have approximately 27 answers on average for each triplet of images.

3.1   Discussion on the Crowd-Sourced Information

We analyse the collected information about the perceived similarities of images to define the ground-truth. We start with the removing a minimum and a maximum assessment for each triplet $q, \bar{o}_i, o_i$. Numbers of respondents are published after removing these extreme assessments. We then analyse the mean and the standard deviation of the answers for each triplet.

We observe even extreme triplets $q, \bar{o}_i, o_i$ such that the respondents have very different opinions. The maximum standard deviation is 32.7 in case of the triplet with an average answer 53.9 and assessed by 30 respondents. This is not surprising, considering the way of the triplet creation, i.e., the focus on different objects $\bar{o}_i, o_i$ placed at the same position of $\bar{d}_{LOF}(q^{10})$ and $d(q^{10})$ ranking, respectively. Another example of a triplet assessed with a large variance is visualised in Fig. 4a. We have visualised all triplets assessed with a large variance and found the assessments quite natural as the similarities $sim(q, \bar{o}_i)$ and $sim(q, o_i)$ are quite subjective in all these cases.

Another extreme is figured by a triplet assessed by 24 people who all returned the answer 50, i.e., that both images $\bar{o}_i, o_i$ are equally similar to q even though $\bar{o}_i \neq o_i$. We have revealed that images $\bar{o}_i, o_i$ in the triplets assessed with low variance and an average answer close to 50 are always the near duplicates which make the crowd-sourced information natural as well.

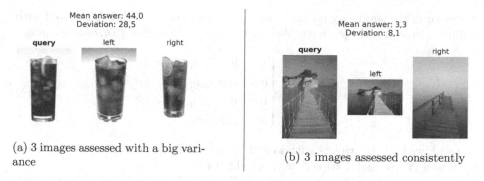

(a) 3 images assessed with a big variance

(b) 3 images assessed consistently

Fig. 4. Examples of images assessed in an extreme ways by the respondents

All triplets $q, \bar{o}_i, o_i$ with no clear preference of people on a more similar image to q out of $\bar{o}_i, o_i$ can hardly be used to improve the similarity models. From this point of view, the more interesting are triplets assessed by respondents clearly and with rather a low standard deviation. The most extreme triplet out of 150 examined was assessed by 29 people with an average answer 0.6 and a standard deviation 2. Similar case of triplet is visualised in Fig. 4b. These triplets suggest a suitable space to investigate the reasons for the differences in $\bar{d}_{LOF}(q^{10})$ and $d(q^{10})$ rankings.

3.2 Ground-Truth Deriving

We use 2 different approaches to determine which of the images $\bar{o}_i, o_i$ is more similar to q using the crowd-sourced data.

First, we summarise the number of answers smaller than 50, bigger than 50, and equal to 50, for each triplet $q, \bar{o}_i, o_i$. The more similar image to q out of $\bar{o}_i, o_i$ is determined as the one preferred by more of the respondents. In other words, this ground-truth takes into account just the side to which the respondents shifted the slider in the web application and ignores the scale of how much they shifted it. If both images $\bar{o}_i, o_i$ are assessed as more similar to q by the same number of respondents or the most of the answers are 50, both images are marked as equally similar to q in this ground-truth which we denote GT_{count}.

The second type of the ground-truth uses the average assessment over the answers, and we remind 2 extreme assessments were already removed. If the average is smaller than 50, the left-hand image is labelled as more similar to q, and if it is bigger than 50, the right-hand image is labelled as more similar to q. If the average answer is 50, both images are marked as equally similar to q in this ground-truth which we denote GT_{avg}.

Having GT_{count} and GT_{avg} ground-truths, we also consider their enhancement by incorporating a degree of compliance over the respondent answers. Specifically, if the standard deviation $\sigma(q, \bar{o}_i, o_i)$ of answers on a triplet $q, \bar{o}_i, o_i$ is small, it is more important to have a similarity model that selects the more similar image out of $\bar{o}_i, o_i$ to q in compliance with the ground-truth. Conversely, the error of the similarity model is not so serious in case of triplets assessed with a high degree of a subjectivity. Weight $w(q, \bar{o}_i, o_i)$ of triplet $q, \bar{o}_i, o_i$ is assigned:

$$w(q, \bar{o}_i, o_i) = \begin{cases} 1 & \text{if } \sigma(q, \bar{o}_i, o_i) < 10 \\ 0.8 & \text{if } \sigma(q, \bar{o}_i, o_i) < 20 \\ 0.6 & \text{if } \sigma(q, \bar{o}_i, o_i) < 30 \\ 0.4 & \text{otherwise} \end{cases} \tag{3}$$

In total, we have 15 triplets with weight 1; 70 triplets with weight 0.8; 61 triplets with weight 0.6, and 4 triplets with weight 0.4.

In total, we have 4 ground-truths: GT_{count}, GT_{avg}, and their variants with the weighted importance of the triplets: $GT_{count\text{-}weighted}$ and $GT_{avg\text{-}weighted}$.

4   Contribution of $\bar{d}_{LOF}$ to the Search Effectiveness

Let us consider a triplet of images q, o_1, o_2 such that the similarity $sim(q, o_1)$ is bigger than $sim(q, o_2)$ according to a specific ground-truth.

We first analyse the rankings $d(q^{10})$ and $\bar{d}_{LOF}(q^{10})$ and compute the number of correct orders of o_1, o_2 according to the GT_{count}. Since the GT_{count} marks 17 pairs of objects o_1, o_2 equally similar to q, we use 133 triplets out of 150 prepared. The Euclidean function d orders correctly just 54 out of 133 pairs o_1, o_2 with respect to q, i.e., 41%. Conversely, the data-dependent function $\bar{d}_{LOF}$ orders correctly 85 out of 133 pairs o_1, o_2, i.e., 64%. This is a reasonable result since we have prepared the triplets of images with a focus on differences in the $d(q^{10})$ and $\bar{d}_{LOF}(q^{10})$ rankings. The result thus well illustrates a positive contribution of the LOF values to the search effectiveness.

We also evaluate the second experiment in which we focus on image o_1 more similar to q out of o_1, o_2, and we find its position in $\bar{d}_{LOF}(q^{10})$ and $d(q^{10})$ ranking, respectively. If the ranking does not contain the image, ∞ is considered. The way of the triplet creation ensures that the positions of o_1 in both rankings are not the same, and we give a point to the ranking that contains o_1 at the lower position. This approach is motivated by a fact that the similar images to q should be generally at the lower positions of the ranking than those less similar. The normalised score of the rankings is summarised in Table 2. The $\bar{d}_{LOF}(q^{10})$ ranking contains more similar images at lower positions than $d(q^{10})$ ranking in case of comparisons with all 4 types of the ground-truth. The biggest contribution of $\bar{d}_{LOF}$ function is observed with respect to the $GT_{count\text{-}weighted}$: ranking $\bar{d}_{LOF}(q^{10})$ contains o_1 at a lower position in 63% of (the weighted) cases.

Finally, we move from the analysis of 150 triplets q, o_1, o_2 to the comparison of whole 45 rankings $\bar{d}_{LOF}(q^{10})$ and $d(q^{10})$ made for 45 query objects (see Sect. 2.3). The average Levenshtein distance of 45 rankings $\bar{d}_{LOF}(q^{10})$ and $d(q^{10})$ is 3.34 with the standard deviation 1.97. The average Spearman distance is 11.53 with the standard deviation 7.5. To verify which of the rankings $\bar{d}_{LOF}(q^{10})$ and $d(q^{10})$ fits better the human perception, we have selected 30 pairs of rankings in random and let people to select the more satisfying one. Option of the equal satisfaction

Table 2. Scores of the ranking $\bar{d}_{LOF}(q^{10})$ given by data-dependent distance function and scores of the $d(q^{10})$ ranking given by the Euclidean distance function, considering all types of the ground-truth

Ground-truth	Score of $\bar{d}_{LOF}(q^{10})$ ranking (%)	Score of $d(q^{10})$ ranking (%)
GT$_{count}$	60	40
GT$_{count-weighted}$	63	37
GT$_{avg}$	57	43
GT$_{avg-weighted}$	58	42

was included as well. We have collected answers about each ranking pair from 10 respondents. The $\bar{d}_{LOF}(q^{10})$ ranking is picked as the better one in case of 19 query objects out of 30 (63%). The $d(q^{10})$ ranking is better assessed 7 times (23%), and both rankings are assessed equally in 4 cases (13%). We have also observed much stronger consensus of the respondents who agreed that $\bar{d}_{LOF}(q^{10})$ ranking is better. On the contrary, if $d(q^{10})$ ranking is preferred, it is usually a tight preference.

Figure 5 and 6 visualise the first 8NN from the $d(q^{10})$ and $\bar{d}_{LOF}(q^{10})$ ranking in the second and third rows, respectively. In both cases, $\bar{d}_{LOF}(q^{10})$ is assessed as a better one by the respondents.

5 Scalable Data-Dependent Distance Based on Sketches

Distance function $\bar{d}_{LOF}$ cannot be used to search most of the contemporary datasets due to the quadratic complexity of LOF$(o), o \in X$ evaluation. Moreover, LOF(o) values should be recomputed when the dataset X is modified.

We propose a different approach to estimate spatial densities $\delta(o)$ used in the Krumhansl's data-dependent distance function $\bar{d}(.,.)$. Our approach is based on the binary sketches of $o \in X$ which are the bit-strings of length λ approximating the search space. While many sketching transformations exist [6,11,13,16] and sketches compared by the Hamming distance are successfully used to speed up the similarity search, we use a specific sketching technique to express $\delta(o)$.

We use sketching technique [12] that defines sketches using λ instances of the *Generalised hyperplane partitioning (GHP)* [17] illustrated in Fig. 7a. Each instance of the GHP defines one bit $i : 0 \leq i < \lambda$ of all sketches $sk(o), o \in X$ as it splits the dataset X into 2 parts: objects $o \in X$ closer to the *pivoting object* $p_1^i \in D$ have the bit i set to 1, and objects o closer to the *pivoting object* $p_2^i \in D$ have the bit i set to 0. The geometric distance function $d(.,.)$ is utilised here. Pivoting objects p_1^i, p_2^i are selected for each bit $i : 0 \leq i < \lambda$ so that:

1. Each bit i splits the dataset X into *unbalanced* parts such that approximately $b \cdot |X|$ objects for a fixed $b \in (0.5, 1)$ are closer to p_1^i than to p_2^i.
2. GHP instances defining sketches are as much independent as possible, i.e., pairwise Pearson correlations of bits of sketches $sk(o), o \in X$ are close to 0.

Fig. 5. Example of 8NN defined by the Euclidean distance function d (1st row), and data-dependent functions $\bar{d}_{LOF}$ and $\bar{d}_{sk}$, respectively (the 2nd and 3rd row)

The heuristic to define sketches $sk(o), o \in D$ with these properties is adopted from [12]. We emphasise that once the sketching transformation is learned, the object to sketch transformation requires just 2λ distance $d(.,.)$ computations where λ is the length of sketches. This is usually by several orders of magnitude less than $\mathcal{O}(|X|)$ distance computations required to evaluate LOF(o).

The sketches with unbalanced bits [12] are strongly related to the density $\delta(o)$: Each bit i of sketches defines the smaller part of the dataset $|X|$ by means of the GHP. The minority of $o \in X$ has the bit i set to 0. Also, the bits of sketches are (almost) uncorrelated [12], i.e., statistically independent. Each 0 in sketch $sk(o)$ of $o \in X$ thus expresses that o is in a minor part of the dataset according to an instance of the GHP which is almost independent on the other bits. Objects $o \in X$ with many zeros in their sketch $sk(o)$ thus tend to be outliers within X. This phenomenon is illustrated in Fig. 7b where the dataset of 35 objects is depicted with several instances of the GHP splitting it to the parts of size 7 and 28 objects (i.e., $b = 0.8$). Two instances of the GHP producing bits i, j with the Pearson correlation -0.07 are emphasised. Just one outlying object in the blue area is separated by these two GHP instances.

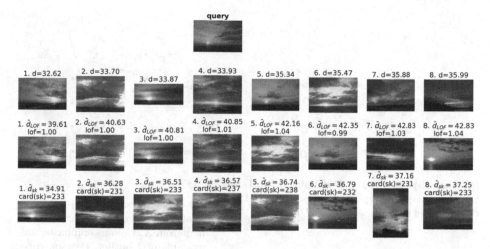

Fig. 6. Example of 8NN defined by the Euclidean distance function d (1st row), and data-dependent functions $\bar{d}_{LOF}$ and $\bar{d}_{sk}$, respectively (the 2nd and 3rd row)

We define the *cardinality* $card(sk(o))$ of $sk(o)$ as a number of bits set to 1 in the sketch. Further, we assume that the lower the cardinality of $sk(o)$, the less dense region around the object o as a consequence of its outlierness. This assumption is reasonable for data with the Gaussian distance density as well as for the most of the other real-life datasets.

To set suitable parameters λ and b, we evaluate the Pearson correlation coefficient of the $LOF(o)$ and $card(sk(o))$ values for a sample of 10,000 randomly selected descriptors $o \in X$ using all 12 combinations of parameters $\lambda \in \{128, 192, 256\} \wedge b \in \{0.8, 0.85, 0.9, 0.95\}$. The most significant correlation -0.69 is observed for $\lambda = 256 \wedge b = 0.9$, so we adopt these parameters.

We express the density $\delta(o)$ using the sketch cardinality as follows, for the numerical reasons. Please notice that 230.4 is the mean cardinality over sketches with $\lambda = 256 \wedge b = 0.9$ since $256 \cdot 0.9 = 230.4$.

$$\delta(o) = card(sk(o)) - 230.4 \qquad (4)$$

The substitution of Eq. 4 to Eq. 1 defines the data-dependent distance function $\bar{d}_{sk}$. We set β in Eq. 1 in the same way as described in Sect. 2.3 and we get value $\beta = 0.4$.

6   Contribution of Efficient $\bar{d}_{sk}$ to the Search Effectiveness

We conduct the main experiments with $\bar{d}_{sk}$ analogically to those reported for $\bar{d}_{LOF}$. We denote $\bar{d}_{sk}(q^{10})$ a list of 10NN of q defined by $\bar{d}_{sk}$ function. We first inspect the ranking given by $\bar{d}_{sk}$ function to compute the number of correct orders of o_1, o_2 according to their similarity to q defined by the GT_{count}. We just have to use a rank of 100 nearest neighbours here since $\bar{d}_{sk}(q^{10})$ often does not

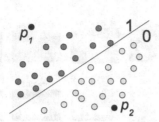

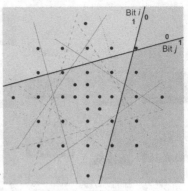

(a) Two objects $p_1, p_2 \in D$ defining an instance of the generalised hyperplane partitioning (GHP), and thus a bit of sketches $sk(o), o \in D$

(b) Unbalanced ($b = 0.8$) low correlated bits tend to separate outliers from X. Colours emphasize an example of 1 outlier. Pearson correlation of bits i and j is $\approx$ -0.07

Fig. 7. Definition of bits of sketches $sk(o), o \in D$ to identify outliers within the dataset X. Notice that many (λ) instances of the GHP is used.

contain none of the objects o_1, o_2. The $\bar{d}_{sk}$ function correctly orders 79 out of 133 pairs o_1, o_2 (59%). We remind that $d(q^{10})$ and $\bar{d}_{LOF}(q^{10})$ rankings correctly order 54 (41%) and 85 (64%) out of 133 pairs o_1, o_2, respectively.

We also compare the whole rankings $\bar{d}_{sk}(q^{10})$ and $d(q^{10})$. The average *Levenshtein* distance of $d(q^{10})$ and $\bar{d}_{sk}(q^{10})$ rankings is 9.23, and the mean *Spearman* distance of the rankings is 74.17. Both distances are much larger than in case of $d(q^{10})$ and $\bar{d}_{LOF}(q^{10})$ comparison where they are 3.34 and 11.53, respectively.

Examples of $\bar{d}_{sk}(q^{10})$ are visualised in the last rows of Fig. 5 and 6. These rankings seem to provide even better order than $\bar{d}_{LOF}(q^{10})$ rankings provided in the second rows.

7   Conclusion

We studied the Krumhansl's Distance density model [10] to better estimate the similarity perceived by humans, compared to the traditional geometric similarity models. We gathered 4 thousand assessments of the image similarities and investigated the veracity of two implementations of the Distance density model: one based on the Local Outlier Factor (LOF), and our proposal that uses the bit-string sketches with unbalanced bits. We have observed significant contributions to the similarity search effectiveness in case of both implementations. The similarity search with the LOF values requires a pre-processing of the searched dataset that has a quadratic time complexity, which is infeasible for most of the current datasets. Conversely, the sketch-based implementation requires an efficient linear dataset pre-processing. Usage of the sketches in this way also opens a space for the future work. While we use them to improve the similarity search effectiveness, they have been proposed to speed up the search. The natural continuation is thus a development of a sketch-based search technique that would improve both, the search effectiveness as well as the efficiency. Also, other density estimation techniques such as Hubness and intrinsic dimensionality can be considered for a comparison with the sketches and LOFs in future.

References

1. Aryal, S., Ting, K.M., Haffari, G., Washio, T.: MP-dissimilarity: a data dependent dissimilarity measure. In: 2014 IEEE International Conference on Data Mining, ICDM, Shenzhen, China, pp. 707–712. IEEE Computer Society (2014)
2. Aryal, S., Ting, K.M., Washio, T., Haffari, G.: Data-dependent dissimilarity measure: an effective alternative to geometric distance measures. Knowl. Inf. Syst. **53**(2), 479–506 (2017)
3. Aryal, S., Ting, K.M., Washio, T., Haffari, G.: A comparative study of data-dependent approaches without learning in measuring similarities of data objects. Data Min. Knowl. Discov. **34**(1), 124–162 (2020)
4. Aryal, S., Ting, K.M., Wells, J.R., Washio, T.: Improving iForest with relative mass. In: Tseng, V.S., Ho, T.B., Zhou, Z.-H., Chen, A.L.P., Kao, H.-Y. (eds.) PAKDD 2014, Part II. LNCS (LNAI), vol. 8444, pp. 510–521. Springer, Cham (2014). https://doi.org/10.1007/978-3-319-06605-9_42
5. Breunig, M.M., Kriegel, H.P., Ng, R.T., Sander, J.: LOF: identifying density-based local outliers. ACM SIGMOD Rec. **29**(2), 93–104 (2000)
6. Cao, Y., et al.: Binary hashing for approximate nearest neighbor search on big data: a survey. IEEE Access **6**, 2039–2054 (2018)
7. Donahue, J., et al.: DeCAF: a deep convolutional activation feature for generic visual recognition. In: Proceedings of the 31th International Conference on Machine Learning, ICML, China, pp. 647–655 (2014)
8. Křenková M.: Probability of outliers and its effects on effectiveness of similarity searching (2021). https://is.muni.cz/th/ssb4c/. Bachelor's thesis, Masaryk University, Faculty of Informatics, Brno, supervisor Pavel Zezula
9. Krizhevsky, A., Sutskever, I., Hinton, G.E.: ImageNet classification with deep convolutional neural networks. In: Advances in Neural Information Processing Systems, vol. 25, pp. 1097–1105. Curran Associates, Inc. (2012)
10. Krumhansl, C.L.: Concerning the applicability of geometric models to similarity data: the interrelationship between similarity and spatial density. Psychol. Rev. **85**(5), 445–463 (1978)
11. Mic, V., Novak, D., Zezula, P.: Designing sketches for similarity filtering. In: 2016 IEEE 16th International Conference on Data Mining Workshops (ICDMW), pp. 655–662 (2016)
12. Mic, V., Novak, D., Zezula, P.: Sketches with unbalanced bits for similarity search. In: Beecks, C., Borutta, F., Kröger, P., Seidl, T. (eds.) SISAP 2017. LNCS, vol. 10609, pp. 53–63. Springer, Cham (2017). https://doi.org/10.1007/978-3-319-68474-1_4
13. Muller-Molina, A.J., Shinohara, T.: Efficient similarity search by reducing I/O with compressed sketches. In: Proceedings of the 2nd International Workshop on Similarity Search and Applications, pp. 30–38 (2009)

14. Santini, S., Jain, R.C.: Similarity measures. IEEE Trans. Pattern Anal. Mach. Intell. **21**(9), 871–883 (1999)
15. Tversky, A.: Features of similarity. Psychol. Rev. **84**(4), 327–352 (1977)
16. Vadicamo, L., Mic, V., Falchi, F., Zezula, P.: Metric embedding into the hamming space with the n-simplex projection. In: Amato, G., Gennaro, C., Oria, V., Radovanović, M. (eds.) SISAP 2019. LNCS, vol. 11807, pp. 265–272. Springer, Cham (2019). https://doi.org/10.1007/978-3-030-32047-8_23
17. Zezula, P., Amato, G., Dohnal, V., Batko, M.: Similarity Search - The Metric Space Approach. Advances in Database Systems, vol. 32. Kluwer (2006)

Generalized Relative Neighborhood Graph (GRNG) for Similarity Search

Cole Foster[✉], Berk Sevilmis, and Benjamin Kimia

Brown University, Providence, RI 02912, USA
{cole_foster,benjamin_kimia}@brown.edu

Abstract. Similarity search for information retrieval on a variety of datasets relies on a notion of neighborhood, frequently using binary relationships such as the kNN approach. We suggest, however, that the notion of a neighbor must recognize higher-order relationship, to capture neighbors in all directions. Proximity graphs, such as the Relative Neighbor Graphs (RNG), use *trinary* relationships which capture the notion of direction and have been successfully used in a number of applications. However, the current algorithms for computing the RNG, despite widespread use, are approximate and not scalable. This paper proposes a hierarchical approach and novel type of graph, the Generalized Relative Neighborhood Graph (GRNG) for use in a pivot layer that then guides the efficient and exact construction of the RNG of a set of exemplars. It also shows how to extend this to a multi-layer hierarchy which significantly improves over the state-of-the-art methods which can only construct an approximate RNG.

Keywords: Generalized relative neighborhood graph · Incremental index construction · Scalable search

1 Introduction

The vast majority of generated data in our society is now in digital form. The data representation has evolved beyond numbers and strings to complex objects. Organization and retrieval have likewise evolved from cosine similarity in vector spaces through inverted files (Google, Yahoo, Microsoft, etc.), to either embedding complex objects in Euclidean spaces or to the use of similarity metrics. The task of similarity search, namely, finding the "neighbors" of a given query based on similarity, is a fundamental building block in application domains such as information retrieval (web search engines, e-commerce, museum collections, medical image processing), pattern recognition, data mining, machine learning, and recommendation systems.

Formally, consider the set of all objects of interest $\mathcal{X}$, hereby referred to as points, data points, or exemplars, and let $\mathcal{S} \subset \mathcal{X}$ be a dataset containing N such objects. Let $d(x, y)$ denote a metric that captures the distance, or the extent

The support of NSF award 1910530 is gratefully acknowledged.

© The Author(s), under exclusive license to Springer Nature Switzerland AG 2022
T. Skopal et al. (Eds.): SISAP 2022, LNCS 13590, pp. 133–149, 2022.
https://doi.org/10.1007/978-3-031-17849-8_11

of dissimilarity, between $x, y \in \mathcal{X}$. The focus of this work is search in a *metric space*, *i.e.*, where the metric satisfies $d(x, y) = 0 \Leftrightarrow x = y$, $d(x, y) = d(y, x)$, and $d(x, z) \leq d(x, y) + d(y, z)$. Some approaches first embed the metric space in a Euclidean space, such as hashing, quantization, CNN, *etc.*, but this can distort relative distances. We define a hierarchical index structure for similarity search in a metric space.

In absence of an embedding space, notions of proximity, neighborhood, and topology are constructed through a graph. The two most popular graphs are the kNN graph [4], where each element is connected to its k nearest neighbors, and the Minimum Spanning Tree (MST) which is the spanning tree (connected tree involving all nodes) that has the least cumulative sum of distances over all links. However, the kNN graph is not necessarily connected: in clustered data, the k closest neighbors may be to one side of an element so that the kNN may not faithfully represent the spatial neighborhood, Fig. 1(c), in that only connections to one side are represented. Connectivity can be achieved with a sufficiently high choice of k, but that is at the expense of over-representing neighboring connections elsewhere, Fig. 2(a, b). A much better choice that captures the spatial layout in all "directions" is using a class of *proximity graphs*, which define a spatial neighborhood for every pair of points x_1 and x_2, and a connection is made if this spatial neighborhood does not contain any other points (also referred to as *empty-neighborhood graphs*). For example, a *Gabriel Graph* (GG) [8] connects two points $x_1, x_2 \in \mathcal{S}$ if the sphere with diameter $x_1 x_2$ is empty, or $d^2(x_3, x_1) + d^2(x_3, x_2) \geq d^2(x_1, x_2)$, $\forall x_3 \in \mathcal{S}$. Another important example is the *Relative Neighborhood Graph* (RNG) [12, 21] which connects x_1 and $x_2 \in S$ if the $lune(x_1, x_2)$, namely, the intersection of the two spheres of radius $x_1 x_2$ through centers x_1 and x_2, is empty, *i.e.*, if

$$\max(d(x_3, x_1), d(x_3, x_2)) \geq d(x_1, x_2), \forall x_3 \in \mathcal{S}. \qquad (1)$$

Other proximity graphs of interest include the Half-Space Graph (HSG), which is a superset of RNG and a t-spanner [1], the *Delaunay Triangulation* (DT) graph [3], and the β-skeleton graph [14]. Proximity graphs generally require consideration of all members x_3 of S for each pair (x_1, x_2) of S, and as such require $O(N^3)$ for naive construction. Note that 1NN $\subset$ MST $\subset$ RNG $\subset$ GG $\subset$ DT. See Fig. 1.

We adopt the use of RNG not only because *(i)* it is connected, but also because *(ii)* it is parameter free, in contrast to kNN, where k has to be specified, Tellez [20] where "b" and "t" have to be defined, and NSG [7] where "R" has to be defined, and also *(iii)* the RNG is a relatively sparse graph, unlike other choices presented in Fig. 1. Figure 9(e) shows the out degree of RNG grows very slowly with intrinsic dimension.

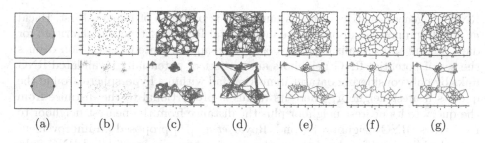

Fig. 1. (a) (top) Two points have an RNG connection if the "lune" between them does not contain other points. (bottom) Two points have a Gabriel Graph (GG) connection if the circle with the line segment between the points as diameter is empty. A comparison of graphs for representing both uniformly distributed points in $\mathcal{R}^2$ (top) and clustered data (bottom). (b) Points in 2D, (c) kNN, k = 8, (d) Tellez [20] b = 4, t = 4, (e) NSG [7], R = 8, (f) RNG, and (f) GG.

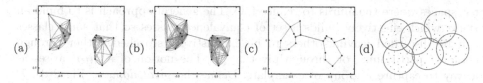

Fig. 2. The kNN connectivity is only based on distance between two elements and not on geometric distribution, (a) k = 5 and (b) k = 8. In contrast, the RNG (c) captures local geometry without regard to distance and requires no parameters. (d) Pivots (red dots) and associated radii define a pivot domain (red discs). (Color figure online)

There are a large number of applications that use the RNG. In graph-based visualization of large image datasets for browsing and interactive exploration, the RNG captures the local structure of the manifold [15–17]. In urban planning theory, RNGs have been used to model topographical arrangements of cities and the road networks. In internet networks, Escalante *et al.* [5] found that broadcasting over the RNG network is superior to blind flooding. De Vries *et al.* [22] propose to use the RNG to reveal related dynamics of page-level social media metrics. Han *et al.* [11] aims to improve the efficiency of a Support Vector Machine (SVM) classifier by using the RNG to extract probable support vectors from all the training samples. Goto *et al.* [9] use the RNG to reduce a training dataset consisting of handwritten digits to 10% of its original size. A related and more recent area is the selection of training data for Convolutional Neural Networks (CNNs) where the RNG is used to reduce the underlying redundancy of the dataset [18].

Despite such widespread use of RNG, there is not a large literature on efficient construction of the RNG in metric spaces. In Euclidean spaces, the notions of angle and direction allow for an efficient implementation, *e.g.*, an $O(N \log N)$ for N points in $\mathcal{R}^2$ [19], an $O(N)$ for uniformly distributed points in a rectangle [13], and an $O(N^2)$ for higher dimensions [19]. The construction of the

RNG for general metric spaces is limited to two groups of papers. First, Hacid *et al.* [10] propose an approximate incremental RNG construction algorithm for data mining and visualization purposes. This approximate construction defines the set of potential RNG neighbors and the set of potentially invalidated RNG links by only considering dataset items that fall within a hypersphere around the query's nearest neighbor, where its radius is proportional to the distance from the query to its nearest neighbor plus the distance from the nearest neighbor to its furthest RNG neighbor. Second, Rayar *et al.* [15] proposed an improvement over Hacid's algorithm by defining the set of potentially invalidated RNG links by the Lth edge neighbors of the query. While both these methods work in any metric space and provide significant speed-up over naive construction, they are *approximate* and thus lose all guarantees provided by the RNG, and make a significant number of errors, as will be shown by Table 1.

The main computational challenge in searching metric spaces is to reduce the number of distance computations which are expensive, in contrast to vector spaces where the aim is to reduce I/O. The general approach is to build an *index* which effectively builds a set of equivalence classes so that some classes can be discarded leaving others to be exhaustively searched, either through compact partitioning or through pivoting [2]. The notion of a *pivot* arises as a way to capture a group of exemplars. Define the *pivot domain*, Fig. 2(d), $\mathcal{D}$ of pivot p_i and domain radius r_i as, $\mathcal{D}(p_i, r_i) = \{x \in \mathcal{S} \mid d(x, p_i) \leq r_i\}$. While pivots do not necessarily need to be members of S, in a metric space which cannot generate new members a pivot is also an exemplar/data point. A sufficient number of pivots $\mathcal{P} = \{p_1, p_2, ..., p_M\} \subset \mathcal{S}$ are required to cover $\mathcal{S}$, *i.e.*, $\mathcal{S} = \bigcup_{i=1}^{M} \mathcal{D}(p_i, r_i)$. Observe that the knowledge of $d(x, p_i)$ bounds $d(x, y)$ for $y \in S_i$ as $d(y, p_i) - r_i \leq d(x, y) \leq d(y, p_i) + r_i$ using the triangle inequality. In the absence of an embedding Euclidean structure the triangle inequality is the only constraint available for relative ranking of distances between triplets of points. For simplicity we take $r_i = r$ in this paper.

The key aim of this paper is to design a hierarchical index that allows for the construction of the exact RNG and allows for efficient search of RNG neighbors of a given query Q. The contribution of the paper is to show that in a two-layer configuration of pivots and exemplars (data points) a novel graph structure, the Generalized Relative Neighborhood Graph (GRNG), allows for efficient and exact construction of RNG of the data points. Note that the RNG is a special case of GRNG when its parameter $r = 0$. In addition, we also show that the GRNG of any coarse-layer of pivots can guide the exact construction of the GRNG of any fine-layer pivots. This allows for a highly efficient, scalable, hierarchical construction involving multiple layers (for a dataset of 26 million points in $\mathcal{R}^2$ ten layers is optimal [6]). Observe that construction is incremental so that the index can be dynamically updated. Given a query, a search process locates it in the hierarchy by examining the coarsest layers, discarding all the exemplar domains for a majority of the pivots and then moving on to the next layers where finer-scale pivot children of a few select coarse-scale pivots need to be considered. This process is then repeated to the lowest layer, the exemplar domain. The query is then located in the RNG and its RNG neighbors are identified. The search process is highly efficient and logarithmic in the number of exemplars in all dimensions, Fig. 9(b, d).

The incremental construction of the index relies on the search component described above to locate the query in each layer, but in addition, in each layer new connections must be made and existing connections must be validated. The construction is done off-line in contrast to search which is typically done on-line. While the construction is exponential in both the number of exemplars and dimensions for uniformly distributed data, for practical applications where the data is clustered, the construction cost behaves much better. The experimental results summarized in Table 1 show that while our method gives the exact RNG neighbors, it is substantially faster in both constructing the RNG and in searching it.

2   Incremental Construction of the RNG

The incremental approach to constructing RNG assumes that $RNG(\mathcal{S})$ is available and computes $RNG(\mathcal{S} \cup Q)$ from it. The query Q is the newest element: *(i)* *Localize Q within $\mathcal{S}$:* finding the RNG Neighbors of Q. The naive approach would consider for all $x_i \in \mathcal{S}$ whether $\exists x_j \in lune(Q, x_i)$; all x_i with empty lunes are RNG neighbors of Q. Note that this involves $O(N^2)$ operations where $N = |\mathcal{S}|$, and this is clearly not scalable, and *(ii)* *Adding Q to the dataset:* When the task is search, the first step finds the RNG neighbors. If Q needs to be added, additionally all pairs of existing links between x_i and x_j need to be validated, whether $Q \in lune(x_i, x_j)$ in which case x_i and x_j are no longer RNG neighbors. This operation is on the order of $O(\alpha N)$ where α is the average out degree of the RNG, typically a small number. Thus, the localization step is significantly more computationally intensive than the validation step.

The remedy to indexing complexity is organization. Specifically, when exemplar groups are represented by pivots, many inferences can take place at the level of pivot domains without computing distances between Q and exemplars. The basic idea in this paper is to construct conditions on pivots that have implications for efficient incremental construction of RNG of exemplars. This is organized in seven stages: *i)* In Stages I, II, and III entire pivot domains $\mathcal{D}(p_i, r_i)$ or a significant number of exemplars x_i are discarded from considering RNG neighbor relations with Q by just measuring $d(Q, p_i)$; *ii)* Stages IV, V, and VI: pivots are used in invalidating potential RNG links with the remaining exemplars; *iii)* Stage VII: pivots are used to exclude entire domains during the RNG validation process of existing links. What relationship between p_i and p_j can prevent the formation of a RNG link between x_i and x_j?

Theorem 1. *Consider exemplars $x_i \in \mathcal{D}(p_i, r_i)$ and $x_j \in \mathcal{D}(p_j, r_j)$. Then*

$$\begin{cases} d(p_k, p_i) < d(p_i, p_j) - (2r_i + r_j) \\ d(p_k, p_j) < d(p_i, p_j) - (r_i + 2r_j) \end{cases} \Rightarrow \max(d(p_k, x_i), d(p_k, x_j)) < d(x_i, x_j)$$

$$(2)$$

This theorem, whose proof is in the full paper [6], states that a pivot p_k that falls in a lune defined by the intersection of the sphere at p_i with radius $d(p_i, p_j) - (2r_i + r_j)$ and the sphere at p_j with radius $d(p_i, p_j) - (r_i + 2r_j)$ also falls in the RNG lune of x_i and x_j, thereby invalidating the potential RNG link between x_i and x_j, *without computing $d(p_k, x_i)$ and $d(p_k, x_j)$!* This is a proximity relationship between p_i, p_j, and p_k, which effectively defines a novel type of graph.

Definition 1. *(Generalized Relative Neighborhood Graph (GRNG)): Two pivots $p_i, p_j \in \mathcal{P}$ have a GRNG link iff no pivots $p_k \in \mathcal{P}$ can be found inside the generalized lune defined by,*

$$\begin{cases} d(p_k, p_i) < d(p_i, p_j) - (2r_i + r_j) & \text{(3a)} \\ d(p_k, p_j) < d(p_i, p_j) - (r_i + 2r_j). & \text{(3b)} \end{cases}$$

Observe that GRNG($\mathcal{P}$) is just the RNG when $r_i = 0$, $\forall i$, thus it is a generalization of it, Fig. 3. Also, note that GRNG($\mathcal{P}$) is a superset of RNG($\mathcal{P}$) since lune(p_i, p_j) is larger than the generalized-lune(p_i, p_j), abbreviated as G-lune(p_i, p_j). This implies that the larger r_i and r_j are, the denser the graph is, until it is effectively the complete graph. This places a constraint on how large r_i and r_j can be. Furthermore, it is easy to show that GRNG($\mathcal{P}$) is a connected graph. In practice, all pivots share the same uniform radius, *i.e.*, $r_i = r, \forall i$. The single parameter r is the minimum for which the union of all pivot domains cover $\mathcal{S}$. Thus, the number of pivots M and r are inversely related. In what follows $d(Q, p_i), i = 1, 2, \ldots, M$ is computed.

Stage I: Pivot-Pivot Interaction: The most important implication of the GRNG($\mathcal{P}$) via Theorem 1, is that a lack of a GRNG link between p_i and p_j invalidates all potential links between their constituents. Stage I therefore begins by locating the pivot parents of Q in $\mathcal{P}$. If Q has no parents, Q is added to the set of pivots $\mathcal{P}$ and GRNG($\mathcal{P}$) is updated. Otherwise, Q can only have RNG links with the common GRNG neighbors of *all* of Q's parents. See Fig. 4.

Stage II: Query-Pivot Interaction: Stage I removes entire pivot domains from interacting with Q, namely, those exemplars in the domain of pivots that do not have GRNG links to *all* parents of Q. Note, however, that the GRNG lune is significantly reduced in size due to the increased radii, in comparison with RNG, *i.e.*, by $2r_i + r_j, r_i + 2r_j$ on each side. This stage enlarges the G-lune by considering Q itself as a virtual parent pivot with $r_Q = 0$.

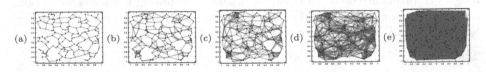

Fig. 3. GRNG of a set of 200 points in $[-1, 1]^2$ where all $r_i = r$ and for different selection of r: (a) $r = 0$, (b) $r = 0.01$, (c) $r = 0.02$, (d) $r = 0.04$, and (e) $r = 0.419$. When r exceeds $\frac{1}{6}$ the maximum distance between points it is the complete graph (e).

Proposition 1. *If p_k is in the G-lune of (p_i, r_i) and $(Q, r_Q = 0)$, i.e.,*

$$\begin{cases} d(Q, p_k) < d(Q, p_i) - r_i & \text{(4a)} \\ d(p_i, p_k) < d(Q, p_i) - 2r_i. & \text{(4b)} \end{cases}$$

Then, p_k is also in the RNG lune(Q, x_i) $\forall x_i \in \mathcal{D}(p_i, r_i)$, thereby invalidating it, i.e., $\max(d(p_k, Q), d(p_k, x_i)) < d(Q, x_i)$.

This proof is in the full paper [6]. Note that since Q is not really a pivot, we cannot simply lookup *GRNG* neighbors of it. Rather, Eqs. 4 must be explicitly checked for all pivots p_i that survive the elimination round of Stage I. Thus, additional entire pivot domains are eliminated, Fig. 4.

Stage III: Pivot-Exemplar Interaction: This stage is symmetric with Stage II by enlarging the G-lune, but instead of using Q as a virtual pivot, an exemplar is used a virtual, zero-radius pivot. These exemplar are constituents x_j of surviving pivots p_j.

Proposition 2. *If a pivot p_k falls in the G-lune of a parent (p_i, r_i) of Q and $(x_j, r_j = 0)$, i.e.,*

$$\begin{cases} d(p_k, p_i) < d(p_i, x_j) - 2r_i & \text{(5a)} \\ d(p_k, x_j) < d(p_i, x_j) - r_i, & \text{(5b)} \end{cases}$$

then $\max(d(p_k, Q), d(p_k, x_j)) < d(Q, x_j)$ and Q cannot have a RNG link with x_j.

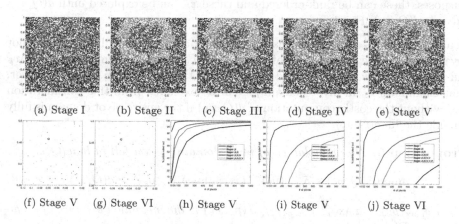

(a) Stage I   (b) Stage II   (c) Stage III   (d) Stage IV   (e) Stage V

(f) Stage V   (g) Stage VI   (h) Stage V   (i) Stage V   (j) Stage VI

Fig. 4. The savings achieved by Stages I–VI for a GRNG-RNG Hierarchy with $M = 200$ pivots on a dataset of $N = 10,000$ uniformly distributed points in $[-1, 1]^2$ where the green area shows remaining exemplars after each stage. (f), (g), (i), and (j) are zoomed in. (Color figure online)

This proof is in the full paper [6]. In Stage III, then, for all parents of Q, (p_i, r_i), and each exemplar x_j of the remaining pivots p_j, Eqs. 5 are checked which if valid rule out the exemplar x_j. Note that once a p_k is found that eliminates x_j, the process stops, so it is judicious to pick p_k in order of distance to p_i as closer pivots are more likely to fall in the G-lune of p_i and x_j, Fig. 4.

Stage IV: Pivot-Mediated Exemplar-Exemplar Interactions: The aim of the next three stages is to prevent brute-force examination of all exemplars x_k potentially invalidating RNG link(Q,x_i) by falling in lune(Q, x_i). In Stage IV only pivots are checked, $i.e.$, whether pivot p_k satisfies

$$\max\left(d\left(p_k, Q\right), d\left(p_k, x_i\right)\right) < d\left(Q, x_i\right), \quad k = 1, 2, ..., M. \tag{6}$$

Observe that only p_k for which $d(p_k, Q) < d(Q, x_i)$ need to be considered, and for those $d(p_k, x_i) < d(Q, x_i)$ is checked. Note that if one p_k satisfies this, link(Q, x_j) is invalidated and the process is stopped, Fig. 4.

Stage V: Exemplar-Mediated Exemplar-Exemplar Interactions: In this stage, all the exemplars x_k which may invalidate the potential RNG link between Q and x_i are explored by checking

$$\max\left(d\left(Q, x_k\right), d\left(x_i, x_k\right)\right) < d\left(Q, x_i\right). \tag{7}$$

Observe that since the process stops if one x_k falls in the lune, so it is judicious to begin with a select group of x_k that would more likely fall in the lune(Q, x_i). First, the closest neighbors of x_i can be found by consulting the RNG neighbors of x_i and neighbors of neighbors, and so on until $d(x_i, x_k)$ exceeds $d(Q, x_i)$. Second, since some distances $d(Q, x_k)$ have been computed and cached for other purposes, these can be rank-ordered and these x_k can be explored until $d(Q, x_k)$ exceeds $d(Q, x_j)$, Fig. 4.

Stage VI: RNG Link Verification: If the potential RNG link(Q, x_i) is not invalidated by the select group of exemplars x_k, the entire remaining set of x_k must exhaustively be considered to complete the verification. Note, however, that exemplars x_k in pivot domain p_k can be excluded from this consideration and without the costly computation of $d(Q, x_k)$ if the entire pivot domain is fully outside the lune(Q, x_i):

Proposition 3. *No exemplar x_k of pivot domain p_k can fall in lune(Q,x_i) if*

$$\max(d\left(Q, p_k\right) - \delta_{\max}(p_k), d\left(x_i, p_k\right) - \delta_{\max}(p_k)) \geq d(Q, x_i), \tag{8}$$

where $\delta_{\max}(p_k) = \max_{\forall x_k, d(x_k, p_k) \leq r_k} d\left(p_k, x_k\right)$ is the maximum distance of exemplar $x_k \in \mathcal{D}(p_k, r_k)$ from p_k.

This proof can be found in the full paper [6]. For the remaining pivot domains, the computation of $d(Q, x_k)$ can still be avoided for some exemplar x_k:

Algorithm 1. RNG Localization for Query Q in GRNG-RNG Hierarchy.

Input: Query Q, pivots $\mathcal{P}$, radius r_i for $p_i \in \mathcal{P}$, GRNG($\mathcal{P}$), children $C(p_i)$ for
$p_i \in \mathcal{P}$, max child distance $\delta_{max}(p_i)$ for $p_i \in \mathcal{P}$, exemplar $\mathcal{X}$, RNG(X),
parents $P(x_i)$ for $x_i \in \mathcal{X}$, GRNG neighbors GRNG(x_i) for $x_i \in \mathcal{X}$.

Output: RNG neighbors of Q, Parents of Q, GRNG neighbors of Q.

1 **begin**

2   **Stage 1:** Find parents $P(Q) = \{p_i \in \mathcal{P} : d(Q, p_i) \leq r_i\}$. Collect potential
GRNG neighbors of Q as $\mathcal{A}(\mathcal{P}) = \bigcup_{p_i \in P(Q)}$ GRNG(p_i). If $|P(Q)| = 0$,
$\mathcal{A}(\mathcal{P}) = \mathcal{P}$.

3   **Stage 2:** Find GRNG(Q) by validating all potential neighbors $p_j \in \mathcal{A}(\mathcal{P})$.
If no $p_k \in \mathcal{P}$ satisfies both $d(Q, p_k) < d(Q, p_j) - r_j$ and
$d(p_j, p_k) < d(Q, p_j) - 2r_j$, then p_j is added to GRNG(Q).

4   **Stage 3:** Collect potential RNG neighbors of Q as $\mathcal{A}(\mathcal{X}) = \bigcup_{p_i \in P(Q)} C(p_i)$.
Remove $x_j \in \mathcal{A}(\mathcal{X})$ if any $p_j \in P(x_j)$ is not in GRNG(Q). Remove
$x_j \in \mathcal{A}(\mathcal{X})$ if any $p_i \in P(Q)$ is not in GRNG(x_j).

5   **Stage 4:** Consider invalidation of link(Q, x_j) for $x_j \in \mathcal{A}(\mathcal{X})$ by checking
$p_k \in GRNG(Q)$ for interference. If any p_k satisfies both $d(Q, p_k) < d(Q, x_j)$
and $d(x_j, p_k) < d(Q, x_j)$, then x_j is removed from $\mathcal{A}(\mathcal{X})$.

6   **Stage 5:** Consider invalidation of link(Q, x_j) for $x_j \in \mathcal{A}(\mathcal{X})$ by checking
$x_k \in \mathcal{A}(\mathcal{X})$ for interference. If any x_k satisfies both $d(Q, x_k) < d(Q, x_j)$ and
$d(x_j, x_k) < d(Q, x_j)$, then x_j is removed from $\mathcal{A}(\mathcal{X})$.

7   **Stage 6:** Consider invalidation of link(Q, x_j) for $x_j \in \mathcal{A}(\mathcal{X})$ by performing
exhaustive check for interference. Use $\delta_{max}(p_k)$ and $C(p_k)$ for $p_k \in \mathcal{P}$ with
Propositions 3 and 4 to narrow down the set of potentially interfering points
x_k. If no x_k satisfies both $d(Q, x_k) < d(Q, x_j)$ and $d(x_j, x_k) < d(Q, x_j)$, then
x_j is added to RNG(Q).

8 **end**

Proposition 4. *Any exemplar x_k in the pivot domain of p_k for which*

$$\max(d(Q, p_k) - d(x_k, p_k), d(x_i, p_k) - d(x_k, p_k)) \geq d(Q, x_i) \qquad (9)$$

falls outside lune(Q, x_i).

The proof is in the full paper [6]. Any exemplar x_k which is not ruled out
by Proposition 3 and 4 must now be explicitly considered. If none are in the
lune(Q, x_i), then link(Q, x_i) is validated.

Stage VII: Existing RNG Link Validation: The above six stages locate Q
in the RNG and identify its RNG neighbors. This is sufficient for a RNG search
query. However, if the dataset $\mathcal{S}$ is to be augmented with Q, a final check must
be made as to which existing RNG links would be removed by the presence of Q.
While this is a brute force $O(\alpha N)$ operation, it is important to avoid computing
$d(Q, x_i)$ for all $x_i \in \mathcal{S}$. Observe that Q does not threaten links that are "too far"
from it. This notion can be implemented if two parameters are maintained, one
for exemplars and one for pivots:

$$\bar{\mu}_{\max}(x_i) = \max_{x_j \in RNG(x_i)} d(x_i, x_j), \mu_{\max}(p_i) = \max_{d(x_i, p_i) \leq r_i} [\bar{\mu}_{\max}(x_i) + d(x_i, p_i)].$$

(10)

Proposition 5. *A query Q does not invalidate RNG links at x_i if $d(Q, x_i) \geq$ $\bar{\mu}_{\max}(x_i)$. A query Q does not invalidate any RNG link of any exemplars $x_i \in$ $\mathcal{D}(p_i, r_i)$, if $d(Q, p_i) > \mu_{\max}(p_i)$.*

The proof is in the full paper [6]. This proposition suggests a three-step procedure: (i) remove entire pivot domains if $d(Q, p_i) \geq \mu_{\max}(p_i)$; (ii) remove all exemplars in the remaining pivot domains for which $d(Q, x_i) \geq \bar{\mu}_{\max}(x_i)$; (iii) check the RNG condition explicitly for the remaining x_i and any x_j it links to. This completes the incremental update of $\mathcal{S}$ to $\mathcal{S} \cup \{Q\}$.

Experimental Results. The improvements due to this two-layer GRNG-RNG configuration are examined in experiments by varying dimensions and number of exemplars. Figure 5 examines the number of distance computations required for construction and search per stage as a function of the number of pivots. Observe that the first stage cost increases linearly while the remaining stages experience an exponential drop. This is also observed for search distances per query. The total cost thus has an optimum for each. Since construction is offline while search is online, the number of pivots is optimized for the latter. Figure 5(c) examines the search costs for different dimensions. It is clear that search time rises exponentially with increasing dimension. Observe from Fig. 5(b) that additional pivots would have enjoyed the exponential drop in all stages except for Stage I which involves GRNG Construction. If the cost of this stage as a function of M can be lowered, the overall cost will be decreased dramatically. The next section proposes a two-layer scheme for constructing GRNG using a coarser GRNG in the same way the RNG construction was guided by a GRNG.

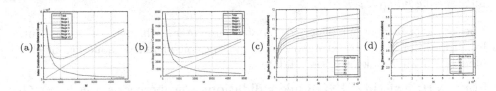

Fig. 5. Stage-by-stage distance computations for construction (a) and search (b) across different numbers of pivots M for N = 102,400 exemplars uniformly distributed in 2D. Comparison of our GRNG-RNG hierarchy for RNG construction (c) and search (d) to a Brute Force RNG algorithm that precomputes all distances.

3   Incremental Construction of the GRNG

The question naturally arises whether the construction of the GRNG of the pivot layer itself can benefit from a two-layer pivot-based indexing approach similar to the construction of the same for the RNG of the exemplars. Formally, let $\bar{\mathcal{P}} = \{(\bar{p}_i, \bar{r}_i)|i = 1, 2, \ldots, \bar{M}\}$ denote pivots obtained from the previous section; refer to these as *fine-scale pivots* to distinguish them from the *coarse-scale pivots* $\mathcal{P} = \{(P_i, r_i)|i = 1, 2, \ldots, M\}$. The idea is for each coarse-scale pivot p_i to represent a number of fine-scale pivots $\bar{p}_i$. Define the *Relative Pivot Domain* $\mathcal{D}(p_i, r_i)$ as the set of all fine-scale domain pivots $(\bar{p}_i, \bar{r}_i)$ whose entire exemplar domain is within a radius of r_i, i.e., $d(p_i, \bar{p}_i) \leq r_i - \bar{r}_i$. In this scenario, a query Q is either a fine-scale pivot for now with r_Q matching that of other fine-scale pivots, or it can be considered a fine-scale pivot with zero radius. The query computes $d(Q, p_i), i = 1, 2, \ldots, M$ and if $d(Q, p_i) < r_i - r_Q$, p_i is a parent of Q. The question then arises as to what kind of graph structure for the coarse-scale pivots can efficiently locate a query in the GRNG of the fine-scale pivots. The following shows that the GRNG of coarse-scale pivots can accomplish this:

Stage I: "Coarse-Scale Pivot" - "Coarse-Scale Pivot" Interactions:

Theorem 2. *Consider two fine-scale pivots* $(\bar{p}_i, \bar{r}_i) \in \mathcal{D}(p_i, r_i)$ *and* $(\bar{p}_j, \bar{r}_j) \in \mathcal{D}(p_j, r_j)$. *Then, if* (p_i, r_i) *and* (p_j, r_j) *do not share a GRNG link,* $(\bar{p}_i, \bar{r}_i)$ *and* $(\bar{p}_j, \bar{r}_j)$ *cannot have a GRNG link either.*

The proof is in the full paper [6]. This theorem, in analogy to Theorem 1 of the previous section, allows for the efficient localization of a query Q for search in stating that the fine-scale GRNG neighbors of Q are only among children of coarse-scale GRNG neighbors of Q's parents, thus, removing entire pivot domains of non-neighbors, see Fig. 6.

Stage II: Query - "Coarse-Scale Pivot" Interactions: In this stage, (Q, r_Q) is considered as a virtual pivot.

Proposition 6. *The query* Q *does not form GRNG links with any children* $(\bar{p}_i, \bar{r}_i)$ *of those coarse-scale pivots* (p_i, r_i) *that do not form a GRNG link with* Q *when considered as a virtual pivot with* $r_Q = 0$. *The proof is in the full paper [6].*

Stage III: "Coarse-Scale Pivot" - "Fine-Scale Pivot" Interactions: This stage is mirror symmetric to Stage II, except that instead of treating Q as a virtual coarse-scale pivot, a specific fine-scale pivot $(\bar{p}_j, \bar{r}_j)$ is considered a virtual pivot.

Proposition 7. *If* $(\bar{p}_j, \bar{r}_j)$ *does not form a coarse-scale GRNG link with a parent* (p_i, r_i) *of* Q, *then* $(\bar{p}_j, \bar{r}_j)$ *does not form a fine-scale GRNG link with* (Q, r_Q).

The proof is simply an application of Theorem (2) with $(\bar{p}_j, \bar{r}_j)$ considered as both a fine-scale and a coarse-scale pivot. This third stage rules out all the remaining fine-scale pivots which are not a GRNG neighbor of **all** Q's parents, Fig. 6 (Fig. 7).

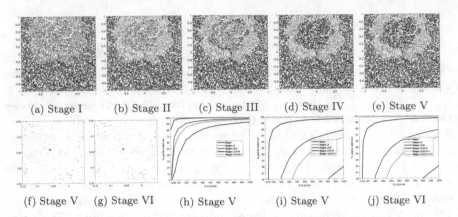

(a) Stage I   (b) Stage II   (c) Stage III   (d) Stage IV   (e) Stage V

(f) Stage V   (g) Stage VI   (h) Stage V   (i) Stage V   (j) Stage VI

Fig. 6. The savings achieved by Stages I–VI for a GRNG-GRNG Hierarchy of $M = 200$ pivots with radius $r = 0.005$ on a dataset of $10{,}000$ uniformly distributed points in $[-1, 1]^2$ where the green area shows remaining exemplars after each stage. (f), (g), (i), and (j) are zoomed in. (Color figure online)

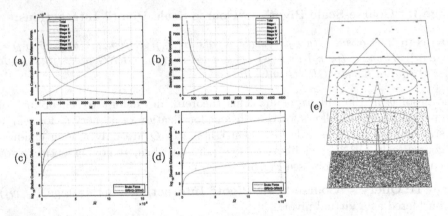

Fig. 7. Stage by stage analysis for GRNG-GRNG hierarchy for $\bar{M} = 102{,}400$ uniformly distributed fine-scale pivots in 2D as a function of M, the number of coarse-scale pivots. The number of distance computations for construction (a) and search (b) show Stage I is increasing with M while other stages exponentially decay with an optimum for each in total. The improvements of GRNG-GRNG with respect to brute-force as a function of M for construction (c) and search (d) distances is significant. (e) The monotonically increasing Stage I in (a–b) suggest using a multi-layer hierarchy.

Stage IV: "Coarse-Scale Pivot"–Mediated "Fine-Scale Pivot" Interactions: All the GRNG links between the remaining fine-scale pivots and Q must now be investigated. In Stage IV only coarse-scale pivots are considered as potential occupiers of the G-lune by probing

$$
\begin{cases}
d\left(p_k, Q\right) < d\left(Q, \bar{p}_{\bar{j}}\right) - \left(2\bar{r}_Q + \bar{r}_{\bar{j}}\right) & \text{(11a)} \\
d\left(p_k, \bar{p}_{\bar{j}}\right) < d\left(Q, \bar{p}_{\bar{j}}\right) - \left(\bar{r}_Q + 2\bar{r}_{\bar{j}}\right). & \text{(11b)}
\end{cases}
$$

Since $d(Q, \bar{p}_{\bar{j}}) - (2r_Q + \bar{r}_{\bar{j}})$ is a known value, only pivots p_k closer to Q than this value need to be considered. Similarly, for $d(\bar{p}_{\bar{j}}, \bar{r}_{\bar{j}}) \in \mathcal{D}(p_j, r_j)$, observe that $d(p_k, \bar{p}_{\bar{j}}) \geq d(p_k, p_j) - (r_j - \bar{r}_{\bar{j}})$, so that if $d(p_k, p_j) \geq d(Q, \bar{p}_{\bar{j}}) - (r_Q + 2\bar{r}_{\bar{j}}) + (r_j - \bar{r}_{\bar{j}})$, then Eq. (11b) does not hold and there is no need to consider such p_k. Thus, very few p_k are actually considered, Fig. 6.

Stage V: "Fine-Scale Pivot" – Mediated "Fine-Scale Pivot" Interactions: Those links between Q and $\bar{p}_{\bar{j}}$ that survive the pivot test must now test against occupancy of G-lune$(Q, \bar{p}_{\bar{j}})$ by exemplars $\bar{p}_{\bar{k}}$. In this stage, a select group of $\bar{p}_{\bar{k}}$, namely those close to Q and $\bar{p}_{\bar{j}}$ which are more likely to be in G-lune$(Q, \bar{p}_{\bar{j}})$ are considered, leaving the rest to Stage VI. Specifically, these are the $k = 25$ nearest neighbors of Q and $\bar{p}_{\bar{j}}$, Fig. 6.

Stage VI: "Fine-Scale Pivot" "Fine-Scale Pivot" Interactions: Very few fine-scale pivots $\bar{p}_{\bar{j}}$ remain at this stage. These need to be validated with all other fine-scale pivots $\bar{p}_{\bar{k}}$. However, the following proposition prevents consideration of a majority of them. Define

$$\delta_{\max}(p_k) = \max_{\forall \bar{p}_{\bar{k}}, \, d(p_k, \bar{p}_{\bar{k}}) \leq (r_k - \bar{r}_{\bar{k}})} d(p_k, \bar{p}_{\bar{k}}). \tag{12}$$

Proposition 8. *All fine-scale pivots* $(\bar{p}_{\bar{k}}, \bar{r}_{\bar{k}}) \in \mathcal{D}(p_k, r_k)$ *satisfying*

$$\begin{cases} d(Q, p_k) - \delta_{\max}(p_k) \geq d\left(Q, \bar{p}_{\bar{j}}\right) - \left(2\bar{r}_Q + \bar{r}_{\bar{j}}\right) & \text{(13a)} \\ d\left(\bar{p}_{\bar{j}}, p_k\right) - \delta_{\max}(p_k) \geq d\left(Q, \bar{p}_{\bar{j}}\right) - \left(2\bar{r}_{\bar{j}} + \bar{r}_Q\right) & \text{(13b)} \end{cases}$$

fall outside the G-lune$(Q, \bar{p}_{\bar{j}})$, for a query $(Q, \bar{r}_Q)$ and a fine-scale pivot $(\bar{p}_{\bar{j}}, \bar{r}_{\bar{j}})$.

The proof is in the full paper [6]. This proposition excludes entire pivot domains from the validation process. The following proposition further restricts the remaining sets.

Proposition 9. *All fine-scale pivots* $(\bar{p}_{\bar{k}}, \bar{r}_{\bar{k}}) \in \mathcal{D}(p_k, r_k)$ *satisfying*

$$\begin{cases} d(Q, p_k) - d(p_k, \bar{p}_{\bar{k}}) \geq d\left(Q, \bar{p}_{\bar{j}}\right) - \left(2\bar{r}_Q + \bar{r}_{\bar{j}}\right) & \text{(14a)} \\ d\left(\bar{p}_{\bar{j}}, p_k\right) - d(p_k, \bar{p}_{\bar{k}}) \geq d\left(Q, \bar{p}_{\bar{j}}\right) - \left(\bar{r}_Q + 2\bar{r}_{\bar{j}}\right), & \text{(14b)} \end{cases}$$

falls outside the GRNG-lune$(Q, \bar{p}_{\bar{j}})$ for a query $(Q, \bar{r}_Q)$ and a fine-scale pivot $(\bar{p}_{\bar{j}}, \bar{r}_{\bar{j}})$.

The proof is in the full paper [6]. After the majority of fine-scale pivots $(\bar{p}_{\bar{k}}, \bar{r}_{\bar{k}})$ have been eliminated, the remaining ones must test the two GRNG conditions. For efficiency, if first condition $d(Q, \bar{p}_{\bar{k}}) < d(Q, \bar{p}_{\bar{j}} - (2\bar{r}_Q + \bar{r}_{\bar{j}})$ does not hold, the second condition $d(\bar{p}_{\bar{j}}, \bar{p}_{\bar{k}}) < d(Q, \bar{p}_{\bar{j}} - (\bar{r}_Q + 2\bar{r}_{\bar{j}})$ need not be tested, Fig. 6.

Stage VII: "Coarse-Scale Pivot" – "Fine-Scale Pivot" Validations: The incremental construction requires checking which existing GRNG links may be invalidated by the addition of Q. Define first,

$$\begin{cases} \bar{\mu}_{\max}(\bar{p}_{\bar{i}}) = \max_{\bar{p}_{\bar{j}}, \mathrm{GRNG}(\bar{p}_{\bar{i}})} \left[d\left(\bar{p}_{\bar{i}}, \bar{p}_{\bar{j}}\right) - (2\bar{r}_{\bar{i}} + \bar{r}_{\bar{j}}) \right] & \text{(15a)} \\[2ex] \mu_{\max}(p_i) = \max_{\forall (\bar{p}_{\bar{i}}, \bar{r}_{\bar{i}}) \in \mathcal{D}(p_i, r_i)} \left[\bar{\mu}_{\max}(\bar{p}_{\bar{i}}) + d(p_i, \bar{p}_{\bar{i}}) \right]. & \text{(15b)} \end{cases}$$

Proposition 10. *The insertion of Q does not invalidate any GRNG links involving fine-scale pivot $\bar{p}_{\bar{i}}$ for which*

$$d(Q, \bar{p}_{\bar{i}}) \geq \bar{\mu}_{\max}(\bar{p}_{\bar{i}}). \tag{16}$$

Furthermore, the insertion of Q does not interfere with the GRNG link involving fine-scale pivots $(\bar{p}_{\bar{i}}, \bar{r}_{\bar{i}}) \in \mathcal{D}(p_i, r_i)$ if

$$d(Q, p_i) \geq \mu_{\max}(p_i). \tag{17}$$

The proof is in the full paper [6]. The proposition suggests a three-step approach to examining existing links: (i) Remove all coarse-scale pivot domains p_i satisfying Eq. 17; (ii) Remove all fine-scale pivot domains $(\bar{p}_{\bar{i}}, \bar{r}_{\bar{i}})$ satisfying Eq. 16; (iii) For any remaining fine-scale pivot $(\bar{p}_{\bar{i}}, \bar{r}_{\bar{i}})$ connecting with $(\bar{p}_{\bar{j}}, \bar{r}_{\bar{j}})$, if Q is in the G-lune$(\bar{p}_{\bar{i}}, \bar{p}_{\bar{j}})$, then the link needs to be removed.

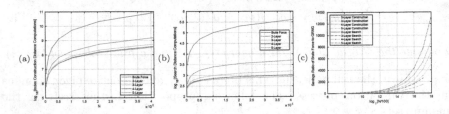

Fig. 8. Comparing the efficiency of multi-layer GRNG hierarchies on 2D uniformly distributed data to a Brute Force algorithm that would precompute all pairwise distances (a) for RNG construction or precompute all N distances to dataset members (b) for search. (c) The ratio of distance computation savings across N and number of layers.

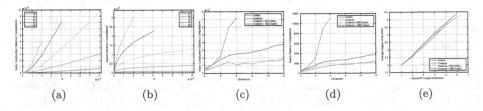

Fig. 9. The distance computations for index construction (a) and search (b) increases as a function of number of exemplars and dimensions. However, with clustered data (c) (d), even with outliers, both construction costs and search distances increase much less rapidly. (e) The average degree of the RNG is related to the intrinsic dimensionality.

Table 1. Results for real world datasets. (top) Corel, $N = 68,040$ in 57D, (middle) MNIST, $N = 60,000$ instances with 64D embeddings obtained through a neural network, and (bottom) LA, $N = 1,073,727$ instances in 2D. Accuracy is established by comparison to the brute-force construction for the first two datasets, but for the last dataset, both the brute-force method and the algorithm by *Hacid et al.* are impractical to run on a dataset of such size. The accuracy of Rayar *et al.* in this case is found by comparing to our method. The last 100 data points are reserved as a test set for search.

Dataset	Algorithm	Total links	Extra (+) & Missing (−) Links	Average degree	Search distances	Index construction distances
Corel $N = 68k$	Hacid *et al.*	212,211	+21,802/−4	6.2378	177,972.36	9,823,840,198,726
	Rayar *et al.*	190,908	+535/−40	5.6116	169,575.08	6,432,673,175
	Ours	190,413	+0/−0	5.5971	43,729.20	1,611,369,217
MNIST $N = 60k$	Hacid *et al.*	118,248	+3,778/−3	3.9416	87,713.10	1,430,022,984,523
	Rayar *et al.*	114,893	+865/−445	3.8298	88,172.04	2,639,416,420
	Ours	114,473	+0/−0	3.8158	10,058.90	407,689,553
LA $N = 1M$	Hacid *et al.*	Impractical				
	Rayar *et al.*	1,277,369	+3,254/−33,706	2.3793	2,147,498.42	1,153,035,099,784
	Ours	1,307,821	-	2.4360	1,020.71	1,042,175,220

4 Experiments

Experiments on uniformly distributed and clustered synthetic data in $\mathcal{R}^d$ show the effectiveness of the proposed approach. Note that for all datasets where brute-force is possible, the RNG has been validated for exactness. Figure 8(a) shows that our method is effective in uniformly distributed data and a hierarchy helps, although the optimal number of layers depends on N. Figure Fig. 8(b) shows that search is extremely efficient and is essentially logarithmic in N. Figure 9 shows that construction costs are exponential in N and dimension d for uniform data (but search remains logarithmic), in contrast to clustered data where both construction and search costs are well-behaved, Fig. 9(c, d). Figure 9(e) shows that the connectivity of RNG is effectively linear in intrinsic dimension of the data. Experiments on several real-world datasets, namely, COREL, MNIST, and LA. For MNIST, a neural network trained using triplet loss was used to reduce the 784D Euclidean representation into 64D. The results are shown in Table 1. These results show that our method is significantly more efficient while also producing the exact RNG.

References

1. Chavez, E., et al.: Half-space proximal: a new local test for extracting a bounded dilation spanner of a unit disk graph. In: Anderson, J.H., Prencipe, G., Wattenhofer, R. (eds.) OPODIS 2005. LNCS, vol. 3974, pp. 235–245. Springer, Heidelberg (2006). https://doi.org/10.1007/11795490_19
2. Chávez, E., Navarro, G., Baeza-Yates, R., Marroquín, J.L.: Searching in metric spaces. ACM Comput. Surv. (CSUR) **33**(3), 273–321 (2001)
3. Delaunay, B.: Sur la sphère vide. A la mémoire de Georges Voronoï. Bulletin de l'Académie des Sciences de l'URSS, pp. 793–800 (1934)

4. Dong, W., Moses, C., Li, K.: Efficient k-nearest neighbor graph construction for generic similarity measures. In: Proceedings of the 20th International Conference on World Wide Web, pp. 577–586 (2011)
5. Escalante, O., Pérez, T., Solano, J., Stojmenovic, I.: RNG-based searching and broadcasting algorithms over internet graphs and peer-to-peer computing systems. In: The 3rd ACS/IEEE International Conference on Computer Systems and Applications, p. 17. IEEE (2005)
6. Foster, C., Sevilmis, B., Kimia, B.: Generalized Relative Neighborhood Graph (GRNG) for Similarity Search. arXiv preprint (2022)
7. Fu, C., Xiang, C., Wang, C., Cai, D.: Fast approximate nearest neighbor search with the navigating spreading-out graph. Proc. VLDB Endow. **12**(5), 461–474 (2019)
8. Gabriel, K.R., Sokal, R.R.: A new statistical approach to geographic variation analysis. Syst. Zool. **18**(3), 259–278 (1969)
9. Goto, M., Ishida, R., Uchida, S.: Preselection of support vector candidates by relative neighborhood graph for large-scale character recognition. In: 2015 13th International Conference on Document Analysis and Recognition (ICDAR), pp. 306–310 (2015)
10. Hacid, H., Yoshida, T.: Incremental neighborhood graphs construction for multidimensional databases indexing. In: Kobti, Z., Wu, D. (eds.) AI 2007. LNCS (LNAI), vol. 4509, pp. 405–416. Springer, Heidelberg (2007). https://doi.org/10.1007/978-3-540-72665-4_35
11. Han, D., Han, C., Yang, Y., Liu, Y., Mao, W.: Pre-extracting method for SVM classification based on the non-parametric K-NN rule. In: 2008 19th International Conference on Pattern Recognition, pp. 1–4. IEEE (2008)
12. Jaromczyk, J.W., Toussaint, G.T.: Relative neighborhood graphs and their relatives. Proc. IEEE **80**(9), 1502–1517 (1992)
13. Katajainen, J., Nevalainen, O., Teuhola, J.: A linear expected-time algorithm for computing planar relative neighbourhood graphs. Inf. Process. Lett. **25**(2), 77–86 (1987)
14. Kirkpatrick, D.G., Radke, J.D.: A framework for computational morphology. In: Machine Intelligence and Pattern Recognition, vol. 2, pp. 217–248. Elsevier (1985)
15. Rayar, F., Barrat, S., Bouali, F., Venturini, G.: An approximate proximity graph incremental construction for large image collections indexing. In: Esposito, F., Pivert, O., Hacid, M.-S., Raś, Z.W., Ferilli, S. (eds.) ISMIS 2015. LNCS (LNAI), vol. 9384, pp. 59–68. Springer, Cham (2015). https://doi.org/10.1007/978-3-319-25252-0_7
16. Rayar, F., Barrat, S., Bouali, F., Venturini, G.: Incremental hierarchical indexing and visualisation of large image collections. In: 24th European Symposium on Artificial Neural Networks, Computational Intelligence and Machine Learning (2016)
17. Rayar, F., Barrat, S., Bouali, F., Venturini, G.: A viewable indexing structure for the interactive exploration of dynamic and large image collections. ACM Trans. Knowl. Discov. Data (TKDD) **12**(1), 1–26 (2018)
18. Rayar, F., Goto, M., Uchida, S.: CNN training with graph-based sample preselection: application to handwritten character recognition. In: 2018 13th IAPR International Workshop on Document Analysis Systems (DAS), pp. 19–24. IEEE (2018)
19. Supowit, K.J.: The relative neighborhood graph, with an application to minimum spanning trees. J. ACM (JACM) **30**(3), 428–448 (1983)

20. Tellez, E.S., Ruiz, G., Chavez, E., Graff, M.: Local search methods for fast near neighbor search. arXiv preprint arXiv:1705.10351 (2017)
21. Toussaint, G.T.: The relative neighbourhood graph of a finite planar set. Pattern Recogn. **12**(4), 261–268 (1980)
22. de Vries, N.J., Arefin, A.S., Mathieson, L., Lucas, B., Moscato, P.: Relative neighborhood graphs uncover the dynamics of social media engagement. In: Li, J., Li, X., Wang, S., Li, J., Sheng, Q.Z. (eds.) ADMA 2016. LNCS (LNAI), vol. 10086, pp. 283–297. Springer, Cham (2016). https://doi.org/10.1007/978-3-319-49586-6_19

A Ptolemaic Partitioning Mechanism

Richard Connor[(✉)]

University of St Andrews, St Andrews, Scotland
rchc@st-andrews.ac.uk

Abstract. For many years, exact metric search relied upon the property of triangle inequality to give a lower bound on uncalculated distances. Two exclusion mechanisms derive from this property, generally known as pivot exclusion and hyperplane exclusion. These mechanisms work in any proper metric space and are the basis of many metric indexing mechanisms. More recently, the Ptolemaic and four-point lower bound properties have been shown to give tighter bounds in some subclasses of metric space.

Both triangle inequality and the four-point lower bound directly imply straightforward *partitioning* mechanisms: that is, a method of dividing a finite space according to a fixed partition, in order that one or more classes of the partition can be eliminated from a search at query time. However, up to now, no partitioning principle has been identified for the Ptolemaic inequality, which has been used only as a filtering mechanism. Here, a novel partitioning mechanism for the Ptolemaic lower bound is presented. It is always better than either pivot or hyperplane partitioning. While the exclusion condition itself is weaker than Hilbert (four-point) exclusion, its calculation is cheaper. Furthermore, it can be combined with Hilbert exclusion to give a new maximum for exclusion power with respect to the number of distances measured per query.

Keywords: Metric search · Partitioning · Ptolemaic inequality · Supermetric space

1   Background and Related Work

The context of interest is querying a large finite space (S, d) which is a subset of an infinite metric space (U, d).

In most general terms, querying the space (S, d) with query $q \in U$ is the task of finding a subset $\{s \leftarrow S \mid d(q, s) \leq t\}$, for some value t which gives a suitable size of solution set. It is generally assumed that $|S|$ is large or the cost of applying the function d is high, and so the simple solution of applying $d(q, s)$ to all $s \in S$ is intractable [1,10].

Table 1 gives a summary of these and other notations used throughout the article.

© The Author(s), under exclusive license to Springer Nature Switzerland AG 2022
T. Skopal et al. (Eds.): SISAP 2022, LNCS 13590, pp. 150–163, 2022.
https://doi.org/10.1007/978-3-031-17849-8_12

Table 1. Notation used throughout

Symbols	Meaning
(U, d)	An infinite metric space with domain U and distance d
(S, d)	A large finite space $S \subset U$ over which search is performed
P	A small reference set $P \subset U$, usually $P \subset S$
$u, u_0, u_1, \ldots$	Elements of the infinite domain U
$s, s_0, s_1, \ldots$	Elements of the finite domain S
$p, p_0, p_1, \ldots$	Elements of the reference set P
M	A fixed radius used to define a partition with a given $p \in P$
q, t	A query $q \in U$ associated with a numeric query threshold t
$\mathcal{P}$	A partition of S defined according to distances to P
$\mathcal{S}$	A class of $\mathcal{P}$ which may be excluded given a particular q, t
$\mathcal{Q}$	A subset of U defined according to a particular q, t
$\mathbb{R}^n$	An n-dimensional real domain
ℓ_2	The Euclidean distance metric
τ	A numeric parameter of the Ptolemaic partitioning mechanism ($\tau \geq 0.5$, typically $\tau \approx 1$)

1.1 Filtering and Partitioning

All metric search solutions rely upon algebraic properties of (U, d). A relatively small set of distinguished reference points $P = \{p_0, \ldots, p_m\}$ (typically, $P \subset S$) is used to avoid direct calculation of $d(q, s)$, after the distances $d(s, P)$ and $d(q, P)$ have been calculated. $d(s, P)$ is calculated ahead of query time, during a pre-processing phase. Two types of usage are distinguished as follows:

filtering: given a query $q \in U$, a specific datum $s \in S$, and the distances $d(q, P)$ and $d(s, P)$, it may be possible to determine that $d(q, s) > t$ for some t without having to calculate $d(q, s)$.

partitioning: given a partition $\mathcal{P}$ of S determined at pre-processing time with respect to $d(S, P)$, and the distances $d(q, P)$, it may be possible to determine that some classes of $\mathcal{P}$ do not contain any elements s such that $d(q, s) \leq t$.

Both types of mechanism have their place in metric search, see [1,10] for many examples. Filtering approaches however imply linear-time solutions, whereas partitioning can be used to construct an indexing mechanism, typically where a very large data set is recursively partitioned, in order to achieve a sub-linear search time.

For filtering, the algebraic properties are required to give a lower-bound on the distance $d(q, s)$ with reference to the sets of distances $d(q, P)$ and $d(s, P)$. For partitioning, a further requirement is to identify a partition that can be determined at pre-processing time, of which one or more classes may be excluded at query time according to $d(q, P)$.

Table 2 shows partitioning mechanisms which derive from various known lower-bound properties. The contribution of this paper is a novel partitioning mechanism for Ptolemaic inequality, shown in bold type in the table. Until now, such a partitioning mechanism has been missing from the literature.

Table 2. Five different partition functions and their corresponding exclusion conditions. In all cases the partition criterion is used to form a distinguished subset of S at pre-processing time, for all $s \in S$. The exclusion condition is evaluated with respect to the query q and a query radius t. Row 5 summarises the novel contribution of this paper.

	Underlying property	Partition criterion	Exclusion condition
1	triangle inequality	$d(s,p) \le M$	$d(q,p) > M + t$
2	triangle inequality	$d(s,p) \ge M$	$d(q,p) < M - t$
3	triangle inequality	$d(s,p_0) \le d(s,p_1)$	$d(q,p_0) - d(q,p_1) > 2t$
4	four-point lower bound	$d(s,p_0) \le d(s,p_1)$	$\frac{d(q,p_0)^2 - d(q,p_1)^2}{d(p_0,p_1)} > 2t$
5	**Ptolemaic inequality**	$d(s,p_0) \le d(s,p_1)$ $\land\ d(s,p_1) \ge \tau d(p_0,p_1)$	$d(q,p_0) - d(q,p_1) > t/\tau$

The remainder of this section introduces some necessary preliminaries. In Sect. 2 the underlying geometry of the partition mechanism is given, and Sect. 3 gives its formal definition. Section 4 gives a quantitative analysis of its value.

1.2   Subclasses of Metric Space

Properties (1–3) listed in Table 2 are possessed by all proper metric spaces. Property (4) is found only in *supermetric* spaces [2], which include all spaces which are isometrically embeddable in Hilbert space[1], while property (5) is found in any Hadamard space[2].

Any Hilbert-embeddable space is also a Hadamard space; although Hadamard spaces are a little more general, it is not clear that any practical non-Hilbert spaces fall in this category. Details of Hilbert spaces are elaborated in [4]; in this context it is sufficient to know that the following classes of metric space are members of both classes: Euclidean, Cosine, Jensen-Shannon, Quadratic Form, Triangular, and Mahalanobis spaces[3]. Furthermore, the square root of any proper metric gives a space in both classes. The partition mechanism described here is thus applicable to any of these spaces.

---

[1] See e.g. https://en.wikipedia.org/wiki/Hilbert_space.
[2] See e.g. https://en.wikipedia.org/wiki/Hadamard_space.
[3] For appropriate formulations; see [4].

1.3   Ptolemaic and Four-Point Lower Bounds

The Ptolemaic inequality was identified for use as a distance lower-bound for certain metric spaces in [6], and used further in a number of studies for example [7,8]. For any four objects $u_0, u_1, u_2, u_3 \in U$, the Ptolemaic inequality states:

$$d(u_0, u_2) \cdot d(u_1, u_3) \leq d(u_0, u_1) \cdot d(u_2, u_3) + d(u_1, u_2) \cdot d(u_3, u_0)$$

In $(\mathbb{R}^n, \ell_2)$ this is more simply stated as the product of the lengths of the diagonals of any quadrilateral being no greater than the sum of the products of the pairs of opposing sides. Given this property, a lower bound on the distance $d(q, s)$ can be determined whenever, for two reference values p_0, p_1, all the distances $d(s, p_0), d(s, p_1), d(q, p_0), d(q, p_1)$ and $d(p_0, p_1)$ are known. This lower bound is much tighter than those available via simple triangle inequality, and has been used to great effect for filtering objects during search, particularly in the context of a very expensive distance function [8]. The mechanisms used to incorporate this lower bound into metric search techniques include the Ptolemaic pivot table, the Ptolemaic PM-Tree, and the Ptolemaic M-Index [7]. In all cases, the inequality is used as an extra filtering mechanism superimposed onto an existing filtering or partitioning structure.

The four-point lower bound property, and the Hilbert exclusion mechanism, were first identified in [2], and investigated further in [4,5]. Any supermetric space (U, d) has the four-point property: for any four objects $u_0, u_1, u_2, u_3 \in U$, there exists a tetrahedron with vertices $u_0', u_1', u_2', u_3' \in \mathbb{R}^3$ where the distances between pairs of points are preserved, i.e. $d(u_i, u_j) = \ell_2(u_i', u_j')$.

The four-point property thus implies the Ptolemaic property, but not vice-versa.

The four-point lower-bound property applies to the case where five of the six edge lengths of a tetrahedron are known. In this case, two adjacent faces of the tetrahedron can be constructed. A lower bound of the unknown distance is obtained by notionally rotating these faces around their common edge to minimise the final edge length, which occurs when a planar tetrahedron is formed.

1.4   Projection into 2-Dimensional Space

Together these properties imply that if the Ptolemaic inequality is applied to a quadrilateral in two dimensions, when that quadrilateral has been formed according to five distances measured among four objects in a supermetric space, then the inequality applies also to the original space. Figure 1 shows an example of this.

The figure shows a projection in $(\mathbb{R}^2, \ell_2)$ of four objects p_0, p_1, s_0 and s_1 selected from a supermetric space (U, d). All distances other than $d(s_0, s_1)$ have been calculated in (U, d). The projections of objects p_0 and p_1 are plotted at the points $(0, 0)$ and $(0, d(p_0, p_1))$ respectively[4]. The projections of objects s_0 and s_1 are plotted at the unique points above the X-axis which preserve their

---

[4] This choice is arbitrary, any two points which preserve $d(p_0, p_1)$ could be used.

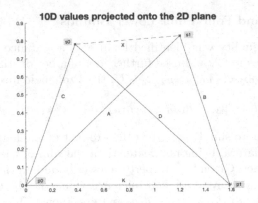

Fig. 1. Four objects p_0, p_1, s_0, s_1 selected from a supermetric space are projected onto a 2D plane according to the known distances K, A, B, C, D. Although $d(s_0, s_1)$ is not known, it is known that a tetrahedron with these four vertices exists in 3 dimensions. By the four-point lower bound, $d(s_0, s_1) \geq X$. By the Ptolemaic lower bound in 2 dimensions, $X \geq \frac{AD - BC}{K}$

distances from p_0 and p_1. The supermetric properties imply that the tetrahedron p_0, p_1, s_0, s_1 must exist in $(\mathbb{R}^3, \ell_2)$, therefore the unknown distance $d(s_0, s_1)$ is lower-bounded by the sixth edge of the planar tetrahedron plotted in $(\mathbb{R}^2, \ell_2)$.

By the four-point lower bound property, $d(s_0, s_1) \geq X$. By the Ptolemaic lower-bound property, $X \geq \frac{AD - BC}{K}$. Therefore, in the original supermetric space, $d(s_0, s_1) \geq \frac{AD - BC}{K}$. For the rest of this article, only 2D projections like these are considered, where two distinguished reference objects p_0, p_1 are used to form a planar projection of the rest of the data set, and rely on the Ptolemaic property with the context of planar quadrilaterals. This restricts the outcome to Hilbert-embeddable spaces, although as noted this is not a significant practical restriction.

It is worth noting that while the derivation and correctness of the mechanism rely upon the existence of the 2D projection, the projection itself does not require to be calculated. As shown in Table 2, the calculations required are restricted to simple calculations over distances measured in the original space.

2   The Underlying Geometry

Partitioning mechanisms differ from filtering in that, for each possibility of exclusion, it is necessary to identify two subsets of the universal space:

1. a *static* subset $\mathcal{S}$, which can be identified and indexed during the pre-processing of the finite data set, and
2. a *dynamic* subset $\mathcal{Q}$, which is identified only after the query and (typically) its associated search radius become apparent.

Exclusion of $\mathcal{S}$ can be performed when every element of $\mathcal{Q}$ is separated by at least the search radius from every element of $\mathcal{S}$. In the following section objects denoted by s and q are referred to, representing elements of $\mathcal{S}$ and $\mathcal{Q}$ respectively.

2.1   2D Geometry

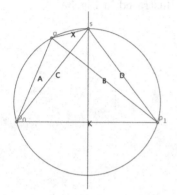

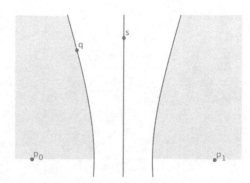

(a) Four points p_0, p_1, s, q on a 2D plane.

(b) For any q' in the shaded area, $d(q', s) \geq \tau |A - B|$.

Fig. 2. In (a), line segments among the points are annotated by their lengths. s is chosen according to the parameter $\tau = C/K$, and q is a point on the circle defined by p_0, p_1 and s. q is the unique point with $X = \tau(B - A)$. The regions shown in the figure represent regions of the original, potentially non-Euclidean, space; the inequalities established are generally applicable to the original space.

Figure 2a shows four points p_0, p_1, q and s drawn on a plane. These points represent the 2D projections of two reference (or pivot) values p_0, p_1, a query value q and a potential solution value s. The figure is annotated with line segments labelled $A - D$, K and X, where the labels represent the lengths of the respective lines. K is the inter-pivot distance, and X is a lower bound of the unknown distance $d(q, s)$.

For the moment, values have been chosen such that

- $C = D$
- the parameter τ defines the ratio C/K
- point q lies on the same circle as p_0, p_1 and s

The Ptolemaic inequality states

$$BC \leq AD + KX$$

so in this case:

$$X \geq \tau(B - A)$$

The boundary of this region defines a hyperbola with foci p_0, p_1 and semi-major axis $X/2\tau$, as shown in Fig. 2b. It follows that any point within the shaded region is at least distance X from the point s.

As q, p_0, p_1 and s are co-circular, q is the unique closest point on the (left-hand) hyperbola to s and $X = \tau(B - A)$. The line segment sq is therefore perpendicular to the tangent of the hyperbola at q. As the gradient of the tangent is negative, it follows that any point above and to the right of s is further than X from any point to the left of the hyperbola, as illustrated in Fig. 3a.

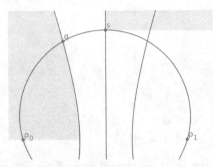

(a) The shaded area to the right of the central axis contains points which are at least $d(q, s)$ from that on the left.

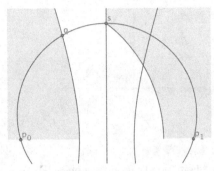

(b) The shaded area here also contains contains points which are at least $d(q, s)$ from that on the left.

Fig. 3. The shaded area to the left of each central axis denotes the locus defined by $d(q', p_0) - d(q', p_1) > \tau t$ for any $q' \in U$. In both cases, for any $s' \in S$ in the shaded area to the right of the central axis, $d(q', s') > t$.

However, the static partition can be extended to include more of the finite search space, by including any value $s' \in S$ to the right of the central axis where also $d(s', p_0) \geq d(s, p_0)$, as illustrated in Fig. 3b. This not only increases the cardinality of the potentially excluded subset, but also avoids the requirement to calculate the 2D projection.

The static and dynamic classes represented in Fig. 3b are now formally defined as

$$\mathcal{S} = \{s' \leftarrow S \mid d(s', p_0) \geq d(s', p_1) \quad \wedge \quad d(s', p_0) \geq \tau d(p_0, p_1)\}$$
$$\mathcal{Q} = \{q' \leftarrow U \mid d(q', p_1) - d(q', p_0) > t/\tau\}$$

with the property that it is impossible for any element $q' \in \mathcal{Q}$ to be within distance t of any element $s' \in \mathcal{S}$.

The validity of this extension seems evident from the illustration in Fig. 3b, but this needs to be demonstrated for the general case. A full justification of its correctness is included in an extended version of this paper available at [3].

3   The Partition Mechanism

The addition of the criterion $d(s', p_0) \geq \tau d(p_0, p_1)$ to the static partition allows further exclusion potential relying on the normal triangle inequality method, i.e. if $d(q, p_0) < \tau d(p_0, p_1) - t$. This extension to the exclusion criterion is illustrated in Fig. 4a.

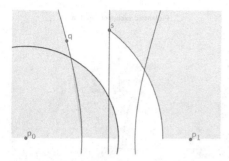
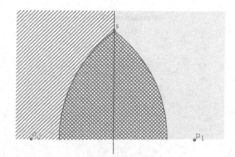

(a) The locus $d(p_0, q) < d(p_0, s) - t$ can be included in Q.

(b) The locus $d(s, p_{\{0,1\}}) < \tau d(p_0, p_1)$ forms the final partition class.

Fig. 4. Extending the exclusion criteria, and the final partition

Furthermore, when also including the symmetric opposite criteria, the static partition now defines three subclasses as shown in Fig. 4b. It may further be noted that the third of these subclasses may also independently excluded if $d(q, p_0)$ or $d(q, p_1) \geq \tau K + t$, again relying only on triangle inequality.

So finally, according to the geometry established in Sect. 2.1, a static partition $\{S_1, S_2, S_3\}$ of S can be established for a pair of reference points p_0, p_1 with $K = d(p_0, p_1)$ and a given value of τ as follows:

$$
\begin{aligned}
S_1 &= \{s \leftarrow S \mid d(s, p_0) \geq d(s, p_1) \quad \wedge \quad d(s, p_0) \geq \tau K\} \\
S_2 &= \{s \leftarrow S \mid d(s, p_0) < d(s, p_1) \quad \wedge \quad d(s, p_1) \geq \tau K\} \\
S_3 &= \{s \leftarrow S \mid d(s, p_0) < \tau K \quad \wedge \quad d(s, p_1) < \tau K\}
\end{aligned}
$$

These static regions are illustrated on the 2D plane in Fig. 4b.

For a given query object q with threshold t, where $A = d(q, p_0)$ and $B = d(q, p_1)$, these classes can be excluded from a search as follows:

$$
\begin{aligned}
S_1 &: \quad B - A > t/\tau \quad \vee \quad A < \tau K - t \\
S_2 &: \quad A - B \geq t/\tau \quad \vee \quad B < \tau K - t \\
S_3 &: \quad A \geq \tau K + t \quad \vee \quad B \geq \tau K + t
\end{aligned}
$$

Note that it is possible for the exclusion of region S_3 to occur in conjunction with that of S_1 or S_2. The mechanism resulting from these definitions is now evaluated in Sect. 4.

4   Evaluation

Before proceeding with a full quantitative evaluation, it is interesting to view graphical representations based on a sample from a particular data set, in order to give a more pragmatic view of the Ptolemaic partition mechanism in comparison with hyperplane (hyperbolic) and Hilbert (four-point) partition mechanisms.

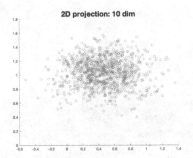

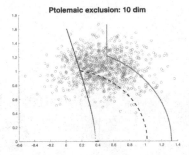

(a) A scatter plot based on randomly selected reference points. p_0 is plotted at $(0,0)$ and p_1 at $(0, d(p_0, p_1))$. The data set is plotted according to the distance of each value from p_0 and p_1.

(b) The boundary of the class $\mathcal{S}_1$ is plotted in red. Values lying to the right of this boundary can be excluded for queries lying to the left of either black boundary.

Fig. 5. Graphical view of the Ptolemaic partition mechanism based on a 2D projection. $\tau = 1.3$ and the query threshold is 0.3.

Figure 5a shows a scatter plot of 1,000 values randomly generated in a 10-dimensional Euclidean space, each projected onto a 2D plane according to their distances from two randomly generated pivot values.

Figure 5b shows the same projection superimposed with one of the partition boundaries of the Ptolemaic partition mechanism with a τ value of 1.3, and a query threshold of 0.3, which is the mean nearest-neighbour distance. The boundary of the static region $\mathcal{S}_1$ is shown in red; those points lying to the right of the red boundary are thus subset to exclusion when either $d(q, p_1) - d(q, p_0) > 1.3 \cdot 0.3$, or if $d(q, p_1) < 1.3 \cdot d(p_0, p_1) - 0.3$. The boundaries of these regions are shown by solid and dotted black lines respectively; every point to the left of either boundary represents a value for $q' \in \mathcal{Q}$ which allows exclusion of the static class.

Figure 6 shows the same plot with boundaries for standard hyperplane and Hilbert exclusion, in 6a and 6b respectively.

It is clear, at least in this case, that the Ptolemaic mechanism always excludes a smaller subset, while the probability of the exclusion being possible is higher. From Fig. 6a it is evident that the dimensionality of the data set challenges hyperplane exclusion, while both Ptolemaic and Hilbert mechanisms continue to remain effective. Finally, while it is not possible to judge the relative efficacy

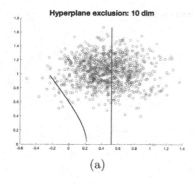
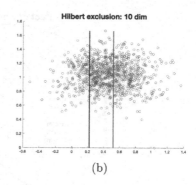

Fig. 6. Equivalent graphical views of hyperplane and Hilbert partition mechanisms. In each case, queries falling to the left of the black line can be used to exclude the subset of data falling to the right of the red line. Again a query threshold of 0.3 has been used. (Color figure online)

of Ptolemaic vs. Hilbert from these diagrams, it can be observed that neither is a proper subset of the other, and it is therefore possible to use both Ptolemaic and Hilbert with respect to the same pair of reference points. This would allow a hybrid mechanism, more effective that either in isolation, based on the same dynamic measurements of $d(q, p_0)$ and $d(q, p_1)$.

4.1 Quantitative Evaluation

Quantitative evaluation is performed over sets of uniformly generated Euclidean data, from between 8 and 20 dimensions. 50k data objects are used and 1k non-intersecting queries are evaluated. The threshold used for each query corresponds to the 5nn distance as pre-calculated over the data.

Experiments were performed over Ptolemaic, Hilbert, and hyperplane mechanisms. For each experiment, a fixed number of reference points was used, and each of the $\binom{n}{2}$ pairs of reference points was used to construct a partition over the space. The single outcome is the mean proportion per query of values that were successfully excluded, this value being between 0 and 1. For the majority of the experiments 10 reference points used, this giving 45 different partitions. Thus all results given correspond to the proportion of the data that can be successfully excluded at cost of only 10 distance calculations per query.

All experiments were performed using MatLab and the code is available[5].

4.2 Choosing τ

First, different values for τ are examined. As mentioned, when $\tau = 0.5$ the mechanism reverts to simple hyperplane exclusion; while a value of less than 0.5 is technically possible, there is no value in such a choice. As τ gets large,

---

[5] https://bitbucket.org/richardconnor/partitions.

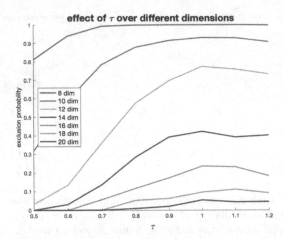

Fig. 7. Probability of successful exclusion for differing values of τ in different dimensions. Note that when $\tau = 0.5$ the mechanism is identical to traditional hyperplane (Hyperbolic) exclusion.

then ever fewer data will be present in the partition which may be excluded, and again the mechanism will become useless. Early tests showed that a value somewhere around 1 is usually close to optimal, although for specific reference point pairs an optimum values of between around 0.8 and 1.2 were observed.

It would in fact be possible to optimise τ based on each particular pair of reference points, which we have not yet investigated thoroughly. In this experiment a fixed value of τ is applied to all partitions, which is possibly more realistic for many scenarios.

Figure 7 shows the results of various values of τ when applied to data of between 8 and 20 dimensions. As can be seen there is a general trend of larger values being better as dimensions increase, but only within quite a small margin; while there is clearly an element of noise in this experiment, the best value in each case is either 1.0 or 1.1, although further investigation is warranted. For further experiments described over the data of different dimensions, the best value of τ found in this experiment was used.

4.3 Evaluation over High Dimensional Data

Having picked a value for τ, outcomes for some different mechanisms over data ranging from 8 to 20 dimensions are given. Four mechanisms are used: Hyperplane (Hyperbolic) exclusion; Hilbert exclusion; Ptolemaic exclusion, and finally a combination of Hilbert and Ptolemaic exclusion.

For this combination, each pair of reference points was used to construct both Ptolemaic and Hilbert partitions, and the union of non-excluded data was calculated. The observation here is that it is possible for different data to be excluded by each mechanism. As the essential query-time cost of performing the

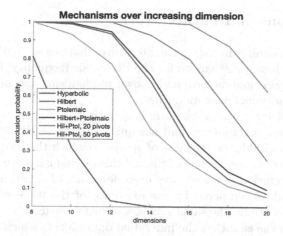

Fig. 8. Performance of different exclusion mechanisms as dimensionality increases, measured as the probability of a non-solution being excluded based on the distances among query and reference values.

exclusions is the cost of the two distance operations and some relatively cheap arithmetic, taking the union of all possible exclusions makes practical sense as the distance calculations are amortised. As Hilbert exclusion always allows exclusion from a superset of queries identified by Hyperbolic exclusion, there is no point in combining that mechanism also.

Figure 8 shows the outcome. As can be seen, while the performance of Hyperbolic exclusion falls rapidly away after around 8–10 dimensions, both Ptolemaic and Hilbert perform much better into the higher dimensional range. Hilbert always performs better than Ptolemaic, which is not very surprising as the four-point lower bound property is stronger then the Ptolemaic inequality, and technically applies to a smaller subset of metric spaces. What is more interesting, however, is that the combination of Ptolemaic and Hilbert gives a strictly better result than Hilbert alone; that is, the data sets identified for exclusion by the two mechanisms are not in a strict subset relation. Again it is noted that the inherent query-time cost of the joint mechanism is very similar to the cost of just one, as in all cases the query to pivot distances calculated are reused in both mechanisms.

The final plots in the graph show the use of 20 and 50 pivot values for the combination mechanism. Although only doubling the number of query-to-pivot distances required, 20 pivots gives $\binom{20}{2}$ i.e. 190 partitions to apply, and as can be seen the increase makes for a much higher exclusion ratio. Similarly, 50 pivots gives 1,225 partitions. The important observation however is that there is a clear degree of orthogonality in the randomly selected partitions, allowing almost perfect exclusion in 12 and 16 dimensions respectively.

5   Conclusions and Future Work

This paper fills a significant gap in the literature, that is a set partition that can be used as an exclusion mechanism for the Ptolemaic inequality; for some years, other distance lower-bounds have had known mechanisms and in this sense the Ptolemaic inequality has been an outlier.

In its simplest form, the mechanism is quantitatively much better than traditional hyperplane partitioning, and not quite as good as Hilbert partitioning. This is almost inevitable, as the class of spaces to which the inequalities can be applied are in a strict subset relation. Should this mechanism have been identified before Hilbert exclusion it would have been deserving of significant excitement, but this is nowadays tempered by the existence of the more effective Hilbert exclusion over essentially the same subclass of metric spaces.

However, it is the case that the individual data objects which the new mechanism excludes are not a proper subset of those identified by Hilbert exclusion, and as shown the two mechanisms may operate in conjunction to give a unified mechanism which, for the same cost of distance calculations against reference points, gives a better exclusion outcome than either in isolation. Particularly in high-dimensional spaces, this therefore gives a further increment in the limit of dimensionality for which exact search can be effective. While the "rule of thumb" used to be that 8–10 dimensions was the effective limit for exact search [9], with the combined mechanism 16 dimensions can be effectively searched while avoiding almost all explicit distance calculations.

Some further avenues are worth exploring. First, it is feasible to calculate individual τ values customised to each particular pair of pivot points, rather than to choose a single value for the whole set. This would be expected to give significant, if incremental, improvement in performance.

Finally, there are many other contexts beyond a simple recursive decomposition of a large data set where such mechanisms can be used. It is therefore of potential value in its own right for this previous gap in knowledge to be filled.

Acknowledgements. The author would like to sincerely thank the anonymous reviewers for their thorough and helpful comments on the submitted version of this article.

References

1. Chávez, E., Navarro, G., Baeza-Yates, R., Marroquín, J.L.: Searching in metric spaces. ACM Comput. Surv. **33**(3), 273–321 (2001). https://doi.org/10.1145/502807.502808. https://dl.acm.org/doi/10.1145/502807.502808
2. Connor, R., Vadicamo, L., Cardillo, F.A., Rabitti, F.: Supermetric search with the four-point property. In: Amsaleg, L., Houle, M.E., Schubert, E. (eds.) SISAP 2016. LNCS, vol. 9939, pp. 51–64. Springer, Cham (2016). https://doi.org/10.1007/978-3-319-46759-7_4
3. Connor, R.: A Ptolemaic partitioning mechanism (2022). https://doi.org/10.48550/ARXIV.2208.09324. https://arxiv.org/abs/2208.09324

4. Connor, R., Cardillo, F.A., Vadicamo, L., Rabitti, F.: Hilbert exclusion: improved metric search through finite isometric embeddings. ACM Trans. Inf. Syst. (TOIS) **35**(3), 1–27 (2016)
5. Connor, R., Vadicamo, L., Cardillo, F.A., Rabitti, F.: Supermetric search. Inf. Syst. **80**, 108–123 (2019)
6. Hetland, M.L.: Ptolemaic indexing. J. Comput. Geom. **6**, 165–184 (2015)
7. Hetland, M.L., Skopal, T., Lokoč, J., Beecks, C.: Ptolemaic access methods: challenging the reign of the metric space model. Inf. Syst. **38**(7), 989–1006 (2013). https://doi.org/10.1016/j.is.2012.05.011. https://www.sciencedirect.com/science/article/pii/S0306437912000786
8. Lokoč, J., Hetland, M.L., Skopal, T., Beecks, C.: Ptolemaic indexing of the signature quadratic form distance. In: Proceedings of the Fourth International Conference on SImilarity Search and APplications, SISAP 2011, pp. 9–16. Association for Computing Machinery, New York (2011). https://doi.org/10.1145/1995412.1995417
9. Weber, R., Schek, H.J., Blott, S.: A quantitative analysis and performance study for similarity-search methods in high-dimensional spaces. In: Proceedings of 24th VLDB, vol. 98, pp. 194–205. Morgan Kaufmann (1998)
10. Zezula, P., Amato, G., Dohnal, V., Batko, M.: Similarity Search: The Metric Space Approach, vol. 32. Springer, Heidelberg (2006). https://doi.org/10.1007/0-387-29151-2

HubHSP Graph: Effective Data Sampling for Pivot-Based Representation Strategies

Stephane Marchand-Maillet[1]([⊠]) and Edgar Chávez[2]

[1] Department of Computer Science, University of Geneva, Geneva, Switzerland
stephane.marchand-maillet@unige.ch
[2] CICESE, Ensenada, Mexico

Abstract. Given a finite dataset in a metric space, we investigate the definition of a representative sample. Such a definition is important in data analysis strategies to seed algorithms (such as k-means) and for pivot-based data indexing techniques. We discuss the geometrical and statistical facets of such a definition.

We propose the Hubness Half Space Partitioning (HubHSP) strategy as an effective sampling heuristic that combines both geometric and statistical constraints. We show that the HubHSP sampling strategy is sound and stable in non-uniform high-dimensional regimes and compares favorably with classical sampling techniques.

Keywords: Dataset sampling · Pivot-based indexing · Local intrinsic dimensionality · Hubness half space partitioning

1 Introduction

Given a dataset in a metric space, the selection of a *representative subset* of the dataset is a common operation in data analysis or for data indexing. It is well known that obtaining a decent approximation of cluster centers prior to running a clustering algorithm such as k-means improves not only the speed of convergence but also the quality of the final result [2].

Pivot-based exact and approximate indexing techniques are based on the prior selection of a *pivot set* which is used in two main mechanisms. Defining pivots as landmarks in the metric space allows to precompute and store distance values from all data to this set and use this information along with the triangle inequality to build an *exclusion criterion* [5].

Pivots may also be used as landmarks to represent the data in permutation-based indexing strategies. The query locates data in its neighborhood by activating pivots and selecting data with similar activation. In both cases the idea is to restrict the number of data for which the exact distance computation is performed [1,3,10]

In the parallel field of data visualization of large data (outside the scope of this paper) the smart sub-sampling of the dataset into a reduced representative subset ensures smooth and accurate display.

T. Skopal et al. (Eds.): SISAP 2022, LNCS 13590, pp. 164–177, 2022.
https://doi.org/10.1007/978-3-031-17849-8_13

In this paper, we first study the approaches for data sampling and the possible constraints that can be set, namely statistical or geometrical. We then propose the Hubness Half Space Partitioning (HubHSP) that builds on the Half Space Partitioning (HSP [4]) to construct a data selector that effectively combines such geometrical and statistical constraints.

We demonstrate empirically the validity and stability of our proposal in various experimental conditions.

2   Dataset Sampling Strategies

Given a N-sized dataset $\mathcal{X} = \{x_i\}_{i \in [\![N]\!]}$ of $\Omega \subseteq \mathbb{R}^D$, classical data sampling strategies are generally either based on statistical or geometric constraints.

2.1   Density-Based Sampling

One natural way to approach dataset re-sampling is from a statistical perspective. Here, the dataset $\mathcal{X}$ is supposed to be a N-sized i.i.d sample of a probability density function (pdf) $f_{\mathcal{X}}$. In other words, $\{x_i\}_{i \in [\![N]\!]}$ is one realization of a set of N independent random variables $\{X_i\}_{i \in [\![N]\!]}$ identically distributed according to this pdf ($X_i \sim f_{\mathcal{X}}$, $i \in [\![N]\!]$).

Re-sampling dataset $\mathcal{X}$ into subset $\mathcal{Y} = \{y_j\}_{j \in [\![n]\!]}$ with $n \leq N$ therefore amounts to make a selection $\mathcal{Y} \subseteq \mathcal{X}$ of n data from $\mathcal{X}$ into $\mathcal{Y}$. In this case a subset of indices $i_j \in [\![N]\!]$ is chosen so that $y_j = x_{i_j} \forall j \in [\![n]\!]$. As shown below, a uniform sampling of indices from within $[\![N]\!]$ guarantees that $\mathcal{Y}$ is also a sample of pdf $f_{\mathcal{X}}$ (i.e. $f_{\mathcal{Y}} = f_{\mathcal{X}}$).

Representation Properties. Maintaining the probability density function of a sample has specific implications. Statistically, a high value of the pdf at a location $x \in \Omega$ makes the likelihood of a sample at this location $P(X_i = x)$ accordingly high.

Conversely, a crude empirical estimate of the value of the pdf at location x, $\hat{f}_{\mathcal{X}}(x)$ is given by the density of samples from $\mathcal{X}$ around x. Classically, the density is defined as the number of objects of interest per unit of volume. Hence, we can define

$$\hat{f}_{\mathcal{X}}(x) = \frac{|\mathcal{X} \cap \mathcal{B}(x, \rho)|}{\text{vol}(\mathcal{B}(x, \rho))} \quad \text{for some small } \rho > 0$$

where we consider the ball $\mathcal{B}(x, \rho) = \{y \in \Omega \mid d(x, y) \leq \rho\}$ as a unit volume. In practice, we only have access to the data from $\mathcal{X}$. Hence the estimate is only non-zero when the ball $\mathcal{B}(x, \rho))$ contains data samples. As a result, we are led to using the k nearest neighbors of x from $\mathcal{X}$ ($\mathcal{V}_{\mathcal{X}}^k(x)$) to estimate the density:

$$\hat{f}_{\mathcal{X}}(x) = \frac{k}{\text{vol}(\mathcal{V}_{\mathcal{X}}^k(x))} \quad \text{for some } k > 0 \tag{1}$$

Note that following the above, the volume $\mathrm{vol}(\mathcal{V}_{\mathcal{X}}^k(x))$ can be the volume of the enclosing ball $(\mathrm{vol}(\mathcal{V}_{\mathcal{X}}^k(x)) = \mathrm{vol}(\mathcal{B}(x,\rho)))$ with ρ the distance to the kth neighbor).

This view justifies that $\hat{f}_{\mathcal{X}}(x) = \hat{f}_{\mathcal{Y}}(x)$ as follows [11]:

Let $\mathrm{P}(x_j \in \mathcal{V}_{\mathcal{X}}^k(x_i)) = p_{j|i}$

then $\mathrm{P}(x_j \in \mathcal{V}_{\mathcal{Y}}^k(x_i)) = \mathrm{P}(x_j \in \mathcal{V}_{\mathcal{X}}^k(x_i), x_j \in \mathcal{Y}) \stackrel{\mathrm{ii}}{=} p_{j|i} \mathrm{P}(x_j \in \mathcal{Y})$.

If we sample uniformly n indices $j \in [\![N]\!]$ then $\mathrm{P}(x_j \in \mathcal{Y}) = \frac{n}{N}$. As a result, $\mathrm{P}(x_j \in \mathcal{V}_{\mathcal{Y}}^k(x_i)) \propto p_{j|i}$ and the normalization ensures that $\hat{f}_{\mathcal{X}}$ and $\hat{f}_{\mathcal{Y}}$ are estimates of the same original density $f_{\mathcal{X}}$. $\qquad\square$

This also pinpoints the fact that since $\mathcal{Y} \subseteq \mathcal{X}$ preserves the original density $f_{\mathcal{X}}$ then $\mathcal{X}$ can be uniformly partitioned into equivalence classes whose representative centers are points $x_j \in \mathcal{Y}$ and the respective radii depend on the local density.

From (1), for a fixed k, $\hat{f}_{\mathcal{X}}$ varies according to the value of $\mathrm{vol}(\mathcal{V}_{\mathcal{X}}^k(x))$. The larger the volume is required to hold the kNN, the lower the density. Hence, based on kNN, the radii of Dirichlet domains[1] in $\mathcal{X}$ centered at $\mathcal{Y}$ adapt to the local density. In that respect, density-based sampling corresponds to nearest neighbor queries with fixed k (i.e. kNN queries).

The direct implication of the above properties is that, if an indexing technique uses the above-defined $\mathcal{Y}$ as representative (pivot) set, then the inverted lists $\mathcal{L}_j$ associated with pivots x_j and defined by[2]

$$\mathcal{L}_j = \{x_i \in \mathcal{X} \mid d(x_i, x_j) \leq d(x_i, x_k) \ \forall x_k \in \mathcal{Y}\}$$

are of constant size ($\mathbf{E}|\mathcal{L}_j| \simeq N/n$). Such a strategy is therefore profitable for indexing where obtaining short inverted lists is desirable for performance and a uniform partition of $\mathcal{X}$ into inverted lists guarantees this minimum.

However, preserving the density of representative samples and therefore creating a non-uniform geometrical partition of the data space is adverse at time of (geometrically) locating the query with respect to the dataset. At the time of locating the query, the relevance of a pivot $x_j \in \mathcal{Y}$ is related to its covering radius (e.g. $\mathrm{vol}(\mathcal{B}(x_j, \rho))$.

Further, given a fixed representation budget of pivots, the highest value for the lower bound for the distance from any query to any pivot is given by a geometrically uniform partition of the space. Emphasizing geometry (rather than density) therefore supports a more robust exclusion mechanism. For the same reason, it is also known that permutation-based indexing schemes that locate data by pivot activation benefit from a uniform partition of the data space by pivots [1].

---

[1] A Dirichlet domain is the generalization of a Voronoi region for high-dimensional spaces. Here, we look at subsets of data from $\mathcal{X}$ closer to a given point in $\mathcal{Y}$ than to any other point in $\mathcal{Y}$.

[2] Here, we allow $x_j \in \mathcal{L}_j$ since generically $\mathcal{Y} \subseteq \mathcal{X}$.

2.2   Geometry-Based Sampling

We therefore investigate the construction of a set of representatives $\mathcal{Y}$ based on geometric constraints. Dataset $\mathcal{X}$ is typically embedded into a domain $\Omega \subset \mathbb{R}^D$ that can be sampled using a D-dimensional regular lattice. Should any element from $\mathcal{X}$ fall into a simplex from the lattice, the center of that simplex (or the closest data from $\mathcal{X}$) may be taken as a representative. Basic examples of such a sampling include regular quantization of the coordinates of the original domain, or after applying some analysis such as PCA to discover (and potentially decimate) uncorrelated coordinates.

Representation Properties. Such a sampling strategy offers the advantage that the representative set $\mathcal{Y}$ lies close to a regular lattice and this regular structure may be exploited by the indexing.

To ensure geometric representation properties for $\mathcal{X}$, the criterion can be expressed as "$\mathcal{Y}$ covers uniformly the convex hull of $\mathcal{X}$", where the covering can be quantified by the k-center criterion:

$$\mathcal{Y} = \operatorname*{argmin}_{\substack{\mathcal{S} \subset \mathcal{X} \\ |\mathcal{S}|=k}} \max_{x \in \mathcal{X}} d(x, \mathcal{S})$$

where, $d(x, \mathcal{S}) = \min_{x' \in \mathcal{S}} d(x, x')$. It is ensuring that data in $\mathcal{X}$ is never far from a sample in $\mathcal{Y}$. This is equivalent to minimizing the diameter of the Dirichlet domains built from $\mathcal{Y}$ of size k in $\mathcal{X}$. In that respect, geometric sampling corresponds to nearest neighbor queries with fixed range ε (i.e. range queries to uncover the εNN). In that case, pivots are associated to a fixed covering radius and inverted lists have lengths adapting to the local density.

3   Homogeneous Space Partitioning

3.1   Half Space Partitioning

In [7,9], we demonstrated that the local degree of the neighborhood graph built using the Half Space Partitioning (HSP) strategy [4] is an accurate proxy for the measurement of local intrinsic dimensionality. This is an important property for designing a geometrically efficient sampling strategy.

Algorithm 1 recalls the construction of the HSP, illustrated for the 2D case in Fig. 1. The HSP strategy partitions the hypersphere around every x_i into cones (see green dashed lines). In the HSP graph, each data point is connected (red edge) with its HSP neighbors and their mutual arrangement and the relationship with the Kissing number correlates their degree with the local dimensionality of the data [9]. Note that there is no upper bound for the distance value from x_i to the next selected HSP neighbor.

The construction of the HSP graph is highly parallel since the neighborhood of every point is computed independently of the rest. While this is a clear computational benefit and makes the HSP graph reproducible however the dataset

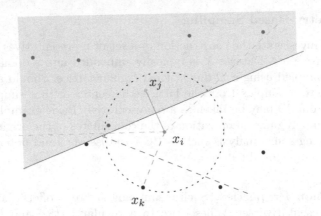

Fig. 1. HSP construction and discarding strategy. The (red) center data x_i chooses its closest (green) neighbor x_j as HSP neighbor and discards all data closer to x_j than to itself (shaded half-space). x_k will be selected as next closest neighbor (as symbolized by the dashed circle) and the next half-space (below the blue dashed line) discarded, until no neighbor of x_i remains (Color figure online)

Algorithm 1. HSP graph construction

1: **procedure** HSP($\mathcal{X}$)   ▷ Half-space partitioning
2: **for** every point $x_i \in \mathcal{X}$ **do**
3:      **while** not all data in $\mathcal{X}$ is discarded **do**
4:          Select the next nearest neighbor $x_j \in \mathcal{X}$ not already discarded
5:          Add x_j as HSP-neighbor of x_i
6:          Discard any data x_k from $\mathcal{X}$ that is closer to x_j than to x_i

---

is given, it makes the structure of the HSP graph unpredictable, apart from its properties arising from sphere packing.

In particular, no control is applied over the indegree of every node (the number of edges pointing *to* every node). As a result, there is no guarantee for a strong overlap of the HSP neighborhoods of 2 close points. Further, the specific structure of the HSP graph is sensitive to any data perturbation that would flip the order in which data appears as nearest neighbors of each other. In a setting where we use a point neighborhood as its representative, we would rather like to introduce correlation between neighborhoods of close points so as to:

- ensure that 2 close points share representatives (geometric consistency)
- obtain a compact, stable and sound representative sample of the data (statistical consistency)
- minimize the overall number of representatives

Here, we propose the "Hubness-HSP" (HubHSP for short) as a graph spanner over $\mathcal{X}$ supporting the selection of a representative set $\mathcal{Y}$. We first propose the rationale for its construction and then derive the actual construction algorithm.

We finally study and experimentally investigate the properties of the resulting HubHSP spanner for dataset sampling.

We wish to define the HubHSP as a structure that supports the selection of a representative set, while maintaining the favorable geometric properties of the HSP: x_j being selected as a neighbor of x_i means that x_j represents the vicinity of x_i and we wish to concentrate this representation into a given budget of representatives $\mathcal{Y}$. The base adaptation is therefore to install a control over the indegree of the nodes in the HubHSP. By enforcing nodes with high indegree, we create "centrality hubs[3]" that can be used to define representatives $\mathcal{Y}$ from the full set $\mathcal{X}$.

We therefore define a "hubness factor" h_j at every node x_j, which corresponds to its indegree during construction. Hence $\sum_j h_j = N$ and the challenge is to allocate h_j values so as to obtain concentrated hubs.

We build the graph following the aggregative compounding principle (see Fig. 2): a new data is matched with its HubHSP neighbors (line 9 in Algorithm 2) according to the HSP geometry while maintaining the most concentrated hubness by privileging existing hubs. Hence, at an intermediate stage, a data x_i is connected to the strongest current hub x_j from within its vicinity, and activates the HSP half-plane point discarding strategy.

Algorithm 2. Hubness HSP graph construction

1: **procedure** HUBHSP($\mathcal{X}$)
2:    $h_i \leftarrow 0 \ \forall i$ ▷ Initialize hubness to 0
3:    $Q.\text{push}(x_{\text{start}})$ ▷ Initialize Q with x_{start}
4:    **while** Q is not empty **do**
5:        $x_i \leftarrow Q.\text{pop}()$ ▷ Next data point in the chain
6:        $Q.\text{push}(\mathcal{V}(x_i))$ ▷ Next data to consider in the chain
7:        C_i is the circle centered at x_i through its closest neighbor
8:        **while** not all data in $\mathcal{X}$ is discarded **do**
9:            Select the neighbor x_j of x_i with maximum current hubness
10:            Add x_j as HSP-neighbor of x_i
11:            $h_j \leftarrow h_j + 1$ ▷ Increase hubness of x_j
12:            $\tilde{x}_j \leftarrow \text{Proj}_{C_i}(x_j)$ ▷ Project x_j onto C_i
13:            Discard any data x_l from $\mathcal{X}$ that is closer to $\tilde{x}_j$ than to x_i

---

We comment the main lines of Algorithm 2:

- Line 9: the current data x_i inspects a given vicinity $\mathcal{V}(x_i)$ (e.g. its 100-NN neighborhood) and finds the data x_j of current maximal hubness $h_j = \max_{x_k \in \mathcal{V}(x_i)} h_k$.
- Lines 10–11: x_j is added as neighbor to x_i by creating an edge (x_i, x_j) and therefore increasing the hubness (indegree) h_j of x_j.

---

[3] Here, centrality relates mainly to notion of degree centrality.

– Line 12: The natural distance-based selection in the HSP guarantees geometrical consistency [4]. This is not used anymore and to restore consistency, selected neighbors are projected onto the sphere C_i centered at x_i and containing the closest neighbor of x_i (blue circle in Fig. 2). In practice, this is done by proper normalization of vector $[x_i, x_j]$ into vector $[x_i, \tilde{x}_j]$ (see Annex).

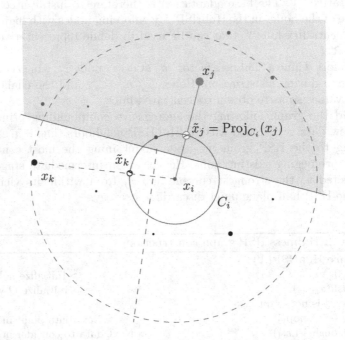

Fig. 2. HubHSP construction and discarding strategy. The current (red) center data x_i chooses its (green) neighbor x_j of highest hubness (size of the data point) as HubHSP neighbor from its vicinity $\mathcal{V}(x_i)$ (red dashed circle). It projects this data onto $\tilde{x}_j$ on the largest empty circle (blue circle) and discards all data closest to $\tilde{x}_j$ than to itself (shaded half-space). x_k will then be selected as next non-discarded neighbor of highest hubness and the next half-space (left to the blue dashed line, bisector of $[x_i, \tilde{x}_k]$) discarded, until no neighbor of x_i remains non-discarded (Color figure online)

The main practical adaptations from the HSP construction strategy are:

1. data is selected by *decreasing hubness* rather than *increasing distance*
2. because of 1. above, the selection of neighbors for x_i (line 4 in Algorithm 1) has to happen within the pre-defined vicinity $\mathcal{V}(x_i)$
3. because of 1. above, to maintain geometric consistency, points are projected onto a sphere of minimal radius around x_i before selection
4. since we now create a chain during the construction of the HubHSP (using Q), a starting point has to be defined.

The first and main benefit of this adaptation is the creation of a hubness index h_j per datum (node in the HubHSP graph). The hubness index h_j is the indegree of node x_j in the HubHSP graph. h_j counts how many data x_i have x_j as HubHSP neighbor. A node with high hubness is therefore an interesting candidate for the representative subset. This provides a sound and natural strategy for the selection of $\mathcal{Y}$ by simply selecting nodes in decreasing order of their indegree.

As a result, the HubHSP graph combines two properties. From its inheritance from the HSP process, the outdegree of every node reflects the local geometry (intrinsic dimensionality) of the data [9]. Through the hubness, the indegree of each node is now correlated with the statistical properties of the data.

Since in practice we need to define (limit) the vicinity $\mathcal{V}(x_i)$ from where the HubHSP neighbors are selected (line 9 in Algorithm 2), the construction of this set impacts the resulting properties of the HubHSP graph.

- if $\mathcal{V}(x_i) = \mathcal{V}^k_{\mathcal{X}}(x_i)$, the kNN neighborhood of x_i in $\mathcal{X}$, the span of this set is driven by the local density, as discussed above. Hence, the kNN-based HubHSP graph reflects the local density of data via arc lengths, on top of reflecting its geometry via outdegree.
- if $\mathcal{V}(x_i) = \mathcal{V}^\varepsilon_{\mathcal{X}}(x_i)$, the εNN neighborhood of x_i in $\mathcal{X}$, the span of this set is immune from the local density and it is the indegree of every neighbor that reflects this density.

Hence, the HubHSP graph adds to the HSP graph the encoding of the local density either via arc lengths (kNN) or indegree (εNN).

3.2 Complexity

The base complexity of the HubHSP construction algorithm is $O(N^2D)$. It mimics that of the computation of any neighborhood graph as it is dominated by selection of candidate neighbors (line 9 in Algorithm 2). Such a complexity may classically be reduced by a pre-indexing of these neighborhoods. In Sect. 4, we present results against baselines whose base complexities are of the same order.

3.3 Generic Metric Spaces

Our discussion and illustration have been concerned with metric space (Ω, d) where $\Omega \subset \mathbb{R}^D$ and $d(.,.)$ is the Euclidean distance function. All definitions provided here rely on the existence of a proper distance function and therefore do generalize to other metric spaces. The precise study of the properties obtained when constructing the HubHSP in these metric spaces is out of the scope of this paper and is left for an extension.

4   Experiments

We now experiment under various conditions and compare to relevant baselines.

4.1 Dataset

To highlight the properties of our proposal, we use data with various properties in terms of density and dimension D. As a base reference, we generate 2 artificial dataset with uniform distribution $\mathcal{U}^{100K \times 2}$ and $\mathcal{U}^{100K \times 10}$, containing 100'000 data of dimension $D = 2$ and $D = 10$, respectively. Note that in this case, the dataset of dimension 10 with 100'000 data is rather sparse.

To depart from the uniform distribution, we generate 2 dataset $\mathcal{N}^{100K \times 2}$ and $\mathcal{N}^{100K \times 10}$ with the same parameters but from a centered normal distribution. While uniformity makes the density of the data the same at every point in space, the Normal distribution induces an exponential variation of the density across the space.

As a more realistic dataset, we use the 500'000 first data of the ANN SIFT (base set) benchmark [8]. In this case $D = 128$, inducing a very sparse set. We also use a dataset of Flow Cytometry data containing $N = 470'995$ $D = 18$-dimensional data. This data is known by definition to aggregate in dense localized clusters (see Fig. 3 for a 2D glance). Its distribution is therefore far from uniform with large unpopulated parts of the space.

In all cases, we set the size n of the sample to 1% of the original size N. We fixed $k = 1000$ and $\varepsilon = 20$ to create the base neighborhoods ($\mathcal{V}_\mathcal{X}^k(x_i)$ and $\mathcal{V}_\mathcal{X}^\varepsilon(x_i)$ respectively) over which the HubHSP graph is built.

4.2 Baselines

Random. As discussed above, a uniform sampling of the data indices ensures the preservation of the statistical properties (density) of the data into the sample.

Farthest First Traversal (FFT). In contrast, this geometrical strategy aims at spreading the representative set across the dataset by approximating the k-center problem [6]. Using this strategy it is expected that the representative samples lie close to a regular grid.

Note that due to the concentration of distance phenomenon, this strategy loses its rationale in high dimensions.

k-means ++ [2] adds a random component to the above FFT strategy by making it most likely but not a strict choice, depending on the density of the data. k-means ++ is therefore interesting since it offers theoretical bounds in representation and mixes geometrical and statistical constraints, as we aim to do here.

4.3 Measures and Results

We use the following measures to assess the characteristics of our proposed sampling. Results are reported in Table 1.

Table 1. Evaluation measures across dataset and techniques. Top section: empty sphere. Middle section: lengths of inverted lists (standard deviation). Bottom section: Maximum distance. Values between parenthesis are standard deviation values

	$\mathcal{U}^{100K\times10}$	$\mathcal{U}^{100K\times2}$	$\mathcal{N}^{100K\times10}$	$\mathcal{N}^{100K\times2}$	SIFT$^{500K\times128}$	FlowCyto$^{471K\times18}$
Random	100.95 (16.72)	**3.19 (1.69)**	182.99 (39.85)	**7.47 (7.24)**	250.35 (47.76)	146.48 (47.64)
FFT	147.51 (4.85)	5.75 (0.54)	330.13 (12.77)	19.37 (5.03)	359.20 (6.33)	321.67 (26.19)
k-means++	107.97 (14.32)	4.12 (1.36)	200.93 (39.88)	13.20 (10.88)	265.47 (38.37)	178.04 (64.88)
HHSP (kNN)	108.76 (10.51)	4.25 (1.78)	170.28 (18.32)	10.69 (10.42)	244.77 (35.84)	146.37 (38.61)
HHSP (eNN)	**94.66 (15.88)**	3.32 (1.45)	**151.47 (31.20)**	9.91 (4.20)	**203.26 (58.11)**	**115.20 (40.76)**
Random	46.47	53.76	59.60	54.27	86.53	66.34
FFT	76.04	23.05	340.66	149.93	329.60	530.15
k-means++	47.97	36.15	77.93	69.09	112.12	90.99
HHSP (kNN)	33.25	35.34	**24.21**	**37.97**	60.11	53.05
HHSP (eNN)	**33.17**	54.26	27.20	51.65	**56.91**	**36.88**
Random	100.38 (18.96)	3.17 (1.71)	180.76 (43.61)	7.55 (8.15)	247.86 (53.62)	145.92 (51.40)
FFT	106.68 (17.56)	**2.51 (1.00)**	240.60 (37.13)	7.79 (3.14)	296.86 (40.41)	218.95 (34.87)
k-means++	100.6 (18.52)	2.78 (1.34)	183.64 (41.57)	6.41 (3.88)	249.60 (50.90)	146.72 (44.19)
HHSP (kNN)	98.51 (19.36)	2.69 (1.16)	**175.17 (47.62)**	**6.32 (5.59)**	245.89 (52.23)	147.88 (59.17)
HHSP (eNN)	**96.85 (19.57)**	3.17 (1.62)	175.90 (48.16)	7.30 (12.11)	**239.22 (56.73)**	**138.20 (53.47)**

The empty sphere measure (top section) quantifies the uniformity of the sampling by measuring the diameter of the largest empty sphere lying between samples. In practice it is the maximum distance between 2 neighboring samples.

Since we wish an equipartition of the space by samples, the smaller this value is, the better the quality of the sample. We report the mean and also measure uniformity of this allocation by reporting the standard deviation (between parenthesis).

We see that in the most basic conditions ($\mathcal{U}^{100K \times 2}$) all sampling strategies perform similarly. When the dimension increases (e.g. $\mathcal{U}^{100K \times 10}$), the data becomes sparser and geometrical techniques (such as FFT) fail. Our proposal is able to consistently reduce the value of the measure while keeping the variance at a comparable level.

The length of inverted lists (middle section) is an indicator of the uniformity of the allocation of representative to the data. In practice, since we use Dirichlet domains to define the lists, the average list length is simply the ratio between the size of the data and the sample ($\mathbf{E}|\mathcal{L}_j| = N/n$) so only the standard deviation is reported. The smaller this value, the more uniform the partition is.

We clearly see the same trend of lower variance in the length of inverted lists and therefore more stability in the allocation of representative data.

The maximum distance (bottom section) between a data and its representative is rather based on the data. It is a geometric indicator of how well every data is represented by the sample. Ideally, every data should find a representative in its vicinity so again, the smaller this value is, the better. We report the mean and also measure uniformity of this allocation by reporting the standard deviation (between parenthesis).

This measure shows that the HubHSP hubness allocates representatives closer to each data than other strategies. This is understood by the ability of the HubHSP to exploit better the statistical and geometrical properties of the data to allocate better a fixed budget of n representative data. This is made clear in the most adverse setting of high-dimensional non-uniform data (which corresponds to real dataset).

Figure 3 proposes a visual intuition of the allocation of representatives in low-dimensional non-uniform data. The resulting samples (red points) are shown over the data (green points) for all baselines and for the HubHSP. An ideal sampling should show regularity (to avoid redundancy) and respect the data density.

Whereas random sampling (top left) is inefficient by allocating redundant representative samples, the FFT (top right) is inefficient by being blind to the local density. k-means $++$ (lower left) proposes an adequate mix of statistical and geometrical sampling but clearly the HubHSP (lower right) adds a form of regularity that removes local density artifacts due to random sampling and explains the effectiveness in terms of geometrical partitioning (Dirichlet domains) of the data.

Finally, Fig. 4 shows an histogram of the corresponding hubness values h_j. A very large majority of these values are zero, which demonstrates the ability

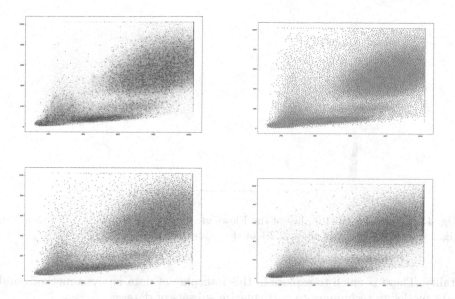

Fig. 3. Sampling strategies by the baselines and the HubHSP over a 2D slice of the FlowCyto dataset (FlowCyto$^{471k \times 2}$) as a low-dimensional non-uniform example. In each scatter plot, the dataset is shown in green and selected representatives are shown in red. [top left] Random uniform, [Top right] FFT, [Lower left] k-means ++, [Lower right] HubHSP (ours) (Color figure online)

of the HubHSP to concentrate its indegree into only a minority of large values (since $\sum_j h_j = N$). This indicates that only a small percentage of data in $\mathcal{X}$ then compete for entering $\mathcal{Y}$.

5 Conclusion

Subsampling a finite dataset may be considered from either a statistical or geometrical perspectives. Classical strategies focus on either of these. Based on the capability of the HSP graph to correlate with the local intrinsic dimensionality we proposed the HubHSP to generate a sound data selection criterion combining geometrical and statistical properties.

We demonstrate the ability of the HubHSP graph construction algorithm as a modification of the HSP graph construction to indicate a sound and stable selection of data as representative. We compare with classical selection algorithm and show that the HubHSP is able to create a more robust and effective sampling by a better exploitation of geometrical constraints on top of statistical sampling.

More generally, this work relates the ability of graph spanners to mirror and combine geometrical and statistical properties of non-uniform point clouds in high dimensions. In [9] diffusion over neighborhood graphs was used to exhibit that structure exploiting the link between connectivity (resp degree) and cen-

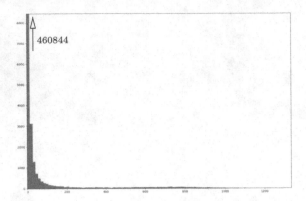

Fig. 4. Hubness for the 2D slice of the FlowCyto dataset (FlowCyto$^{471k \times 2}$) shown in Fig. 2 [Lower right]. Only about 2.2% of the values are non-zero.

trality. There is much to explore in this interplay of data analysis methods and data modeling techniques to particularize subsets of dataset.

Acknowledgments. This work is partly funded by the Swiss National Science Foundation under grant number 207509 "Structural Intrinsic Dimensionality".

Annexes

HubHSP Projection. The HSP selects its neighbors based on increasing distance after discarding half-planes. Since the neighbors selected by the HubHSP can occur in random order of their distance values from the central point x_i, it is critical to consider them as projected over a common sphere centered at x_i.

The most canonical choice is the sphere C_i including the first neighbor x_l of x_i. Note $\rho_i = d(x_l, x_i)$ its radius (the distance between x_i and its closest neighbor), then a point x_j is projected as $\tilde{x}_j$ onto C_i by:

$$\tilde{x}_j = \text{Proj}_{C_i}(x_j) = \underset{x \in C_i}{\text{argmin}}\, d(x, x_j) = x_i + \rho_i \frac{x_j - x_i}{d(x_j, x_i)}$$

Main Mathematical Symbols

Ω Ambient space	$f_{\mathcal{X}}$ True pdf of the dataset
$\mathcal{X}, \mathcal{Y}$ Main dataset, representative set	$\hat{f}_{\mathcal{X}}$ Empirical density of the dataset
$[\![N]\!]$ Set of indices $\{1 \cdots N\}$	$\mathcal{V}_{\mathcal{X}}^k(x)$ k-closest neighbors of x in $\mathcal{X}$
$d(.,.)$ distance function	$\mathcal{V}_{\mathcal{X}}^\varepsilon(x)$ ε-neighbors of x ($= \mathcal{B}(x, \varepsilon) \cap$
$\mathcal{B}(x, \rho)$ Ball centered at x of radius ρ	$\mathcal{X}$)
	$\mathcal{L}_j$ Inverted list for x_j
$\text{Proj}_C(x)$ Projection of x onto C	$\mathbf{E}X$ Expectation of variable X

References

1. Amato, G., Esuli, A., Falchi, F.: A comparison of pivot selection techniques for permutation-based indexing. Inf. Syst. **52**, 176–188 (2015). https://doi.org/10.1016/j.is.2015.01.010
2. Arthur, D., Vassilvitskii, S.: K-means++: the advantages of careful seeding. In: Proceedings of the Eighteenth Annual ACM-SIAM Symposium on Discrete Algorithms, SODA 2007, pp. 1027–1035. Society for Industrial and Applied Mathematics, USA (2007)
3. Bustos, B., Navarro, G., Chávez, E.: Pivot selection techniques for proximity searching in metric spaces. Pattern Recogn. Lett. **24**, 2357–2366 (2003)
4. Chavez, E., et al.: Half-space proximal: a new local test for extracting a bounded dilation spanner of a unit disk graph. In: Anderson, J.H., Prencipe, G., Wattenhofer, R. (eds.) OPODIS 2005. LNCS, vol. 3974, pp. 235–245. Springer, Heidelberg (2006). https://doi.org/10.1007/11795490_19
5. Chávez, E., Navarro, G., Baeza-Yates, R., Marroquín, J.L.: Searching in metric spaces. ACM Comput. Surv. **33**(3), 273–321 (2001)
6. Dasgupta, S., Long, P.M.: Performance guarantees for hierarchical clustering. J. Comput. Syst. Sci. **70**, 555–569 (2005). Farthest First Traversal for Pivot Selection
7. Hoyos, A., Ruiz, U., Marchand-Maillet, S., Chávez, E.: Indexability-based dataset partitioning. In: Amato, G., Gennaro, C., Oria, V., Radovanović, M. (eds.) SISAP 2019. LNCS, vol. 11807, pp. 143–150. Springer, Cham (2019). https://doi.org/10.1007/978-3-030-32047-8_13
8. Jégou, H., Douze, M., Schmid, C.: Product quantization for nearest neighbor search. IEEE Trans. Pattern Anal. Mach. Intell. **33**(1), 117–128 (2011)
9. Marchand-Maillet, S., Pedreira, O., Chávez, E.: Structural intrinsic dimensionality. In: Reyes, N., et al. (eds.) SISAP 2021. LNCS, vol. 13058, pp. 173–185. Springer, Cham (2021). https://doi.org/10.1007/978-3-030-89657-7_14
10. Ruiz, G., Chávez, E., Ruiz, U., Tellez, E.S.: Extreme pivots: a pivot selection strategy for faster metric search. Knowl. Inf. Syst. **62**(6), 2349–2382 (2020). https://doi.org/10.1007/s10115-019-01423-5
11. Terrell, G.R., Scott, D.W.: Variable kernel density estimation. Ann. Stat. **20**(3), 1236–1265 (1992)

Indexing and Clustering

Graph Edit Distance Compacted Search Tree

Ibrahim Chegrane[1,3]([⊠]), Imane Hocine[1,2], Saïd Yahiaoui[1], Ahcene Bendjoudi[1], and Nadia Nouali-Taboudjemat[1]

[1] CERIST, Research Center on Scientific and Technical Information,
16306 Ben Aknoun, Algiers, Algeria
{syahiaoui,abendjoudi,nnouali}@cerist.dz
[2] Ecole Nationale Supérieure d'Informatique,
BP 68M, 16309 Oued-Smar, Alger, Algeria
bi_hocine@esi.dz
[3] CoBIUS Lab, Department of Computer Science, University of Sherbrooke,
Sherbrooke, QC, Canada
ibrahim.chegrane@usherbrooke.ca

Abstract. We propose two methods to compact the used search tree during the graph edit distance (GED) computation. The first maps the node information and encodes the different edit operations by numbers and the needed remaining vertices and edges by BitSets. The second represents the tree succinctly by bit-vectors. The proposed methods require 24 to 250 times less memory than traditional versions without negatively influencing the running time.

Keywords: Graph Edit Distance (GED) · Compacted GED search space

1 Introduction

The Graph Edit Distance (GED) is a well-known metric used to compute the degree of dissimilarity between two graphs g_1 and g_2. It is generally used in pattern recognition [12], such as handwriting recognition [9] and document analysis [4]. The GED is defined as the minimum-cost sequence of edit operations needed to transform graph g_1 into graph g_2 [3]. The allowed operations are insertion, deletion, and substitution, which are applied on vertices and their corresponding edges. The GED computation is an NP-hard problem [13]. It has an exponential time complexity due to the exponential size of the generated search tree.

Bunke and Allermann were the precursors for solving the GED problem [3]. The authors used an A* based algorithm where the search tree is generated dynamically. In [8], the authors proposed an approximation for the GED problem called *A*-Beamsearch*. By limiting the size of the A* priority queue to a certain size s. To speed up the A* search process, [10] presents an effective heuristic that gives the estimated cost h and concludes a lower bound. This heuristic, called bipartite heuristic [9], has been discussed and improved in [11] and [2] to compute a more accurate lower bound. Authors in [1] proposed an approach called (DF_GED)

© The Author(s), under exclusive license to Springer Nature Switzerland AG 2022
T. Skopal et al. (Eds.): SISAP 2022, LNCS 13590, pp. 181–189, 2022.
https://doi.org/10.1007/978-3-031-17849-8_14

based on the Depth-First Search (DFS) to reduce the amount of used memory space. It proposes an alternative to the A* algorithm without addressing the underlying data structure and data representation. In [6], a tree-based approximate approach that gives near-optimal results is proposed. Gouda and Hassaan in [7] proposed an edge-based DFS method called CSI_GED.

Existing methods [1,6,10] mainly focus on reducing the time complexity by using parallel techniques or heuristics which provide approximate results without addressing the used data structure. In this work we attempt to reduce the memory space inherent to the GED computation by proposing two methods to compact the GED search tree. First, we compact each field used in its nodes based on an efficient mapping to encode the information of the different edit operations. A single number encodes the hole edit operation including its type and involved vertices, and a BitSet encodes the needed remaining vertices and edges. This mapping allows us to represent each path as a sequence of numbers. Second, the search tree is represented succinctly by bit-vectors where only the active nodes are stored and all the ancestor parents are deleted. Our work is independent of the search tree algorithms. Therefore, the proposed approach represents a general framework that can be used with both algorithms based on best first search (A*) or on depth-first search (B&B). Experiments on well-known benchmarks show the efficiency of our proposed methods. It confirms that our methods reduce the memory used by a factor of 24x to 250x. Moreover, they do not negatively influence the running time. It generally gets the same processing time as traditional algorithms, and may achieve twice faster times with some benchmarks.

The rest of this paper is organized as follows. In Sect. 2, we present the search tree used to solve the GED problem. In Sect. 3, we describe our methods. Section 4 outlines the obtained results. Finally, conclusions are given in Sect. 5.

2   The Data Structure Used to Solve the GED Problem

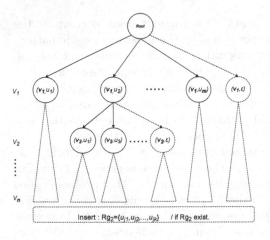

Fig. 1. Vertex edit operations in the search tree.

The GED search tree represents the mapping of the vertices of the first graph g_1 with the vertices of the second graph g_2 using the three edit operations: substitution, deletion and insertion. It generates for each vertex $v_i \in V_1$ all the possible substitutions with other vertices $u_j \in V_2$, and also the deletion of v_i. At the end, if there are still vertices in V_2, we insert them in one single operation. In addition to the list OPEN that is used in the tree exploration process.

The following information is associated with each node:

1. A pointer to keep relationships with its parent (to construct the edit path).
2. The vertex edit operation: The two involved vertex from g_1 and g_2; (v_i, u_j), (v_i, ϵ) or (ϵ, u_j). The vertex information may contain a weight or labels.
3. The implied edges operation which are either added or calculated directly.
4. The real cost g: the sum of costs from the root to this intermediate node.
5. The estimated cost h from this intermediate node to the leaf.
6. The remaining vertices of g_1: At each level l, each outgoing path has the same vertex v_l from g_1 and a different w_j from g_2 plus one deletion node. So it suffices to store the last index of the processed vertex (See Fig. 1).
7. The remaining vertices of g_2: We keep a list of non-processed vertices.
8. The remaining edges of g_1 and g_2: If we compute them, the processing time will increase. In contrast, we increase memory space needed if we store them.

3 Compacted Search Tree for the GED Problem

To compact the data structure presented in Sect. 2, we present two methods:

3.1 Compacted Method 1: GED Compacted Search Tree (_CT)

The idea is to compact each separate field needed (the vertex edit operations). Our work is inspired by a cost matrix proposed in [9,10]. The cost matrix represents all the combinations of edit operations between the vertices of the two graphs g_1 and g_2. Using this matrix model, we propose the *Edit Operations Matrix* to index all possible operations. The proposed matrix is divided into four regions (See Table 1). The top left region represents substitutions between g_1 and g_2. The far-right column represents the deletions from g_1, while the bottom line represents the insertions in g_2. The last region of the bottom-right cell is useless. We assign to each cell a unique number. We begin from the top left of the matrix by 0 and, each time, we increment by 1 till we finish at the bottom right of the matrix. Therefore, instead of manipulating the vertex edit operations, we use the unique *id* assigned to each edit operation (See Table 1). Each node in the tree uses the *ids* from the edit operation matrix. This avoids manipulating the entire vertices of edit operations. We do not need to store this matrix. We only generate each vertex edit operation *id* based on the indices of the vertices from g_1 and g_2.

Table 1. Vertex operation matrix id.

	0	1	2	...	(m-1)	m
0	0	1	2	...	m-1	m
1	$(1 \times m) + 1$	$(1 \times m) + 2$	$(1 \times m) + 3$	...	$(1 \times m) + m$	$(1 \times m) + (m+1)$
2	$(2 \times m) + 2$	$(2 \times m) + 3$	$(2 \times m) + 4$	...	$(2 \times m) + (m+1)$	$(2 \times m) + (m+2)$
(n-1)	$((n-1) \times m) + (n-1)$	$((n-1) \times m) + (n-1) + 1$	$((n-1) \times m) + (n-1) + 2$	...	$((n-1) \times m) + m + (n-1) - 1$	$((n-1) \times m) + m + (n-1)$
n	$(n \times m) + (n)$	$(n \times m) + (n) + 1$	$(n \times m) + (n) + 2$	...	$(n \times m) + m + (n) - 1$	$(n \times m) + m + (n)$

The ids in the Edit Operations Matrix: Let n,m be the number of vertices of g_1, g_2 respectively. The *id* of an edit operation that involves the vertex i form g_1 and the vertex j from g_2 (the indices begin from 0) can be given by the following equation: $id(i,j) = (i \times m) + (i + j)$, so we can write it in the following form: $id(i,j) = (m + 1) \times i + j$. In Table 1, it is clear that the column m concerns operations of the deletion, and the row n concerns those of the insertion. Hence, in the case of deletion a vertex v_i, we set $j = m$. In contrast, we set $i = n$ if we insert a given v_j. Therefore, the vertex edit operations are given as follow:

– Substitution: $get\_id\_sub(i,j) = (m+1) \times i + j$
– Deletion: $get\_id\_del(i) = (m+1) \times i + m$
– Insertion: $get\_id\_ins(j) = (m+1) \times n + j$

Get i and j the Involved Vertices form the Edit Operation $id(i,j)$: From the *id* of a given edit operation, we need to find the type of that operation and its involved vertices. Note that, we only have the following three values: *id*, n and m. The index i of the vertex in g_1 is given by:

$$i = \left\lfloor \frac{id(i,j)}{(m+1)} \right\rfloor = \left\lfloor \frac{(m+1) \times i + j}{(m+1)} \right\rfloor$$

The index j of a vertex in g_2 is given by:

$$j = id(i,j) \bmod (m+1) = ((m+1) \times i + j) \bmod (m+1)$$

After getting i and j values, we deduct the edit operation by checking if:

– $i < n$ & $j < m$, then it is a substitution between v_i from g_1 and u_j from g_2.
– $i < n$ & $j = m$, then it is a deletion of the vertex v_i from g_1.
– $i = n$ & $j < m$, then it is an insertion of the vertex u_j in g_2.

Get the Complete Edit Path: When the search process finds a solution, we need to reconstruct the whole path of edit operations including vertices and edges. For each edit operation *id* in the edit path $\lambda(g_1, g_2) = \{id_{e1}, id_{e2}, ..., id_{ek}\}$, we retrieve the type of the edit operation and the involved vertices. Then, we extract the implied edges and add them to the final path solution.

The List of the Remaining Vertices and Edges: The remaining vertices and edges at each node are represented by a separate BitSet. A bitvector is created for each remaining list. Initially, all the bits are set to 1. Each node is assigned a copy of its parent BitSet with a 0 in the processed node position.

3.2   Compacted Method 2: Path Representation Using BitSets (_CB)

We benefit from the mapping of the first method where paths are represented by suits of numbers. We represent these paths by BitSets. Each path will be compacted. Moreover, we keep only the active nodes in the search tree, and we delete all the ancestor parents. A path is the succession of nodes related by pointers that contain ids. Assuming that b the size of the pointer equals the size of the edit operation id, we need $2b \times k$ bits to represent a path of k operations. This can be reduced to only a few bits when representing a path by a BitSet.

In the first method, each path is represented as follows $\lambda(g_1, g_2) = \{id_{e1}, id_{e2}, ..., id_{ek}\}$. For example, $path(g_1, g_2) = \{2, 6, 8, ...\}$. We encode this path by a BitSet, where each edit operation id is represented in the BitSet by 1 in its position. For the ids $(2, 6, 8)$, in the BitSet we put 1 at the 2nd,6th, and 8th positions; and all other bits are set to 0. Hence, the $path(g_1, g_2) = \{2, 6, 8, ...\}$ is represented as BitSets like $path(g_1, g_2) = [0, 0, 1, 0, 0, 0, 1, 0, 1, ...]$. Each partial or complete path (at inner or leaf node) is represented by its own BitSet.

During the searching process, we keep only the nodes (paths) that are not treated yet. We do not need the ancestor nodes from the root to the final treated node (inner or leaf node), because all the ids of the edit operations are in the BitSet of the final treated node. Figure 2 illustrates the search tree using BitSets.

The BitSet Size Needed by Nodes at Each Level of the Tree: Each node in the search tree generates at most $m + 1$ child (m is the number of vertices of g_2), where the outgoing are composed by only one vertex from g_1 combined with the other vertices of g_2 plus its own deletion (see Fig. 1). As shown in Table 1, in each row of the edit operations matrix, one vertex v_i from g_1 is substituted with all the vertices of g_2, and deleted at last. The first row contains the ids from 0 to m, the second from $m+1$ to $2m+1$, etc.

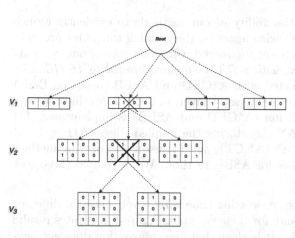

Fig. 2. The search tree using bites array.

At the first level of the tree, each node, can so be represented by a BitSet having the same size as the first column in the matrix which is $m + 1$. At the second level, each node, requires the size of the second column of the matrix $(m + 1)$ that allows to index the ids of the second vertex from g_1, combined with the rest of vertices from g_2 (m) plus one deletion. We also need to keep all the path in the second level. Thus, we add the BitSet of the first level. As a result, the size is $2 \times (m + 1)$. As a general rule, each node has to keep the information of its previous parents. Therefore, we need a BitSet of $l \times (m + 1)$ bits in each node at the level l. We should notice that we have a sparse BitSet. All the positions contain the value 0, except the one representing the id of the edit operation associated with the node. Hence, if desired, one can compress the

Table 2. Setting cost for vertex and edge edit operations.

	Vertex			Edge		
	Sub	Del	Ins	Sub	Del	Ins
Setting 1	2	4	4	1	1	1
Setting 2	2	4	4	1	2	2
Setting 3	6	2	2	3	1	1

Table 3. Datasets information.

Dataset	NB graphs	mean #nodes	mean degree	min #nodes	max #nodes
PAH	94	20.7	20.4	10	28
Mao	68	18.4	2.1	11	27

BitSet [5]. The other information needed during the searching process, such as g, h values and remaining vertices and edges, are kept at each node.

4   Tests and Experiments

In this section, we investigate the ability of our methods to efficiently reduce the used memory space, and see their impact on the running time. Our program is written in JAVA 1.8. Our tests are conducted using one core of one computing node of IBNBADIS Cluster, *with a RAM memory limited to 16 GB*. The two proposed methods implemented with A*GED and ASBB (based on B&B) approaches are compared using the datasets[1] given in Table 3. We have a total of 8 methods. Each basic algorithm (A*GED and ASBB) is implemented: (1) computing the implied edges (A*), (2) storing the implied edges (A*Edge), (3) using compacting method 1 on A* (A*_CT), and (4) using compacting method 2 on A* (A*_CB). The same goes for ASBB method. We have used three cost settings[2] (Table 2).

Time Processing Results: The processing time is relatively close for different methods tested for A*, ASBB and, for their variants. Figure 3 illustrates results for Mao and Grec20 benchmarks. It is clear that the compaction does not negatively influence the processing time. Since the PAH Benchmark is difficult to solve, we do our experiment with only ASBB algorithm using only setting 1. The results are in hours as follow: *basic ASBB: 42.50 h, ASBB_CT: 21.92 h* and *ASBB_CB: 20.98 h*. We notice clearly that the compacted methods speed up the processing time to twice because they manipulate only ids with elementary operations (number and bits).

Memory Space Results: To measure the space used by the program, we use the open source *MemoryMeter*[3]. Figure 4 illustrates the memory space used by A*, ASBB and their four implementations with compaction to solve the problem of exact GED for Mao and Grec20 datasets. Storing the implied edges (A*/ASBB

---

[1] Download from https://gdc2016.greyc.fr/#ged.

[2] These settings were used in the competition https://gdc2016.greyc.fr/#ged.

[3] MemoryMeter: https://github.com/jbellis/jamm.

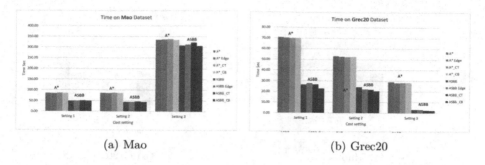

(a) Mao   (b) Grec20

Fig. 3. The running time for A*, ASBB with compaction on Mao, and Grec20.

Edge), as expected, increases a little bit the used memory space. It is very clear that the compaction improves the used memory space. Our first method A*_CT achieves an average gain of 4.33, 3.57 less memory with respectively Mao and Grec20. Whereas, ASBB_CT method gets an average gain of 1.73, 164 for the same datasets. Our second method (A*/ASBB)_CB achieves remarkable good results. We clearly see the power of this method to reduce the memory space better than basic algorithms, where it gains an average of 24 less memory with A*_CB, and 250x less with ASBB_CB. Figure 5 illustrates the gain factor of the used memory space between basic and compacted algorithms.

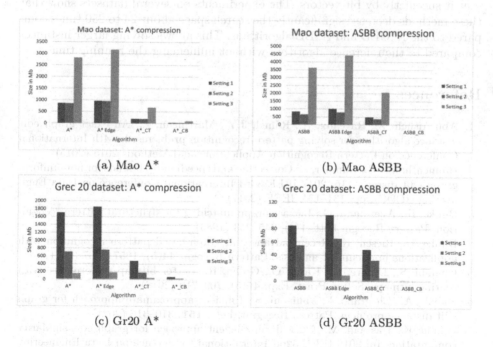

(a) Mao A*   (b) Mao ASBB

(c) Gr20 A*   (d) Gr20 ASBB

Fig. 4. The memory space occupied by each method on the used datasets.

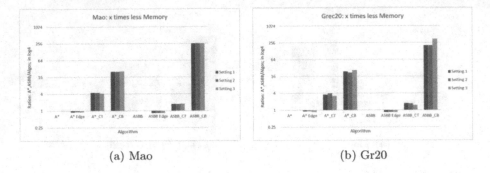

(a) Mao   (b) Gr20

Fig. 5. The ratio of used memory space between basic and compacted algorithms.

5   Conclusion

The exact GED problem has exponential space and time complexity. This work focuses on the memory space of the search tree used to solve this problem. We proposed to compact this tree using an intelligent mapping to represent the different edit operations, and BitSets to represent the needed remaining vertices and edges. Moreover, instead of storing the traditional search tree, we represent it succinctly by bit-vectors. The experiments on several datasets show that these methods decrease significantly the search space about 24 to 250 times compared to the A*GED and ASBB algorithms. This allows solving larger instances compared to the reference algorithm without influencing the running time.

References

1. Abu-Aisheh, Z., Raveaux, R., Ramel, J.Y., Martineau, P.: An exact graph edit distance algorithm for solving pattern recognition problems. In: 4th International Conference on Pattern Recognition Applications and Methods 2015 (2015)
2. Blumenthal, D.B., Gamper, J.: Correcting and speeding-up bounds for non-uniform graph edit distance. In: 2017 IEEE 33rd International Conference on Data Engineering (ICDE), pp. 131–134. IEEE (2017)
3. Bunke, H., Allermann, G.: Inexact graph matching for structural pattern recognition. Pattern Recogn. Lett. **1**(4), 245–253 (1983)
4. Bunke, H., Riesen, K.: Recent advances in graph-based pattern recognition with applications in document analysis. Pattern Recogn. **44**(5), 1057–1067 (2011)
5. Chambi, S., Lemire, D., Kaser, O., Godin, R.: Better bitmap performance with roaring bitmaps. Softw. Pract. Exp. **46**(5), 709–719 (2016)
6. Dabah, A., Chegrane, I., Yahiaoui, S.: Efficient approximate approach for graph edit distance problem. Pattern Recognit. Lett. **151**, 310–316 (2021)
7. Gouda, K., Hassaan, M.: Csi_ged: an efficient approach for graph edit similarity computation. In: 2016 IEEE 32nd International Conference on Data Engineering (ICDE), pp. 265–276. IEEE (2016)

8. Neuhaus, M., Riesen, K., Bunke, H.: Fast suboptimal algorithms for the computation of graph edit distance. In: Yeung, D.-Y., Kwok, J.T., Fred, A., Roli, F.,
   de Ridder, D. (eds.) SSPR /SPR 2006. LNCS, vol. 4109, pp. 163–172. Springer,
   Heidelberg (2006). https://doi.org/10.1007/11815921_17
9. Riesen, K., Bunke, H.: Approximate graph edit distance computation by means of
   bipartite graph matching. Image Vis. Comput. **27**(7), 950–959 (2009)
10. Riesen, K., Fankhauser, S., Bunke, H.: Speeding up graph edit distance computa-
    tion with a bipartite heuristic. In: MLG (2007)
11. Riesen, K., Fischer, A., Bunke, H.: Computing upper and lower bounds of graph
    edit distance in cubic time. In: El Gayar, N., Schwenker, F., Suen, C. (eds.) ANNPR
    2014. LNCS (LNAI), vol. 8774, pp. 129–140. Springer, Cham (2014). https://doi.
    org/10.1007/978-3-319-11656-3_12
12. Vento, M.: A long trip in the charming world of graphs for pattern recognition.
    Pattern Recogn. **48**(2), 291–301 (2015)
13. Zeng, Z., Tung, A.K., Wang, J., Feng, J., Zhou, L.: Comparing stars: on approxi-
    mating graph edit distance. Proc. VLDB Endow. **2**(1), 25–36 (2009)

Clustering by Direct Optimization
of the Medoid Silhouette

Lars Lenssen[(✉)] and Erich Schubert

Informatik VIII, TU Dortmund University, 44221 Dortmund, Germany
{lars.lenssen,erich.schubert}@tu-dortmund.de

Abstract. The evaluation of clustering results is difficult, highly dependent on the evaluated data set and the perspective of the beholder. There are many different clustering quality measures, which try to provide a general measure to validate clustering results. A very popular measure is the Silhouette. We discuss the efficient medoid-based variant of the Silhouette, perform a theoretical analysis of its properties, and provide two fast versions for the direct optimization. We combine ideas from the original Silhouette with the well-known PAM algorithm and its latest improvements FasterPAM. One of the versions guarantees equal results to the original variant and provides a run speedup of $O(k^2)$. In experiments on real data with 30000 samples and $k = 100$, we observed a 10464× speedup compared to the original PAMMEDSIL algorithm.

1   Introduction

In cluster analysis, the user is interested in discovering previously unknown structure in the data, as opposed to classification where one predicts the known structure (labels) for new data points. Sometimes, clustering can also be interpreted as data quantization and approximation, for example k-means which aims at minimizing the sum of squared errors when approximating the data with k average vectors, spherical k-means which aims to maximize the cosine similarities to the k centers, and k-medoids which minimizes the sum of distances when approximating the data by k data points. Other clustering approaches such as DBSCAN [6,15] cannot easily be interpreted this way, but discover structure related to connected components and density-based minimal spanning trees [16].

The evaluation of clusterings is a challenge, as there are no labels available. While many internal ("unsupervised", not relying on external labels) evaluation measures were proposed such as the Silhouette [14], Davies-Bouldin index, the Variance-Ratio criterion, the Dunn index, and many more, using these indexes for evaluation suffers from inherent problems. Bonner [4] noted that "none of the many specific definitions [...] seems best in any general sense", and results are subjective "in the eye of the beholder" as noted by Estivill-Castro [7]. While these

Part of the work on this paper has been supported by Deutsche Forschungsgemeinschaft (DFG) – project number 124020371 – within the Collaborative Research Center SFB 876 "Providing Information by Resource-Constrained Analysis" project A2.

T. Skopal et al. (Eds.): SISAP 2022, LNCS 13590, pp. 190–204, 2022.
https://doi.org/10.1007/978-3-031-17849-8_15

claims refer to clustering methods, not evaluation methods, we argue that these do not differ substantially: each internal cluster evaluation method implies a clustering algorithm obtained by enumeration of all candidate clusterings, keeping the best. The main difference between clustering algorithms and internal evaluation then is whether or not we know an efficient optimization strategy. K-means is an optimization strategy for the sum of squares evaluation measure, while the k-medoids algorithms PAM, and Alternating are different strategies for optimizing the sum of deviations from a set of k representatives.

In this article, we focus on the evaluation measure known as Silhouette [14], and discuss an efficient algorithm to optimize a variant of this measure, inspired by the well-known PAM algorithm [8,9] and FasterPAM [18,19].

2   Silhouette and Medoid Silhouette

The Silhouette [14] is a popular measure to evaluate clustering validity, and performs very well in empirical studies [2,5]. For the given samples $X = \{x_1, \ldots, x_n\}$, a dissimilarity measure $d : X \times X \mapsto \mathbb{R}$, and the cluster labels $L = \{l_1, \ldots, l_n\}$, the Silhouette for a single element i is calculated based on the average distance to its own cluster a_i and the smallest average distance to another cluster b_i as:

$$s_i(X, d, L) = \frac{b_i - a_i}{\max(a_i, b_i)}, \text{ where}$$
$$a_i = \text{mean} \{d(x_i, x_j) \mid l_j = l_i\}$$
$$b_i = \min_{k \neq l_i} \text{mean} \{d(x_i, x_j) \mid l_j = k\}.$$

The motivation is that ideally, each point is much closer to the cluster it is assigned to, than to another "second closest" cluster. For $b_i \gg a_i$, the Silhouette approaches 1, while for points with $a_i = b_i$ we obtain a Silhouette of 0, and negative values can arise if there is another closer cluster and hence $b_i < a_i$. The Silhouette values s_i can then be used to visualize the cluster quality by sorting objects by label l_i first, and then by descending s_i, to obtain the Silhouette plot. However, visually inspecting the Silhouette plot is only feasible for small data sets, and hence it is also common to aggregate the values into a single statistic, often referred to as the Average Silhouette Width (ASW):

$$S(X, d, L) = \frac{1}{n} \sum_{i=1}^{n} s_i(X, d, L).$$

Hence, this is a function that maps a data set, dissimilarity, and cluster labeling to a real number, and this measure has been shown to satisfy desirable properties for clustering quality measures (CQM) by Ackerman and Ben-David [1].

A key limitation of the Silhouette is its computational cost. It is easy to see that it requires all pairwise dissimilarities, and hence takes $O(N^2)$ time to compute – much more than popular clustering algorithms such as k-means.

For algorithms such as k-means and k-medoids, a simple approximation to the Silhouette is possible by using the distance to the cluster center respectively medoids $M = \{M_1, \ldots, M_k\}$ instead of the average distance. For this "simplified

Silhouette" (which can be computed in $O(Nk)$ time, and which Van der Laan et al. [20] called medoid-based Silhouette) we use

$$s'_i(X, d, M) = \frac{b'_i - a'_i}{\max(a'_i, b'_i)}, \text{ where}$$
$$a'_i = d(x_i, M_{l_i})$$
$$b'_i = \min_{k \neq l_i} d(x_i, M_k).$$

If each point is assigned to the closest cluster center (optimal for k-medoids and the Silhouette), we further know that $a'_i \leq b'_i$ and $s_i \geq 0$, and hence this can further be simplified to the *Medoid Silhouette*

$$\tilde{s}_i(X, d, M) = \frac{d_2(i) - d_1(i)}{d_2(i)} = 1 - \frac{d_1(i)}{d_2(i)}.$$

where d_1 is the distance to the closest and d_2 to the second closest center in M. For $d_1(i) = d_2(i) = 0$, we add a small ε to $d_2(i)$ to get $\tilde{s} = 1$. The Average Medoid Silhouette (AMS) then is defined as the average

$$\tilde{S}(X, d, M) = \frac{1}{n} \sum_{i=1}^{n} \tilde{s}_i(X, d, M).$$

It can easily be seen that the optimum clustering is the (assignment of points to the) set of medoids such that we minimize an "average relative loss":

$$\arg\max_M \tilde{S}(X, d, M) = \arg\min_M \text{mean}_i \frac{d_1(i)}{d_2(i)}.$$

For clustering around medoids, we impose the restriction $M \subseteq X$; which has the benefit of not restricting the input data to be numerical (e.g., $X \subset \mathbb{R}^d$, as in k-means), and allowing non-metric dissimilarity functions d.

3   Related Work

The Silhouette [14] was originally proposed along with Partitioning Around Medoids (PAM, [8,9]), and indeed k-medoids already does a decent job at finding a good solution, although it does optimize a different criterion (the sum of total deviations). Van der Laan et al. [20] proposed to optimize the Silhouette by substituting the Silhouette evaluation measure into the PAM SWAP procedure (calling this PAMSIL). Because they recompute the loss function each time (as opposed to PAM, which computes the change), the complexity of PAMSIL is $O(k(N - k)N^2)$, since for each of $k \cdot (N - k)$ possible swaps, the Silhouette is computed in $O(N^2)$. Because this yields a very slow clustering method, they also considered the Medoid Silhouette instead (PAMMEDSIL), which only needs $O(k^2(N - k)N)$ time (but still considerably more than PAM).

Schubert and Rousseeuw [18,19] recently improved the PAM method, and their FastPAM approach reduces the cost of PAM by a factor of $O(k)$, making the method $O(N^2)$ by the use of a shared accumulator to avoid the innermost loop. In this work, we will combine ideas from this algorithm with the PAMMEDSIL approach above, to optimize the Medoid Silhouette with a swap-based local search, but a run time comparable to FastPAM. But we will first perform a theoretical analysis of the properties of the Medoid Silhouette, to show that it is worth exploring as an alternative to the original Silhouette.

4   Axiomatic Characterization of Medoid Clustering

We follow the axiomatic approach of Ackerman and Ben-David [1], to prove the value of using the Average Medoid Silhouette (AMS) as a clustering quality measure (CQM). Kleinberg [11] defined three axioms for clustering functions and argued that no clustering algorithm can satisfy these desirable properties at the same time, as they contradict. Because of this, Ackermann and Ben-David [1] weaken the original Consistency Axiom and extract four axioms for clustering quality measures: *Scale Invariance* and *Richness* are defined analogously to the Kleinberg Axioms. We redefine the CQM axioms [1] for medoid-based clustering.

Definition 1. *For given data points $X = \{x_1, \ldots, x_n\}$ with a set of k medoids $M = \{m_1, \ldots, m_k\}$ and a dissimilarity d, we write $x_i \sim_M x_{i'}$ whenever x_i and $x_{i'}$ have the same nearest medoid $n_1(i) \subseteq M$, otherwise $x_i \nsim_M x_{i'}$.*

Definition 2. *Dissimilarity d' is an M-consistent variant of d, if $d'(x_i, x_{i'}) \leq d(x_i, x_{i'})$ for $x_i \sim_M x_{i'}$, and $d'(x_i, x_{i'}) \geq d(x_i, x_{i'})$ for $x_i \nsim_M x_{i'}$.*

Definition 3. *Two sets of medoids $M, M' \subseteq X$ with a distance function d over X, are isomorphic, if there exists a distance-preserving isomorphism $\phi : X \to X$, such that for all $x_i, x_{i'} \in X$, $x_i \sim_M x_{i'}$ if and only if $\phi(x_i) \sim_{M'} \phi(x_{i'})$.*

Axiom 1 (Scale Invariance). *A medoid-based clustering quality measure f satisfies scale invariance if for every set of medoids $M \subseteq X$ for d, and every positive λ, $f(X, d, M) = f(X, \lambda d, M)$.*

Axiom 2 (Consistency). *A medoid-based clustering quality measure f satisfies consistency if for a set of medoids $M \subseteq X$ for d, whenever d' is an M-consistent variant of d, then $f(X, d', M) \geq f(X, d, M)$.*

Axiom 3 (Richness). *A medoid-based clustering quality measure f satisfies richness if for each set of medoids $M \subseteq X$, there exists a distance function d over X such that $M = \arg\max_M f(X, d, M)$.*

Axiom 4 (Isomorphism Invariance). *A medoid-based clustering quality measure f is isomorphism-invariant if for all sets of medoids $M, M' \subseteq X$ with distance d over X where M and M' are isomorphic, $f(X, d, M) = f(X, d, M')$.*

Batool and Hennig [3] prove that the ASW satisfies the original CQM axioms. We prove the first three adapted axioms for the Average Medoid Silhouette. The fourth, Isomorphism Invariance, is obviously fulfilled, since AMS is based only on dissimilarites, just as the ASW [3].

Theorem 1. *The AMS is a* scale invariant *clustering quality measure.*

Proof. If we replace d with λd, both $d_1(i)$ and $d_2(i)$ are multiplied by λ, and the term will cancel out. Hence, $\tilde{s}_i$ does not change for any i:

$$\tilde{S}(X, \lambda d, M) = \tfrac{1}{n}\sum_{i=1}^{n} \tilde{s}_i(X, \lambda d, M) = \tfrac{1}{n}\sum_{i=1}^{n} \tfrac{\lambda d_2(i) - \lambda d_1(i)}{\lambda d_2(i)}$$
$$= \tfrac{1}{n}\sum_{i=1}^{n} \tfrac{d_2(i) - d_1(i)}{d_2(i)} = \tfrac{1}{n}\sum_{i=1}^{n} \tilde{s}_i(X, d, M) = \tilde{S}(X, d, M).$$

Theorem 2. *The AMS is a* consistent *clustering quality measure.*

Proof. Let dissimilarity d' be a M-consistent variant of d. By Definition 2: $d'(x_i, x_{i'}) \leq d(x_i, x_{i'})$ for all $x_i \sim_M x_{i'}$, and $\min_{x_i \not\sim_M x_{i'}} d'(x_i, x_{i'}) \geq \min_{x_i \not\sim_M x_{i'}} d(x_i, x_{i'})$. This implies for all $i \in \mathbb{N}$: $d'_1(i) \leq d_1(i), d'_2(i) \geq d_2(i)$ and it follows:

$$\frac{d_1(i)}{d_2(i)} - \frac{d'_1(i)}{d'_2(i)} \geq 0 \quad \Leftrightarrow \quad \frac{d'_2(i) - d'_1(i)}{d'_2(i)} - \frac{d_2(i) - d_1(i)}{d_2(i)} \geq 0$$

which is equivalent to $\forall_i \; \tilde{s}_i(X, d', M) \geq \tilde{s}_i(X, d, M)$, hence $\tilde{S}(X, d', M) \geq \tilde{S}(X, d, M)$, i.e., AMS is a consistent clustering quality measure.

Theorem 3. *The AMS is a* rich *clustering quality measure.*

Proof. We can simply encode the desired set of medoids M in our dissimilarity d. We define $d(x_i, x_j)$ such that it is 0 if trivially $i = j$, or if x_i or x_j is the first medoid m_1 and the other is not a medoid itself. Otherwise, let the distance be 1.

For M we then obtain $\tilde{S}(X, d, M) = 1$, because $d_1(i) = 0$ for all objects, as either x_i is a medoid itself, or can be assigned to the first medoid m_1. This is the maximum possible Average Medoid Silhouette. Let $M' \neq M$ be any other set of medoids. Then there exists at least one missing $x_i \in M \backslash M'$. For this object $\tilde{s}_i(X, d, M) = 0$ (as its distance to all other objects is 1, and it is not in M'), and hence $\tilde{S}(X, d, M') < 1 = \tilde{S}(X, d, M)$.

5   Direct Optimization of Medoid Silhouette

PAMSIL [20] is a modification of PAM [8,9] to optimize the ASW. For PAMSIL, Van der Laan [20] adjusts the SWAP phase of PAM by always performing the SWAP that provides the best increase in the ASW. When no further improvement is found, a (local) maximum of the ASW has been achieved. However, where the original PAM efficiently computes only the change in its loss (in $O(N - k)$ time for each of $(N - k)k$ swap candidates), PAMSIL computes the entire ASW in $O(N^2)$ for every candidate, and hence the run time per iteration increases to $O(k(N-k)N^2)$. For a small k, this yields a run time that is cubic in the number of objects N, and the algorithm may need several iterations to converge.

5.1   Naive Medoid Silhouette Clustering

PAMMEDSIL [20] uses the Average Medoid Silhouette (AMS) instead, which can be evaluated in only $O(Nk)$ time. This yields a SWAP run time of $O(k^2(N - k)N)$ (for small $k \ll N$ only quadratic in N). As Schubert and Rousseeuw [18,19] were able to reduce the run time of PAM to $O(N^2)$ per iteration, we modify the PAMMEDSIL approach accordingly to obtain a similar speedup. The SWAP algorithm of PAMMEDSIL is shown in Algorithm 1.

Algorithm 1: PAMMEDSIL SWAP: Iterative improvement

1 $S' \leftarrow$ Simplified Silhouette sum of the initial solution M
2 **repeat**
3 $\quad$ $(S'_*, M_*) \leftarrow (0, \text{null})$
4 $\quad$ **foreach** $m_i \in M = \{m_1, \ldots, m_k\}$ **do** $\qquad$ // each medoid
5 $\quad\quad$ **foreach** $x_j \notin \{m_1, \ldots, m_k\}$ **do** $\qquad$ // each non-medoid
6 $\quad\quad\quad$ $(S', M') \leftarrow (0, M\backslash\{m_i\} \cup \{x_j\})$
7 $\quad\quad\quad$ **foreach** $x_o \in X = \{x_1, \ldots, x_n\}$ **do**
8 $\quad\quad\quad\quad$ $S' \leftarrow S' + s'_o(X, d, M')$ $\qquad$ // Simplified Silhouette
9 $\quad\quad\quad$ **if** $S' > S'_*$ **then** $(S'_*, M_*) \leftarrow (S', M')$ // keep best swap found
10 $\quad$ **if** $S'_* \geq S'$ **then break**
11 $\quad$ $(S', M) \leftarrow (S'_*, M_*)$ $\qquad$ // perform swap
12 **return** $(S'/N, M)$

5.2   Finding the Best Swap

We first bring PAMMEDSIL up to par with regular PAM. The trick introduced with PAM is to compute the change in loss instead of recomputing the loss, which can be done in $O(N - k)$ instead of $O(k(N - k))$ time if we store the distance to the nearest and second centers, as the latter allows us to compute the change if the current nearest center is removed efficiently. In the following, we omit the constant parameters X and d for brevity. We denote the previously nearest medoid of i as $n_1(i)$, and $d_1(i)$ is the (cached) distance to it. We similarly define $n_2(i)$, $d_2(i)$, and $d_3(i)$ with respect to the second and third nearest medoid. We briefly use d'_1 and d'_2 to denote the new distances for a candidate swap. For the Medoid Silhouette, we can compute the change when swapping medoids $m_i \in \{m_1, \ldots, m_k\}$ with non-medoids $x_j \notin \{m_1, \ldots, m_k\}$:

$$\Delta\tilde{S} = \frac{1}{n} \sum_{o=1}^{n} \Delta\tilde{s}_o(M, m_i, x_j)$$

$$\Delta\tilde{s}_o(M, m_i, x_j) = \tilde{s}_o(M\backslash\{m_i\} \cup \{x_j\}) - \tilde{s}_o(M)$$

$$= \frac{d'_2(i) - d'_1(i)}{d'_2(i)} - \frac{d_2(i) - d_1(i)}{d_2(i)} = \frac{d_1(i)}{d_2(i)} - \frac{d'_1(i)}{d'_2(i)}.$$

Clearly, we only need the distances to the closest and second closest center, before and after the swap. Instead of recomputing them, we exploit that only one medoid can change in a swap. By determining the new values of d'_1 and d'_2 using cached values only, we can save a factor of $O(k)$ on the run time.

In the PAM algorithm (where the change would be simply $d'_1 - d_1$), the distance to the *second* nearest is cached in order to compute the loss change if the current medoid is removed, without having to consider all $k - 1$ other medoids: the point is then either assigned to the new medoid, or its former second closest. To efficiently compute the change in Medoid Silhouette, we have to take this one step further, and additionally need to cache the identity of the second closest center and the distance to the *third* closest center (denoted d_3). This is beneficial if, e.g., the nearest medoid is replaced. Then we may have, e.g., $d'_1 = d_2$ and $d'_2 = d_3$, if we can distinguish these cases.

Algorithm 2: Change in Medoid Silhouette, $\Delta\tilde{s}_o(M, m_i, x_j)$

1 **if** $m_i = n_1(o)$ **then**   // nearest is replaced

2 | **if** $d(o,j) < d_2(o)$ **then return** $\frac{d_1(o)}{d_2(o)} - \frac{d(o,j)}{d_2(o)}$ // xj is new nearest

3 | **if** $d(o,j) < d_2(o)$ **then return** $\frac{d_1(o)}{d_2(o)} - \frac{d_2(o)}{d(o,j)}$ // xj is new second

4 | **else return** $\frac{d_1(o)}{d_2(o)} - \frac{d_2(o)}{d_3(o)}$

5 **else if** $m_i = n_2(o)$ **then**   // second nearest is replaced

6 | **if** $d(o,j) < d_1(o)$ **then return** $\frac{d_1(o)}{d_2(o)} - \frac{d(o,j)}{d_1(o)}$ // xj is new nearest

7 | **if** $d(o,j) < d_3(o)$ **then return** $\frac{d_1(o)}{d_2(o)} - \frac{d_1(o)}{d(o,j)}$ // xj is new second

8 | **else return** $\frac{d_1(o)}{d_2(o)} - \frac{d_1(o)}{d_3(o)}$

9 **else**

10 | **if** $d(o,j) < d_1(o)$ **then return** $\frac{d_1(o)}{d_2(o)} - \frac{d(o,j)}{d_1(o)}$ // xj is new nearest

11 | **if** $d(o,j) < d_2(o)$ **then return** $\frac{d_1(o)}{d_2(o)} - \frac{d_1(o)}{d(o,j)}$ // xj is new second

12 | **else return** 0

The change in Medoid Silhouette is then computed roughly as follows: (1) If the new medoid is the new closest, the second closest is either the former nearest, or the second nearest (if the first was replaced). (2) If the new medoid is the new second closest, the closest either remains the former nearest, or the second nearest (if the first was replaced). (3) If the new medoid is neither, we may still have replaced the closest or second closest; in which case the distance to the third nearest is necessary to compute the new Silhouette. Putting all the cases (and sub-cases) into one equation becomes a bit messy, and hence we opt to use pseudocode in Algorithm 2 instead of an equivalent mathematical notation. Note that the first term is always the same (the previous loss), except for the last case, where it canceled out via $0 = \frac{d_1(o)}{d_2(o)} - \frac{d_1(o)}{d_2(o)}$. As this is a frequent case, it is beneficial to not have further computations here (and hence, to compute the change instead of computing the loss). Clearly, this algorithm runs in $O(1)$ if $n_1(o)$, $n_2(o)$, $d_1(o)$, $d_2(o)$, and $d_3(o)$ are known. We also only compute $d(o,j)$ once. Modifying PAMMEDSIL (Algorithm 1) to use this computation yields a run time of $O(k(N-k)N)$ to find the best swap, i.e., already $O(k)$ times faster. But we can further improve this approach.

5.3 Fast Medoid Silhouette Clustering

We now integrate an acceleration added to the PAM algorithm by Schubert and Rousseeuw [18,19], that exploits redundancy among the loop over the k medoids to replace. For this, the loss change $\Delta\tilde{S}(m_i, x_j)$ is split into multiple components: (1) the change by removing medoid m_i (without choosing a replacement), (2) the change by adding x_j as an additional medoid, and (3) a correction term if both operations occur at the same time. The first factors can be computed in $O(kN)$, the second in $O(N(N-k))$, and the last factor is 0 if the removed medoid is neither of the two closest, and hence is also in $O(N^2)$. This then yields an algorithm that finds the best swap in $O(N^2)$, again $O(k)$ times faster.

The first terms (the removal of each medoid $m_i \in M$) are computed as:

$$\Delta \tilde{S}^{-m_i} = \sum\nolimits_{n_1(o)=i} \frac{d_1(o)}{d_2(o)} - \frac{d_2(o)}{d_3(o)} + \sum\nolimits_{n_2(o)=i} \frac{d_1(o)}{d_2(o)} - \frac{d_1(o)}{d_3(o)}, \qquad (1)$$

while for the second we compute the addition of a new medoid $x_j \notin M$

$$\Delta \tilde{S}^{+x_j} = \sum_{o=1}^{n} \begin{cases} \frac{d_1(o)}{d_2(o)} - \frac{d(o,j)}{d_1(o)} & \text{if } d(o,j) < d_1(o) \\ \frac{d_1(o)}{d_2(o)} - \frac{d_1(o)}{d(o,j)} & \text{else if } d(o,j) < d_2(o) \\ 0 & \text{otherwise.} \end{cases}$$

Combining these yields the change:

$$\Delta \tilde{S}(m_i, x_j) = \Delta \tilde{S}^{+x_j} + \Delta \tilde{S}^{-m_i}$$

$$+ \sum_{\substack{o \text{ with} \\ n_1(o)=i}} \begin{cases} \frac{d(o,j)}{d_1(o)} + \frac{d_2(o)}{d_3(o)} - \frac{d_1(o)+d(o,j)}{d_2(o)} & \text{if } d(o,j) < d_1(o) \\ \frac{d_1(o)}{d(o,j)} + \frac{d_2(o)}{d_3(o)} - \frac{d_1(o)+d(o,j)}{d_2(o)} & \text{else if } d(o,j) < d_2(o) \\ \frac{d_2(o)}{d_3(o)} - \frac{d_2(o)}{d(o,j)} & \text{else if } d(o,j) < d_3(o) \\ 0 & \text{otherwise} \end{cases}$$

$$+ \sum_{\substack{o \text{ with} \\ n_2(o)=i}} \begin{cases} \frac{d_1(o)}{d_3(o)} - \frac{d_1(o)}{d_2(o)} & \text{if } d(o,j) < d_1(o) \\ \frac{d_1(o)}{d_3(o)} - \frac{d_1(o)}{d_2(o)} & \text{else if } d(o,j) < d_2(o) \\ \frac{d_1(o)}{d_3(o)} - \frac{d_1(o)}{d(o,j)} & \text{else if } d(o,j) < d_3(o) \\ 0 & \text{otherwise.} \end{cases}$$

It is easy to see that the additional summands can be computed by iterating over all objects x_o, and adding their contributions to accumulators for $n_1(o)$ and $n_2(o)$. As each object o contributes to exactly two cases, the run time is $O(N)$. This then gives Algorithm 3, which computes $\Delta \tilde{S}^{+x_j}$ along with the sum of $\Delta \tilde{S}^{-m_i}$ and these correction terms in an accumulator array. The algorithm needs $O(k)$ memory for the accumulators in the loop, and $O(N)$ additional memory to store the cached n_1, n_2, d_1, d_2, and d_3 for each object.

This algorithm gives the same result,but FastMSC ("Fast Medoid Silhouette Clustering") is $O(k^2)$ faster than the naive PAMMEDSIL.

5.4   Eager Swapping and Random Initialization

We can now integrate further improvements by Schubert and Rousseeuw [19]. Because doing the best swap (steepest descent) does not appear to guarantee finding better solutions, but requires a pass over the entire data set for each step, we can converge to local optima much faster if we perform every swap that yields an improvement, even though this means we may repeatedly replacing the same medoid. For PAM they called this eager swapping, and named the variant FasterPAM. This does not improve theoretical run time (the last iteration will always require a pass over the entire data set to detect convergence), but empirically reduces the number of iterations substantially. It will no longer find the same results, but there is no evidence that a steepest descent is beneficial over

---

Algorithm 3: FastMSC: Improved SWAP algorithm

1 **repeat**
2   **foreach** x_o **do** compute $n_1(o), n_2(o), d_1(o), d_2(o), d_3(o)$
3     $\Delta\tilde{S}^{-m_1}, \ldots, \Delta\tilde{S}^{-m_i} \leftarrow$ compute loss change removing m_i using (1)
4     $(\Delta\tilde{S}^*, m^*, x^*) \leftarrow (0,\text{null},\text{null})$
5   **foreach** $x_j \notin \{m_1, \ldots, m_k\}$ **do**   // each non-medoid
6        $\Delta\tilde{S}_i, \ldots, \Delta\tilde{S}_k \leftarrow (\Delta\tilde{S}^{-m_1}, \ldots, \Delta\tilde{S}^{-m_i})$ // use removal loss
7        $\Delta\tilde{S}^{+x_j} \leftarrow 0$ // initialize shared accumulator
8   **foreach** $x_o \in \{x_1, \ldots, x_n\}$ **do**
9           $d_{oj} \leftarrow d(x_o, x_j)$ // distance to new medoid
10   **if** $d_{oj} < d_1(o)$ **then**   // new closest
11             $\Delta\tilde{S}^{+x_j} \leftarrow \Delta\tilde{S}^{+x_j} + d_1(o)/d_2(o) - d_{oj}/d_1(o)$
12             $\Delta\tilde{S}_{n_1(o)} \leftarrow \Delta\tilde{S}_{n_1(o)} + d_{oj}/d_1(o) + d_2(o)/d_3(o) - \frac{d_1(o)+d_{oj}}{d_2(o)}$
13             $\Delta\tilde{S}_{n_2(o)} \leftarrow \Delta\tilde{S}_{n_2(o)} + d_1(o)/d_3(o) - d_1(o)/d_2(o)$
14   **else if** $d_{oj} < d_2(o)$ **then**   // new first/second closest
15             $\Delta\tilde{S}^{+x_j} \leftarrow \Delta\tilde{S}^{+x_j} + d_1(o)/d_2(o) - d_1(o)/d_{oj}$
16             $\Delta\tilde{S}_{n_1(o)} \leftarrow \Delta\tilde{S}_{n_1(o)} + d_1(o)/d_{oj} + d_2(o)/d_3(o) - \frac{d_1(o)+d_{oj}}{d_2(o)}$
17             $\Delta\tilde{S}_{n_2(o)} \leftarrow \Delta\tilde{S}_{n_2(o)} + d_1(o)/d_3(o) - d_1(o)/d_2(o)$
18   **else if** $d_{oj} < d_3(o)$ **then**   // new second/third closest
19             $\Delta\tilde{S}_{n_1(o)} \leftarrow \Delta\tilde{S}_{n_1(o)} + d_2(o)/d_3(o) - d_2(o)/d_{oj}$
20             $\Delta\tilde{S}_{n_2(o)} \leftarrow \Delta\tilde{S}_{n_2(o)} + d_1(o)/d_3(o) - d_1(o)/d_{oj}$
21       $i \leftarrow \text{argmax}\,\Delta\tilde{S}_i$
22       $\Delta\tilde{S}_i \leftarrow \Delta\tilde{S}_i + \Delta\tilde{S}^{+x_j}$
23   **if** $\Delta\tilde{S}_i > \Delta\tilde{S}^*$ **then** $(\Delta\tilde{S}^*, m^*, x^*) \leftarrow (\Delta\tilde{S}, m_i, x_j)$
24   **break outer loop if** $\Delta\tilde{S}^* \leq 0$
25   swap roles of medoid m^* and non-medoid x^* // perform swap
26    $\tilde{S} \leftarrow \tilde{S} + \Delta\tilde{S}^*$
27 **return** $\tilde{S}, M$

---

choosing the first descent found. The main downside to this is, that it increases the dependency on the data ordering, and hence is best used on shuffled data when run repeatedly. Similarly, we will study a variant that eagerly performs the first swap that improves the AMS as FasterMSC ("Fast and Eager Medoid Silhouette Clustering").

Also, the classic initialization with PAM BUILD now becomes the performance bottleneck, and Schubert and Rousseeuw [19] showed that random initialization in combination with eager swapping works very well.

6   Experiments

We next evaluate clustering quality, to show the benefits of optimizing AMS. We report both AMS and ASW, as well as the supervised measures Adjusted Random Index (ARI) and Normalized Mutual Information (NMI). Afterward, we study the scalability, to verify the expected speedup for our algorithm FastMSC.

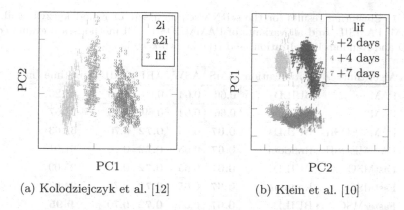

(a) Kolodziejczyk et al. [12]   (b) Klein et al. [10]

Fig. 1. Different kind of mouse embryonic stem cells (mESCs). For both datasets we have done PCA and plot the first two principal components. (a) shows 704 mESCs grown in three different conditions and (b) 2717 mESCs at the moment of LIF withdrawal, 2 days after, 4 days after, and 7 days after.

6.1   Data Sets

Since it became possible to map gene expression at the single-cell level by RNA sequencing, clustering on these has become a popular task, and Silhouette is a popular evaluation measure there. Single-cell RNA sequencing (scRNA-seq) provides high-dimensional data that requires appropriate preprocessing to extract information. After extraction of significant genes, these marker genes are validated by clustering of proper cells.

We explore two larger sample size (by scRNA standards) scRNA-sequencing data sets of mouse embryonic stem cells (mESCs) publicly available. Kolodziejczyk et al. [12] studied 704 mESCs with 38561 genes grown in three different conditions (2i, a2i and serum). Klein et al. [10] worked on the influence leukemia inhibitory factor (LIF) withdrawal on mESCs. For this, he studied a total of 2717 mESCs with 24175 genes. The data included 933 cells after LIF-withdrawal, 303 cells two days after, 683 cells 4 days after, and 798 cells 7 days after. We normalize each cell by total counts over all genes, so that every cell has a total count equal to the median of total counts for observations (cells) before normalization, then we perform principal component analysis (PCA) and use the first three principal components for clustering. Fig. 1 visualizes the first two principal components of these data sets and the obtained labels. To test the scalability of our new variants, we need larger data sets. We use the well-known MNIST data set, with 784 features and 60000 samples (PAMSIL will not be able to handle this size in reasonable time). We implemented our algorithms in Rust, extending the `kmedoids` package [17], wrapped with Python, and we make our source code available in this package. We perform all computations in the same package, to avoid side effects caused by comparing too different implementations [13]. We run 10 restarts on an AMD EPYC 7302 processor using a single thread, and evaluate the average values.

Table 1. Clustering results for the scRNA-seq data sets of Kolodziejczyk et al. [12] for PAM, PAMSIL, and all variants of PAMMEDSIL. All methods are evaluated for BUILD and Random initialization, and true known $k = 3$.

Algorithm	Initialization	AMS	ASW	ARI	NMI	Run time (ms)
PAM	BUILD	0.66	0.64	0.69	0.65	18.26
PAM	Random	0.66	0.64	0.69	0.65	22.67
PAMMEDSIL	BUILD	**0.67**	0.65	**0.72**	0.70	62.63
PAMMEDSIL	Random	**0.67**	0.65	**0.72**	0.70	61.91
FastMSC	BUILD	**0.67**	0.65	**0.72**	0.70	25.09
FastMSC	Random	**0.67**	0.65	**0.72**	0.70	24.67
FasterMSC	BUILD	**0.67**	0.65	**0.72**	0.70	**9.95**
FasterMSC	Random	**0.67**	0.65	**0.72**	0.70	10.95
PAMSIL	BUILD	0.61	**0.66**	**0.72**	**0.71**	12493.86
PAMSIL	Random	0.61	**0.66**	**0.72**	**0.71**	16045.47

6.2 Clustering Quality

We evaluated all methods with PAM BUILD initialization and a random initialization. To evaluate the relevancy of the Average Silhouette Width and the Average Medoid Silhouette, we compare true labels using the Adjusted Rand Index (ARI) and Normalized Mutual Information (NMI), two common measures in clustering. On the data set from Kolodziejczyk shown in Table 1, the highest ARI is achieved by the direct optimization methods for AMS and ASW. The different initialization provide the same results for all methods. We get a much faster run time for the AMS variants compared to the ASW optimization. For FasterMSC, we obtain the same ARI as for PAMSIL with 1255× faster run time and only a 0.01 lower NMI. As expected, AMS and ASW are optimal by those algorithms, that optimize for this measure, but because the measures are correlated, those that optimize AMS only score 0.01 worse on the ASW. Interestingly the total deviation used by PAM appears to be slightly more correlated to AMS than ASW in this experiment. Given the small difference, we argue that AMS is a suitable approximation for ASW, at a much reduced run time.

Since there were no variations in the resulting medoids for the different restarts of the experiment, we can easily compare single results visually. Figure 2b compares the results of PAMMEDSIL and PAMSIL, showing which points are clustered differently than in the given labels. Both clusters are similar, with class 1 captured better in one, classes 2 and 3 better in the other result. Table 2 shows the clustering results for the scRNA-seq data sets of Klein et al. [10]. In contrast to Kolodziejczyk's data set, we here obtain a higher ARI for PAMSIL than for the AMS optimization methods. We get only the same high ARI and NMI for AMS optimization as for PAM, but a slightly higher ASW. However, FasterMSC is 16521× faster than PAMSIL.

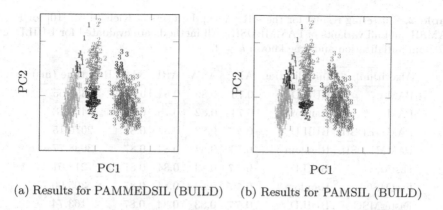

(a) Results for PAMMEDSIL (BUILD)   (b) Results for PAMSIL (BUILD)

Fig. 2. Clustering results for the scRNA-seq data sets of Kolodziejczyk et al. [12] for PAMMEDSIL and PAMSIL. All correctly predicted labels are colored by the corresponding cluster and all errors are marked as black. (Color figure online)

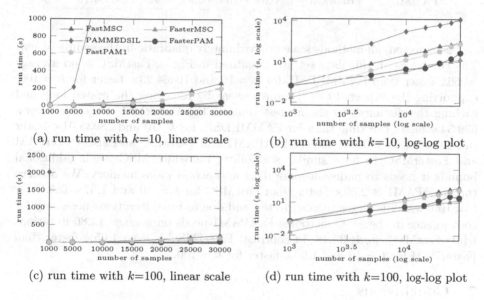

(a) run time with $k=10$, linear scale   (b) run time with $k=10$, log-log plot

(c) run time with $k=100$, linear scale   (d) run time with $k=100$, log-log plot

Fig. 3. Run time on MNIST data (time out 24 h)

6.3   Scalability

To evaluate the scalability of our methods, we use the well-known MNIST data, which has 784 variables (28×28 pixels) and 60000 samples. We use the first $n = 1000, \ldots, 30000$ samples and compare $k = 10$ and $k = 100$. Due to its high run time, PAMSIL is not able to handle this size in a reasonable time. In addition to the methods for direct AMS optimization, we evaluate the FastPAM1 and FasterPAM implementation. For all methods we use random initialization.

Table 2. Clustering results for the scRNA-seq data sets of Klein et al. [10] for PAM, PAMSIL and all variants of PAMMEDSIL. All methods are evaluated for BUILD and Random initialization and true known $k = 4$.

Algorithm	Initialization	AMS	ASW	ARI	NMI	Run time (ms)
PAM	BUILD	0.75	0.82	0.84	0.87	355.55
PAM	Random	0.74	0.82	0.78	0.80	476.18
PAMMEDSIL	BUILD	**0.77**	0.83	0.84	0.87	2076.15
PAMMEDSIL	Random	**0.77**	0.83	0.84	0.87	3088.77
FastMSC	BUILD	**0.77**	0.83	0.84	0.87	212.01
FastMSC	Random	**0.77**	0.83	0.84	0.87	305.00
FasterMSC	BUILD	**0.77**	0.83	0.84	0.87	163.74
FasterMSC	Random	**0.77**	0.83	0.84	0.87	**122.63**
PAMSIL	BUILD	0.67	**0.84**	**0.95**	**0.92**	2026025.10
PAMSIL	Random	0.67	0.84	0.93	0.91	1490354.10

As expected, all methods scale approximately quadratic in the sample size n. The run times on this data set are visualized in Fig. 3. FastMSC is on average 50.66x faster than PAMMEDSIL for $k = 10$ and 10464.23× faster for $k = 100$, supporting the expected $O(k^2)$ improvement by removing the nested loop and caching the distances to the nearest centers. For FasterMSC we achieve even 639.34× faster run time than for PAMMEDSIL for $k=10$ and 78035.01× faster run time for $k=100$. We expect FastPAM1 and FastMSC and also FasterPAM and FasterMSC to have similar scalability; but since MSC needs additional bounds it needs to maintain more data and access more memory. We observe that FastPAM1 is 2.50× faster than FastMSC for $k = 10$ and 1.57× faster for $k = 100$, which is larger than expected and due to more iterations necessary for convergence in the MSC methods: FastPAM1 needs on average 14.86 iterations while FastMSC needs 33.48. In contrast, FasterMSC is even 1.65× faster than FasterPAM for $k = 10$ and 1.96× faster for $k = 100$.

7   Conclusions

We showed that the Average Medoid Silhouette satisfies desirable theoretical properties for clustering quality measures, and as an approximation of the Average Silhouette Width yields desirable results on real problems from gene expression analysis. We propose a new algorithm for optimizing the Average Medoid Silhouette, which provides a run time speedup of $O(k^2)$ compared to the earlier PAMMEDSIL algorithm by avoiding unnecessary distance computations via caching of the distances to the nearest centers and of partial results based on FasterPAM. This makes clustering by optimizing the Medoid Silhouette possible on much larger data sets than before. The ability to optimize a variant of the popular Silhouette measure directly demonstrates the underlying problem that any internal cluster evaluation measure specifies a clustering itself.

References

1. Ackerman, M., Ben-David, S.: Measures of clustering quality: a working set of axioms for clustering. In: Advances in Neural Information Processing Systems (NIPS 2008), pp. 121–128 (2008). https://proceedings.neurips.cc/paper/2008/hash/beed13602b9b0e6ecb5b568ff5058f07-Abstract.html
2. Arbelaitz, O., Gurrutxaga, I., Muguerza, J., Pérez, J.M., Perona, I.: An extensive comparative study of cluster validity indices. Pattern Recognit. **46**(1), 243–256 (2013). https://doi.org/10.1016/j.patcog.2012.07.021
3. Batool, F., Hennig, C.: Clustering with the average silhouette width. Comput. Stat. Data Anal. **158**, 107190 (2021). https://doi.org/10.1016/j.csda.2021.107190
4. Bonner, R.E.: On some clustering techniques. IBM J. Res. Devel. **8**(1), 22–32 (1964). https://doi.org/10.1147/rd.81.0022
5. Brun, M., et al.: Model-based evaluation of clustering validation measures. Pattern Recognit. **40**(3), 807–824 (2007). https://doi.org/10.1016/j.patcog.2006.06.026
6. Ester, M., Kriegel, H.P., Sander, J., Xu, X.: A density-based algorithm for discovering clusters in large spatial databases with noise. In: International Conference on Knowledge Discovery and Data Mining, KDD'96, pp. 226–231 (1996). https://dl.acm.org/doi/10.5555/3001460.3001507
7. Estivill-Castro, V.: Why so many clustering algorithms – a position paper. SIGKDD Explor. **4**(1), 65–75 (2002). https://doi.org/10.1145/568574.568575
8. Kaufman, L., Rousseeuw, P.J.: Clustering by means of medoids. In: Statistical Data Analysis Based on the L_1 Norm and Related Methods. North-Holland (1987)
9. Kaufman, L., Rousseeuw, P.J.: Clustering large applications (program CLARA). In: Finding Groups in Data. Wiley (1990). https://doi.org/10.1002/9780470316801.ch3
10. Klein, A., et al.: Droplet barcoding for single-cell transcriptomics applied to embryonic stem cells. Cell **161**, 1187–1201 (2015). https://doi.org/10.1016/j.cell.2015.04.044
11. Kleinberg, J.: An impossibility theorem for clustering. In: Advances in Neural Information Processing Systems (NIPS 2002), vol. 15, pp. 463–470 (2002). https://papers.nips.cc/paper/2002/hash/43e4e6a6f341e00671e123714de019a8-Abstract.html
12. Kolodziejczyk, A., et al.: Single cell RNA-sequencing of pluripotent states unlocks modular transcriptional variation. Cell Stem Cell **17**(4), 471–485 (2015). https://doi.org/10.1016/j.stem.2015.09.011
13. Kriegel, H.-P., Schubert, E., Zimek, A.: The (black) art of runtime evaluation: are we comparing algorithms or implementations? Knowl. Inf. Syst. **52**(2), 341–378 (2016). https://doi.org/10.1007/s10115-016-1004-2
14. Rousseeuw, P.J.: Silhouettes: a graphical aid to the interpretation and validation of cluster analysis. J. Comput. Appl. Math. **20**, 53 (1987). https://doi.org/10.1016/0377-0427(87)90125-7
15. Schubert, E., Sander, J., Ester, M., Kriegel, H.P., Xu, X.: DBSCAN revisited, revisited: why and how you should (still) use DBSCAN. ACM Trans. Database Syst. **42**(3), 1–21 (2017). https://doi.org/10.1145/3068335
16. Schubert, E., Hess, S., Morik, K.: The relationship of DBSCAN to matrix factorization and spectral clustering. In: Lernen, Wissen, Daten, Analysen (2018)
17. Schubert, E., Lenssen, L.: Fast k-medoids clustering in Rust and Python. J. Open Source Softw. **7**(75), 4183 (2022). https://doi.org/10.21105/joss.04183

18. Schubert, E., Rousseeuw, P.J.: Faster k-medoids clustering: improving the PAM, CLARA, and CLARANS algorithms. In: Amato, G., Gennaro, C., Oria, V., Radovanović, M. (eds.) SISAP 2019. LNCS, vol. 11807, pp. 171–187. Springer, Cham (2019). https://doi.org/10.1007/978-3-030-32047-8_16
19. Schubert, E., Rousseeuw, P.J.: Fast and eager k-medoids clustering: O(k) runtime improvement of the PAM, CLARA, and CLARANS algorithms. Inf. Syst. **101**, 101804 (2021). https://doi.org/10.1016/j.is.2021.101804
20. Van der Laan, M., Pollard, K., Bryan, J.: A new partitioning around medoids algorithm. J. Stat. Comput. Simul. **73**(8), 575–584 (2003). https://doi.org/10.1080/0094965031000136012

Automatic Indexing for Similarity Search in ELKI

Erich Schubert[✉]

TU Dortmund University, Dortmund, Germany
erich.schubert@tu-dortmund.de

Abstract. Many data mining algorithms are distance-based and may benefit from using a database index accelerating the similarity search. Examples include clustering algorithms such as DBSCAN, nearest-neighbor classification, and the local outlier factor (LOF). However, choosing the appropriate index requires some knowledge and experience, so it commonly is left to the user, or there is a default value known to work for many. In this article, we discuss a system that contains a query optimizer for such queries that can automatically choose and create an appropriate index. It can reuse suitable indexes that are already present, and it comes with memory management that can also automatically drop an unused auto-created index when memory is scarce. The system is integrated into the ELKI data mining framework version 0.8.0, released along with this paper, and will be used automatically by many algorithms in the toolkit.

1 Introduction

Distance-based data mining algorithms often involve some search of relevant neighbors, either for all objects in a given radius (e.g., DBSCAN [7,9]) or for the k nearest neighbors (e.g., kNN classification, kNN outlier, LOF [6], and many other local outlier detectors [12]). Such algorithms can benefit substantially from index acceleration [8]. A more rare search is priority search, where the nearest neighbors are to be returned in ascending order, but there is no fixed threshold on either how many neighbors are needed, or the maximum radius. Incremental priority search is a generalization of both (if we stop at a particular radius, we have the result of a radius search; if we stop after k elements, we have a k nearest neighbor search). But it usually is more costly than the other two because it has to manage more open search paths that the other searches with given thresholds can discard early. Priority search is also useful for implementing filter and *filter-refinement* strategies; for example, we can use it to find the k nearest objects that additionally satisfy some constraint, or we can use priority search with a distance lower bound, and perform a more expensive distance computation for the candidates found this way. By the lower bounding property, the distance to the kth farthest refined object can be used to terminate the priority search while guaranteeing exact results (for details on this search strategy, see Seidl and

T. Skopal et al. (Eds.): SISAP 2022, LNCS 13590, pp. 205–213, 2022.
https://doi.org/10.1007/978-3-031-17849-8_16

Kriegel [13]). For example, we can use a cheap lower bound to find candidate graphs, then use graph edit distance for refinement in post-processing until the desired number of exact results are below the lower bound of the remainder [2].

2 Queries Supported

In this work, we focus on three particular queries (although ELKI also has support for, e.g., reverse k-nearest neighbor search), each for a query object q and a distance function d:

Range Search: given ε, return all database objects x that satisfy $d(x, q) \leq \varepsilon$. In particular, for Euclidean distance, this may also be called a radius search and should not be confused with rectangular interval searches, which sometimes may also be called range searches in literature.

k-nearest Neighbor Search: given k, return all database objects x that satisfy $d(x, q) \leq k$-dist(q), where k-dist(q) is the smallest distance such that at least k results are returned. In the case of ties, all results are to be included. Hence the result may contain more than k objects.

Incremental Priority Search: return an *iterator* that allows incrementally retrieving neighbor objects, ordered increasingly by $d(x, q)$, without having to specify neither the radius ε nor the number of results k beforehand.

Since the last is a less commonly used query (albeit it can answer both of the above query types), it warrants additional discussion. To illustrate the challenges of priority search, consider that we may even be further interested in approximate priority search, where objects are returned only in approximately increasing order. The exact distance to the candidate may still be unknown, but the searcher may have an upper and lower bound and further a lower bound for all objects not yet returned. E.g., in the cover tree, a set of points is represented by a ball cover. The distance to the ball center and the radius imply a lower and upper bound for the ball contents; the radius yields an accuracy estimate. The smallest lower bound of the open candidates lower bounds all remaining results. In a filter-refinement search, this may allow us to guarantee that we have found all results and hence stop the search early. In other cases, we may use this to find filtered k-nearest neighbors, skipping over candidates that do not have the desired property, e.g., to find the nearest open shops when indexed only by distance, omitting closed locations.

For such complicated searches, the ELKI API `PrioritySearcher` for priority search includes the following methods:

`advance()` advance the search to the next object
`getApproximateDistance()` to get a distance approximation
`getApproximateAccuracy()` to get an accuracy of the approximation
`getLowerBound()` to get a lower bound for the current candidate
`getUpperBound()` to get an upper bound for the current candidate

`computeExactDistance()` to get or compute the exact distance to a candidate
`allLowerBound()` to get a lower bound to all remaining results
`decreaseCutoff(radius)` to allow the searcher to drop candidates

Unfortunately (and this adds to the complexity of using this API), many of
these values may be unknown (then returning "not a number"), depending on
the index used. The cover tree is a nice example that provides all of these bounds,
but for example, the vantage point tree will often not have upper bounds.

Above API uses the iterator pattern, with the searcher object always pointing
to the current candidate instead of returning candidate objects. This design
reduces the number of object allocations, which considerably improves runtime
for Java due to the cost of object initialization and garbage collection. A similar
design is employed by many libraries for primitive collections for the same reason.
When implemented in a language that can return more complex structures on
the stack, a different design may be possible – or when Java gets value types.

An example of using this API can be found in the ELKI CFSFDP tutorial[1]
to find the nearest point of higher density is as follows:

```
double dist = Double.POSITIVE_INFINITY, tmp;
for(searcher.search(q); searcher.valid(); searcher.advance()) {
  if(density.intValue(searcher) > dens
     && (tmp = searcher.computeExactDistance()) < dist) {
    nearest.set(searcher.decreaseCutoff(dist = tmp));
} }
```

We begin searching at object q and process candidates by their approximated
increasing distance. Whenever finding an object of higher density, we update the
cutoff distance until the search stops. At this point, no unprocessed object may
be closer to the candidate stored in `nearest`. But in contrast to regular nearest
neighbor search we were able to skip over neighbors, and in contrast to range
search we did not have to know the search radius beforehand.

3   Automatic Index Acceleration

The key to automatic index acceleration is the need to plan. As it is technically
impossible to know the future, we have to rely on the developer to declare what
is needed. For example, a developer may need the k nearest neighbors only of a
single point (in which case it will likely not be beneficial to construct an index
automatically). In other cases he may need all pairwise distances later (and
hence, computing a full distance matrix would be reasonable), and in another
case, he may need the k nearest neighbors for each data sample and for each
k in a particular range (in which case it is likely best to compute the nearest
neighbors for the largest k of interest and store them).

Current commercial databases rarely support such queries, nor much acceler-
ated data mining, but are primarily useful for selecting, extracting, and preparing

---

[1] The full tutorial is at https://elki-project.github.io/tutorial/cfsfdp.

data. Much more index acceleration for similarity search is found in open-source systems such as the widely known scikit-learn and the less known Smile. But in scikit-learn, for example, distance-based methods have to actively create the index (either by instantiating a nearest neighbor searcher or by inheriting from it), and then perform a bulk query for best performance. The user has little control over the index search, besides some pass-through options. Because of this rather poor architecture, the DBSCAN class of scikit-learn has the options `algorithm` (`ball_tree`, `kd_tree`, or `brute`) and `leaf_size` that control the index (and not DBSCAN); and an extension to the neighbor searcher requires adding new options to DBSCAN. The index is not reused across multiple invocations.

For ELKI, we wanted a better decoupling of database indexes and algorithms. In the earlier versions of ELKI [11], there would be a `Database` object that allows the developer to obtain query searchers, and that would be responsible for creating all indexes before invoking the algorithm. In this version of ELKI, we add automatic index generation, and the developer interacts with a specialized class, the `QueryBuilder`, which follows the known builder design pattern. The API requires the developer to specify the necessary parameters (distance function, query type, but also additional constraints), the system then either chooses an available index of the database that supports this query, or invokes the `QueryOptimizer` that is responsible for creating a suitable index automatically. This split into two is desirable separation of concerns. At the same time, it gives more control to the user, who can either (1) add suitably optimized indexes to the database before calling the algorithm, (2) control or replace the query optimizer and define a custom optimization strategy without having to touch the algorithm classes. An algorithm developer, on the other hand, does not have to take care of indexing parameters to pass on to the searcher. The developer can provide additional needs to the query builder, useful, e.g., to verify the correctness a new index, or to fall back to alternative strategies and manual index selection. For example, the developer can (1) explicitly request a linear scan, (2) request exact results even when an approximate index is available, (3) accept only optimized queries, (4) asking for all answers to be precomputed and cached (for multiple uses), or (5) ask for cheap optimizations only if only a few points will be queried. For distance queries, algorithms can declare that they (6) will need almost all pairwise distances but also (7) request to not cache a distance matrix if they – as in hierarchical clustering – are going to keep a working copy.

For example, the ELKI implementation of DBSCAN uses a very simple call:

```
new QueryBuilder<>(relation, distance).rangeByDBID(epsilon)
```

to obtain a searcher for the ε range neighbors of database objects. When expaning clusters in DBSCAN, we search for neighbors using:

```
rangeQuery.getRange(startObjectID, epsilon, neighbors.clear())
```

where we recycle the output array `neighbors` to reduce garbage collection costs.

The following is the query builder call in the LOF algorithm:

```
new QueryBuilder<>(relation, distance).precomputed().kNNByDBID(k)
```

which indicates that we need a k-nearest neighbor search by object ID, and that the results are to be precomputed and cached (#4 above, because the LOF algorithm also uses the k-distance of neighbors to compare local densities). Neighbors of an object are then simply obtained (from the cache) by

```
KNNList neighbors = knnSearcher.getKNN(curr, k);
```

Searches in ELKI are strongly typed – the above examples query by object ID which allows the system to precompute results, for example, which is not possible if we had requested a search by objects (e.g., by a coordinate).

4   Choosing the Index Automatically

Depending on the parameters, distances, and data dimensionality, the ELKI optimizer will currently choose between a k-d-tree [4], a cover tree [5], or a vp-tree [14], and can automatically precompute nearest neighbors or add a full distance matrix. Details can be found in the class EmpiricalQueryOptimizer, which may be updated as new benchmarks lead to better heuristics.

For Euclidean distance, other Minkowski norms, and squared Euclidean distance, the k-d-tree usually performed best in low-dimensional data (we use a lightweight implementation that does not store bounding boxes, but by keeping an array of bounds per dimension still uses multidimensional bounds as suggested by Arya and Mount [1]. For priority search, the performance is much worse (as these bounds need to be copied for each branch, rather than updated via the stack), and other indexes may outperform the k-d-tree.

For other metrics, the vantage point tree (vp-tree, [14]) usually outperformed the cover tree in our current experiments, so it will usually take precedence.

For distances that are not metric (besides the squared Euclidean distance mentioned above), we currently do not have an automatic solution. But other functionality such as precomputation remains active.

5   Automatic Garbage Collection

It would be possible to have the index disappear when the searcher is no longer in use; either automatic by the Java garbage collector, or even more explicitly by implementing the AutoCloseable interface and the Java try with resources mechanism, as used for closing files. But in data mining, it is very common that we want to run an algorithm multiple times with different parameters or random restarts. In such cases, we want to be able to reuse the index. Hence we decided to use the WeakReference API of Java, and keep a weak reference to the index. This allows the Java system to garbage collect unused indexes when memory is low while keeping reusable indexes around across multiple restarts of an algorithm in many cases. In ELKI, this is handled by the `Hierarchy` API, which allows to attach objects to others in a hierarchy without polluting the objects' API, and without requiring the objects to implement a particular API. This method is also used to, for example, attach evaluation results to an algorithm result, or to attach metadata. For automatic indexing, we (weakly) attach the automatic indexes to the indexed data by

```
Metadata.hierarchyOf(relation).addWeakChild(index);
```

so they can easily be rediscovered; or deleted if the indexed relation is deleted.

Table 1. Best average query performance per index. Note that many data sets are high-dimensional and hence difficult for the k-d-tree.

Index	Parameters	Runtime relative to best		
		Average	Median	Maximum
k-nearest-neighbor search				
k-d	leafsize = 2 split = midpoint	18.50	1.83	148.07
cover	leafsize = 20	2.92	1.81	12.04
vp	leafsize = 1 samples = 10	1.55	1.17	3.41
auto		1.48	1.12	3.55
Range search				
cover	leafsize = 40	24.82	14.84	90.78
k-d	leafsize = 1 split = midpoint	2.17	1.11	12.77
auto		1.87	1.61	4.79
vp	leafsize = 1 samples = 10	1.79	1.66	4.41
Incremental priority search				
k-d	leafsize = 10 split = midpoint	33.83	4.26	268.47
auto		1.25	1.83	1.83
cover	leafsize = 10	1.23	1.06	1.88
vp	leafsize = 10 samples = 10	1.21	1.12	1.77

6   Experiments

In Table 1 we show the results of some benchmarks using data sets from the MultiView [10] data collection. We use ALOI color histograms of 27, 63, 77, and 216 dimensions. Additionally, we include a dataset of US zip codes, projected to Euclidean space. We measure the average run time of 5 restarts, different k, different query radii, and Euclidean and Manhattan distance (no other distances yet). Scores are normalized by the best (average) performance on each data set. We report the average relative performance, median relative performance, as well as worst relative performance. We report only the best performance (by average) for each index across the parameter sweep included. These results need to be carefully interpreted because we used the same data sets to choose the heuristics of the query optimizer (before this benchmark, and we also incorporated our own experience – otherwise the automatic index would likely always win this benchmark if we had used these exact results). We would like to point out that the automatic indexer will also use the k-d-tree, despite it not scoring very well in this benchmark; the main reason why the k-d-tree does not look good appears to be the high dimensionality. Had we only used the 2 dimensional ZIP code data set, the k-d-tree would have won. Furthermore, the k-d-tree is the only index that directly works with squared Euclidean distance; the metric indexes would need to run with Euclidean distance instead, then re-square the results. A second caveat is that the parameter sweeps may be unfair to methods such as the cover tree that have fewer parameters than others.

We observe that the heuristic implemented in ELKI appears to do a decent job at automatically choosing a suitable index, at least on the data sets investigated so far. Nevertheless, careful tuning of the index can still lead to a 1.8 to 4.8× speedup if a particularly poor configuration is hit (there may also be some measurement noise included here). Looking at the median instead gives the impression that most of the time, most indexes work comparatively well (we included only well-performing indexes, the R*-tree [3] for example performed much worse, but it also is designed as a page-oriented on-disk index, and we are benchmarking in-memory performance here). There are a few exceptions to this rule: as we can see, our implementation of the cover tree appears to have issues with range searching; this will need further investigation. The k-d-tree performs significantly worse in priority search, for the state-keeping reason explained above along with the dimensionality of the data. We do not yet have a bounding-box k-d-tree included here, which may be beneficial in this case. Overall, it appears that the incremental priority search is the most challenging search scenario here, and worth further research.

7   Limitations

Not all algorithms benefit from this automatic indexing. For example, the standard k-means algorithm needs to find the closest centers for each data point, but there are rather few centers ($k \ll N$ usually), and they change every iteration. Index-accelerated techniques for k-means, for example using the k-d-tree, exist; but require modification of the indexes to store additional aggregates.

Last but not least, when benchmarking algorithms, the user may want to disable automatic indexing and take manual control. In many cases, this will be trivially possible by simply pre-creating the desired indexes, as ELKI will then use them. But it is possible to globally disable automatic indexing by setting the elki.optimizer environment variable to an optimizer that never adds indexes, (e.g., by passing `-Delki.optimizer=no` on the command line; where `no` here is an alias for the class `DisableQueryOptimizer`). Similarly, a developer can plug in a custom optimizer class and explore other mechanisms by providing an own implementation of the `QueryOptimizer` interface, or extending the existing classes to override part of the functionality.

8 Conclusion

In this paper we discuss various aspects of implementing automatic indexing in a data mining toolkit, beginning with the need to support different queries, complex query types such as an approximate incremental priority search, and the need to design a suitable API for these queries that expose the partially missing information to the developer. We demonstrate that with some simple heuristics we may be able to select indexes that work well enough for many use cases. The source code of ELKI is developed as open-source on Github, at https://github.com/elki-project/elki.

References

1. Arya, S., Mount, D.: Algorithms for fast vector quantization. In: Data Compression Conference, DCC, pp. 381–390 (1993). https://doi.org/10.1109/DCC.1993.253111
2. Bause, F., Blumenthal, D.B., Schubert, E., Kriege, N.M.: Metric indexing for graph similarity search. In: Similarity Search and Applications, SISAP, pp. 323–336 (2021). https://doi.org/10.1007/978-3-030-89657-7_24
3. Beckmann, N., Kriegel, H., Schneider, R., Seeger, B.: The R*-tree: an efficient and robust access method for points and rectangles. In: ACM SIGMOD International Conference on Management of Data, pp. 322–331 (1990). https://doi.org/10.1145/93597.98741
4. Bentley, J.L.: Multidimensional binary search trees used for associative searching. Commun. ACM **18**(9), 509–517 (1975). https://doi.org/10.1145/361002.361007
5. Beygelzimer, A., Kakade, S.M., Langford, J.: Cover trees for nearest neighbor. In: International Conference Machine Learning, ICML, pp. 97–104 (2006). https://doi.org/10.1145/1143844.1143857
6. Breunig, M.M., Kriegel, H., Ng, R.T., Sander, J.: LOF: identifying density-based local outliers. In: ACM SIGMOD International Conference on Management of Data, pp. 93–104. ACM (2000). https://doi.org/10.1145/342009.335388
7. Ester, M., Kriegel, H., Sander, J., Xu, X.: A density-based algorithm for discovering clusters in large spatial databases with noise. In: Knowledge Discovery and Data Mining, KDD, pp. 226–231 (1996)
8. Kriegel, H., Schubert, E., Zimek, A.: The (black) art of runtime evaluation: are we comparing algorithms or implementations? Knowl. Inf. Syst. **52**(2), 341–378 (2017). https://doi.org/10.1007/s10115-016-1004-2
9. Schubert, E., Sander, J., Ester, M., Kriegel, H., Xu, X.: DBSCAN revisited, revisited: why and how you should (still) use DBSCAN. ACM Trans. Database Syst. 42(3), 19:1–19:21 (2017). https://doi.org/10.1145/3068335
10. Schubert, E., Zimek, A.: ELKI multi-view clustering data sets based on the Amsterdam library of object images (ALOI). Zenodo (2010). https://doi.org/10.5281/zenodo.6355684

11. Schubert, E., Zimek, A.: ELKI: a large open-source library for data analysis - ELKI release 0.7.5 "heidelberg" (2019). CoRR abs/1902.03616, arxiv.org/abs/1902.03616
12. Schubert, E., Zimek, A., Kriegel, H.: Local outlier detection reconsidered: a generalized view on locality with applications to spatial, video, and network outlier detection. Data Min. Knowl. Discov. **28**(1), 190–237 (2014). https://doi.org/10.1007/s10618-012-0300-z
13. Seidl, T., Kriegel, H.: Optimal multi-step k-nearest neighbor search. In: ACM SIGMOD International Conference on Management of Data, pp. 154–165 (1998). https://doi.org/10.1145/276304.276319
14. Yianilos, P.N.: Data structures and algorithms for nearest neighbor search in general metric spaces. In: Symposium on Discrete Algorithms, SODA, pp. 311–321 (1993)

Approximate Nearest Neighbor Search on Standard Search Engines

Fabio Carrara$^{(\boxtimes)}$ (ID), Lucia Vadicamo (ID), Claudio Gennaro (ID),
and Giuseppe Amato (ID)

ISTI CNR, Pisa, Italy
{fabio.carrara,lucia.vadicamo,claudio.gennaro,
giuseppe.amato}@isti.cnr.it

Abstract. Approximate search for high-dimensional vectors is commonly addressed using dedicated techniques often combined with hardware acceleration provided by GPUs, FPGAs, and other custom in-memory silicon. Despite their effectiveness, harmonizing those optimized solutions with other types of searches often poses technological difficulties. For example, to implement a combined text+image multimodal search, we are forced first to query the index of high-dimensional image descriptors and then filter the results based on the textual query or vice versa. This paper proposes a text surrogate technique to translate real-valued vectors into text and index them with a standard textual search engine such as Elasticsearch or Apache Lucene. This technique allows us to perform approximate kNN searches of high-dimensional vectors alongside classical full-text searches natively on a single textual search engine, enabling multimedia queries without sacrificing scalability. Our proposal exploits a combination of vector quantization and scalar quantization. We compared our approach to the existing literature in this field of research, demonstrating a significant improvement in performance through preliminary experimentation.

Keywords: Surrogate text representation · Inverted index · Approximate search · High-dimensional indexing · Very large databases

1 Introduction

A key aspect that determined the success of the web was undoubtedly the arrival on the scene of search engines. Although in the beginning, the technology of the vector space model on which they are based was not immune to problems such as spam web pages, they were very efficient, scalable, and flexible. Not surprisingly, it was relatively easy to enhance and integrate them with other technologies such as hyperlink analysis (PageRank) and term proximity.

Underlying the power of search engines are inverted indexes, which in turn exploit the sparseness of the representation of documents to be retrieved. Unfortunately, artificial intelligence models produce learned vectors that are difficult

T. Skopal et al. (Eds.): SISAP 2022, LNCS 13590, pp. 214–221, 2022.
https://doi.org/10.1007/978-3-031-17849-8_17

to deal with using inverted indexes. Neural networks for image or text representations, such as GeM [14] or BERT [7] to mention a few, produce high-dimensional dense vectors that are usually compared with the cosine similarity. This sprouted the development of solutions to solve maximum inner product search problems efficiently. Commonly used data structures exploit inverted indexes in combination with data partitioning techniques, such as Voronoi partition or proximity graphs, to restrict the search to a fraction of the database. Although existing solutions for high-dimensional vector search have proven great performance in terms of speed and accuracy [10–12], they still have drawbacks. Their implementation is often hardwired to run on main memory as a dense vector search system and nothing more. Most of them are not a proper database system, so multimodal queries such as images and text cannot be resolved. For example, search for all images similar to a given example image and match certain tags. Other limitations include extensive use of RAM or a lack of mature and transparent mechanisms to ensure scalability, such as fault-tolerance or load balancing. In contrast, NoSQL databases, such as Elasticsearch, can scale horizontally as the data size grows.

In this work, we tackle the problem of maximum inner product search of high-dimensional real-valued vectors using full-text search engines and Surrogate Text Representations (STRs)—a family of transformations to encode metric data into synthetic texts. We contextualize our work in the area of data structures for similarity search of dense vectors in secondary memory. All data structures based on metric spaces (such as M-Tree [6]) would be suitable in theory for this task. However, in this work, we focus mainly on those optimized explicitly for working with dense real-valued vectors. Many efficient vector similarity search approaches based on data partitioning techniques (such as [10–12]) use dedicated implementations of access structures such as inverted indexes. STR-based methods, on the other hand, rely on transformations that sparsify data and encode it as small sets of codewords indexed on standard text engines [2,4,9]. These approaches are successfully used to solve multimodal queries for combined text search with image similarity [1,3].

We propose an improved approach combining Voronoi partitioning and STRs. Specifically, we associate a posting list to each Voronoi cell and use STRs to generate the entries of each posting list. Our proposal enables the exploitation of off-the-shelf text search engines, thus supporting combined text+image multimodal search that relies only on text retrieval technologies and platforms without implementing dedicated access methods. Code to reproduce experiments is available at https://github.com/fabiocarrara/str-encoders.

2   Surrogate Text Representation

As we explained in the introduction, our goal is to index and retrieve feature vectors by leveraging commercially available search engines.

Our primary objective is to define a family of transformations that map a feature vector into a textual representation. Of course, we also require that such transformations preserve the proximity relations between the data as much as possible, i.e., maps similar feature vectors to similar textual documents. To achieve this, we need a transformation $f : \mathbb{R}^d \to \mathbb{N}^m$ that maps each original vector $\boldsymbol{y}$ into a vector $\overline{\boldsymbol{y}}$ whose components are integer-valued. Indeed, the core idea is then interpreting $\overline{\boldsymbol{y}}$ as a term frequency vector with respect to a codebook $\mathcal{C} = \{\tau_1, \ldots, \tau_m\}$ of m terms. The text document associated with the vector $\boldsymbol{y}$ will be a space-separated concatenation of the codebook terms so that τ_i is repeated a number of times equal to $\overline{y}_i$. We indicate with $T_{f,\mathcal{C}}(\cdot)$ the overall transformation from the original vectors to the text documents, which depends on both the function f and the used codebook $\mathcal{C}$. For example if $f(\boldsymbol{y}) = \overline{\boldsymbol{y}} = [2,0,1,3]$ and $\mathcal{C} = \{\text{"A", "B", "C", "D"}\}$ then the text document associated to $\boldsymbol{y}$ will be $T_{f,\mathcal{C}}(\boldsymbol{y}) = $"A A C D D D". The rationale of this approach is that a full-text search engine based on the *vector space model* [15] will generate a vector representation of the text by counting the number of occurrences of the words in it, i.e., the term frequencies (TF). Therefore, the abstract transformation f represents a function that exactly generates the vectors that are internally represented by the search engine in the case of the simple TF-weighting scheme.

Since this approach is based on transforming the components of a vector $\boldsymbol{y}$ into the term frequencies of a synthetic text document, the employed transformation f should output a vector $\overline{\boldsymbol{y}}$ with positive components (no search engine admits negative TFs even though this in principle would be possible). Moreover, it should provide sparse vectors to ensure having a large number of zero components in the TF vectors and thus a good inverted index efficiency.

These assumptions form the basis of a family of approaches based on what is known as *Surrogate Text Representation* (STR) [4,9]. STR approaches differ primarily in the steps used to deal with negative values, sparsification, and the final real-to-integer discretization. Moreover, it is worth noting that these approaches are designed to solve Maximum Inner Product Searches, where the cosine similarity or the inner product is used to assess the similarity of the original feature vectors. Indeed, this similarity is approximated by the inner product between the associated TF vectors in the vector space model employed by the text search engine.

3   Voronoi Partitioning STR

In this work, we propose a STR technique that employs a Voronoi partitioning of the original features space and a specific codebook for each Voronoi cell. In a nutshell, we use a k-means data partitioning to assign feature vectors to Voronoi cells corresponding to a set of centroids $\{\boldsymbol{c}_1, \ldots, \boldsymbol{c}_k\}$, and then we use a different STR transformation for each Voronoi cell. Specifically, we build a codebook $\mathcal{C}_i = \{\tau_{i,1}, \ldots, \tau_{i,m}\}$ for the i-th cell, and we transforms the vectors in that cell using $T_{f,\mathcal{C}_i}$.

As space transformation f, we employed modified versions of two state-of-the-art STR approaches: the Deep Permutation STR [2] and the Scalar Quantization STR [4] that we briefly review below.

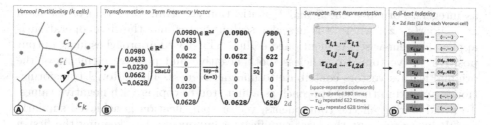

Fig. 1. Overview of the proposed VP-SQ surrogate text representation method. (**A**) The database is Voronoi-partitioned using k-means, and (**B**) elements of each partition are encoded into sparse term-frequency vectors using a surrogate text representation technique (SQ in this case, that produces $2d$-dimensional vectors with n non-zero components). (**C**) Surrogate documents are created by repeating tokens of partition-specific codebooks. (**D**) Documents are indexed using a full-text search engine; all the codebooks form a vocabulary of $2kd$ terms, and each database element is present in exactly n posting lists among the $2d$ ones related to the Voronoi cell containing the element.

Deep Permutation (DP) STR. The term frequency vector $\overline{y} = f_{\text{DP}}(y)$ is obtained from the original vector y by assigning an integer importance value from 1 to n to the top-n components of y and dropping (setting to zero) all other components. Formally, $\overline{y}_i = \max(r_i - d + n, 0)$, where r_i is the 1-based rank of $\overline{y}_i$ when sorting the components of y in ascending order (e.g., $r = 1$ for the minimum-valued component, and $r = d$ for the maximum-valued one), and d is the dimensionality of the vector. For example, given a real-valued vector $y = [0.5, -0.7, 2.45, -1.2]$, the vector with the ranks in ascending order is $r = [3, 1, 4, 2]$, thus for $n = 2$, $\overline{y}_1 = \max(3 - 4 + 2, 0) = 1$, $\overline{y}_2 = \max(1 - 4 + 2, 0) = 0$, and so on, finally getting $f_{\text{DP}}(y) = [1, 0, 2, 0]$. This formulation was initially thought for non-negative (post-ReLU) neural network activations and assigns less importance to negative values that, however, contribute to informativeness in the general case. Thus, Amato et al. [2] proposed to apply the Concatenated Rectified Linear Unit (CReLU) transformation [16], which simply makes an identical copy of vector elements, negates it, concatenates both the original vector and its negation, and then applies ReLU altogether. Formally, $y^+ = \text{CReLU}(y) = \text{ReLU}([y, -y])$, where the $\text{ReLU}(\cdot) = \max(\cdot, 0)$ is applied element-wise. For example, given $y = [0.5, -0.7, 2.49, -1.2]$, its transformed version is $y^+ = [0.5, 0, 2.49, 0, 0, 0.7, 0, 1.2]$. To avoid the imbalance towards positive activations at the expense of negative ones, we use the CReLU transformation before applying f_{DP}. Following the previous example, $f_{\text{DP}}(y^+) = [0, 0, 2, 0, 0, 0, 0, 1]$ for $n = 2$.

Scalar Quantization (SQ) STR. The DP method transforms real-valued components into integer-valued ones but completely disregards the value of the original component and how much it contributes to the inner product computation. On the other hand, the SQ method can retain this information. The SQ STR simply applies Scalar Quantization to vector components to store them as integers. Formally, the Scalar Quantization is a transformation of the form $z \rightarrow \mathrm{floor}(s \cdot z)$, where s is a scalar scaling factor and the floor operation is applied element-wise. As mentioned earlier, STR-based approaches must output positive TF vectors. Nonetheless, both negative and positive elements of the original feature vectors contribute to informativeness. The CReLU transformation is applied in the SQ approach as a first step to coping with negative values. To avoid storing all the components, vector sparsification is achieved similarly to DP by zeroing out the least significant components, i.e., keeping the first-n largest components of $\mathrm{CReLU}(\boldsymbol{y})$. For example, for $n = 2$ the sparsified version of the $\mathrm{CReLU}(\boldsymbol{y})$ considered above will be $[0, 0, 2.49, 0, 0, 0, 0, 1.2]$. Then, the final term frequency vector is obtained after scaling and truncation (zero values are left untouched); for $s = 10$, the corresponding SQ of the vector $\boldsymbol{y}$ would be $f_{\mathrm{SQ}}(\boldsymbol{y}) = [0, 0, 24, 0, 0, 0, 0, 12]$.

Note that DP and SQ only differ in the definition of the function f used to associate term frequency vectors to the original feature vectors. However, both these approaches are limited by construction to using a codebook that contains exactly $m = 2d$ terms if using the CReLU, d if using the ReLU, where d is the dimension of the original feature vectors. This means that the total number of posting lists in the inverted index is limited by the dimensionality d as well, which may compromise the efficiency of the search (e.g., if d is too small compared to the size of the dataset, then the inverted index may have few posting lists, but each contains a large fraction of the original dataset). For example, dimensionality reduction techniques (e.g., PCA) are often used to reduce high-dimensional vectors without a considerable loss of effectiveness. However, we may have no advantage in using the DP and SQ STR techniques to index and search these reduced vectors on a large scale.

We propose to use Voronoi Partitioning (VP) on top of the DP and SQ approaches, allowing the disentanglement of the cardinality of the codebook from d and hence the tuning of the number of posting lists. Indeed, our extension of DP and SQ approaches, which we named VP-DP and VP-SQ, allow producing an inverted index with $m = k * 2d$ posting lists, where the number of partitions k can be tuned to guarantee a higher level of efficiency. We obtain k centroids in the original vector space using k-means clustering. Each data vector $\boldsymbol{y}$ is transformed as $T_{f,c_i}(\boldsymbol{y})$, where i is the index of its closest centroid, $\mathcal{C}_i = \{\tau_{i,1}, \ldots, \tau_{i,m}\}$ is a specific codebook associated to the centroid $\boldsymbol{c}_i$, and f is either f_{SQ} or f_{DP}. Note that each object will be stored in exactly n posting lists related to its closest centroid. Figure 1 shows an example for VP-SQ.

To process a query $\boldsymbol{x}$, we first compute its P closest centroids, $\boldsymbol{c}_{i_1}, \ldots, \boldsymbol{c}_{i_P}$, and then we transform the query vector into the text document obtained by concatenating the texts $T_{f,\mathcal{C}_{i_h}}(\boldsymbol{x})$ for all $h = 1, \ldots, P$. This corresponds to accessing nP posting lists, i.e., n posting lists for the P Voronoi cells closest to the query.

4   Experiments

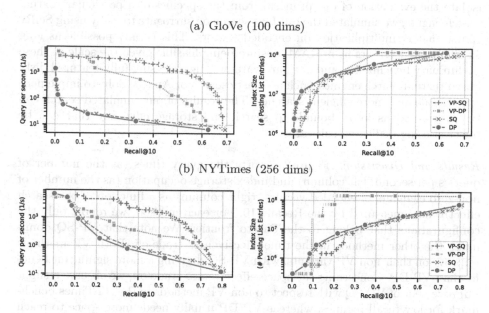

(a) GloVe (100 dims)

(b) NYTimes (256 dims)

Fig. 2. Time (Query per seconds, left column, top-right is better) and Space Efficiency (n. of elements, right column, bottom-right is better) versus Effectiveness (Recall@10). We only plot configurations belonging to the Pareto frontier.

Datasets. We adopt the GloVe-100 and NYTimes-256 benchmarks for maximum inner product search prepared by Aumüller et al. [5] for a preliminary evaluation of the proposed methods. GloVe-100 [13] is a collection of more than one million 100-dimensional real-valued vectors representing word embeddings learned in an unsupervised fashion. NYTimes-256 [8] is a collection of 280k 256-dimensional real-valued vectors containing bag-of-word-derived document representations of NYTimes news articles. Both datasets provide a set of 10k test queries and the corresponding 100 nearest neighbors for each query. We normalize all vectors to the unitary L_2 norm to implement the intended scoring function (cosine similarity) as the inner product between vectors.

Tested Configurations. We encoded all vectors (data and queries) using DP, SQ, VP-DP, and VP-SQ, obtaining surrogate term-frequencies vectors as sparse integer matrices. For VP-SQ and VP-DP, we vary the number of k-means centroids $k \in \{128, 256, 512, 1024, 2048, 4096, 8192\}$ and the number of voronoi cells accessed at query-time $P \in \{1, 2, 5, 10, 25, 50\}$. For SQ and VP-SQ, we use a scalar quantization factor $s = 10^5$. For all methods, we vary the number of kept elements n for each vector from 1% to 100% of the original vector dimensionality d. For simplicity, we skip the configurations providing a query throughput lower than ten queries per second (query time > 100 ms).

Implementation Details. We perform experiments on a Ubuntu 20.04 server with Intel(R) Core(TM) i9-9900K CPU @ 3.60GHz and 64GB of RAM. To isolate the evaluation of our proposal from the specifics of a particular textual search engine, we simulated the full-text search on surrogate texts by using SciPy sparse matrix multiplication on encoded vectors. This is only possible as long as all encoded vectors fit in RAM; despite being feasible given the scale of these preliminary benchmarks and our hardware, we suggest using fully-featured disk-based textual search engines, such as Elasticsearch or Apache Solr, to implement larger-scale and more efficient searches. The results of our simulated search can be interpreted as lower bounds to search and storage efficiency that can be boosted using dedicated software.

Results and Discussion. Figure 2 reports the query times (as the number of queries per second, left column) and index storage occupation (as the number of non-zero elements of encoded vectors, right column) as a function of the search effectiveness measured by the Recall@10. For each method, we report only the configurations that belong to the Pareto frontier. We note that VP-SQ dominates the other methods in the time-effectiveness trade-off. Both VP methods improve on their non-VP variants, with VP-SQ deriving a more significant benefit than VP-DP. Concerning the space-effectiveness trade-off, we observe a slight improvement of VP-SQ with respect to non-VP methods in the NYTimes benchmark for low recall regimes, whereas VP-DP usually needs more space to reach higher recalls.

5   Conclusions

In this paper, we proposed a new method for out-of-core similarity search of dense vectors. We mainly target those who need to scale over large amounts of data using an integrated search framework based on a standard search engine. Compared to the state of the art, we improved the performance of surrogate text-based techniques that had the major limitation of working with codebooks constrained by the dimensionality of the dense vectors to be searched.

A key aspect of our approach entails the combination of vector partitioning technique with existing approaches allowing us to expand the codebook used for indexing and thus better fine-tune performance. In the near future, we plan to try to improve our technique by using artificial intelligence-based approaches to learn vector sparsification without sacrificing too much search accuracy.

Acknowledgements. This work was partially funded by AI4Media - A European Excellence Centre for Media, Society, and Democracy (EC, H2020 n. 951911).

References

1. Amato, G., et al.: The VISIONE video search system: exploiting off-the-shelf text search engines for large-scale video retrieval. J. Imaging **7**(5), 76 (2021)
2. Amato, G., Bolettieri, P., Carrara, F., Falchi, F., Gennaro, C.: Large-scale image retrieval with elasticsearch. In: The 41st International ACM SIGIR Conference on Research & Development in Information Retrieval, pp. 925–928 (2018)
3. Amato, G., et al.: VISIONE at video browser showdown 2022. In: THornór Jónsson, B., et al. (eds.) MMM 2022. LNCS, vol. 13142, pp. 543–548. Springer, Cham (2022). https://doi.org/10.1007/978-3-030-98355-0_52
4. Amato, G., Carrara, F., Falchi, F., Gennaro, C., Vadicamo, L.: Large-scale instance-level image retrieval. Inf. Process. Manage. **57**(6), 102100 (2020)
5. Aumüller, M., Bernhardsson, E., Faithfull, A.: ANN-benchmarks: a benchmarking tool for approximate nearest neighbor algorithms. Inf. Syst. **87**, 101374 (2020)
6. Ciaccia, P., Patella, M., Zezula, P.: M-tree: an efficient access method for similarity search in metric spaces. In: Vldb, vol. 97, pp. 426–435 (1997)
7. Devlin, J., Chang, M.W., Lee, K., Toutanova, K.: BERT: pre-training of deep bidirectional transformers for language understanding. In: Proceedings of the 2019 Conference of the North American Chapter of the Association for Computational Linguistics: Human Language Technologies, Vol. 1 (Long and Short Papers), pp. 4171–4186 (2019)
8. Dua, D., Graff, C.: UCI machine learning repository (2017). http://archive.ics.uci.edu/ml
9. Gennaro, C., Amato, G., Bolettieri, P., Savino, P.: An approach to content-based image retrieval based on the Lucene search engine library. In: Lalmas, M., Jose, J., Rauber, A., Sebastiani, F., Frommholz, I. (eds.) ECDL 2010. LNCS, vol. 6273, pp. 55–66. Springer, Heidelberg (2010). https://doi.org/10.1007/978-3-642-15464-5_8
10. Jegou, H., Douze, M., Schmid, C.: Product quantization for nearest neighbor search. IEEE Trans. Pattern Anal. Mach. Intell. **33**(1), 117–128 (2010)
11. Johnson, J., Douze, M., Jégou, H.: Billion-scale similarity search with GPUs. IEEE Trans. Big Data **7**(3), 535–547 (2019)
12. Malkov, Y.A., Yashunin, D.A.: Efficient and robust approximate nearest neighbor search using hierarchical navigable small world graphs. IEEE Trans. Pattern Anal. Mach. Intell. **42**(4), 824–836 (2018)
13. Pennington, J., Socher, R., Manning, C.D.: GloVe: global vectors for word representation. In: Empirical Methods in Natural Language Processing (EMNLP), pp. 1532–1543 (2014)
14. Revaud, J., Almazan, J., Rezende, R., de Souza, C.: Learning with average precision: training image retrieval with a listwise loss. In: International Conference on Computer Vision, pp. 5106–5115. IEEE (2019)
15. Salton, G., McGill, M.J.: Introduction to Modern Information Retrieval. McGraw-Hill Inc, New York (1986)
16. Shang, W., Sohn, K., Almeida, D., Lee, H.: Understanding and improving convolutional neural networks via concatenated rectified linear units. In: Proceedings of the 33rd International Conference on Machine Learning. ICML 2016, vol. 48, pp. 2217–2225. JMLR.org (2016)

Evaluation of LID-Aware Graph Embedding Methods for Node Clustering

Dušica Knežević(✉) [ID], Jela Babić [ID], Miloš Savić [ID], and Miloš Radovanović [ID]

Department of Mathematics and Informatics, Faculty of Sciences,
University of Novi Sad, Trg Dositeja Obradovića 4, 21000 Novi Sad, Serbia
{lucy,jelab,svc,radacha}@dmi.uns.ac.rs

Abstract. Data generated by everyday applications may appear in different forms. Various important and frequently used machine learning and data mining techniques have been designed assuming the tabular data form. To apply those techniques to graph structured data, it necessary to form graph embeddings. The crucial moment in creating a graph embedding is to choose the best embedding technique that preserves all the vital information when converting a graph into its tabular representation. Determining the best approach requires some form of evaluation of the internal qualities of potential embeddings and their utility in concrete applications. In this paper, we present a comparative evaluation of graph embeddings when used to cluster graph nodes in the embedded space. The examined graph embedding methods are node2vec and two recently proposed extensions of this algorithm based on local intrinsic dimensionality. The results of both intrinsic and external clustering evaluation on real-world graphs indicate that LID-aware extensions improve node clustering, especially when detecting a small number of clusters.

Keywords: Clustering · Graph embedding · LID-aware node2vec

1 Introduction

In the era of big data large amounts of information are produced that require analysis and data mining (DM). Information from sources such as social media and sensors from IoT devices can be used to identify patterns, trends, and new insights that can help with evidence-based decision making and strategic planning. This data can also be used to train predictive models with machine learning (ML) algorithms. There is a variety of ways to organize and store large-scale data: tables, graphs, time series, etc. Numerous data processing techniques developed in the last decades in the research communities of ML and DM usually require input data in tabular form. In the case of graph-structured data, this requirement necessitates transformation of the original data into a suitable format.

The main task of graph embedding methods is to transform graph data into tabular data without losing essential information, but also without explicitly specifying which two nodes are connected by an edge in the produced embedding.

© The Author(s), under exclusive license to Springer Nature Switzerland AG 2022
T. Skopal et al. (Eds.): SISAP 2022, LNCS 13590, pp. 222–233, 2022.
https://doi.org/10.1007/978-3-031-17849-8_18

It is expected that the application of a graph embedding method before applying ML or DM algorithms produces equal or better results than algorithms natively designed for graphs. The process of graph analysis is then conditioned by the quality of the produced embedding. It should be emphasized that this approach may also face potential problems characteristic for tabular data forms such as the curse of dimensionality.

Tabular data is represented by rows and columns. Columns are features used to describe objects of interest that correspond to rows in the table. The number of columns is the dimensionality of the space in which data is located. When creating the tabular representation in the form of a graph embedding, one of the main problems is to select the suitable value for dimensionality. The measure used to represent the minimal number of features required to describe a point of information in the space is called intrinsic dimensionality (ID). Intrinsic dimensionality is usually viewed as a concept related to the entire dataset, and corresponding ID measures are typically used in dimensionality reduction algorithms. The use of such global ID measures is not always suitable because data dimensionality may vary locally for different parts of a dataset. Local intrinsic dimensionality (LID) was introduced by shifting the focus of ID estimation from the global data view to the data space around a data point [1,6]. A recent paper by Savić et al. [16] addresses the issue of using LID-related measures in the context of graph embedding generation. The authors proposed NC-LID, a LID-related measure for quantifying the discriminative power of the shortest path distance with respect to natural communities of nodes as their intrinsic localities. Based on this measure, new extensions of the node2vec [4] graph embedding algorithm have been introduced and evaluated by examining to what extent the produced embeddings preserve the structure of input graphs. This paper expands the evaluation given in [16], with the main motivation to analyze the proposed node2vec extensions for the particular application to node clustering.

Clustering is the task of dividing data points into a number of groups (clusters) where similar data points are in the same cluster, and more distant points reside in separate clusters. In terms of graph analysis we use nodes as data points. In other words, clusters in a graph are groups of similar nodes (similar by the shortest-path distance or some other node similarity metric). By performing clustering validation over identified clusters, it is possible to compare the quality of the used embedding methods. The clustering method used in this paper is KMeans [11] which is the most commonly used algorithms to cluster tabular data. KMeans belongs to the group of partitional clustering algorithms in the sense that it generates a single partition with a specified number of non-overlapping clusters. Clustering validation can be intrinsic and external. Intrinsic evaluation focuses on the cohesion of identified clusters based on a distance measure. In our analysis the Silhouette score [15] is used to measure cluster cohesiveness. In external evaluation, identified clusters are compared to explicitly stated node groups determined by labels assigned to nodes. For this purpose we use Normalized Mutual Information [9].

The rest of the paper is structured as follows. A brief summary of analyzed graph embedding methods is given in Sect. 2. In the following Sect. 3 we describe methods and measures used to evaluate graph embeddings in the context of node clustering. The obtained results are presented in Sect. 4. The last section concludes the paper and gives directions for future work.

2   Graph Embedding Methods

The embedding algorithms we analyze belong to the class of random walk algorithms. The random walk approach has become a common technique for the graph embedding problem in recent studies [3]. The main idea of random walk based graph embedding algorithms is to sample a certain number of random walks emanating from each node in a graph. In the case of the node2vec algorithm, the random walks are treated as ordinary sets over the alphabet of node identifiers. This means that the problem of generating graph embeddings is essentially reduced to the problem of generating text embeddings.

The node2vec algorithm is an improvement of DeepWalk [14] with the main idea to use biased random walks. The algorithm is based on finding the best neighborhood selection strategy that allows seamless interpolation between depth first search (DFS) and breadth first search (BFS) when creating a random walk. Node2vec depends on two parameters: p and q. These parameters control how fast the algorithm explores and exits the neighborhood of a given starting node. The p parameter (return parameter) controls the probability of returning to the previous node in the walk. The q parameter (in-out parameter) controls how closely the walk resembles the DFS or BFS exploration strategy. The generated walks are then passed to the Word2Vec algorithm [12], which creates the desired graph embedding.

The aforementioned paper by Savić et al. [16] has raised the question of a different direction to graph embedding generation in which hyperparameters controlling random walk sampling are not globally fixed, but personalized per node and edge with automatic adjustments from initially stated base values. Inspired by the LID model introduced by Houle [6–8], the authors first defined the NC-LID measure for quantifying the discriminatory power of the shortest-path distance considering natural communities [10] of nodes as their intrinsic localities. The lowest possible value of NC-LID is equal to zero and corresponds to the case in which the shortest-path distance perfectly separates the natural community of a node from the rest of the graph. Higher NC-LID values imply more structurally complex natural communities. The authors then proposed two LID-aware node2vec variants (lid-n2v-rw and lid-n2v-rwpq) in which personalized hyperparameters are adjusted according to NC-LID values.

Lid-n2v-rw is the first LID-aware node2vec modification that is focused on the personalization of the number of random walks sampled per node, and the length of random walks. The number of random walks for an arbitrary node

n is computed by the equation $\lfloor(1 + \text{NC-LID}(n)) \cdot B\rfloor$, where B is the base number of random walks (by default $B = 10$). Additionally, the length of random walks sampled for n is equal to $\lfloor W/(1 + \text{NC-LID}(n))\rfloor$ (by default $W = 80$). This means that more random walks are sampled for nodes with more complex natural communities. Additionally, random walks for such nodes are shorter in order to keep the computational budget approximately constant and to lower the probability of "escaping" from their natural communities.

Lid-n2v-rwpq is the second variant of LID-aware node2vec and it considers a more biased approach to graph embedding construction. The main idea is to personalize p and q parameters controlling biases during the random walk sampling. The base values of p and q are $p_b = 1$, and $q_b = 1$, by default. The lid-n2v-rwpq variant incorporates the following adjustments of p and q for a pair of nodes x and y, denoted by $p(x, y)$ and $q(x, y)$, respectively, where x is the node on which the random walk currently resides and y is one of its neighbors:

1. If x is in the natural community of y then $p(x, y) = p_b$, otherwise $p(x, y) = p_b + \text{NC-LID}(y)$. This adjustment lowers the probability of transitioning between different natural communities.
2. If y is in the natural community of x then $q(x, y) = q_b$, otherwise $q(x, y) = q_b + \text{NC-LID}(x)$. This rule increases the probability of staying within more complex natural communities.

3   Evaluation Methods

The evaluation of clustering algorithms applied to graph embeddings can be done in two ways depending on whether nodes have explicit labels indicating cluster assignments (external evaluation) or not (intrinsic evaluation). Let O denote the partitioning of nodes into clusters according to explicit labels and let C be the partitioning of nodes obtained by a clustering algorithm applied to a graph. Then, the similarity between O and C can be obtained by computing partitioning similarity metrics such as normalized mutual information (NMI). Additionally, clustering algorithms can be intrinsically evaluated without having explicit labels by computing metrics reflecting cohesiveness of obtained clusters, such as the Silhouette score.

The Silhouette score indicates how similar data point d (node in our case) is to its own cluster c compared to other identified clusters. It calculates the average distance of d to data points in c and the average distance of d to data points in all other clusters. Its values range from -1 to 1. In our evaluation, the Silhouette score is used as the measure of intrinsic clustering validation being one of the most commonly used indices for assessing clustering quality. Higher Silhouette scores indicate better clustering quality suggesting a more adequate graph embedding for the purpose of clustering, which enables us to examine the impact of graph embedding algorithms in this particular task.

NMI is the normalized variant of the mutual information measure. It is calculated for two partitions of data points into clusters and its value varies from 0, meaning that sets have no mutual information, to 1 which denotes perfect correlation between sets. The value of NMI does not depend on the label naming scheme. Clustering partitions we compare by computing NMI are the following:

- the partition induced by explicit labels present in graph data,
- partitions obtained by community detection on original graphs, and
- partitions identified by KMeans clustering of graph embeddings.

The KMeans algorithm requires parameter K which is the number of non-overlapping clusters that will be detected in the given dataset. In particular, we use the number of detected communities and the number of explicitly stated labels in the original graph. Additionally, we include fixed values for K from $\{2, 3, 4, 5, 10\}$. In our evaluation we rely on the implementation of KMeans from the scikit-learn library [13]. The greedy modularity clustering algorithm [2] implemented in the NetworkX library [5] is used for detecting communities.

4 Results

This section describes the results of the comparison between clustering on graph embeddings obtained by node2vec and its two LID-aware variants. The experimental corpus of datasets used for the evaluation is the same as in [16] and consists of five citation networks (Cora, Cora ML, Citeseer, DBLP and Pubmed), two Amazon datasets (Amazon electronics computers and Amazon electronics photo), and one small social network (Zachary karate club). All datasets from the corpus are explicitly labeled.

The results of our analysis indicate that the best results, in terms of NMI and Silhouette scores, are obtained when embeddings are generated for dimensionality equal to 10. Other parameters can be seen in Table 1. These node2vec parameters are determined by reconstructing graphs from embeddings according to Euclidean distance and comparing reconstructed graphs to original ones. It should be emphasized that we use the same values of hyperparameters for our LID-elastic node2vec extensions (base values of p and q as in Table 1) in order to have an unbiased comparison to node2vec. The best value of K in KMeans varies between datasets. In case of Zachary karate club the best K is 2, for Cora ML $K = 7$, Citeseer $K = 6$, Amazon electronics photo $K = 8$, Amazon electronics computers $K = 10$, DBLP $K = 4$, Pubmed $K = 3$, and Cora $K = 70$.

4.1 Intrinsic Evaluation

Figure 1 shows Silhouette scores for node2vec, lid-n2v-rw and lid-n2v-rwpq for KMeans when K values ($K \leq 10$) are chosen such that the Silhouette score is maximal possible. It can be seen that the highest Silhouette score for the majority of datasets is obtained for embeddings generated by lid-n2v-rw. The largest difference in the Silhouette score can be observed for Cora ML where LID-aware node2vec variants have significantly higher values compared to node2vec. Lid-n2v-rwpq is the best performing embedding algorithm for Zachary karate

Table 1. The best values of embedding parameters p and q for node2vec and its LID-aware variants.

Dataset	node2vec		lid-n2v-rw		lid-n2v-rwpq	
	p	q	p	q	p	q
Zachary karate club	0.25	2	0.25	2	0.25	2
Cora	4	0.25	4	0.25	4	0.25
Cora ML	4	0.25	4	0.25	4	0.25
Citeseer	0.5	0.25	0.5	0.25	0.5	0.25
Amazon electronics computers	4	0.5	4	0.5	4	0.5
Amazon electronics photo	4	0.5	4	0.5	4	0.5
DBLP	4	1	4	1	4	1
Pubmed	2	0.5	2	0.5	2	0.5

club and Pubmed. The original node2vec is the best option only for one dataset (Cora). Thus, it can be concluded that clusters obtained from LID-aware variants of node2vec are more cohesive suggesting that LID-aware extensions improve the node clustering process.

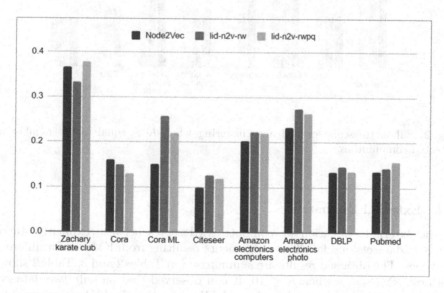

Fig. 1. The best Silhouette scores for KMeans clustering when $K \leq 10$.

Values of Silhouette scores for KMeans clustering when K is equal to the number of communities detected by the greedy modularity optimization (GMO) are shown in Fig. 2. For 6 datasets from our experimental corpus, Silhouette scores for different graph embedding methods are very similar. Only for 2 datasets (Zachary and Citesser) we have that node2vec performs slightly better than its LID-aware variants. The number of detected communities is larger than 100 for all datasets except Zacahary where GMO detected 3 clusters. With a larger number of smaller clusters, Silhouette scores tend to have higher values. Consequently, it can be concluded that the intrinsic evaluation for the best K that is lower than or equal to 10 is more reliable than the same evaluation when $K > 100$ for to two reasons: (1) it is hard to expect an extremely large number of clusters in our datasets considering their size, and (2) for large K the obtained Silhouette scores are almost equal indicating that the clustering results do not depend on the used graph embedding method.

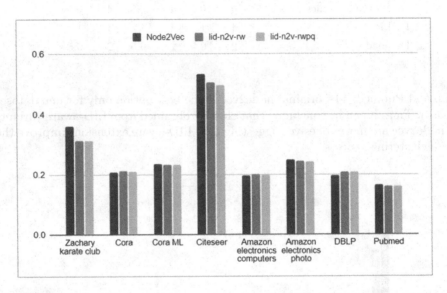

Fig. 2. Silhouette score for KMeans clustering when K is equal to the number of detected communities.

4.2   External Evaluation

In the external evaluation we compute NMI scores between explicitly stated labels in datasets and labelling assignments resulting from KMeans for different K values. The obtained results are summarized in Tables 2 and 3. Table 2 shows the best NMI scores when $K \leq 10$. It can observed that on only two datasets (DBLP and Cora) node2vec has higher NMI scores than its LID-aware variants. For other datasets one of the LID-aware variants is the best performing algorithm. Considerable improvements in the NMI score are present for 3 graphs (Pubmed, Citeseer and Zachary) where NMI of LID-aware variants is higher by 0.1 than NMI of node2vec.

NMI scores when K is equal to the number of clusters detected by GMO are given in Table 3. The largest NMI for Amazon electronics photo is achieved

Table 2. NMI scores for explicit labels and labeling assignments obtained from KMeans for the best $K \leq 10$.

Dataset	node2vec	lid-n2v-rw	lid-n2v-rwpq
Zachary karate club	0.693	0.826	0.727
Cora	0.545	0.523	0.418
Cora ML	0.548	0.583	0.597
Citeseer	0.489	0.577	0.572
Amazon electronics computers	0.554	0.554	0.569
Amazon electronics photo	0.649	0.675	0.657
DBLP	0.557	0.478	0.471
Pubmed	0.368	0.479	0.483

by two algorithms, node2vec and lid-n2v-rw. However, on the same dataset lid-n2v-rwpq has slightly lower NMI indicating that all three algorithms perform similarly. The situation is similar for other datasets where NMI of the best performing algorithm is not considerably higher than NMI of two other alternatives. For 2 datasets (DBLP, Pubmed) node2vec achieves the highest NMI, lid-n2v-rw is also the best option for 2 datasets (Cora and Amazon electronics computers), whereas lid-n2v-rwpq reaches the highest NMI for 3 datasets. The best NMI score per dataset considering both cases (when $K \leq 10$ and K equal to the number of detected clusters) is indicated in Table 4, where it can be seen that for 6 out of 8 datasets LID-elastic node2vec extensions outperform the original node2vec.

Table 3. NMI scores for explicit labels and labeling assignments from KMeans when K is equal to the number of detected communities.

Dataset	node2vec	lid-n2v-rw	lid-n2v-rwpq
Zachary karate club	0.727	0.826	0.861
Cora	0.546	0.548	0.545
Cora ML	0.640	0.639	0.651
Citeseer	0.857	0.855	0.858
Amazon electronics computers	0.403	0.404	0.401
Amazon electronics photo	0.489	0.489	0.486
DBLP	0.574	0.557	0.557
Pubmed	0.574	0.529	0.523

We also examined the correlation between Silhouette and NMI scores for LID-aware node2vec variants. Figure 3 shows the highest Silhouette and NMI across all datasets from our experimental corpus. It can be seen that those

Table 4. The best NMI score per dataset.

Dataset	Best NMI score	Method
Zachary karate club	0.861	lid-n2v-rwpq
Cora	0.548	lid-n2v-rw
Cora ML	0.651	lid-n2v-rwpq
Citeseer	0.858	lid-n2v-rwpq
Amazon electronics computers	0.569	lid-n2v-rwpq
Amazon electronics photo	0.675	lid-n2v-rw
DBLP	0.574	node2vec
Pubmed	0.574	node2vec

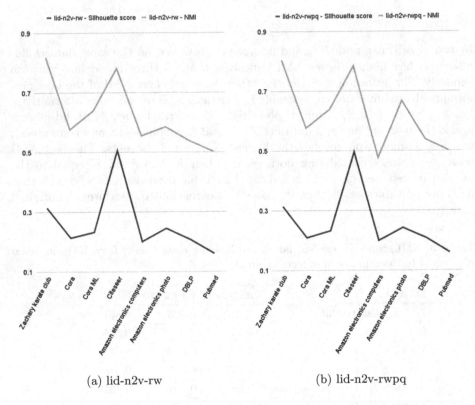

(a) lid-n2v-rw   (b) lid-n2v-rwpq

Fig. 3. Comparison of maximal Silhouette and NMI scores across all datasets.

two metrics are perfectly correlated, i.e. larger Silhouette score implies larger NMI. Consequently, it can be concluded that the metric we selected for intrinsic evaluation is consistent with the metric used for external evaluation. This is also evident in the results of the evaluation itself:

1. for a small number of detected clusters ($K \leq 10$) LID-aware node2vec variants perform better than pure node2vec according to both intrinsic and external evaluation, while
2. for a large number of detected clusters corresponding to the number of communities detected by GMO all three algorithms achieve similar performance.

5   Conclusion and Future Work

The main focus of this paper was on the evaluation of LID-aware graph embedding methods when they are used prior to node clustering. Both intrinsic and external evaluation of KMeans were conducted on embeddings produced by pure node2vec and two its LID-aware extensions that personalize hyperparameters controlling random walk sampling. For the purpose of intrinsic evaluation we selected the Silhouette score to quantify cohesiveness of clusters. The external evaluation was based on NMI considering labels explicitly given in datasets and label assignments obtained by KMeans for different K values.

The obtained results indicate that LID-aware node2vec extensions in general achieve better intrinsic and external evaluation scores, especially when detecting a small number of clusters (equal to or less than 10). In the case of a large number of clusters, corresponding to the number of communities detected by greedy modularity optimization applied directly to graphs, all three examined graph embedding algorithms achieve comparable evaluation scores. The intrinsic evaluation should be considered more reliable since external evaluation depends on explicitly assigned labels that do not necessarily represent natural clusters. However, it was shown that the selection of metrics in different evaluation methods gives consistent results.

Regarding future work, our evaluation could be expanded by including additional datasets, community detection algorithms and other clustering algorithms designed for tabular data (e.g., agglomerative hierarchical clustering, DBSCAN, etc.). LID-aware extensions evaluated in this paper are based on local community detection, but in addition we could also detect communities globally. For example, an additional parameter controlling the probability of a random walk leaving a global community could be incorporated into LID-aware extensions of node2vec. In this way we force random walks to stay within the global community of a starting node. Furthermore, this idea might as well be expanded to overlapping communities where special attention is given to nodes belonging to multiple communities.

Acknowledgments. This research is supported by the Science Fund of the Republic of Serbia, #6518241, AI – GRASP. The authors would like to thank the anonymous reviewers for their insightful suggestions and comments that helped improve the quality of the paper.

References

1. Amsaleg, L., et al.: Estimating local intrinsic dimensionality. In: Proceedings of the 21th ACM SIGKDD International Conference on Knowledge Discovery and Data Mining, p. 29–38. KDD 2015, Association for Computing Machinery, New York (2015). https://doi.org/10.1145/2783258.2783405
2. Clauset, A., Newman, M.E.J., Moore, C.: Finding community structure in very large networks. Phys. Rev. E **70**(6) (2004). https://doi.org/10.1103/physreve.70.066111
3. Goyal, P., Ferrara, E.: Graph embedding techniques, applications, and performance: a survey. Knowl.-Based Syst. **151**, 78–94 (2018). https://doi.org/10.1016/j.knosys.2018.03.022
4. Grover, A., Leskovec, J.: Node2vec: scalable feature learning for networks. In: Proceedings of the 22nd ACM SIGKDD International Conference on Knowledge Discovery and Data Mining, p. 855–864. KDD 2016, Association for Computing Machinery, New York (2016). https://doi.org/10.1145/2939672.2939754
5. Hagberg, A.A., Schult, D.A., Swart, P.J.: Exploring network structure, dynamics, and function using networkx. In: Varoquaux, G., Vaught, T., Millman, J. (eds.) Proceedings of the 7th Python in Science Conference, pp. 11–15. Pasadena, CA (2008)
6. Houle, M.E.: Dimensionality, discriminability, density and distance distributions. In: 2013 IEEE 13th International Conference on Data Mining Workshops, pp. 468–473 (2013). https://doi.org/10.1109/ICDMW.2013.139
7. Houle, M.E.: Local intrinsic dimensionality I: an extreme-value-theoretic foundation for similarity applications. In: Beecks, C., Borutta, F., Kröger, P., Seidl, T. (eds.) Similarity Search and Applications, pp. 64–79. Springer International Publishing, Cham (2017). https://doi.org/10.1007/978-3-319-68474-1_5
8. Houle, M.E.: Local intrinsic dimensionality III: density and similarity. In: Satoh, S., et al. (eds.) SISAP 2020. LNCS, vol. 12440, pp. 248–260. Springer, Cham (2020). https://doi.org/10.1007/978-3-030-60936-8_19
9. Kvalseth, T.O.: On normalized mutual information: measure derivations and properties. Entropy **19**(11) (2017). https://doi.org/10.3390/e19110631
10. Lancichinetti, A., Fortunato, S., Kertész, J.: Detecting the overlapping and hierarchical community structure in complex networks. New J. Phys. **11**(3), 033015 (2009). https://doi.org/10.1088/1367-2630/11/3/033015
11. MacQueen, J.B.: Some methods for classification and analysis of multivariate observations. In: Cam, L.M.L., Neyman, J. (eds.) Proceedings of the Fifth Berkeley Symposium on Mathematical Statistics and Probability, vol. 1, pp. 281–297. University of California Press (1967)
12. Mikolov, T., Chen, K., Corrado, G., Dean, J.: Efficient estimation of word representations in vector space. In: 1st International Conference on Learning Representations, ICLR 2013, Scottsdale, Arizona, USA, 2–4 May 2013, Workshop Track Proceedings (2013). http://arxiv.org/abs/1301.3781
13. Pedregosa, F., et al.: Scikit-learn: machine learning in Python. J. Mach. Learn. Res. **12**, 2825–2830 (2011)
14. Perozzi, B., Al-Rfou, R., Skiena, S.: Deepwalk: Online learning of social representations. In: Proceedings of the 20th ACM SIGKDD International Conference on Knowledge Discovery and Data Mining, p. 701–710. KDD 2014, Association for Computing Machinery, New York (2014). https://doi.org/10.1145/2623330.2623732

15. Rousseeuw, P.J.: Silhouettes: a graphical aid to the interpretation and validation of cluster analysis. J. Comput. Appl. Math. **20**, 53–65 (1987). https://doi.org/10.1016/0377-0427(87)90125-7

16. Savić, M., Kurbalija, V., Radovanović, M.: Local intrinsic dimensionality and graphs: towards LID-aware graph embedding algorithms. In: Reyes, N., et al. (eds.) SISAP 2021. LNCS, vol. 13058, pp. 159–172. Springer, Cham (2021). https://doi.org/10.1007/978-3-030-89657-7_13

Similarity-Based Unsupervised Evaluation of Outlier Detection

Henrique O. Marques[1]([✉]) [ID], Arthur Zimek[1] [ID], Ricardo J. G. B. Campello[2] [ID], and Jörg Sander[3] [ID]

[1] University of Southern Denmark, Odense, Denmark
`oli@sdu.dk`, `zimek@imada.sdu.dk`
[2] University of Newcastle, Callaghan, Australia
`ricardo.campello@newcastle.edu.au`
[3] University of Alberta, Edmonton, Canada
`jsander@ualberta.ca`

Abstract. The evaluation of unsupervised algorithm results is one of the most challenging tasks in data mining research. Where labeled data are not available, one has to use in practice the so-called internal evaluation, which is based solely on the data and the assessed solutions themselves. In unsupervised cluster analysis, indices for internal evaluation of clustering solutions have been studied for decades, with a multitude of indices available, based on different criteria. In unsupervised outlier detection, however, this problem has only recently received some attention, and still very few indices are available. In this paper, we provide a new internal index based on criteria different from the ones available in the literature. The index is based on a (generic) similarity measure to efficiently evaluate candidate outlier detection solutions in a completely unsupervised way. We evaluate and compare this index against existing indices in terms of quality and run time performance using collections of both real and synthetic datasets.

Keywords: Outlier detection · Unsupervised evaluation · Validation · Model selection

1 Introduction

Outlier detection is one of the central tasks of data mining. This task aims to identify observations that are considered exceptional in some sense. In many applications, such observations deserve much more attention than those considered normal, as they might reveal important phenomena, such as traffic accidents [13], network intrusion attacks [2], credit card frauds [1], sensor failures [33], or diseases affecting human health [3].

The techniques for outlier detection can be categorized into supervised, semi-supervised, and unsupervised techniques. Supervised techniques assume that enough observations labeled as inliers and outliers are available to describe both

© The Author(s), under exclusive license to Springer Nature Switzerland AG 2022
T. Skopal et al. (Eds.): SISAP 2022, LNCS 13590, pp. 234–248, 2022.
https://doi.org/10.1007/978-3-031-17849-8_19

classes using a classifier. In the semi-supervised scenario, a few labeled outliers might even be available, but they are not sufficient to describe the outlier class. In this scenario, also referred to as "novelty detection", the techniques assume that only inlier observations are available, and these previously known inliers are used to obtain a model using one-class classification techniques [39]. When no labeled data are available at all, one has to use unsupervised techniques, which do not assume any prior knowledge or examples of outliers and inliers [10].

In this work, we focus on unsupervised outlier detection scenarios. In this scenario it is difficult to precisely and generally define a notion of "outlierness". Some definitions in the literature seek to capture the broader idea of what constitutes an outlier. For example, the classical definition by Barnett and Lewis [6] describes an outlier as "an observation (or subset of observations) which appears to be inconsistent with the remainder of that set of data". However, how and when an observation qualifies as "inconsistent" is subjective and depends on the application scenario and the algorithm used.

Due to the inherent subjectivity of the unsupervised outlier detection scenario, a wide variety of algorithms have emerged to capture the different possible notions of outlier. Each of these algorithms, naturally, is more or less appropriate depending on the application scenario. The selection of an algorithm for a particular application should be guided based on the quality of its results in that application. However, with no precise definition of outliers nor labeled examples to compare with the algorithms' results, it is far from trivial to make a quality assessment. This problem is inherent to unsupervised learning. It has been investigated for decades in the data clustering domain [21,22,43], but has only recently received some attention in outlier detection [29,30,46].

In practical applications of data clustering the related problem of unsupervised evaluation of the results is tackled by using some kind of quantitative index, called internal validation indices [22]. These indices are called internal as they do not make use of any external information (such as class labels). The quality assessment of a clustering solution is based solely on the solution and the data themselves. Most of these indices are also relative as they can compare different clustering solutions and point out which one is better in relative terms. The possible applications for such indices go far beyond only providing an unsupervised quality estimate for the solutions. The most basic application is model selection, i.e., to use the quality estimates provided by the index to select the most suitable algorithm and/or choosing the appropriate configuration of parameters for the algorithm. Due to the variety of indices that have been proposed over the past few decades in the clustering literature [42], these indices can also be employed in more sophisticated applications, for example, to build ensembles of validation indices [23,43].

Although internal indices have been extensively studied and shown to be effective and useful tools in the unsupervised clustering domain, they are still in their infancy in outlier detection. The lack of diversity of indices is especially critical in this scenario. Due to the natural subjectivity of this context, no single index can capture all possible facets of the unsupervised outlier detection problem. Therefore, relying on multiple indices can be very important. Furthermore, the low diversity of indices available makes it very difficult to employ them in more sophisticated applications, restricting their application mostly to the fundamental tasks of model selection and unsupervised evaluation. In fact, the lack of internal indices for unsupervised outlier detection has already been acknowledged in the literature as an obstacle to the development of advanced ensemble selection methods [46]. Therefore, the development of indices supported on different grounds is essential also to unlock the full potential of applications for these indices. In this paper, we aim to aid in bridging this gap by proposing a new internal, relative evaluation measure for unsupervised outlier detection. The index uses the similarity of the observations as the basis to formulate its criterion, relying on the common intuition that outliers are dissimilar from the other observations. The use of similarities is very in line with most unsupervised outlier detection algorithms that detect outliers based on distances involving their neighbors. The use of a similarity measure also makes the index very convenient for applications in unstructured data (*e.g.*, texts, images, and graphs), where it is often tricky to explicit the data in a good feature set. At the same time, our proposed index is more computationally efficient than existing ones.

We organize the remainder of this paper as follows. In Sect. 2, we discuss the typical approaches in the literature for the evaluation of the results in unsupervised outlier detection, including the external evaluation and other indices in the literature for internal evaluation. In Sect. 3, we introduce our similarity-based index for internal evaluation, SIREOS. Finally, we evaluate this index in Sect. 4 and conclude the paper in Sect. 5.

2   Related Work

In the literature on unsupervised outlier detection, the common procedure for the evaluation of the results makes use of previously labeled datasets. In this scenario, referred to as external evaluation or validation, the labels are not used by the algorithms themselves, but rather merely to assess their results. The labeling or ranking produced by the algorithm is compared with the correct and previously known labeling (ground truth) using quality measures, such as precision-at-n and ROC AUC curve [10,36]. These external evaluation procedures have been essential in the outlier detection literature. Comparative studies have taken advantage of them to evaluate how algorithms compare to each other [10,16]. Such procedures are fundamental to assess the current state of the art in the area. However, they make sense only in controlled experiments, as in the aforementioned comparative studies. The premise of a fully labeled dataset makes it entirely unsuitable for practical applications of unsupervised learning.

Internal evaluation, which is the focus of this paper, provides a quality estimate of the results without the requirement of a fully labeled dataset. This subject, however, has been neglected for a long time in outlier detection and was brought to the community's attention only in 2013 [46]. Shortly after, Marques *et al.* [30] proposed IREOS, the first index for the internal evaluation of outlier detection results. The index takes advantage of maximum margin classifiers (*e.g.*, SVM and KLR [17]) to formulate a criterion based on the separability of the observations labeled as outliers in the candidate solution. Although the publication of IREOS was a breakthrough in the area, in its first version the index was only able to evaluate top-n (binary) solutions, *i.e.*, solutions in which a subset of n observations are labeled as outliers, while the remaining $N - n$ observations are labeled as inliers. Most algorithms, however, do not label observations as outliers or inliers, but assign scores to each observation representing its degree of outlierness. Another major limitation of the index was its inability to scale on large datasets. These limitations have been addressed in the fuller developed version of IREOS [29], where it was extended to the more general scenario of the evaluation of outlier detection scorings. In addition, the authors introduced speedup techniques to compute an approximation of the index in a small fraction of the original runtime.

In the same paper [29], the authors also introduced a baseline measure, the "Laplacian Score". This baseline measure was originally proposed as a filter method for feature selection [19]. The authors took advantage of the fact that this feature selection method ranks the features according to their importance. They treated the candidate solutions as a set of features (each candidate outlier detection solution corresponds to one feature), such that the method can rank the candidate solutions according to their importance. Note that the authors used this measure only as a baseline to evaluate IREOS. Laplacian Score is not a fully developed and explored index and is not based on a solid theoretical basis.

Two additional indices were proposed by Goix [14]. The indices are based on existing Excess-Mass (EM) [15] and Mass-Volume (MV) [11] curves. These statistical tools are used to measure the quality of a scoring function in terms of level sets. The main idea behind the index assumes that the level sets of a scoring function are estimates of the level sets of the density. Therefore, the collection of level sets of an optimal scoring function coincides with that related to the underlying density distribution of the data. This distribution, however, is generally unknown in practice, and the MV and EM curves need to be estimated using Monte-Carlo approximations. A major drawback is that Monte-Carlo approximations make good estimates only on datasets with low dimensionality ($d \leq 8$). The authors extend these criteria to high-dimensional datasets by applying feature bagging on the dataset. They sample small subsets of the features, evaluate the results produced in each feature sampling individually and aggregate these individual evaluations. This approach, however, has the inconvenience of the need to re-execute the algorithm/parameter in the different feature samplings to evaluate the candidate solution provided by that algorithm.

3   Internal Evaluation of Outlier Detection

3.1   Problem Statement

The problem of internal evaluation of outlier detection has already been formalized in [29,30]. Here, we revise this formulation as we use the same notation in the remaining of this paper. Let $\mathbf{X} = \{\mathbf{x}_1, \cdots, \mathbf{x}_N\}$ be an unlabeled dataset containing N d-dimensional feature vectors, $\mathbf{x}_i$, and assume that one or more unsupervised outlier detection algorithms will produce, for this dataset, a collection Ω of n_Ω candidate outlier detection solutions, $\Omega = \{\omega_1, \cdots, \omega_{n_\Omega}\}$, which one wants to evaluate in the absence of labels. Solutions $\omega_{(.)}$ produced by unsupervised outlier detection algorithms can be given in different formats. The most common format is a scoring $\mathbf{y} = \{y_1, \cdots, y_N\}$, $y_i \in \mathbb{R}^+$, where y_i represents the outlier score associated with the observation $\mathbf{x}_i$, which reflects the degree of outlierness of $\mathbf{x}_i$. This type of solution allows objects $\mathbf{x}_i$ to be sorted and ranked according to their degree of outlierness y_i. When the number of outliers n is known, one can establish a threshold in the ranking in order to select a subset $\mathbf{S} \subset \mathbf{X}$, $|\mathbf{S}| = n$, containing the top-n objects that are labeled as outliers. When represented in this format, we refer to $\omega_{(.)}$ as binary, top-n solutions. In this particular case of binary top-n solutions, the number of different possible solutions is finite. The set containing all possible labeling realizations $\mathbb{U}_\omega$ contains $\binom{N}{n}$ solutions.

Given a collection Ω of candidate solutions ω_i, whether they are scoring solutions or top-n solutions, we want to independently and quantitatively measure the quality of each individual candidate solution, e.g., (i) to assess their statistical significance when compared to the null hypothesis of a random solution; or (ii) to compare them in relative terms so that the best candidates, corresponding to more suitable models (algorithms, parameters), can be selected.

3.2   Internal Evaluation of Top-n Outlier Detection

In the seminal work on internal evaluation of outlier detection [30], the authors introduced a framework for Internal, Relative Evaluation of Outlier Solutions (IREOS). IREOS is based on a measure of separability $p(\cdot)$ given by a maximum margin classifier. In order to quantify the quality of a candidate solution $\mathbf{S}$, the index computes the average separability of the observations $\mathbf{x}_i$ labeled as outliers in that solution:

$$I(\mathbf{S}) = \frac{1}{n} \sum_{\mathbf{x}_i \in \mathbf{S}} p(\mathbf{x}_i), \tag{1}$$

The intuition behind the index is that outliers are observations with a higher degree of separability. Therefore, the higher the average degree of separability of the candidate outliers, the better the solution.

The labeling of a subset of n observations as outliers, given by a candidate solution $\mathbf{S}$, can be viewed as a sample of size n from the dataset. Therefore, the mean of the separability of these n observations, $I(\mathbf{S})$, can be seen as a sample mean. The Central Limit Theorem (CLT) guarantees that the sampling distribution of the sample mean is normally distributed, as long as the sample size, n, is not critically small. For this reason, we can assume that the distribution of IREOS follows, at least approximately, a Normal distribution:

$$I \sim \mathcal{N}(E\{I\}, Var\{I\}) \tag{2}$$

We can also evoke the CLT to derive the mean and variance of the distribution of IREOS, for example, to assess the statistical significance of a candidate solution when compared to the null hypothesis of a random solution. The mean $E\{I\}$ of the distribution is computed as:

$$E\{I\} = \frac{1}{|\mathbb{U}_\omega|} \sum_{\mathbf{S}\in\mathbb{U}_\omega} I(\mathbf{S}), \tag{3}$$

and the variance $Var\{I\}$ as:

$$Var\{I\} = \frac{1}{n^2|\mathbb{U}_\omega|} \sum_{\mathbf{S}\in\mathbb{U}_\omega} \sum_{\mathbf{x}_i\in\mathbf{S}} (p(\mathbf{x}_i) - E\{I\})^2 \tag{4}$$

Note, however, that although $\mathbb{U}_\omega$ is finite for binary top-n solutions, the number of $p(\cdot)$ computations required to calculate these statistics becomes computationally prohibitive even for moderate datasets. In practice, the index statistics are estimated using Monte-Carlo simulations.

3.3 Internal Evaluation of Outlier Detection Scorings

As most unsupervised outlier detection algorithms provide the solution ω in the format of outlier scoring $\mathbf{y}$, instead of a binary, top-n solution $\mathbf{S}$, weights are introduced in the original formulation of the index (Eq. (1)) to make it suitable for the evaluation of outlier scorings [29]:

$$IREOS(\omega) = \frac{\sum_{i=1}^{N} p(\mathbf{x}_i)w_i}{\sum_{i=1}^{N} w_i}, \tag{5}$$

The intuition behind using weights in the index is that these weights w_i are associated with the outlier scorings of the observations $\mathbf{x}_i$, such that solutions assigning higher (lower) outlier scores to observations with higher (lower) separabilities result in larger values of index, indicating that these are better solutions. However, the fact that various outlier detection algorithms produce scores on completely different scales requires some kind of normalization to compare solutions provided by different algorithms. By using the framework for outlier scoring normalization proposed by Kriegel et al. [26], the original outlier scores ($\mathbf{y}$) can be transformed into the interval $[0, 1]$ in a way that they can be interpreted as outlier probabilities. The resulting normalized outlier scores, $w(\cdot)$, can then be used in Eq. (5).

3.4 Similarity-Based Internal Evaluation of Outlier Detection

The framework IREOS [30] was originally proposed to perform the internal evaluation of outlier detection solutions using maximum margin classifiers. The use of classifiers other than the maximum margin classifiers to compute the separabilities $p(\cdot)$ was acknowledged by the authors [29] as a possible topic for future research. Here, however, we propose the use of other measures in the framework that are not tied to classifiers. In fact, the separability measure $p(\cdot)$ provided by classifiers has been acknowledged in the literature as the main criticism of the index [10, 29, 47], as it can be computationally very demanding to compute the separability by training classifiers. Similarity is a less complex (both in terms of computational requirements and in terms of expressiveness) measure. In this paper, we explore the usefulness of this simpler measure to evaluate candidate outlier detection solutions with a Similarity-based Internal, Relative Evaluation of Outlier Solutions (SIREOS). The use of similarity relies on the common intuition that outliers are observations somehow dissimilar from the others. Therefore, we expect that in a good solution, a suitable measure of the similarity of the observations labeled as outliers to the rest of the dataset will be low, whereas, in a poor solution, this similarity should be higher.

In order to evaluate the candidate solutions, we define the similarity-based measure to be used in the place of $p(\cdot)$ as:

$$ s(\mathbf{x}_i) = \frac{1}{(N-1)} \sum_{\mathbf{x}_j \in (\mathbf{X} \backslash \mathbf{x}_i)} \mathbf{K}(\mathbf{x}_i, \mathbf{x}_j), \tag{6} $$

where $\mathbf{K}(\mathbf{x}_i, \mathbf{x}_j)$ measures the similarity between $\mathbf{x}_i$ and $\mathbf{x}_j$. The possibilities for the function $\mathbf{K}(\mathbf{x}_i, \mathbf{x}_j)$ are diverse, and the choice depends on the nature of the data and the application scenario. In the literature, there are several similarity measures designed for the different pattern of data, *e.g.*, cosine for high-dimensional datasets [40], dynamic time warping (DTW) for time series [31], simple matching coefficient (SMC) for categorical data [40], graph edit distance (GED) for graphs [35], structural similarity (SSIM) for images [44], and so on. In the context of unstructured data, modern machine learning techniques (*e.g.*, deep learning) have shown an advantage over traditional techniques [34] as they can internally learn representations without the need of crafted feature engineering. In this context, where it is often tricky to explicitly represent the data by a good feature set in advance, these well-established similarity measures make the index computation possible without needing to map the data into a feature space (including latent spaces learned as part of models to be evaluated).

Given a similarity function $\mathbf{K}(\mathbf{x}_i, \mathbf{x}_j)$, the measure $s(\mathbf{x}_i)$ presented in Eq. (6) can be readily plugged into Eq. (5), resulting in the new index proposed here:

$$ SIREOS(\omega) = \frac{\sum_{i=1}^{N} s(\mathbf{x}_i) w_i}{\sum_{i=1}^{N} w_i}, \tag{7} $$

Note that in contrast to the original index, where the larger the index (better separabilities), the better the solution, here, as we use a similarity-based measure and we expect outliers to have low similarity to the other observations, the lower the index, the better the solution.

4   Evaluation

In our experiments, we evaluate our index in terms of quality and runtime against other competitors, namely, IREOS [29], Laplacian Score [29], Excess-Mass (EM) [14], and Mass-Volume (MV) [14] curves. In order to measure the quality of the index, we performed an experiment involving model selection. Using the quality assessments of the solutions computed by indices, we selected the best solution of each dataset according to their respective scores. The quality of these solutions is then independently assessed with respect to the ground truth, *i.e.*, in a supervised way. We compute the Area Under the ROC Curve (ROC AUC) of the outlier scores in the selected solutions against the labels in the ground truth. The objective is to compare the assessments of the solutions with respect to the ground truth and the quality assessments of the solutions provided by the indices. We expect good indices to have a positive correlation with the assessments with respect to the ground truth, *i.e.*, good solutions according to the index should also be considered good according to the ground truth.

For runtime experiments, we measure the total running time of each index to evaluate a single solution, and report the average runtime over 5 experiments. The experiments were performed in a machine with 16 GB RAM and processor Quad-Core Intel Core i7, 2.7 GHz. All the implementations used in our experiments had the source code provided by the own authors of the indices. In order to perform a fair runtime comparison involving codes in the same language, we implemented our own Python version of IREOS, which was originally available in Java. All our codes, as well as pointers to the third-party codes, are available in a repository at https://github.com/homarques/SIREOS.

4.1   Datasets

In our experiments, we use a collection of 24 real-world datasets previously used for internal evaluation of outlier detection results [29]. This collection is composed of 23 datasets from a publicly available outlier detection repository [10], with the addition of 4 datasets as used in the IREOS study [30], namely, Isolet, Multiple Features, Optical Digits, and Vowel. We excluded those datasets for which none of the outlier detection algorithms could find at least one solution with at least 0.75 of ROC AUC, namely Annthyroid, Wilt, and WPBC. The inclusion of these datasets in the previous studies [10, 29] was important because the authors were also evaluating the suitability of datasets for outlier detection benchmarking. As none of these datasets seemed suitable for outlier detection, their inclusion would only lead to noise in the evaluation of our experiments.

For each dataset, we selected 10 candidate solutions from a vast collection of results produced by varying the parameter neighborhood size k (between 1 and 100) of 13 different algorithms, namely: COF [41], FastABOD [27], INFLO [24], KDEOS [37], KNN [32], KNNW [4,5], LDOF [45], LDF [28], LOF [8], LoOP [25], ODIN [18], SimplifiedLOF [38], and GLOSH [9]. The selection was made by ensuring that the selected solutions keep an interval as equally spaced as possible between solutions in terms of their ROC AUC values.

In addition to the collection of real-world datasets, we also use a collection of synthetic datasets to measure the total run time of the indices evaluated. The datasets were obtained using the generator proposed in [20], varying the number of dimensions from 2 to 128 $\{2, 4, 8, 16, 32, 64, 128\}$ and the number of points from 2,000 to 128,000 using the same progression of dimensionality. When varying the number of dimensions, the dataset size is fixed with 4,000 objects. For the different sizes of the datasets, we set the dimension to 8.

4.2   Parameters

For the similarity function used in our experiments, we choose the Radial Basis Function (RBF), as it is one of the most effective and popular similarity functions:

$$\mathbf{K}(\mathbf{x}_i, \mathbf{x}_j) = e^{-\frac{||\mathbf{x}_i - \mathbf{x}_j||^2}{2t}}, \tag{8}$$

using t equal to the 0.01 quantile of the pairwise distances, based on preliminary experiments. This empirical rule of thumb was applied across all the data sets.

Since for many of the datasets the computation of the exact IREOS is prohibitive, we adopt the authors' approximation with $k = 250$, as it provided a good trade-off between speed and accuracy in their experiments in [29]. For the optional mechanism for modeling clumps in IREOS, we use $m_{cl} = \sqrt{5\% \cdot N}$, as recommend by the authors in fully unsupervised scenarios when domain-specific information about whether/how clumps should be modeled is not available.

As the datasets used in our experiments are not low dimensional and EM/MV curves can only be computed in low dimensional data ($d \leq 8$), we use the feature bagging algorithm proposed by the authors with their suggested parameters, $m = 50$ and $d = 5$, $i.e.$, 50 draws of 5 features. The volume in spaces of dimension 5 was estimated using 30,000 Monte-Carlo approximations.

4.3   Results

The results of the experiment involving model selection are summarized in Fig. 1, showing the average ranking of the different indices according to their selected

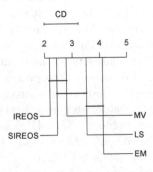

Fig. 1. Average ranking of the indices according to the solutions selected by them.

solutions. The length of the upper bar (CD) indicates the critical difference of the well-known Friedman/Nemenyi statistical test [12] at significance level $\alpha = 0.05$. The CD diagram shows that, on average, IREOS, SIREOS and MV select the best solutions, with no statistically significant difference between them. By using IREOS or SIREOS to select the best solution, one would choose the best solution according to the ground truth in 12 out of the 24 datasets. In comparison, MV makes the best recommendation in only 8 of the 24 datasets.

It is interesting to note that the top performers (SIREOS, IREOS, and MV) appear to be complementary in that they often don't elect the same solution as best, indicating an interesting path for an ensemble of validation indices. In order to get a better sense of these results, we show box plots of the distribution of the ROC AUC values for all candidate solutions for each dataset in Fig. 2. The position of the solutions selected by the top performing indices are indicated by special symbols in the plots. An overlapping of symbols involving the best solution chosen by these indexes occurs only in 12 out of 24 datasets. In the other 12 times, one of the indices selected alone a solution that is superior.

In the second group in terms of performance, with a significant difference from the first, LS and EM select the best solution w.r.t. the ground truth, respectively, in 5 and 6 times out of the 24 datasets.

Figure 3a shows the total runtime as a function of the (synthetic) dataset size. In the smaller datasets ($N \le 16,000$), most of the indices have similar runtime. The exceptions are the EM and MV curves due to the runtime of the Monte-Carlo simulations dominating the total runtime on small datasets. As expected, as the number of points increases, the difference in the runtime of the

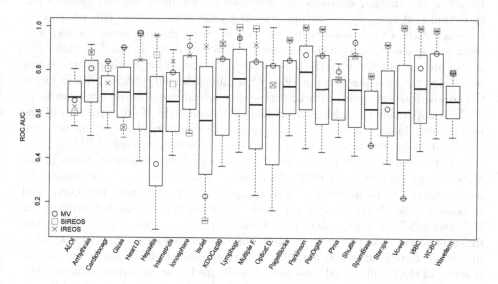

Fig. 2. Distribution of the ROC AUC values for all candidate solutions used in the model selection experiments (real-world data). The position of the solutions selected by the indices as best are indicated by their respective special symbols.

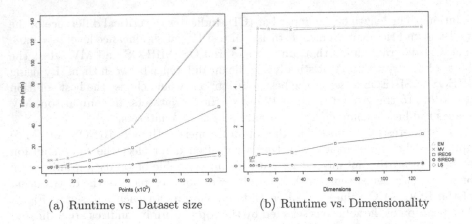

(a) Runtime vs. Dataset size   (b) Runtime vs. Dimensionality

Fig. 3. Runtime as a function of the dataset size and dataset dimensionality.

indices becomes clearer. The two top-performers in terms of runtime are LS and SIREOS, with LS having the advantage of working in the 1-dimensional space of the outlier scoring instead of the 8-dimensional space of the dataset. Also, as the size of the dataset increases, the gap between the runtimes of EM and MV and the runtimes of the other indices becomes larger.

Figure 3b shows the total runtime as a function of the dimensionality. EM and MV show a competitive runtime for small dimensions ($d < 8$), faster than IREOS, since feature sampling is not required for small dimensional datasets. However, the runtime dramatically increases as the dimensionality exceeds the threshold that triggers the feature sampling procedure. Beyond this point, runtime is invariant to dimensionality because feature sampling forces the index to work in a space of constant dimensionality. The invariance in the dimensionality is also present in LS, due to the index working in the outlier scoring space. When measuring the runtime as a function of the dimensionality, LS and SIREOS are the top performers again, with LS having the advantage of being invariant to it.

It is important to highlight that EM, MV, and IREOS are estimates of the real indices. Therefore, they have parameters that control the trade-off between the accuracy in the index calculation and the runtime: in the case of EM and MV curves, the number of Monte-Carlo simulations and the number of draws in the feature bagging, and for IREOS, the number of neighbors used to compute the separability. The parameters used to compare the runtime were the same used to compare the effectiveness in the model selection experiment. In addition, for EM and MV, the outlier detection algorithm needs to be re-executed in the different feature samplings to evaluate the candidate solution provided by that algorithm. In our runtime experiment above, we used the KNN algorithm [32], as it is one of the simplest and most used algorithms in the literature. However, the runtime for the EM and MV indices can increase (decrease) in case of a different choice. Also, all the indices/algorithms followed standard implementations. They all could benefit from using appropriate data structures, such as a Kd-Tree [7].

5   Conclusions

In this paper, we presented SIREOS, a similarity-based index for the internal evaluation of outlier detection solutions. The index is built on the framework for Internal, Relative Evaluation of Outlier Solutions (IREOS), addressing a major issue of the original index proposed within this framework, its computational cost. In our experiments, we compared SIREOS against the original IREOS as well as against other indices from the literature w.r.t. quality and runtime performance. In terms of quality, SIREOS exhibited top performance, statistically tied with IREOS and MV. In terms of runtime, however, SIREOS performed much better than both indices, regardless of dimensionality or dataset size.

We can see similarity as a proxy to separability, but it should also be noted that separability is more complex not only computationally but also in expressiveness. It is easy to imagine two examples where an outlier is equally far away from its neighbors in both cases, but the separability would be evaluated as different, e.g., as the outlier can be separated from other observations by a linear boundary in one case while requiring a non-linear boundary in the other. The experiments showed that the two indices do not always agree, but do not differ significantly in quality over many datasets. Hence SIREOS is adding variation to the portfolio of existing indices. On the other hand, the generic similarity-based index proposed here is ready to use with a variety of similarity measures and thus can incorporate rich semantics itself. However, this would require an extended study with different data types.

It is important to remember that the evaluated indices are supported on different grounds. Although some perform better than others, they are rather complementary and all of them can still be important. Relying on multiple indices can be an important tool to deal with the many facets of the unsupervised outlier detection problem. Furthermore, combining these indices may be another interesting topic for future work, where we can explore more sophisticated applications of such indices, such as ensemble selection for outlier detection ensembles, or building ensembles of validation indices.

Acknowledgement. This work has partly been funded by NSERC Canada, and the Independent Research Fund Denmark in the project "Reliable Outlier Detection".

References

1. Adewumi, A.O., Akinyelu, A.A.: A survey of machine-learning and nature-inspired based credit card fraud detection techniques. Int. J. Syst. Assur. Eng. Manag. **8**(2), 937–953 (2017)
2. Ahmad, Z., Khan, A.S., Shiang, C.W., Abdullah, J., Ahmad, F.: Network intrusion detection system: a systematic study of machine learning and deep learning approaches. Trans. Emerg. Telecommun. Technol. **32**(1), e4150 (2021)
3. Alaverdyan, Z., Jung, J., Bouet, R., Lartizien, C.: Regularized Siamese neural network for unsupervised outlier detection on brain multiparametric magnetic resonance imaging. Med. Image Anal. **60** (2020)

4. Angiulli, F., Pizzuti, C.: Fast outlier detection in high dimensional spaces. In: Elomaa, T., Mannila, H., Toivonen, H. (eds.) PKDD 2002. LNCS, vol. 2431, pp. 15–27. Springer, Heidelberg (2002). https://doi.org/10.1007/3-540-45681-3_2
5. Angiulli, F., Pizzuti, C.: Outlier mining in large high-dimensional data sets. IEEE Trans. Knowl. Data Eng. **17**(2), 203–215 (2005)
6. Barnett, V., Lewis, T.: Outliers in Statistical Data, 3rd edn. Wiley, Hoboken (1994)
7. Bentley, J.L.: Multidimensional binary search trees used for associative searching. Commun. ACM **18**(9), 509–517 (1975)
8. Breunig, M.M., Kriegel, H., Ng, R.T., Sander, J.: LOF: identifying density-based local outliers. In: SIGMOD Conference, pp. 93–104. ACM (2000)
9. Campello, R.J.G.B., Moulavi, D., Zimek, A., Sander, J.: Hierarchical density estimates for data clustering, visualization, and outlier detection. ACM Trans. Knowl. Discov. Data **10**(1), 5:1–5:51 (2015)
10. Campos, G.O., et al.: On the evaluation of unsupervised outlier detection: measures, datasets, and an empirical study. Data Min. Knowl. Discov. **30**(4), 891–927 (2016)
11. Clémençon, S., Jakubowicz, J.: Scoring anomalies: a M-estimation formulation. In: AISTATS. JMLR Workshop and Conference Proceedings, vol. 31, pp. 659–667 (2013)
12. Demsar, J.: Statistical comparisons of classifiers over multiple data sets. J. Mach. Learn. Res. **7**, 1–30 (2006)
13. Djenouri, Y., Zimek, A., Chiarandini, M.: Outlier detection in urban traffic flow distributions. In: ICDM, pp. 935–940. IEEE Computer Society (2018)
14. Goix, N.: How to evaluate the quality of unsupervised anomaly detection algorithms? CoRR abs/1607.01152 (2016)
15. Goix, N., Sabourin, A., Clémençon, S.: On anomaly ranking and excess-mass curves. In: AISTATS. JMLR Workshop and Conference Proceedings, vol. 38 (2015)
16. Goldstein, M., Uchida, S.: A comparative evaluation of unsupervised anomaly detection algorithms for multivariate data. PLoS ONE **11**(4), 1–31 (2016)
17. Hastie, T., Tibshirani, R., Friedman, J.H.: The Elements of Statistical Learning: Data Mining, Inference, and Prediction, 2nd edn. Springer, Heidelberg (2009). https://doi.org/10.1007/978-0-387-84858-7
18. Hautamäki, V., Kärkkäinen, I., Fränti, P.: Outlier detection using k-nearest neighbour graph. In: ICPR (3), pp. 430–433. IEEE Computer Society (2004)
19. He, X., Cai, D., Niyogi, P.: Laplacian score for feature selection. In: NIPS, pp. 507–514 (2005)
20. Iglesias, F., Zseby, T., Ferreira, D.C., Zimek, A.: MDCGen: multidimensional dataset generator for clustering. J. Classif. **36**(3), 599–618 (2019)
21. Iglesias, F., Zseby, T., Zimek, A.: Absolute cluster validity. IEEE Trans. Pattern Anal. Mach. Intell. **42**(9), 2096–2112 (2020)
22. Jain, A.K., Dubes, R.C.: Algorithms for Clustering Data. Prentice-Hall, Hoboken (1988)
23. Jaskowiak, P.A., Moulavi, D., Furtado, A.C.S., Campello, R.J.G.B., Zimek, A., Sander, J.: On strategies for building effective ensembles of relative clustering validity criteria. Knowl. Inf. Syst. **47**(2), 329–354 (2016)
24. Jin, W., Tung, A.K.H., Han, J., Wang, W.: Ranking outliers using symmetric neighborhood relationship. In: Ng, W.-K., Kitsuregawa, M., Li, J., Chang, K. (eds.) PAKDD 2006. LNCS (LNAI), vol. 3918, pp. 577–593. Springer, Heidelberg (2006). https://doi.org/10.1007/11731139_68
25. Kriegel, H., Kröger, P., Schubert, E., Zimek, A.: LoOP: local outlier probabilities. In: CIKM, pp. 1649–1652. ACM (2009)

26. Kriegel, H., Kröger, P., Schubert, E., Zimek, A.: Interpreting and unifying outlier scores. In: SDM, pp. 13–24. SIAM/Omnipress (2011)
27. Kriegel, H., Schubert, M., Zimek, A.: Angle-based outlier detection in high-dimensional data. In: KDD, pp. 444–452. ACM (2008)
28. Latecki, L.J., Lazarevic, A., Pokrajac, D.: Outlier detection with kernel density functions. In: Perner, P. (ed.) MLDM 2007. LNCS (LNAI), vol. 4571, pp. 61–75. Springer, Heidelberg (2007). https://doi.org/10.1007/978-3-540-73499-4_6
29. Marques, H.O., Campello, R.J.G.B., Sander, J., Zimek, A.: Internal evaluation of unsupervised outlier detection. ACM Trans. Knowl. Discov. Data 14(4), 47:1–47:42 (2020)
30. Marques, H.O., Campello, R.J.G.B., Zimek, A., Sander, J.: On the internal evaluation of unsupervised outlier detection. In: SSDBM, pp. 7:1–7:12. ACM (2015)
31. Rakthanmanon, T., et al.: Searching and mining trillions of time series subsequences under dynamic time warping. In: KDD, pp. 262–270 (2012)
32. Ramaswamy, S., Rastogi, R., Shim, K.: Efficient algorithms for mining outliers from large data sets. In: SIGMOD Conference, pp. 427–438. ACM (2000)
33. Ramotsoela, D.T., Abu-Mahfouz, A.M., Hancke, G.P.: A survey of anomaly detection in industrial wireless sensor networks with critical water system infrastructure as a case study. Sensors 18(8), 2491 (2018)
34. Ruff, L., et al.: Deep semi-supervised anomaly detection. In: ICLR (2020)
35. Sanfeliu, A., Fu, K.: A distance measure between attributed relational graphs for pattern recognition. IEEE Trans. Syst. Man Cybern. 13(3), 353–362 (1983)
36. Schubert, E., Wojdanowski, R., Zimek, A., Kriegel, H.: On evaluation of outlier rankings and outlier scores. In: SDM, pp. 1047–1058. SIAM/Omnipress (2012)
37. Schubert, E., Zimek, A., Kriegel, H.: Generalized outlier detection with flexible kernel density estimates. In: SDM, pp. 542–550. SIAM (2014)
38. Schubert, E., Zimek, A., Kriegel, H.: Local outlier detection reconsidered: a generalized view on locality with applications to spatial, video, and network outlier detection. Data Min. Knowl. Discov. 28(1), 190–237 (2014)
39. Swersky, L., Marques, H.O., Sander, J., Campello, R.J.G.B., Zimek, A.: On the evaluation of outlier detection and one-class classification methods. In: DSAA (2016)
40. Tan, P., Steinbach, M.S., Karpatne, A., Kumar, V.: Introduction to Data Mining, 2nd edn. Pearson (2019)
41. Tang, J., Chen, Z., Fu, A.W., Cheung, D.W.: Enhancing effectiveness of outlier detections for low density patterns. In: Chen, M.-S., Yu, P.S., Liu, B. (eds.) PAKDD 2002. LNCS (LNAI), vol. 2336, pp. 535–548. Springer, Heidelberg (2002). https://doi.org/10.1007/3-540-47887-6_53
42. Vendramin, L., Campello, R.J.G.B., Hruschka, E.R.: Relative clustering validity criteria: a comparative overview. Stat. Anal. Data Min. 3(4), 209–235 (2010)
43. Vendramin, L., Jaskowiak, P.A., Campello, R.J.G.B.: On the combination of relative clustering validity criteria. In: SSDBM, pp. 4:1–4:12. ACM (2013)
44. Wang, Z., Bovik, A.C., Sheikh, H.R., Simoncelli, E.P.: Image quality assessment: from error visibility to structural similarity. IEEE Trans. Image Process. 13(4), 600–612 (2004)
45. Zhang, K., Hutter, M., Jin, H.: A new local distance-based outlier detection approach for scattered real-world data. In: Theeramunkong, T., Kijsirikul, B., Cercone, N., Ho, T.-B. (eds.) PAKDD 2009. LNCS (LNAI), vol. 5476, pp. 813–822. Springer, Heidelberg (2009). https://doi.org/10.1007/978-3-642-01307-2_84

46. Zimek, A., Campello, R.J.G.B., Sander, J.: Ensembles for unsupervised outlier detection: challenges and research questions a position paper. SIGKDD Explor. **15**(1), 11–22 (2013)
47. Zimek, A., Filzmoser, P.: There and back again: outlier detection between statistical reasoning and data mining algorithms. WIREs Data Min. Knowl. Discov. **8**(6) (2018)

Learning

FastHebb: Scaling Hebbian Training of Deep Neural Networks to ImageNet Level

Gabriele Lagani[1,2]([✉]), Claudio Gennaro[2], Hannes Fassold[3], and Giuseppe Amato[2]

[1] Department of Computer Science, University of Pisa, 56127 Pisa, Italy
gabriele.lagani@phd.unipi.it
[2] ISTI-CNR, 56124 Pisa, Italy
{gabriele.lagani,claudio.gennaro,giuseppe.amato}@isti.cnr.it
[3] Joanneum Research, 8010 Graz, Austria
hannes.fassold@joanneum.at

Abstract. Learning algorithms for Deep Neural Networks are typically based on supervised end-to-end Stochastic Gradient Descent (SGD) training with error backpropagation (backprop). Backprop algorithms require a large number of labelled training samples to achieve high performance. However, in many realistic applications, even if there is plenty of image samples, very few of them are labelled, and semi-supervised sample-efficient training strategies have to be used. Hebbian learning represents a possible approach towards sample efficient training; however, in current solutions, it does not scale well to large datasets. In this paper, we present *FastHebb*, an efficient and scalable solution for Hebbian learning which achieves higher efficiency by 1) merging together update computation and aggregation over a batch of inputs, and 2) leveraging efficient matrix multiplication algorithms on GPU. We validate our approach on different computer vision benchmarks, in a semi-supervised learning scenario. FastHebb outperforms previous solutions by up to 50 times in terms of training speed, and notably, for the first time, we are able to bring Hebbian algorithms to ImageNet scale.

Keywords: Hebbian learning · Deep learning · Neural networks · Semi-supervised · Sample efficiency · Content-Based Image Retrieval

1 Introduction

In the past few years, Deep Neural Networks (DNNs) have emerged as a powerful technology in the domain of computer vision [10,19]. DNNs started gaining popularity also in the domain of large scale multimedia Content-Based Image Retrieval (CBIR), replacing handcrafted feature extractors [2,36] and using activations of internal layers as feature vectors for similarity search. Learning

---

This work was partially supported by the H2020 project AI4Media (GA 951911).

T. Skopal et al. (Eds.): SISAP 2022, LNCS 13590, pp. 251–264, 2022.
https://doi.org/10.1007/978-3-031-17849-8_20

algorithms for DNNs are typically based on supervised end-to-end Stochastic Gradient Descent (SGD) training with error backpropagation (*backprop*). This approach is considered biologically implausible by neuroscientists [32]. Instead, they propose *Hebbian* learning as a biological alternative to model synaptic plasticity [9].

Moreover, backprop-based algorithms need a large number of labeled training samples in order to achieve high results, which are expensive to gather, as opposed to unlabeled samples. Therefore, researchers started to investigate *semi-supervised* learning strategies, which aim to exploit large amounts of unlabeled data, in addition to the fewer labeled data, for sample efficient learning [5,28]. In this context, a possible direction that has been proposed is to perform an unsupervised pre-training stage on all the available samples, which is then followed by a supervised fine-tuning stage on the few labeled samples only [16,38].

In recent work, Hebbian learning has begun to gain attention from the computer science community as an effective method for unsupervised pre-training, since Hebbian algorithms do not require supervision, achieving promising results in scenarios with scarce labeled data [22,24]. However, current solutions for Hebbian training (such as [3,20,23,25,26,35]) are still limited in terms of computational efficiency, making it difficult to scale to large datasets such as ImageNet [6].

In order to address this issue, we present *FastHebb*, a novel solution for Hebbian training that achieves enhanced efficiency by leveraging two observations. First, when a mini-batch of inputs has to be processed, the weight update corresponding to each input is first computed, and then the various updates are aggregated over the mini-batch; however, update computation and aggregation can be merged together with a significant speedup. Second, Hebbian learning rules can be reformulated in terms of matrix multiplications, which enables to exploit efficient matrix multiplication algorithms on GPU.

We validate our method on various computer vision benchmarks. Since Hebbian algorithms are unsupervised, we consider a semi-supervised training scenario, in which Hebbian learning is used to perform unsupervised network pre-training, followed by fine-tuning with traditional backprop-based supervised learning. We also consider sample efficiency scenarios, in which we assume that only a small fraction of the training data is labeled, in order to study the effectiveness of Hebbian pre-training in scenarios with scarce data. In order to make comparisons with backprop-based methods, we consider Variational Auto-Encoder (VAE) [15,16] pre-training as a baseline for comparisons. We show that our approach achieves comparable results, but with a significant speed-up both in terms of number of epochs, as well as total training time. In particular, our method achieves up to 50x speed-up w.r.t. previous Hebbian learning solutions, allowing to scale up our experiments to ImageNet level. To the best of our knowledge, this is the first time that Hebbian algorithms are applied at such scale.

In summary, our contribution is twofold:

1. We propose a novel efficient solution to Hebbian learning algorithms, with code available online[1];

---

[1] https://github.com/GabrieleLagani/HebbianLearning/tree/fasthebb.

2. We performed extensive experimental evaluation of the performance of our solution on various computer vision benchmarks. In particular, for the first time (to the best of our knowledge) results of Hebbian algorithms on ImageNet are provided.

The remainder of this paper is structured as follows: Sect. 2 introduces some background and related work on Hebbian learning; Sect. 3 presents our FastHebb method; Sect. 4 provides the details of our experimental setup; Sect. 5 presents the results of our experiments; Finally, Sect. 6 outlines some concluding remarks and hints for future work.

2 Background and Related Work

In this section, we illustrate some of the Hebbian learning rules from literature that recently provided promising results, and we describe some related work focusing on the application of such rules on computer vision tasks, in particular in semi-supervised training scenarios. Since a thorough explanation of the Hebbian rules would be outside the scope of this paper, here we just give the update equations of interest, referring the interested reader to the vast literature on the topic [7,9,25–27].

Let us start by considering a neuron, identified by an index i, with weight vector $\mathbf{w}_i$, which receives as input a vector $\mathbf{x}$, and produces a corresponding output y_i. One of the Hebbian approaches that we focus on is the *soft Winner-Takes-All* (SWTA) competitive learning rule [8,25,29], which can be expressed as follows:

$$\Delta \mathbf{w}_i = \eta\, r_i \left(\mathbf{x} - \mathbf{w}_i\right) \tag{1}$$

where η is the learning rate, and the coefficient r_i is a score computed as the *softmax* of the neural activations: $r_i = \frac{e^{y_i/T}}{\sum_j e^{y_j/T}}$. Here, T is the *temperature* parameter of the softmax, which serves to cope with the variance of the activations (the name comes from statistical mechanics, where this operation was first defined). The effect of such a defined score is to allow each neuron to specialize on a different cluster of input patterns.

The other learning rule that we consider is Hebbian Principal Component Analysis (HPCA) [4,14,24,26]:

$$\Delta \mathbf{w}_i = \eta\, y_i \left(\mathbf{x} - \sum_{j=1}^{i} y_j \mathbf{w_j}\right) \tag{2}$$

WTA competition was studied in past work as a possible approach for training relatively shallow neural networks [20,35] (with up to 2–3 hidden layers). The investigation was further extended to deeper networks, and to hybrid architectures where some layers were trained by backprop and others by Hebbian learning [1,26]. Experimental results on CNNs showed promises of HPCA-like learning mechanisms initially with shallow networks [3], and then with deeper networks as well [23,24,26].

Since the HPCA and SWTA learning rules are unsupervised, they have found application in the context of semi-supervised neural network training, in order to perform an unsupervised pre-training stage [22–25]. In particular, they were found to be particularly useful in sample efficient learning scenarios, i.e. situations with scarce availability of labeled data. Related approaches for unsupervised pre-training are based on autoencoding architectures [5,16,28,38]. Results on various computer vision benchmarks suggest that Hebbian pre-training allows to significantly improve performance on such scenarios compared to other unsupervised pre-training methods such as Variational Auto-Encoder (VAE) pre-training [15,16]. Application of Hebbian learning to semi-supervised settings seems a promising direction. Other approaches to semi-supervised learning are based on pseudo-labeling/consistency-based methods [13,34]. However, these methods are not in contrast with unsupervised pre-training, and they could actually be integrated together. This possible future direction will also be highlighted in Sect. 6.

The problem with current Hebbian learning solutions is that they do not scale well to large datasets. Note that, the learning rules mentioned above describe the weight update for a single input $\mathbf{x}$. When there is a batch of inputs to be processed, the weight updates are aggregated over the batch dimension, typically by averaging (or weighted averaging, for SWTA, the weights being the competition scores r_i, check [1,21] for details). Similarly, in a convolutional layer, $\mathbf{x}$ would correspond to a patch extracted from an input at a given offset, and weight updates computed at different offsets need to be aggregated over all the extracted patches. In this contribution, we notice that these two phases (update computation and aggregation) can be merged together, which allows to reformulate Hebbian learning rules more efficiently in terms of matrix multiplications, which are particularly suitable for GPU computation. We show that our solution is able to scale well to large datasets such as ImageNet.

3   Efficient Hebbian Learning with FastHebb Method

Let us start by introducing some preliminary information about the multi-dimensional tensor data that we need to work with, and the notation that will be used in the following.

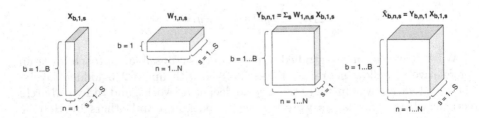

Fig. 1. Types of tensor objects involved in our scenario.

We define a *tensor* simply as a multi-dimensional array of data. In particular, our tensors are three-dimensional. We denote such tensors with capital letters, followed by as many indices as dimensions (three in our case). A dimension of size 1, also known as a *singleton* dimension, is denoted with the symbol 1 as index. Moreover, we adopt the following convention: index $b = 1...B$ denotes the *batch* dimension, index $n = 1...N$ denotes the *neuron* dimension, and index $s = 1...S$ denotes the *size* dimension. Note that the meaning of an index is inferred by the corresponding letter and not by its position. With reference to Fig. 1, the first tensor (from left to right) is a typical input tensor, consisting of a mini-batch of B inputs, each being a vector of size S. The second tensor represents a typical weight matrix, consisting of one weight vector for each of the N neurons, each of size S. The third is a typical output tensor, with each output being a vector on N elements, one for each neuron, and there is one such vector for each of the B elements in the batch. The last is a typical reconstruction tensor, which extends over all the dimensions.

Finally, in order to make the use of matrix multiplication explicit in our formulas, we will use the notation matmul$(\cdot, \cdot)$ as follows:

$$C_{d,e,g} = \sum_f A_{d,e,f} B_{d,g,f} = \sum_f A_{d,e,f} B_{d,f,g} := \mathrm{matmul}(A_{d,e,f}, B_{d,f,g}) \qquad (3)$$

Note that we are taking the tensor product between tensors A and B, identifying index d and contracting index f. This corresponds to a batch matrix multiplication over index d, i.e. mapping d pairs of matrices with indices (e, f) and (f, g), to d matrices with indices (e, g): $(e, f) \times (f, g) \to (e, g)$. If more that three dimensions are present, then the last two denote height and width of the matrices, and all the previous dimensions are considered as batch dimensions (and thus identified). If a batch dimension of one of the multiplied tensors happens to be a singleton, then it undergoes *broadcasting* to match the other tensor dimension, as done in common mathematical frameworks. In all the other cases the corresponding batch dimensions of the two tensors must have the same size (as well as the contracted f dimension). Sums, subtractions, and multiplications by constants over tensor are performed component-wise, but all dimensions must match. Also in this case, a singleton dimension of one tensor undergoes broadcast to match the corresponding dimension of the other tensor (in case of singleton dimensions, and only in this case, correspondence is inferred from the position of the indices).

Using the notation introduced above, we can express the Hebbian rules discussed in this paper, including the aggregation step, as follows:

$$\Delta W_{1,n,s} = \sum_b C_{b,n,1} \Delta W_{b,n,s} = \mathrm{matmul}(C_{n,1,b}, \Delta W_{n,b,s}) \qquad (4)$$

Tensor C represents the coefficients for (weighted) averaging during the update aggregation step. With our notation, we consider the batch index b to run over all the patches extracted from the inputs, and also over all the inputs in the mini-batch. In other words, all the patches extracted from all the images in the mini-batch are considered as a unique larger mini-batch over which aggregation is performed.

Notice that, at this point, update computation and aggregation phases are considered together. In fact, merging these two phases is an essential step towards achieving the performance improvement addressed in this work, as described below. In particular, as the dimension associated with index b is very large, since it runs over all the patches extracted from all the inputs, it would be beneficial to contract this index as soon as possible in our computations, possibly before larger tensors such as $\Delta W_{b,n,s}$ are obtained. We proceed differently depending on the Hebbian rule under consideration.

Hebbian Winner-Takes-All. The (soft-)WTA learning rule can be rewritten as follows:

$$
\begin{aligned}
\Delta W_{1,n,s} &= \eta \sum_b C_{b,n,1} R_{b,n,1} \left(X_{b,1,s} - W_{1,n,s} \right) \\
&= \eta \sum_b (C\,R)_{b,n,1} \left(X - W \right)_{b,n,s} \\
&= \eta \, \mathrm{matmul}\left((C\,R)_{n,1,b},\, (X - W)_{n,b,s} \right)
\end{aligned}
\tag{5}
$$

where $C_{b,n,1} = \frac{R_{b,n,1}}{\sum_b R_{b,n,1}}$.

Note that this formulation requires $O(B\,N\,S)$ complexity both in time and space. In particular, it needs to store a $B \times N \times S$ tensor. All the elements are stored simultaneously in order parallelize operations over each dimension through vectorized or GPU hardware. If the amount of memory required is prohibitive, it is possible to serialize computations over one or more dimensions. However, computational performance can be improved by rewriting:

$$
\begin{aligned}
\Delta W_{1,n,s} &= \eta \sum_b C_{b,n,1} R_{b,n,1} \left(X_{b,1,s} - W_{1,n,s} \right) = \\
&= \eta \sum_b (C\,R)_{b,n,1} X_{b,1,s} - \eta \sum_b (C\,R)_{b,n,1} W_{1,n,s} = \\
&= \eta \, \mathrm{matmul}\left((C\,R)_{1,n,b}, X_{1,b,s} \right) - \eta \sum_b (C\,R)_{b,n,1} W_{1,n,s} = \\
&= \eta \, \mathrm{matmul}\left((C\,R)_{1,n,b}, X_{1,b,s} \right) - \eta\, Q_{1,n,1} W_{1,n,s}
\end{aligned}
\tag{6}
$$

where $Q_{1,n,1} = \sum_b (C\,R)_{b,n,1}$.

By contracting index b early, we have obtained a new formulation that requires only $O(N(B+S))$ space. The time complexity depends on the algorithm employed for matrix multiplication, which can be made lower than $O(BNS)$.

Hebbian Principal Component Analysis. The Hebbian PCA learning rule can be rewritten as follows:

$$\Delta W_{1,n,s} = \eta \frac{1}{B} \sum_b Y_{b,n,1} \left(X_{b,1,s} - \sum_{n'=1}^{n} Y_{b,n',1} W_{1,n',s} \right)$$

$$= \eta \frac{1}{B} \sum_b Y_{b,n,1} \left(X_{b,1,s} - \sum_{n'=1}^{N} L_{n,n'} Y_{b,n',1} W_{1,n',s} \right) \qquad (7)$$

$$= \eta \frac{1}{B} \sum_b Y_{b,n,1} E_{b,n,s}$$

$$= \eta \frac{1}{B} \text{matmul}\left(Y_{n,1,b}, E_{n,b,s} \right)$$

where $E_{b,n,s} = \left(X_{b,1,s} - \sum_{n'=1}^{N} L_{n,n'} Y_{b,n',1} W_{1,n',s} \right)$, and $L_{n,n'}$ is simply a lower-triangular matrix with all ones on and below the main diagonal and all zeros above.

In this case, the computation requires $O(BN^2S)$ space and time, but this can be improved by rewriting:

$$\Delta W_{1,n,s} = \eta \frac{1}{B} \sum_b Y_{b,n,1} \left(X_{b,1,s} - \sum_{n'=1}^{N} L_{n,n'} Y_{b,n',1} W_{1,n',s} \right)$$

$$= \eta \frac{1}{B} \sum_b Y_{b,n,1} X_{b,1,s} - \eta \frac{1}{B} \sum_b Y_{b,n,1} \sum_{n'=1}^{N} L_{n,n'} Y_{b,n',1} W_{1,n',s}$$

$$= \eta \frac{1}{B} \text{matmul}\left(Y_{1,n,b}, X_{1,b,s} \right) - \eta \frac{1}{B} \sum_{n'=1}^{N} \sum_b Y_{b,n,1} Y_{b,n',1} L_{n,n'} W_{1,n',s}$$

$$= \eta \frac{1}{B} \text{matmul}\left(Y_{1,n,b}, X_{1,b,s} \right) - \eta \frac{1}{B} \sum_{n'=1}^{N} \text{matmul}\left(Y_{1,n,b}, Y_{1,b,n'} \right) L_{n,n'} W_{1,n',s}$$

$$= \eta \frac{1}{B} \text{matmul}\left(Y_{1,n,b}, X_{1,b,s} \right) - \eta \frac{1}{B} \sum_{n'=1}^{N} P_{1,n,n'} W_{1,n',s}$$

$$= \eta \frac{1}{B} \text{matmul}\left(Y_{1,n,b}, X_{1,b,s} \right) - \eta \frac{1}{B} \text{matmul}\left(P_{1,n,n'}, W_{1,n',s} \right)$$

$$\qquad (8)$$

Here, $P_{1,n,n'} = \text{matmul}\left(Y_{1,n,b}, Y_{1,b,n'} \right) L_{n,n'}$.

This computation requires $O(N^2 + NS)$ space, and at most $O(BNS + BN^2 + N^2S)$ time.

4   Experimental Setup

In order to validate our method, we performed experiments on various datasets in the computer vision domain. We evaluated both the computing time required by

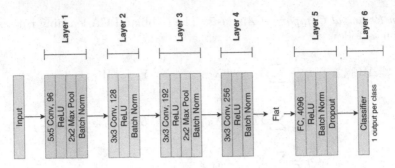

Fig. 2. The neural network used for the experiments.

Hebbian algorithms, with and without the FastHebb optimization, and their performance in sample efficiency scenarios, also making comparisons with backprop-based learning. In the following, we describe the details of our experiments and comparisons, discussing the network architecture and the training procedure.

4.1 Datasets and Sample Efficiency Regimes

The datasets that we considered for our experiments are CIFAR10 [18], CIFAR100, Tiny ImageNet [37], and ImageNet [6]. We performed our experiments in various regimes of label scarcity. We define an s% *sample-efficiency regime* as a scenario in which on s% of the training set elements is assumed to be labeled. We considered 1%, 2%, 3%, 4%, 5%, 10%, 25%, and 100% sample efficiency regimes.

For each of the above regimes, we run our experiments in a semi-supervised training fashion: first, an unsupervised pre-training stage was performed, exploiting the Hebbian learning rules, using all the available training samples; this was followed by a supervised backprop-based fine-tuning stage on the labeled samples only.

4.2 Network Architecture and Training

We considered a six layer neural network as shown in Fig. 2: five deep layers plus a final linear classifier. The various layers were interleaved with other processing stages (such as ReLU nonlinearities, max-pooling, etc.), and the overall architecture was inspired by AlexNet [19].

A similar, but bigger model was used for ImageNet classification, which is shown in Fig. 3.

For each sample efficiency regime, we trained the network with our semi-supervised approach in a classification task. First, we used Hebbian unsupervised pre-training rules in the internal layers. This was followed by the fine tuning stage with SGD training, involving the final classifier as well as the previous layers, in an end-to-end fashion.

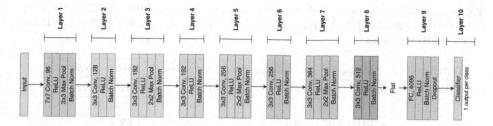

Fig. 3. The bigger neural network used for the experiments on ImageNet.

For each configuration we also created a baseline for comparison. In this case, we used another popular unsupervised method, namely the Variational Auto-Encoder (VAE) [15], for the unsupervised pre-training stage. This was again followed by the supervised end-to-end fine tuning based on SGD. VAE-based semi-supervised learning was also the approach considered in [16].

Both classification accuracy and training time were evaluated and used as metrics for comparisons.

4.3   Details of Training

We implemented our experiments using PyTorch. All the hyperparameters mentioned below resulted from a parameter search aimed at maximizing the validation accuracy on the respective datasets, following the Coordinate Descent (CD) approach [17].

Training was performed in 20 epochs using mini-batches of size 64. No more epochs were necessary, since the models had already reached convergence at that point. Networks were fed input images of size 32×32 pixels, except for the case of ImageNet, where images of size 210×210 were used.

During Hebbian training, the learning rate was set to 10^{-3} (10^{-4} for ImageNet). No L2 regularization or dropout was used, since the learning method did not present overfitting issues.

For VAE training, the network backbone without the classifier acted as encoder, with an extra layer mapping the output to 256 gaussian latent variables, while a specular network branch acted as decoder. VAE training was performed without supervision, in an end-to-end encoding-decoding task, optimizing the β-VAE Variational Lower Bound [11], with coefficient $\beta = 0.5$.

Both for VAE training and for the supervised training stage, based on SGD, the initial learning rate was set to 10^{-3} and kept constant for the first ten epochs, while it was halved every two epochs for the remaining ten epochs. We also used momentum coefficient 0.9, and Nesterov correction. During supervised training, we also used dropout rate 0.5, L2 weight decay penalty coefficient set to $5 \cdot 10^{-2}$ for CIFAR10, 10^{-2} for CIFAR100, $5 \cdot 10^{-3}$ for Tiny ImageNet, and $1 \cdot 10^{-3}$ for ImageNet. Cross-entropy loss was used as optimization metric.

To obtain the best possible generalization, *early stopping* was used in each training session, i.e. we chose as final trained model the state of the network at the epoch when the highest validation accuracy was recorded.

Table 1. Training times on each dataset, for VAE, Hebbian PCA (HPCA), Hebbian PCA with FastHebb (HPCA-FH), soft-WTA (SWTA), and soft-WTA with FastHebb (SWTA-FH) methods.

Dataset	Method	Epoch duration	Num. epochs	Total duration
CIFAR10	VAE	14 s	17	3 m 58 s
	SWTA	4 m 14 s	1	4 m 14 s
	SWTA-FH	18 s	1	**18 s**
	HPCA	6 m 23 s	12	1 h 16 m 36 s
	HPCA-FH	19 s	12	3 m 48 s
CIFAR100	VAE	15 s	15	3 m 45 s
	SWTA	4 m 16 s	1	4 m 16 s
	SWTA-FH	18 s	1	**18 s**
	HPCA	6 m 25 s	7	44 m 55 s
	HPCA-FH	19 s	7	2 m 13 s
Tiny ImageNet	VAE	33 s	20	11 m
	SWTA	9 m 41 s	1	9 m 41 s
	SWTA-FH	41 s	1	**41 s**
	HPCA	14 m 20 s	14	3 h 20 m 40 s
	HPCA-FH	43 s	14	10 m 2 s
ImageNet	VAE	2 h 59 m 19 s	16	47 h 49 m 4 s
	SWTA	105 h 13 m 24 s	3	315 h 40 m 12 s
	SWTA-FH	3 h 38 m 6 s	3	**10 h 54 m 18 s**
	HPCA	155 h 41 m 39 s	3	467 h 4 m 57 s
	HPCA-FH	3 h 39 m 18 s	3	10 h 57 m 54 s

Experiments were performed on an Ubuntu 20.4 machine, with Intel Core I7 10700K Processor, 32 GB Ram, and NVidia Geforce 3060 GPU with 12 GB dedicated memory. The experiments were implemented using the Pytorch package, version 1.8, and Python 3.7.

5   Results and Discussion

In this section, the experimental results obtained with each dataset are presented and analyzed. We report the training times on each dataset, for all the approaches explored. Moreover, we report the classification accuracy in the semi-supervised task, in the various sample efficiency regimes. Experiment results from five independent iterations were averaged, and the differences between methods were tested for statistical significance with a p value of 0.05.

5.1   Training Time Performance Evaluation

Table 1 shows the training time measured on the various datasets, for each of the considered approaches. We measured the average epoch duration, the total

Table 2. Accuracy results on each dataset (top-1 for CIFAR10, and top-5 for the other datasets, since they have many more classes), for the various approaches explored.

Regime	Method	CIFAR10	CIFAR100	Tiny ImageNet	ImageNet
1%	VAE	22.54	12.28	5.55	2.72
	SWTA	30.23	15.30	6.20	6.69
	HPCA	**39.75**	**22.63**	**11.38**	**8.65**
2%	VAE	26.78	15.25	6.74	6.14
	SWTA	36.59	20.76	8.56	11.52
	HPCA	**45.51**	**30.83**	**15.71**	**13.64**
3%	VAE	29.00	16.44	7.74	15.35
	SWTA	41.54	23.69	10.26	15.67
	HPCA	**48.80**	**35.04**	**18.23**	**17.28**
4%	VAE	31.15	17.89	8.45	**23.97**
	SWTA	45.31	26.91	11.52	19.95
	HPCA	**51.28**	**38.89**	**20.55**	20.39
5%	VAE	32.75	18.48	9.29	**29.04**
	SWTA	48.35	29.57	12.55	24.87
	HPCA	**52.20**	**41.42**	**22.46**	23.28
10%	VAE	45.67	23.80	13.51	**43.73**
	SWTA	**58.00**	38.26	16.70	41.54
	HPCA	57.35	**48.93**	**28.13**	34.27
25%	VAE	68.70	52.59	**37.89**	**61.33**
	SWTA	**69.85**	56.26	24.96	59.34
	HPCA	64.77	**58.70**	37.10	56.92
100%	VAE	85.23	**79.97**	**60.23**	76.84
	SWTA	**85.37**	79.80	54.94	76.10
	HPCA	84.38	74.42	53.96	**77.28**

number of training epochs required by each method, and the total training time. The number of epochs is counted by considering the training over when the network performance stops improving. The reported number of epochs refers to the pre-training phase only, and not to the successive fine-tuning, as we observed no statistically significant difference in the duration of the latter phase for different pre-training methods. Training time of FastHebb methods are compared to the previous respective best known solutions for Hebbian learning, that were also based on GPU [26].

We can see that, in terms of total training time, Hebbian methods are almost five times faster than VAE on ImageNet. Among the Hebbian approaches, soft-WTA is faster, thanks to its lower time complexity. Most importantly, as shown form the ImageNet performance results, thanks to the novel optimization, FastHebb algorithms scale gracefully also to large scale datasets.

5.2 Semi-supervised, Sample Efficiency Scenario

Table 2 shows the classification accuracy results obtained on the various dataset, for each of the considered approaches. Top-1 accuracy was used for CIFAR10, and top-5 for all the other datasets, since they have many more classes. Note that, in this case, we show the results for HPCA and soft-WTA, but these are the same with or without the FastHebb optimization. In fact, the optimization does not change the update rule itself.

We can observe that Hebbian approaches perform better than VAE in sample efficiency regimes with very scarce label availability, below 4–5%. In particular, we can observe performance improvements of HPCA of almost 20% in the 5% regime for the CIFAR10 dataset. On the other hand VAE-based pre-training only improves when the available number of labeled training samples for the successive supervised fine-tuning phase becomes larger. When scaling up to ImageNet dataset, we still have a slight advantage of Hebbian methods in scarce data regimes (from 2 to 6%, depending on the regime). However, when higher regimes are considered, the performance of Hebbian pre-training is slightly lower than VAE, but this is compensated, as shown before, by a significant advantage in terms of training time.

6 Conclusions and Future Work

We have shown how the FastHebb approach can be leveraged to optimize running times of Hebbian learning algorithms for DNN training. Thanks to this optimization, we were able to scale Hebbian learning experiments to ImageNet level. To the best of our knowledge, this is the first solution able to bring Hebbian learning to such scale. Experiments in semi-supervised scenarios show the efficacy of Hebbian approaches for unsupervised network pre-training, compared to backprop-based VAE pre-training, both in terms of classification accuracy and training time, especially in sample efficiency scenarios where the labeled data for supervised fine tuning are scarce (less than 4–5% of the overall available data).

As possible future work directions, we suggest to perform further studies of FastHebb on other large-scale application scenarios, such as Content Based Image Retrieval (CBIR) to evaluate the quality of deep features extracted by this method. Preliminary work in this direction is promising [22]. Moreover, further Hebbian rules can also be derived, for example from Independent Component Analysis (ICA) [12] and sparse coding [30,31,33]. Finally, in the context of semi-supervised learning, Hebbian approaches can also be combined with pseudo-labeling and consistency-based methods mentioned in Sect. 2 [13,34].

References

1. Amato, G., Carrara, F., Falchi, F., Gennaro, C., Lagani, G.: Hebbian learning meets deep convolutional neural networks. In: Ricci, E., Rota Bulò, S., Snoek, C., Lanz, O., Messelodi, S., Sebe, N. (eds.) ICIAP 2019. LNCS, vol. 11751, pp. 324–334. Springer, Cham (2019). https://doi.org/10.1007/978-3-030-30642-7_29

2. Babenko, A., Slesarev, A., Chigorin, A., Lempitsky, V.: Neural codes for image retrieval. In: Fleet, D., Pajdla, T., Schiele, B., Tuytelaars, T. (eds.) ECCV 2014. LNCS, vol. 8689, pp. 584–599. Springer, Cham (2014). https://doi.org/10.1007/978-3-319-10590-1_38

3. Bahroun, Y., Soltoggio, A.: Online representation learning with single and multi-layer Hebbian networks for image classification. In: Lintas, A., Rovetta, S., Verschure, P.F.M.J., Villa, A.E.P. (eds.) ICANN 2017. LNCS, vol. 10613, pp. 354–363. Springer, Cham (2017). https://doi.org/10.1007/978-3-319-68600-4_41

4. Becker, S., Plumbley, M.: Unsupervised neural network learning procedures for feature extraction and classification. Appl. Intell. **6**(3), 185–203 (1996)

5. Bengio, Y., Lamblin, P., Popovici, D., Larochelle, H.: Greedy layer-wise training of deep networks. In: Advances in Neural Information Processing Systems, pp. 153–160 (2007)

6. Deng, J., Dong, W., Socher, R., Li, L.J., Li, K., Fei-Fei, L.: ImageNet: a large-scale hierarchical image database. In: 2009 IEEE Conference on Computer Vision and Pattern Recognition, pp. 248–255. IEEE (2009)

7. Gerstner, W., Kistler, W.M.: Spiking Neuron Models: Single Neurons, Populations, Plasticity. Cambridge University Press, Cambridge (2002)

8. Grossberg, S.: Adaptive pattern classification and universal recoding: I. parallel development and coding of neural feature detectors. Biol. Cybern. **23**(3), 121–134 (1976)

9. Haykin, S.: Neural Networks and Learning Machines, 3rd edn. Pearson, London (2009)

10. He, K., Zhang, X., Ren, S., Sun, J.: Deep residual learning for image recognition. In: Proceedings of the IEEE Conference on Computer Vision and Pattern Recognition, pp. 770–778 (2016)

11. Higgins, I., et al.: β-VAE: learning basic visual concepts with a constrained variational framework (2016)

12. Hyvarinen, A., Karhunen, J., Oja, E.: Independent component analysis. Stud. Inform. Control **11**(2), 205–207 (2002)

13. Iscen, A., Tolias, G., Avrithis, Y., Chum, O.: Label propagation for deep semi-supervised learning. In: Proceedings of the IEEE/CVF Conference on Computer Vision and Pattern Recognition, pp. 5070–5079 (2019)

14. Karhunen, J., Joutsensalo, J.: Generalizations of principal component analysis, optimization problems, and neural networks. Neural Netw. **8**(4), 549–562 (1995)

15. Kingma, D.P., Welling, M.: Auto-encoding variational Bayes. arXiv preprint arXiv:1312.6114 (2013)

16. Kingma, D.P., Mohamed, S., Jimenez Rezende, D., Welling, M.: Semi-supervised learning with deep generative models. In: Advances in Neural Information Processing Systems 27, pp. 3581–3589 (2014)

17. Kolda, T.G., Lewis, R.M., Torczon, V.: Optimization by direct search: new perspectives on some classical and modern methods. SIAM Rev. **45**(3), 385–482 (2003)

18. Krizhevsky, A., Hinton, G.: Learning multiple layers of features from tiny images (2009)

19. Krizhevsky, A., Sutskever, I., Hinton, G.E.: ImageNet classification with deep convolutional neural networks. In: Advances in Neural Information Processing Systems 25, pp. 1097–1105 (2012)

20. Krotov, D., Hopfield, J.J.: Unsupervised learning by competing hidden units. Proc. Natl. Acad. Sci. **116**(16), 7723–7731 (2019)

21. Lagani, G.: Hebbian learning algorithms for training convolutional neural networks. Master's thesis, School of Engineering, University of Pisa, Italy (2019). https://etd.adm.unipi.it/theses/available/etd-03292019-220853/

22. Lagani, G., Bacciu, D., Gallicchio, C., Falchi, F., Gennaro, C., Amato, G.: Deep features for CBIR with scarce data using Hebbian learning. arXiv preprint arXiv:2205.08935 (2022)

23. Lagani, G., Falchi, F., Gennaro, C., Amato, G.: Evaluating Hebbian learning in a semi-supervised setting. In: Nicosia, G., et al. (eds.) LOD 2021. LNCS, vol. 13164, pp. 365–379. Springer, Cham (2021). https://doi.org/10.1007/978-3-030-95470-3_28

24. Lagani, G., Falchi, F., Gennaro, C., Amato, G.: Hebbian semi-supervised learning in a sample efficiency setting. Neural Netw. **143**, 719–731 (2021)

25. Lagani, G., Falchi, F., Gennaro, C., Amato, G.: Training convolutional neural networks with competitive Hebbian learning approaches. In: Nicosia, G., et al. (eds.) LOD 2021. LNCS, vol. 13163, pp. 25–40. Springer, Cham (2021)

26. Lagani, G., Falchi, F., Gennaro, C., Amato, G.: Comparing the performance of Hebbian against backpropagation learning using convolutional neural networks. Neural Comput. Appl. **34**(8), 6503–6519 (2022)

27. Lagani, G., et al.: Assessing pattern recognition performance of neuronal cultures through accurate simulation. In: 2021 10th International IEEE/EMBS Conference on Neural Engineering (NER), pp. 726–729. IEEE (2021)

28. Larochelle, H., Bengio, Y., Louradour, J., Lamblin, P.: Exploring strategies for training deep neural networks. J. Mach. Learn. Res. **10**(1), 1–40 (2009)

29. Nowlan, S.J.: Maximum likelihood competitive learning. In: Advances in Neural Information Processing Systems, pp. 574–582 (1990)

30. Olshausen, B.A.: Learning linear, sparse, factorial codes. Massachusetts Institute of Technology, AIM-1580 (1996)

31. Olshausen, B.A., Field, D.J.: Emergence of simple-cell receptive field properties by learning a sparse code for natural images. Nature **381**(6583), 607 (1996)

32. O'Reilly, R.C., Munakata, Y.: Computational Explorations in Cognitive Neuroscience: Understanding the Mind by Simulating the Brain. MIT Press, Cambridge (2000)

33. Rozell, C.J., Johnson, D.H., Baraniuk, R.G., Olshausen, B.A.: Sparse coding via thresholding and local competition in neural circuits. Neural Comput. **20**(10), 2526–2563 (2008)

34. Sellars, P., Aviles-Rivero, A.I., Schönlieb, C.B.: LaplaceNet: a hybrid energy-neural model for deep semi-supervised classification. arXiv preprint arXiv:2106.04527 (2021)

35. Wadhwa, A., Madhow, U.: Bottom-up deep learning using the Hebbian principle (2016)

36. Wan, J., et al.: Deep learning for content-based image retrieval: a comprehensive study. In: Proceedings of the 22nd ACM International Conference on Multimedia, pp. 157–166 (2014)

37. Wu, J., Zhang, Q., Xu, G.: Tiny imagenet challenge. Stanford University, Technical report (2017)

38. Zhang, Y., Lee, K., Lee, H.: Augmenting supervised neural networks with unsupervised objectives for large-scale image classification. In: International Conference on Machine Learning, pp. 612–621 (2016)

Causal Disentanglement with Network Information for Debiased Recommendations

Paras Sheth[1(✉)] [ID], Ruocheng Guo[2] [ID], Kaize Ding[1] [ID], Lu Cheng[1] [ID], K. Selçuk Candan[1] [ID], and Huan Liu[1] [ID]

[1] Arizona State University, Tempe, AZ 85281, USA
{psheth5,kding9,lcheng35,candan,huanliu}@asu.edu
[2] Bytedance AI Lab, London, UK

Abstract. Recommender systems suffer from biases that may misguide the system when learning user preferences. Under the causal lens, the user's exposure to items can be seen as the treatment assignment, the ratings of the items are the observed outcome, and the different biases act as confounding factors. Therefore, to infer debiased preferences and to capture the causal relationship between exposure and the observed ratings, it is essential to account for any hidden confounders. To this end, we propose a novel causal disentanglement framework that decomposes latent representations into three independent factors, responsible for (a) modeling the exposure of an item, (b) predicting ratings, and (c) controlling for hidden confounders. Experiments on real-world datasets validate the effectiveness of the proposed *Causal Disentanglement for DeBiased Recommendations* (D2Rec) model in debiasing recommendations.

Keywords: Causal disentanglement · Social recommendation · Confounders

1 Introduction

Recommender systems recommend new items by inferring user preference from historical interactions. Explicit feedback-based recommender systems, for example, first expose the user to an item and then record their feedback in terms of explicit preference signals, such as ratings. Recent studies, however, have shown that even such explicit feedback-based systems suffer from various biases [19] which misguide the systems to infer inaccurate preferences. For instance, when a recommender system suffers from popularity bias, popular items are more likely to be recommended (or ranked higher) than less popular ones. This type of bias exerts adverse effects on the user and provider's engagement [23]. Effective user and provider engagement necessitates the debiasing of recommender systems.

Causal View of Recommender Systems. In this paper, we argue that an effective approach to address biases may be to look at the recommender system

T. Skopal et al. (Eds.): SISAP 2022, LNCS 13590, pp. 265–273, 2022.
https://doi.org/10.1007/978-3-031-17849-8_21

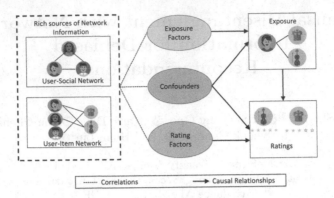

Fig. 1. A social recommender systems from a causal perspective. The figure shows disentangled factors – those for modeling exposure, those for modeling ratings, and those serving as hidden confounders

problem from a causal perspective. Notably, one can consider the exposure mechanism to represent a treatment assignment. The observed ratings can be considered analogous to outcomes [19,21] and actions that influence exposure and the rating mechanisms are similar to confounders. Consequently, we need to control for the effects of unobserved confounders to infer debiased preferences. Since users of a recommender system do not interact with items randomly, we rely on an alternative approach that uses proxies to control for confounders [19,21].

Networks as Proxies for Confounders. In this paper, we argue that user-item interaction and social networks are rich information sources that could act as a suitable proxy to account for confounders. Moreover, as suggested by social influence theory [14], users' existing social relations can influence their future behaviors, for example, by nudging connected users to converge towards similar preferences making networks suitable source for de-confounding.

Need for Disentangled Network Information. Utilizing network information in its entangled may lead the model to learn biased preferences. For instance, herd mentality indicates that a user-item interaction may arise due to an item's popularity. Although the interaction is caused due to the item popularity (a confounding factor), the model may infer this as user preference and recommend similar items to the user [1]. Thus, utilizing network information in entangled form to learn user and item latent representations [18,20] or to account for confounders [11] may result in inaccurate inferences (Fig. 1).

Causal Disentanglement for DeBiased Recommendations (D2Rec). In this paper, we propose a causal disentanglement model for social recommender systems with explicit feedback, coined *Causal Disentanglement for DeBiased Recommendations (D2Rec)*[1]. In particular, D2Rec aims to disentangle the user and item latent representations into three independent factor: confounding fac-

---

[1] Code is available at https://github.com/paras2612/D2Rec.

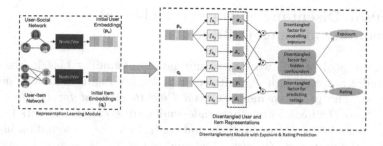

Fig. 2. An overview of the architecture of the proposed D2Rec model.

tors, exposure (treatment) factors, and ratings (outcome) factors. By seperately accounting for the confounders' contribution in the rating and exposure prediction tasks, D2Rec aims to mitigate the confounding bias. The main contributions of this paper can be summarized as

- investigating a novel setting of mitigating confounding bias in social recommender systems with explicit feedback,
- proposing a principled framework that disentangles the latent representations into various factors to mitigate confounding bias in social recommenders,
- demonstrating the effectiveness of the proposed framework on various real-world datasets with comparative analysis.

2 Related Work

Disentangling Representations for Recommendation. To better understand user preferences and identify system defects, the authors of [13] proposed to generate explainable recommendations with the help of a framework that brings transparency to the representation learning process. Another line of work focuses on disentangling latent user representations for news recommendations [9]. The authors of [16] proposed a model for disentangling user and item latent representations into conformity influence and personal interest factors to improve recommendations. Another piece of work [22] focuses on leveraging the user's social relations in learning disentangled representations.

Causal Recommender Systems. Recent work proposed in [11] utilized user's social relations to estimate the exposure along with propensity score and utilized this estimated exposure to mitigate selection bias. Some works, including [21] proposed to leverage the good aspects of popularity bias and deconfound the bad aspects for improving recommendations. Compared to earlier works, our work focuses on leveraging disentanglement to learn a representation of the hidden confounders in the latent space based on all the observed information, including the user's social connections and an item's popularity in the explicit feedback setting, which is more descriptive of a user's preference.

3   Causal Disentanglement for Debiased Recommendations (D2Rec)

The primary goal of this work is to mitigate confounding bias in the social recommender systems with explicit feedback by leveraging auxiliary network information. The proposed model *Causal Disentanglement for DeBiased Recommendations (D2Rec)*, learns three independent disentangled factors from the user and item's latent representations and control for the confounding bias. An overview of the proposed D2Rec can be found in Fig. 2. The approach consists of two key components. First, the representation learning module that learns the initial user and item embeddings from the networks. Second, we propose a novel module, namely, *causal disentanglement module with rating and exposure prediction* that disentangles the previously obtained embeddings into factors used to predict the rating and the exposure for a given user-item pair.

3.1   Representation Learning Module

As mentioned earlier, the auxiliary network information sources contain information about various factors that result in an observed user-item interaction. To capture this information, the first component of D2Rec aims to learn the initial user and item embeddings from the network information.

The representation learning module follows an architecture similar to the Node2Vec [6] architecture. Since the learned representations should capture the neighborhood information, the objective function aims to maximize the log probability of observing a network neighborhood $N_S(k)$ given the node k's latent representation. Thus, the initial embeddings are obtained as:

$$p_u = \max_\phi \sum_{u \in U} \log \Pr\left(N_S(u) \mid \phi(u)\right), \quad q_i = \max_\phi \sum_{i \in I} \log \Pr\left(N_S(i) \mid \phi(i)\right). \quad (1)$$

where $N_S(u)(N_S(i))$ represents the network neighborhood for user u (item i), $\phi(u)(\phi(i))$ represents the feature representation for the user u (item i), U (I) denotes the set of all users (items). This module enables p_u and q_i to successfully learn continuous feature representations of the nodes in the corresponding network. In our model, Node2Vec helps in capturing network features from the corresponding networks to transform each user (or item) into a vector.

3.2   Causal Disentanglement with Rating and Exposure Prediction

Causal Disentanglement. The initial embeddings obtained from Eq. 1 are highly entangled. Thus, the model can learn biased user preferences by utilizing these representations in their current state. To overcome this problem, we propose to use causality-guided disentanglement to learn independent factors with unique functions. In particular, we disentangle the user and item latent representations (p_u and q_i) into three underlying factors α, γ, Δ where α is partially responsible for modeling the exposure (treatment), Δ is partially responsible for predicting the ratings (outcomes), and γ is responsible for the confounding factors that causally affect both the exposure and the ratings. The causal disentanglement module consists of six independent feedfoward neural networks that facilitate the learning of the disentangled factors from the obtained user and item representations, p_u and q_i, respectively. They are α_u, α_i, γ_u, γ_i, Δ_u, and Δ_i, denoting the underlying factors for exposure prediction (α), confounders (γ), and rating prediction (Δ). Formally:

$$\alpha_u = \text{ReLU}(f_{\theta_1}(p_u)); \quad \alpha_i = \text{ReLU}(f_{\theta_2}(q_i)); \quad \gamma_u = \text{ReLU}(f_{\theta_3}(p_u));$$
$$\gamma_i = \text{ReLU}(f_{\theta_4}(q_i)); \quad \Delta_u = \text{ReLU}(f_{\theta_5}(p_u)); \quad \Delta_i = \text{ReLU}(f_{\theta_6}(q_i)). \tag{2}$$

where ReLU represents the nonlinear ReLU activation function, $f_{\theta_k}, k = 1, ..., 6$ denote feedforward neural networks. To enforce independence among the factors, we use an Integral Probability Metric – Maximum Mean Discrepancy (MMD) [5], which is a statistical test to determine whether two samples are from the same distribution. The discrepancy loss [7] is given by:

$$\mathcal{L}_{disc} = \sum_{\{e1,e2\} \in \mathcal{E}} \text{MMD}(e1, e2) \tag{3}$$

where $\mathcal{E} = \{(\alpha_u, \gamma_u), (\alpha_u, \Delta_u), (\gamma_u, \Delta_u), (\alpha_i, \gamma_i), (\gamma_i, \Delta_i), (\alpha_i, \Delta_i)\}$. We leverage the disentangled factors for users and items obtained from Eq. (2) for rating prediction and exposure modeling for user-item pairs. We take each disentangled user factor and perform a Hadamard product ($\odot$) to its counterpart in the item factors to generate a joint user-item representation. We obtain the combined factors, $\alpha_{u,i}$, $\gamma_{u,i}$, and $\Delta_{u,i}$ as follows:

$$\alpha_{u,i} = \alpha_u \odot \alpha_i; \quad \gamma_{u,i} = \gamma_u \odot \gamma_i; \quad \Delta_{u,i} = \Delta_u \odot \Delta_i. \tag{4}$$

We then group $\alpha_{u,i}$, $\gamma_{u,i}$, and $\Delta_{u,i}$ into the following categories: the factors $\alpha_{u,i}$ and $\gamma_{u,i}$ are collectively used for modelling the exposure, and factors $\gamma_{u,i}$ and $\Delta_{u,i}$ are collectively used for modelling the ratings.

Rating Prediction. With the aid of disentanglement, we learn factors from the user and item latent representations that only affect the ratings and are independent of the exposure mechanism and vice versa (since $\Delta_{u,i}$ and $\alpha_{u,i}$ are independent of each other) which helps the rating prediction model to generate debiased recommendations. Also, by explicitly accounting for confounders as inputs to the rating prediction function we adjust for the confounding bias. Given the disentangled representations, we compute the exposure and rating as:

$$\hat{e}_{u,i} = \sigma(\alpha_{u,i} \cdot \gamma_{u,i}), \quad \hat{y}_{u,i} = \text{ReLU}(\gamma_{u,i} \cdot \Delta_{u,i}), \tag{5}$$

where $\cdot$ is the dot product, σ is the sigmoid activation function. Given the predicted exposure and ratings from Eq. (5), the overall objective function is:

$$J(\hat{y}_{u,i}, \hat{e}_{u,i}) = \kappa \cdot \mathcal{L}_{disc} + \mathcal{L}(y_{u,i}, \hat{y}_{u,i}) + \mathcal{L}_e(e_{u,i}, \hat{e}_{u,i}), \tag{6}$$

where we aim to minimize $\mathcal{L}(y_{u,i}, \hat{y}_{u,i})$, which represents the mean squared error in predicting the rating $\mathcal{L} = \sum_{u,i} (y_{u,i} - \hat{y}_{u,i})^2$.

We also aim to minimize $\mathcal{L}_e(e_{u,i}, \hat{e}_{u,i})$, which represents the binary cross-entropy loss formulated as $\mathcal{L}_e = -\sum_{u,i}(e_{u,i} \cdot \log(\hat{e}_{u,i}) + (1 - e_{u,i}) \cdot \log(1 - \hat{e}_{u,i}))$. where $e_{u,i}$ denotes the true exposure for user u and item i, $\hat{e}_{u,i}$ represents the predicted exposure learned from Eq. (5). To ensure independence among factors we maximize the discrepancy loss and use κ to control the effect of discrepancy loss on the overall objective function.

4   Experiments

We conducted a series of experiments to understand whether disentangling the user and item latent features learned from auxiliary network information can help adjust for the confounding bias and result in social recommendations. Ideally, a causal method is evaluated on a test set where treatments are randomly assigned [17]. However, there are no real-world social recommender system datasets for a similar setting. To solve this problem, we follow the standard protocol introduced by [2, 12] to generate pseudo test sets that are debiased in terms of the item popularity. We aim to answer the following research questions:

- **RQ.1** Can disentangling the user and item embeddings with network information help debias recommendations?
- **RQ.2** What are the roles played by the network information and by the disentanglement module concerning the performance of D2Rec, respectively?

4.1   Experimental Setup

Datasets and Evaluation Protocol. For our experiments, we use two representative real-world datasets $Ciao^2$ and $Epinions^3$. Both these datasets are derived from popular social networking websites Ciao and Epinions. These websites allow users to rate multiple items, browse/write reviews, and formulate trust relations among users. Since, we aim to create pesudo debiased test sets, we split each dataset into training and test sets as follows. First, the training samples are randomly sampled from the original data (thus biased). Then, from the rest of the dataset, we create subsets as the debiased test sets by conditioning on item popularity to make each pseudo debiased test set have an equal number of ratings per items. For the evaluation protocol, we employ the widely used Mean Squared Error (MSE) and Mean Absolute Error (MAE) to measure the prediction performance of models. MAE and MSE measure the error in predicting the rating scores. Thus, a lower value of these metrics is preferred.

Baselines. We consider the following representative baselines:

- *NeuMF* [8] utilizes embedding layers and a multi-layer perceptron to learn the user and item latent features.

---

[2] https://www.cse.msu.edu/~tangjili/Ciao.rar.
[3] https://www.cse.msu.edu/~tangjili/Epinions.rar.

Table 1. Comparing the prediction performance of D2Rec with different baselines across 10 runs. Bold represent best results and underlined is the second best.

Dataset	Model	Popularity de-biased test sets							
		Popularity = 2		Popularity = 3		Popularity = 5		Popularity = 10	
		MAE	MSE	MAE	MSE	MAE	MSE	MAE	MSE
Epinions	NeuMF [8]	1.30 ± 0.02	2.74 ± 0.02	1.25 ± 0.02	2.60 ± 0.01	1.23 ± 0.02	2.52 ± 0.01	1.22 ± 0.01	2.47 ± 0.01
	PMF [15]	1.23 ± 0.02	2.91 ± 0.02	1.02 ± 0.01	2.00 ± 0.02	0.91 ± 0.01	1.61 ± 0.02	0.93 ± 0.01	1.55 ± 0.01
	SocialMF [10]	1.37 ± 0.01	3.87 ± 0.02	1.03 ± 0.02	2.30 ± 0.02	0.90 ± 0.02	1.60 ± 0.01	0.86 ± 0.01	1.46 ± 0.01
	GraphRec [4]	0.62 ± 0.02	0.87 ± 0.02	0.65 ± 0.03	0.89 ± 0.02	0.71 ± 0.01	0.96 ± 0.02	0.74 ± 0.01	1.03 ± 0.02
	ConsisRec [20]	**0.62 ± 0.02**	**0.83 ± 0.03**	0.59 ± 0.01	0.83 ± 0.01	0.54 ± 0.02	0.76 ± 0.02	0.51 ± 0.01	0.71 ± 0.01
	IPS-MF [12]	0.99 ± 0.03	1.66 ± 0.02	0.97 ± 0.02	1.57 ± 0.01	0.95 ± 0.02	1.55 ± 0.02	0.94 ± 0.01	1.53 ± 0.01
	CIRS [19]	1.06 ± 0.03	3.34 ± 0.03	0.72 ± 0.02	1.89 ± 0.02	0.48 ± 0.01	0.92 ± 0.01	0.33 ± 0.02	0.54 ± 0.01
	D2Rec (ours)	0.70 ± 0.02	1.47 ± 0.02	**0.48 ± 0.02**	**0.81 ± 0.01**	**0.31 ± 0.02**	**0.43 ± 0.01**	**0.20 ± 0.01**	**0.24 ± 0.01**
Ciao	NeuMF [8]	1.21 ± 0.02	2.40 ± 0.03	1.18 ± 0.02	2.29 ± 0.02	1.15 ± 0.01	2.13 ± 0.02	1.14 ± 0.01	2.07 ± 0.02
	PMF [15]	1.21 ± 0.02	2.77 ± 0.02	0.96 ± 0.03	1.71 ± 0.01	0.80 ± 0.02	1.13 ± 0.01	0.78 ± 0.01	1.08 ± 0.01
	SocialMF [10]	1.40 ± 0.02	4.24 ± 0.04	1.01 ± 0.01	2.23 ± 0.03	0.78 ± 0.02	1.12 ± 0.02	0.74 ± 0.02	0.96 ± 0.01
	GraphRec [4]	0.59 ± 0.03	0.71 ± 0.02	0.65 ± 0.02	0.79 ± 0.01	0.68 ± 0.03	0.82 ± 0.02	0.73 ± 0.01	0.90 ± 0.02
	ConsisRec [20]	0.57 ± 0.03	**0.61 ± 0.02**	0.52 ± 0.02	0.57 ± 0.01	0.51 ± 0.02	0.55 ± 0.01	0.41 ± 0.02	0.33 ± 0.02
	IPS-MF [12]	1.08 ± 0.04	2.00 ± 0.02	1.07 ± 0.02	1.92 ± 0.03	1.04 ± 0.01	1.78 ± 0.02	1.02 ± 0.01	1.71 ± 0.01
	CIRS [19]	0.90 ± 0.03	3.07 ± 0.03	0.51 ± 0.03	1.42 ± 0.02	0.27 ± 0.01	0.55 ± 0.01	0.15 ± 0.02	0.23 ± 0.01
	D2Rec (ours)	**0.43 ± 0.02**	0.72 ± 0.04	**0.23 ± 0.03**	**0.30 ± 0.03**	**0.11 ± 0.01**	**0.08 ± 0.01**	**0.05 ± 0.01**	**0.03 ± 0.01**

- *PMF* [15] models the user preference matrix using low-rank user and item matrices generated with Gaussian priors.
- *SocialMF* [10] uses social networks to model user preferences by adding propagation of each relation into matrix factorization.
- *Graphrec* [4] models the networks (social and interaction) with a GNN.
- *ConsisRec* [20] uses sampling-based attention techniques to solve the social inconsistency problem.
- *IPS-MF* [12] uses inverse propensity scores to alleviate the confounding bias.
- *CIRS* [19] This work uses the predicted exposure as a substitute for confoundersing factors during rating prediction.

4.2 Performance Comparison (RQ.1)

We compare the different baseline models with D2Rec on two real-world datasets *Epinions* and *Ciao* as shown in Table 1. We observe the following for **RQ.1:**

- Overall, D2Rec mostly yields the best performance across all datasets. We attribute the effectiveness of D2Rec to the following reasons: (1) By leveraging rich sources of network information D2Rec can capture multiple aspects of confounding including item popularity. (2) By disentangling the user and item representations into three factors D2Rec is effective in learning unbiased user preferences, resulting in better recommendation performance. (3) By utilizing the contribution of the disentangled confounding factors in rating prediction, D2Rec controls for the confounding bias.
- Among the three types of baselines, the causal recommender systems serve as the strongest baselines in most cases, justifying that accounting for the underlying causal model is effective in mitigating confounding bias for debiasing recommender systems with explicit feedback.

– We believe the discrepancy in error rate of GraphRec occurs due to the over-smoothing issue [3] in GNNs. Over-smoothing can make GraphRec overfit to the unpopular items as they dominate the population.

5   Conclusion and Future Work

This work aims to leverage various sources of network information to debias social recommendations with the aid of causal disentanglement. Under the causal setting, the network information acts as a suitable proxy for the hidden confounders. With the aid of causal disentanglement D2Rec captures multiple aspects of confounding present in the network information which unravels the learned representations into three independent factors. Empirical evaluations on two real-world datasets corroborate the effectiveness of D2Rec. A meaningful direction for future work is extending D2Rec to consider particular aspects of confounding, such as user conformity and item popularity factors.

Acknowledgements. This material is based upon work supported by, or in part by the National Science Foundation (NSF) grants 1909555 and 2200140.

References

1. Abdollahpouri, H., et al.: The unfairness of popularity bias in recommendation. arXiv preprint arXiv:1907.13286 (2019)
2. Bonner, S., et al.: Causal embeddings for recommendation. In: RecSys 2018 (2018)
3. Cai, C., et al.: A note on over-smoothing for graph neural networks. arXiv preprint arXiv:2006.13318 (2020)
4. Fan, W., et al.: Graph neural networks for social recommendation. In: WWW 2019 (2019)
5. Gretton, A., et al.: A kernel two-sample test. JMLR (2012)
6. Grover, A., et al.: Node2vec: scalable feature learning for networks. In: SIGKDD 2016 (2016)
7. Hassanpour, N., et al.: Learning disentangled representations for counterfactual regression. In: ICLR 2019 (2019)
8. He, X., et al.: Neural collaborative filtering. In: WWW 2017 (2017)
9. Hu, L., et al.: Graph neural news recommendation with unsupervised preference disentanglement. In: ACL 2020 (2020)
10. Jamali, M., et al.: A matrix factorization technique with trust propagation for recommendation in social networks. In: RecSys 2010 (2010)
11. Li, Q., et al.: Be causal: de-biasing social network confounding in recommendation. arXiv preprint arXiv:2105.07775 (2021)
12. Liang, D., et al.: Causal inference for recommendation. In: UAI 2016 (2016)
13. Liu, N., et al.: Explainable recommender systems via resolving learning representations. In: CIKM 2020 (2020)
14. Marsden, P.V., et al.: Network studies of social influence. Sociol. Meth. Res. **22**, 127–151 (1993)
15. Mnih, A., et al.: Probabilistic matrix factorization. In: NeurIPS 2008 (2008)

16. Qian, T., et al.: Intent disentanglement and feature self-supervision for novel recommendation. arXiv preprint arXiv:2106.14388 (2021)
17. Shadish, W.R., et al.: Can nonrandomized experiments yield accurate answers? A randomized experiment comparing random and nonrandom assignments. J. Am. Stat. Assoc. **103**, 1334–1344 (2008)
18. Wang, X., et al.: Disentangled graph collaborative filtering. In: SIGIR 2020 (2020)
19. Wang, Y., et al.: Causal inference for recommender systems. In: RecSys 2020 (2020)
20. Yang, L., et al.: ConsisRec: enhancing GNN for social recommendation via consistent neighbor aggregation. In: SIGIR 2021 (2021)
21. Zhang, Y., et al.: Causal intervention for leveraging popularity bias in recommendation. arXiv preprint arXiv:2105.06067 (2021)
22. Zheng, L., et al.: Social recommendation based on preference disentangle aggregation. In: BigDIA 2021 (2021)
23. Zhu, Z., et al.: Popularity-opportunity bias in collaborative filtering. In: WSDM 2021 (2021)

Learned Indexing in Proteins: Substituting Complex Distance Calculations with Embedding and Clustering Techniques

Jaroslav Olha$^{(\boxtimes)}$ (ID), Terézia Slanináková(ID), Martin Gendiar, Matej Antol(ID), and Vlastislav Dohnal(ID)

Faculty of Informatics and Institute of Computer Science, Masaryk University, Botanická 68a, 602 00 Brno, Czech Republic
{olha,xslanin,492606,dohnal}@mail.muni.cz, antol@muni.cz

Abstract. Despite the constant evolution of similarity searching research, it continues to face challenges stemming from the complexity of the data, such as the curse of dimensionality and computationally expensive distance functions. Various machine learning techniques have proven capable of replacing elaborate mathematical models with simple linear functions, often gaining speed and simplicity at the cost of formal guarantees of accuracy and correctness of querying.

The authors explore the potential of this research trend by presenting a lightweight solution for the complex problem of 3D protein structure search. The solution consists of three steps – (i) transformation of 3D protein structural information into very compact vectors, (ii) use of a probabilistic model to group these vectors and respond to queries by returning a given number of similar objects, and (iii) a final filtering step which applies basic vector distance functions to refine the result.

Keywords: Protein database · Embedding non-vector data · Learned metric index · Similarity search · Machine learning for indexing

1 Introduction

The methods and approaches developed by the similarity searching community are used by a wide range of scientific fields, both within computer science and beyond. While some applications require provable accuracy guarantees, verifiable

The publication of this paper and the follow-up research was supported by the ERDF "CyberSecurity, CyberCrime and Critical Information Infrastructures Center of Excellence" (No. CZ.02.1.01/0.0/0.0/16_019/0000822). V. Dohnal—Part of this work was carried out with the support of ELIXIR CZ Research Infrastructure (ID LM2018131, MEYS CR). M. Antol—Computational resources were supplied by the project "e-Infrastruktura CZ" (e-INFRA CZ LM2018140) supported by the Ministry of Education, Youth and Sports of the Czech Republic.

T. Skopal et al. (Eds.): SISAP 2022, LNCS 13590, pp. 274–282, 2022.
https://doi.org/10.1007/978-3-031-17849-8_22

algorithms, or support for complex similarity functions, many of the similarity searching problems emerging in various areas of research do not have such strict formal constraints.

There are multiple similarity search indexes, falling under the umbrella of approximate searching, capable of adjusting to such use cases by lowering their accuracy thresholds or returning partial results. However, in recent years, an entirely new approach has begun to gain traction – the area of data retrieval has started to incorporate various machine learning approaches. Notably, in 2018, Kraska et al. [8] suggested that all conventional index structures could be viewed as models of data distributions, implying that machine and deep learning models could be used in their place. Even though the idea was originally proposed and tested on structured data, this reframing of the problem has already inspired similar work in the realm of unstructured datasets [1,6,12].

To investigate the potential of these approaches further, we have chosen to examine the problem of 3D protein structure similarity search. This is an important open problem in biochemical and medical research, which can be viewed as an instance of similarity searching in non-vector datasets, because similarity between a pair of protein structures is usually calculated using a series of non-trivial, computationally expensive operations.

In this paper, we demonstrate that even a relatively complex interdisciplinary problem such as 3D protein structure retrieval can be tackled with fast and lightweight solutions. We present a simple pipeline where protein structures are first transformed into short vectors and used to train multiple partitioning and classification models – these are linked together to form a learned index structure. The index then answers queries by returning several candidate leaf nodes, and filtering the objects stored therein using basic vector (similarity) functions.

2   Related Work

Learned indexing was first introduced in [8] with the core idea of learning a cumulative distribution function (CDF) to map a key to a record position. This proposition challenged the long-standing paradigm of building indexes solely with classic data structures such as B-trees and allowed for reduction in searching costs. To allow for indexing of large data collections, the authors introduced *Recursive model index (RMI)* – a hierarchical tree index structure of simple interconnected machine learning models, each learning the mapping on a subset of the dataset. RMI is, however, limited to sorted datasets of structured data, and cannot accommodate multi-dimensional data.

The generalization of the learned indexing concept to spatial and low-dimensional data was explored primarily by the *Z-order model* [13], which makes use of the space-filling curve encoding to produce 1D representation of the original data, and *ML-index* [5] which achieves the same with the use of *iDistance*.

Following the architectural design of RMI, we proposed the *Learned metric index (LMI)* [1], which can use a series of arbitrary machine learning models to solve the classification problem by learning a pre-defined partitioning scheme.

This was later extended to a fully unsupervised (data-driven) version introduced in [11], which is utilized in this work.

Protein Representation

To enable computational approaches to the problem of uncovering functional properties of proteins, a great amount of research attention has been directed to creating representative (numerical) embeddings of protein structures. There are two distinct categories of embeddings based on the input data – those that operate with *sequences* and those working with *3D structures*. Sequence embeddings use techniques such as hidden Markov models or various natural language processing methods [2] to derive meaning from protein sequences, treating them as encoded sequences of characters, which is not applicable to our research.

Embeddings representing protein 3D structures are generally less elaborate, since the information content is more robust to begin with. The most common encoding is a protein distance map, which produces a symmetric 2D matrix of pairwise distances between either atoms, groups of atoms or amino acid residues. This distance map can be transformed into a protein contact map, which is a binary image where each pixel indicates whether two residues are within a certain distance from one another or not. Contact maps have been used in conjunction with machine learning techniques for prediction of protein structure [4]. While these techniques are related to our own approach, we produce embeddings that are considerably more compact and reflective of our similarity searching use case, as will be shown in the following sections.

3   Data Domain

We have chosen to test our approach on 3D protein structures for several reasons. First, while protein structure data is very widely used, and the study of this data is vital for almost every area of biochemical research, the issue of efficient search and comparison of protein structures is still unresolved to some extent, with many databases still relying on time-consuming brute-force linear search [10].

Just as importantly, it is clear that the issue of efficient search within this data will only become more crucial and challenging in the next few years – the common dataset of empirically solved protein structures continues to grow exponentially [3], and the computational prediction of protein structures from their sequences has recently seen rapid improvement with the release of AlphaFold 2 in 2021 [7], which has resulted in the publication of hundreds of millions of new reliable 3D protein structures a year later.

Protein structures are sometimes cited as a typical example of complex unstructured data, since they cannot be meaningfully ordered according to any objective criteria (any search method needs to rely on pairwise similarity), and the similarity of two protein structures often cannot be determined by a single vector operation. Typically, protein molecule data are stored using the three-dimensional coordinates of each of their atoms, with the protein randomly oriented in space. In order to compare a pair of protein structures, they first need to

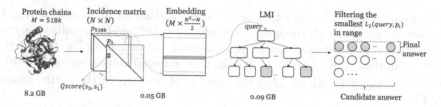

Fig. 1. A diagram of the proposed solution.

Table 1. File size of the protein dataset (518,576 protein chains, database size 8.2 GB) stored using protein embeddings, and build times of two different LMI architectures.

Embedding size ($N \times N$)	File size	Index build time (256-64)	Index build time (128–128)
5×5	16 MB	246 s	184 s
10×10	51 MB	350 s	270 s
30×30	456 MB	927 s	655 s
50×50	1275 MB	2391 s	1814 s

be properly spatially aligned in terms of translation and rotation, and a subset of atoms must be selected for alignment. This typically involves gradual optimization of a spatial distance metric (such as the root-mean-square deviation of all the atom coordinates), which is a computationally expensive process that cannot be directly mapped to a simple vector operation.

Once aligned, the similarity of the proteins can be measured. One commonly used measure of protein similarity is the Q_{score} [9], which is calculated by dividing the number of aligned amino acids in both protein chains by the spatial deviation of this alignment and the total number of amino acids in both chains. Even though this measure is imperfect and not appropriate for all use cases, it is used in several prominent applications, including the PDB's own search engine.

Note that two identical structures have a Q_{score} of 1, and completely different structures have a Q-score of 0: as a result, the score needs to be inverted in order to be used as a distance metric $(d(x, y) = 1 - Q_{score}(x, y))$. In the following sections, we will refer to this inverted value as $Q_{distance}$.

4   Fast Searching in Proteins

We present a pipeline (visualized in Fig. 1) consisting of three separate components: (i) a simple embedding technique for protein data in the PDB format, (ii) the use of a machine-learning-based index – Learned Metric Index (LMI) – to locate a candidate set of similar protein structures, and (iii) fast filtering to produce the final query answer[1].

The embedding we propose divides the protein sequence into N consecutive sections – the positions of the atoms within each section are averaged, and the section is subsequently treated as a single point in space. We then calculate

---

[1] Publicly available prototype at https://disa.fi.muni.cz/demos/lmi-app-protein/.

distances between each pair of these sections, creating an incidence matrix. In this matrix, we prune all the values exceeding a cutoff, and normalize the rest. The matrix is symmetrical and all the diagonal values are 0. The half of this matrix (omitting the main diagonal) is then reduced into a single row in a $M \times (\frac{N^2-N}{2})$ matrix, where M is the number of proteins in the entire dataset (see Fig. 1).

This produces a very compact embedding for all the proteins, and the entire dataset can be represented by a file that is up to two orders of magnitude smaller than the original database – see Table 1.

To reduce the search space to a small number of candidate protein structures, we used the Learned Metric Index (LMI), a tree index structure where each internal node is a learned model trained on a sub-section of data assigned to it by its parent node [1]. Specifically, we used the data-driven version of LMI, where the partitioning is determined in an unsupervised manner. We explored different architectural setups – both in terms of the number of nodes at each level (index breadth), as well as the number of levels (index depth). As the learned models, we explored K-Means, Gaussian Mixture Models, and K-Means in combination with Logistic regression (see [11] for details regarding the model setups). For the sake of compactness, in the experimental evaluation we only present the results achieved with the best-performing setup – a two-level LMI structure with arity of 256 on level 1 and 64 on level 2 (i.e., 256 root descendants, each of them with 64 child nodes), with K-Means chosen as the partitioning algorithm. After LMI is built, we search within it using a query protein structure and return target candidate sets; the size of the candidate sets is determined by a pre-selected stop condition (for instance, a stop condition of 1% of the dataset corresponds to $\sim5,000$ candidate answers per query).

In the final step, we filter the candidate set according to a particular distance function. In our experiments, we have examined filtering based on the Euclidean distance as well as the cosine distance of the vector embeddings, but the filtering step could theoretically be performed using any distance metric, or even the original Q_{score} similarity of the full protein structures. The filtering step returns a subset of the candidate set based on the specified criteria (i.e., kNN or range).

5   Experimental Evaluation

We evaluated our approach using range queries, with 512 randomly chosen protein chains from the dataset used as query objects. In order to compare our results against the ground truth, we needed to know the $Q_{distances}$ (based on Q_{score}) between the 512 protein chains and all the other chains in the database – these distances were kindly provided by the researchers behind [10], where the same 512 objects were used as the pivots for their search engine. The objects were chosen uniformly randomly with respect to protein chain length, which ensures that even very long proteins are represented among our queries (despite constituting a relatively small portion of the dataset).

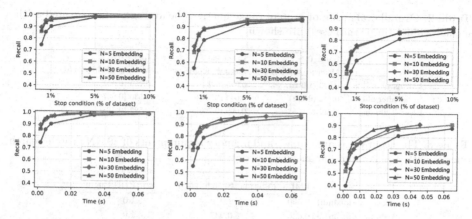

Fig. 2. Evaluation of range queries after LMI search and before filtering, using K-Means and a 256-64 LMI architecture with ranges: 0.1 (left), 0.3 (middle), 0.5 (right).

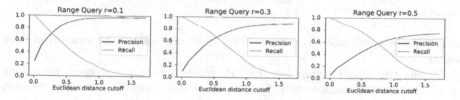

Fig. 3. Effects of filtering on the recall and precision of the candidate set of objects (relative to the ground truth answer).

We expected the performance of our method to deteriorate as the range of the queries expands, since a wider search range would require the method to correctly identify more objects which are less similar. To examine this effect, we have chosen three representative query ranges of 0.1, 0.3 and 0.5 – in a real use case, the range would be chosen by a domain expert based on the particular use case. As a rule of thumb, a range of 0.1 represents a high degree of similarity, while a range of 0.5 represents low (but still biologically significant) similarity; the biological relevance of answers drops sharply beyond this range [10].

First, we evaluated the performance of the LMI, before the filtering step. The recall shown in Fig. 2 pertains to the entire candidate set of objects (i.e. how much of the ground truth answer is contained in the 1%/5%/10% of the dataset returned by the LMI for further filtering).

This figure presents us with two important pieces of information – firstly, it is clear that LMI can reach very high recall even when trained on the smaller 10×10 embedding – this makes the embedding a natural choice for further evaluation, since it is efficient while significantly reducing the memory and CPU costs of training compared with the larger embeddings. It can also be seen that, especially in the lower query ranges which are of most interest to us, the 1% stop condition represents a sensible trade-off between recall and search time, returning

Table 2. Overall evaluation of protein range queries: the average values, as well as the median values (in parentheses) are shown.

	Range 0.1 Mean # of objects: 83	Range 0.3 Mean # of objects: 236	Range 0.5 Mean # of objects: 519
LMI recall	0.973 (1.000)	0.895 (0.999)	0.755 (0.867)
Recall after filtering	0.742 (0.878)	0.649 (0.711)	0.530 (0.637)
F1 after filtering	0.712 (0.855)	0.669 (0.766)	0.592 (0.673)

Table 3. The accuracy, search times, and memory requirements of 30 NN protein search queries with a maximum distance radius of 0.5.

	LMI + Filtering	Sketch-based method	PDB Engine
Accuracy (median)	0.660	1.0	1.0
Accuracy (mean)	0.626	0.937	1.0
Time (median)	0.094 s	2.5 s	183 s
Time (max)	0.145 s	6109 s	14321 s
Index size	87 MB	178 MB	N/A

relatively few candidate objects ($\sim$5,000) while minimizing the amount of false negatives.

During the filtering step (see Fig. 3), recall naturally decreases over time (since the method occasionally filters out relevant answers), while precision improves as the portion of relevant objects in the candidate set increases.

Table 2 shows the final results of the range queries with the best-performing configuration of parameters: embedding size $N = 10$, the K-means clustering model, 256-64 LMI architecture, and filtering after the 1% stop condition using the Euclidean distance metric. The results, especially in the lower query ranges, are very encouraging, although the filtering stage seems to introduce a surprisingly large amount of false negatives by filtering out parts of the correct answer. It is likely that the filtering metric we have chosen was slightly too naïve, and the filtering step could have benefited from a different distance function, or at least a different weighting of the vectors before calculating their Euclidean distance. In the future, this presents a natural point of focus to further improve our results.

Finally, to provide broader context for the pipeline's performance, we have evaluated it against a more conventional, recently-published approach which uses a three-stage search engine comparing bit-strings in the Hamming space ("sketches") to approximate the distance of protein chains [10]. Note that since the sketch-based paper mainly used 30-NN queries limited by the range 0.5, our method needed to be modified in order to perform the same type of query, which resulted in slightly suboptimal results. We have also included the performance of the linear search of the PDB database, as presented in the sketch-based paper. All of these results can be found in Table 3 – while our method clearly does not match the high accuracy of the sketch-based method in this experimental setup, it is faster by at least an order of magnitude, occasionally exceeding 4 orders of magnitude since it does not suffer from an extreme "tail" of worst-case search times caused by evaluation of long proteins.

6   Summary and Conclusions

In an effort to investigate the potential of new data retrieval techniques in the field of similarity searching, we have developed and evaluated a novel approach to the problem of protein structure search, resulting in a short pipeline consisting of a concise vector embedding, learned indexing, and distance-based answer filtering. By successfully applying this approach on a well-established database of 3D protein structures, we have shown that even in a domain that may, at first, seem poorly suited to simple vector-based transformations, a surprising amount of information can be discerned by learned models.

One advantage of our modular approach is that every part of the pipeline can be evaluated separately, allowing experts to identify the weakest spots and alter them based on the current use case and dataset. The experiments presented in this paper serve as a good example – after evaluating each part of our own pipeline, it is clear that we have chosen an overly simplistic filtering method for our data. In the future, we plan to investigate more sophisticated options for vector-based filtering, as well as a completely different approach to reducing the size of query answers.

While it is difficult to compare our work with the state of the art (since there are no direct analogues to our method in the chosen data domain), we have made an effort to modify our method for the fairest possible comparison with a recent, more conventional similarity searching approach in the same domain. In this comparison, our solution, although coming up short in terms of accuracy, is consistently faster by multiple orders of magnitude, and maintains much lower memory requirements.

References

1. Antol, M., Ol'ha, J., Slanináková, T., Dohnal, V.: Learned metric index - proposition of learned indexing for unstructured data. Inf. Syst. **100**, 101774 (2021)
2. Asgari, E., Mofrad, M.R.: Continuous distributed representation of biological sequences for deep proteomics and genomics. PLoS ONE **10**(11), e0141287 (2015)
3. Burley, S.K., et al.: RCSB Protein Data Bank: powerful new tools for exploring 3D structures of biological macromolecules for basic and applied research and education in fundamental biology, biomedicine, biotechnology, bioengineering and energy sciences. Nucleic Acids Res. **49**(D1), D437–D451 (2021)
4. Cheng, J., Baldi, P.: Improved residue contact prediction using support vector machines and a large feature set. BMC Bioinform. **8**(1), 1–9 (2007)
5. Davitkova, A., Milchevski, E., Michel, S.: The ML-index: a multidimensional, learned index for point, range, and nearest-neighbor queries. In: EDBT, pp. 407–410 (2020)
6. Hünemörder, M., Kröger, P., Renz, M.: Towards a learned index structure for approximate nearest neighbor search query processing. In: Reyes, N., et al. (eds.) SISAP 2021. LNCS, vol. 13058, pp. 95–103. Springer, Cham (2021). https://doi.org/10.1007/978-3-030-89657-7_8
7. Jumper, J., et al.: Highly accurate protein structure prediction with AlphaFold. Nature **596**(7873), 583–589 (2021)

8. Kraska, T., Beutel, A., Chi, E.H., Dean, J., Polyzotis, N.: The case for learned index structures. In: Proceedings of the 2018 International Conference on Management of Data, SIGMOD 2018, pp. 489–504. Association for Computing Machinery (2018)

9. Krissinel, E., Henrick, K.: Secondary-structure matching (SSM), a new tool for fast protein structure alignment in three dimensions. Acta Crystallogr. D Biol. Crystallogr. 60(12), 2256–2268 (2004)

10. Mic, V., Raček, T., Křenek, A., Zezula, P.: Similarity search for an extreme application: experience and implementation. In: Reyes, N., et al. (eds.) SISAP 2021. LNCS, vol. 13058, pp. 265–279. Springer, Cham (2021). https://doi.org/10.1007/978-3-030-89657-7_20

11. Slanináková, T., Antol, M., Olha, J., Kaňa, V., Dohnal, V.: Data-driven learned metric index: an unsupervised approach. In: Reyes, N., et al. (eds.) SISAP 2021. LNCS, vol. 13058, pp. 81–94. Springer, Cham (2021). https://doi.org/10.1007/978-3-030-89657-7_7

12. Tian, Y., Yan, T., Zhao, X., Huang, K., Zhou, X.: A learned index for exact similarity search in metric spaces. arXiv preprint arXiv:2204.10028 (2022)

13. Wang, H., Fu, X., Xu, J., Lu, H.: Learned index for spatial queries. In: 2019 20th IEEE International Conference on Mobile Data Management (MDM), pp. 569–574. IEEE (2019)

Self-supervised Information Retrieval Trained from Self-generated Sets of Queries and Relevant Documents

Gianluca Moro[1] ![ORCID], Lorenzo Valgimigli[1(✉)] ![ORCID], Alex Rossi[1], Cristiano Casadei[2], and Andrea Montefiori[2]

[1] Department of Computer Science and Engineering (DISI), University of Bologna, Cesena (FC), Via dell'Università 50, Bologna, Italy
{gianluca.moro,lorenzo.valgimigli}@unibo.it,
alex.rossi6@studio.unibo.it
[2] Maggioli S.P.A. Santarcangelo di Romagna (RN), Via del Carpino 8, Santarcangelo di Romagna, Italy
{cristiano.casadei,andrea.montefiori}@maggioli.it

Abstract. Large corpora of textual data such as scientific papers, patents, legal documents, reviews, etc., represent precious unstructured knowledge that needs semantic information retrieval engines to be extracted. Current best information retrieval solutions use supervised deep learning approaches, requiring large labelled training sets of queries and corresponding relevant documents, often unavailable, or their preparation is economically infeasible for most organizations. In this work, we present a new self-supervised method to train a neural solution to model and efficiently search large corpora of documents against arbitrary queries without requiring labelled dataset of queries and associated relevant papers. The core points of our self-supervised approach are (i) a method to self-generate the training set of queries and their relevant documents from the corpus itself, without any kind of human supervision, (ii) a deep metric learning approach to model their semantic space of relationships, and (iii) the incorporation of a multi-dimensional index for this neural semantic space over which running queries efficiently. To better stress the performance of the approach, we applied it to a totally unsupervised corpus with complex contents of over half a million Italian legal documents.

Keywords: Semantic search · Self-supervised learning · Large italian dataset

1 Introduction

One of today's most crucial challenges is exploiting the implicitly conserved knowledge within massive textual collections [14]. Textual information retrieval (IR) systems, which aim to retrieve semantically related documents against a human query leveraging semantic representation [7, 28, 33], are the core of many everyday applications such as search engines, recommendation systems, and chatbots.

Language models based on deep neural networks got unprecedented success [13, 15, 26] thanks to their ability to create high-quality semantic representations of the

© The Author(s), under exclusive license to Springer Nature Switzerland AG 2022
T. Skopal et al. (Eds.): SISAP 2022, LNCS 13590, pp. 283–290, 2022.
https://doi.org/10.1007/978-3-031-17849-8_23

text, named embedding [39], with no prior feature engineering. However, their quality depends on a priori labelled datasets for the train, namely a set of hand-crafted queries and related documents for each, often missing or unfeasible to craft for many domains. To this end, self-supervised learning methods leverage intrinsic relationships of the dataset to automatically create artificial labels for the train, allowing deep neural networks that need supervision to be deployed on not-supervised domains.

We propose a novel self-supervised method to produce a self-generated artificial labelled dataset for IR, upon which to train a self-supervised neural model. It automatically generates for each textual passage three types of queries to use for the train: (1) non-fluent queries created with tf-idf, (2) fluent queries created using a summarizer, and (3) entity-based queries created using a Named-Entity Recognition (NER) model. We apply our solution to a large collection (half a million) of Italian legal documents[1] with two main issues: (i) the high domain complexity due to the Italian Jurisprudence that counts more than 350000 laws, protocols, policies, and (ii) the lack of labels or direct relationships to exploit. We incorporate in the solution an optimized multi-dimensional index, named Faiss [18], to efficiently retrieve items from the latent space. Extensive results show the ability of our self-supervised IR to model Italian legal documents and retrieve the right ones according to an arbitrary input query, beating the state-of-the-art pretrained model for multilingual semantic search on an unseen test set[2].

2   Related Works

First IR solutions, such as TFiDF [29] or BM25Okapi [31], study words frequencies to score textual similarity [11]. With the arrival of transformers, novel powerful language models [5,30,35,38] showed their ability to represent the semantic of a text with no prior feature engineering [2,27] becoming the neural engine of many state-of-the-art IR systems [1,3] and replacing the RNN [12]. Novel training losses, named *deep metric losses* [19], were proposed to leverage relationships between a given item (*anchor* or a), a semantic similar one (*positive* or p) and a different one (*negative* or n). Contrastive Loss [20] trains a model to minimize the distance between a positive pair (a, p) and maximize it between a negative one (a, n). Triplet Loss [10] improves the contrastive loss, turning the two pairs into a triplet (a, p, n) and forcing the model to place a and p closer than a and n. Many more complex and sophisticated functions have been proposed, leveraging different numbers of positives and negatives, and different grades of positiveness (e.g. soft positive [36]) or negativeness (e.g. hard negative [37])

One drawback is the need of labelled data to define relationships among documents. Several self-supervised training techniques try to address such issue, generating labels automatically from intrinsic relationships of the data [8,9,21,22,34].

In our particular case we do not have any relationships to exploit (e., g., bibliography, citations, references), thus we create artificial queries, using different techniques, as positive items from each sequence of text (*anchor*), to be represented as similar as possible to their source sequences. Thanks to them, we train a deep metric neural IR in a self-supervised learning otherwise impossible to train.

---

[1] Kindly provided by Gruppo Maggioli s.p.a https://www.maggioli.com/en-us.
[2] Web App and appendix at https://disi-unibo-nlp.github.io/projects/SelfIRSisap2022/.

3 Methods

3.1 Self-supervised Query Generation

The text corpus is supplied by Gruppo Maggioli[3] and consists of a dump of 543838 Italian legal documents. Documents have a great variability in length depending on the type ("Doctrine", "Jurisprudence", "Legislation", "Praxis", "Maximaries") and the category ("Balance", "Police", "Contract", ...) they belong to, with an average number of words per document of 897.

First, we clean the dataset discarding all documents without text, reducing the number of documents to 488000. Then we split them into sequences of the same length (64 words) obtaining a total of 6800000 pieces. For each sequence of unstructured text, we create three types of queries: non-fluent, fluent, and entity-based.

For the *Non-fluent queries*, we generate them as unordered sequences of n keywords, leveraging $tf - idf$ which scores each word according to its importance in the given sentence.

$$S(w_d) = log(1 + tf(w_d)) \times log\left(\frac{N}{df(w)}\right) \tag{1}$$

where $tf(w_d)$ is the frequency of the term w in the document d and $df(w)$ is the frequency of the term w in all the N documents in the corpus. We select the n words with the highest score, where n is a random number extracted from a Gaussian distribution $n \sim \mathcal{N}(\mu = 5, \sigma^2)$.

Fluent queries are produced as syntax-correct queries from each passage leveraging the summarization algorithm KL-Sum [16] which greedily adds extracted sentences to the summary, trying to minimize the KL-divergence[4]. Neural solutions as [25] fail due to the need of fine-tuning.

Entities-based queries are single entities among a legislative reference, a location, a name of a person or organization, extracted by using a multilingual NER based on XLM-RoBERTa [4] that we fine-tuned on *I-CAB* dataset [24].

> **Passage:** ...complessivo e, quindi, del corrispettivo dell'*appalto*. Secondo il **T.A.R.** una tale *ipotesi* sarebbe perseguibile soltanto in corso di svolgimento del *servizio*....
> **Non-fluent query:** appalto servizio ipotesi
> **Fluent query:** Secondo il T.A.R. una tale ipotesi sarebbe perseguibile
> **Extracted name entity:** T.A.R.

3.2 Language Model

We use DistilBERT [32], trained for multilingual tasks, where we add a pooling layer generating one single embedding for each passage s_i as the mean of all the token embeddings. We add a dense feed-forward network to map the input tensor to a 512-dimensional space with tanh activation function. The whole system can be formalized with the following equation:

$$e_i = \mathcal{D}(\theta_d, \mathcal{P}(E(\theta_e, s_i))) \tag{2}$$

---

[3] https://www.maggioli.com/it-it.

[4] The implementation is from sumy. https://github.com/miso-belica/sumy.

where $\mathcal{D}, \mathcal{P}, E$ are respectively the dense layer, the pooling layer and the Bert model layer. The θ_d, θ_e represent the trainable parameters of the dense and Bert model layers.

We train the model by leveraging a deep metric loss, namely the multiple negatives ranking loss function [17], ideal for training neural models for retrieval settings with positive pairings (i., e., (query, passage)).

$$MNL = -1/K \sum_{i=1}^{K} \left[S(x_i, y_i) - log \sum_{j=1}^{K} e^{S(x_i, y_j)} \right] \tag{3}$$

where S is a similarity function between sentence embeddings, we use cosine similarity. x and y are elements from the batch where x_i and y_j are similar only for $i = j$.

Furthermore, to improve the training phase, we apply two different techniques: *Hard Negatives* and *Masking*. *Hard Negatives* are negative items, but with a grade of similarity higher than normal negatives. We generate them by extracting from each sequence the top 10 keywords using *TFiDF*. Sequences sharing more than three keywords are considered hard negatives.

Then, we implement a query masking which consists of substituting some words from the passage, also present in the query, with random words. It forces the model to rely less on word matching and more on the semantics of the phrase, already used in different domains [6]. We found that masking the 10% of words gives the best results.

4   Experiments

4.1   Resources and Training Details

We used a workstation equipped with a GPU GeForce RTX 3090 with 24 GB of dedicated memory, and 24 GB of RAM. We used Python3, PyTorch framework Hugging-Face for Deep Learning tasks and Faiss for optimized similarity search.

The model is based on the Sentence Transformer library[5], in particular, we used *distiluse-base-multilingual-cased-v1*. We trained the model for 2 epochs over 8.1 millions triplets composed by 4 million fluent queries, 4 million non-fluent queries, and 100000 of queries composed by specific entities. We used a minibatch size of 64 and a AdamW optimizer [23] with a weight decay of 0.01 and a learning rate of $2e - 05$[6].

4.2   Results

To evaluate the model's performance improvement obtained by our method, we used one large test set (400K passages and 1000 queries) for each type of query, reporting top-1, top-5, and top-10 rank accuracies, from a set of never seen documents (removed from the training pool). The ranking accuracy $rank@n$, normalized and expressed as a percentage, returns the frequency of presence of the associated passage to the input query in the top n retrieved documents.

---

[5] https://github.com/UKPLab/sentence-transformers.
[6] The remaining hyperparameters of the underlying pretrained sentence-transformer are kept at their default settings.

We turned each passage into an embedding leveraging the model to test, and we exploited Faiss to speed up and optimize the similarity research among them against an input query embedding[7]. We compare our self-supervised solution against the same model with no fine-tuning, a state-of-the-art and ready-to-use model for the multilingual semantic search, which represents the only option for neural semantic search in the lack of a labelled dataset. We show the results on the Tables 1, 2, and 3.

Table 1. Fluent queries.

	Baseline	Trained
R@1	28%	**91.6%**
R@5	37%	**96.4%**
R@10	40.5%	**96.7%**

Table 2. Non-fluent queries.

	Baseline	Trained
R@1	33%	**87%**
R@5	35.5%	**94.2%**
R@10	36%	**95.8%**

Table 3. Entity-based queries.

	Baseline	Trained
R@1	0.7%	**49%**
R@5	4%	**72%**
R@10	8%	**78%**

Our solution significantly improves the baseline performances. The three kinds of queries, automatically generated for the train and the test, mimic the queries a user can submit to the system seeking a specific term, documents about some keywords, or expressing a fluent human question.

4.3   Ablations

Table 4. The table reports the results obtained using different pretrained models.

Model	Rank@1	Rank@5	Rank@10
paraphrase-xlm-r-multilingual-v1	52%	57%	57%
xlmr-personal-multilingual	37%	40%	41%
stsb-xlm-r-multilingual	29%	30%	31%
distiluse-base-multilingual-cased-v1	**64%**	**73%**	**75%**
paraphrase-multilingual-MiniLM-L12-v2	35%	38%	39%
paraphrase-multilingual-mpnet-base-v2	40%	45%	45%

We tested different pretrained models from Huggingface[8], training them for 1000 instances using non-fluent queries, and we tested them on a test set of 10K passages. As reported in Table 4, the `distiluse-base-multilingual-cased` is the one with higher performances.

We also investigated different metric losses (Tables 6 and 5), namely *Cosine Similarity Loss*, *Contrastive Loss*, *Triplet Loss* and *Multi Negative Ranking Loss*. The latter gives the best results with fluent and non-fluent queries.

Furthermore, we studied the number of tokens per items: 64 and 128 (Table 8) and the masking percentage (Table 9). The results show that a minor number of tokens increases the performance, and masking the 10% leads to the best results[9].

---

[7] We used *IndexFlatL2*, which allows exact search by L2 norm distance without errors.

[8] https://huggingface.co/.

[9] Both tests are conducted on fluent-queries test set of 400000 items.

Finally, we tested two different approaches to create hard negatives: *Legislative references in common* and *Keywords in common* (Sect. 3.1). In Table 7 we report the results by training the model with fluent queries and evaluated on 400000 sequences. Results empirically prove that hard negatives from keywords help in the model training.

Table 5. Non-fluent queries.

Loss	R1	R5	R10
Baseline	22%	28%	28%
Triplet	30%	34%	35%
Constr	43%	48%	49%
CosSim	52%	64%	65%
MNR	**73%**	**83%**	**84%**

Table 6. Fluent queries.

Loss	R1	R5	R10
Baseline	26%	33%	36%
Triplet	31%	34%	37%
Constr	42%	46%	49%
CosSim	28%	35%	38%
MNR	**44%**	**56%**	**60%**

Table 7. Results with different kinds of hard negatives.

Hard Neg	R1	R5	R10
Random	**65%**	72%	75%
Leg. ref	**65%**	72%	75%
Keywords	**65%**	**74%**	**76%**

Table 8. Different passage lengths.

Loss	R@1	R@2	R@5
64 tokens	**65%**	**72%**	**75%**
128 tokens	44%	56%	60%

Table 9. Different masking percentages.

Masking	R@1	R@5	R@10
0%	65%	74%	76%
10%	**66%**	**75.5%**	**78%**
20%	66%	74.5%	77.5%

5   Conclusion

We presented a novel domain-agnostic self-supervised method to train a neural semantic IR on unsupervised text sets, which automatically generates three kinds of queries for each textual passage: (i) fluent query using a summarizer method, (ii) non-fluent query, selecting with TFiDF the most important keywords, and (iii) entity-based query, using a NER algorithm to extract specific entities. These artificial queries were then employed for training a neural model using existing deep metric learning losses. This solution mitigates the lack of labelled datasets in most domains, which are almost impossible to forge because of the time required and the human economic costs. Indeed, we applied it to a real unlabelled dataset provided by a private Italian company, which is a collection of more than 500000 Italian legal documents with no explicit categories and relationships as required by neural models.

Despite such substantial limitations, thanks to our novel technique, we were capable of training a neural information retriever that significantly improves multilingual distillBERT performances, which is the state-of-the-art solution for semantic search on the multilingual domain. Finally, we performed extensive experiments and ablations studies to assess our architectural choices.

We believe this methodology could be general and exploited for other languages and domains, particularly useful in scenarios with extremely limited or unlabelled text sets. For this purpose, we will perform new studies on new text sets in other languages with scarce or missing labelled text sets.

References

1. Abbasiantaeb, Z., Momtazi, S.: Text-based question answering from information retrieval and deep neural network perspectives: a survey. WIREs Data Min. Knowl. Discov. **11**(6), e1412 (2021)
2. Abend, O., Rappoport, A.: The state of the art in semantic representation. In: ACL (1), pp. 77–89. Association for Computational Linguistics (2017)
3. Cohan, A., Feldman, S., Beltagy, I., Downey, D., Weld, D.S.: SPECTER: document-level representation learning using citation-informed transformers. In: ACL, pp. 2270–2282. Association for Computational Linguistics (2020)
4. Conneau, A., et al.: Unsupervised cross-lingual representation learning at scale. In: ACL, pp. 8440–8451. Association for Computational Linguistics (2020)
5. Devlin, J., Chang, M., Lee, K., Toutanova, K.: BERT: pre-training of deep bidirectional trans-formers for language understanding. In: NAACL-HLT (1), pp. 4171–4186. Association for Computational Linguistics (2019)
6. Domeniconi, G., Masseroli, M., Moro, G., Pinoli, P.: Cross-organism learning method to discover new gene functionalities. Comput. Methods Programs Biomed. **126**, 20–34 (2016)
7. Domeniconi, G., Moro, G., Pagliarani, A., Pasini, K., Pasolini, R.: Job recommendation from semantic similarity of linkedin users' skills. In: ICPRAM, pp. 270–277. SciTePress (2016)
8. Domeniconi, G., Moro, G., Pasolini, R., Sartori, C.: Iterative refining of category profiles for nearest centroid cross-domain text classification. In: Fred, A., Dietz, J.L.G., Aveiro, D., Liu, K., Filipe, J. (eds.) IC3K 2014. CCIS, vol. 553, pp. 50–67. Springer, Cham (2015). https://doi.org/10.1007/978-3-319-25840-9_4
9. Domeniconi, G., Semertzidis, K., López, V., Daly, E.M., Kotoulas, S., Moro, G.: A novel method for unsupervised and supervised conversational message thread detection. In: DATA, pp. 43–54. SciTePress (2016)
10. Dong, X., Shen, J.: Triplet loss in Siamese network for object tracking. In: Ferrari, V., Hebert, M., Sminchisescu, C., Weiss, Y. (eds.) ECCV 2018. LNCS, vol. 11217, pp. 472–488. Springer, Cham (2018). https://doi.org/10.1007/978-3-030-01261-8_28
11. Dumais, S.T.: Latent semantic analysis. Annu. Rev. Inf. Sci. Technol. **38**(1), 188–230 (2004)
12. Fabbri, M., Moro, G.: Dow jones trading with deep learning: the unreasonable effectiveness of recurrent neural networks. In: DATA, pp. 142–153. SciTePress (2018)
13. Formal, T., Piwowarski, B., Clinchant, S.: Match your words! a study of lexical matching in neural information retrieval. In: Hagen, M., et al. (eds.) ECIR 2022. LNCS, vol. 13186, pp. 120–127. Springer, Cham (2022). https://doi.org/10.1007/978-3-030-99739-7_14
14. Frisoni, G., Moro, G., Carbonaro, A.: A survey on event extraction for natural language understanding: Riding the biomedical literature wave. IEEE Access **9**, 160721–160757 (2021)
15. Guo, J., et al.: A deep look into neural ranking models for information retrieval. Inf. Process. Manag. **57**(6), 102067 (2020)
16. Haghighi, A., Vanderwende, L.: Exploring content models for multi-document summariza-tion. In: HLT-NAACL, pp. 362–370. The Association for Computational Linguistics (2009)
17. Henderson, M.L., et al.: Efficient natural language response suggestion for smart reply. CoRR abs/1705.00652 (2017)
18. Johnson, J., Douze, M., Jégou, H.: Billion-scale similarity search with GPUS. IEEE Trans. Big Data **7**(3), 535–547 (2021)
19. Kaya, M., Bilge, H.S.: Deep metric learning: a survey. Symmetry **11**(9), 1066 (2019)
20. Khosla, P., et al.: Supervised contrastive learning. In: NeurIPS (2020)
21. Lample, G., Conneau, A., Denoyer, L., Ranzato, M.: Unsupervised machine translation using monolingual corpora only. In: ICLR (Poster). OpenReview.net (2018)

22. Logeswaran, L., Lee, H.: An efficient framework for learning sentence representations. In: ICLR (Poster). OpenReview.net (2018)

23. Loshchilov, I., Hutter, F.: Decoupled weight decay regularization. In: 7th International Conference on Learning Representations, ICLR 2019, New Orleans, LA, USA, 6–9 May 2019. OpenReview.net (2019). http://openreview.net/forum?id=Bkg6RiCqY7

24. Magnini, B., Lavelli, A., Magnolini, S.: Comparing machine learning and deep learning approaches on NLP tasks for the Italian language. In: LREC, pp. 2110–2119. European Language Resources Association (2020)

25. Moro, G., Ragazzi, L.: Semantic self-segmentation for abstractive summarization of long documents in low-resource regimes. In: AAAI, pp. 11085–11093. AAAI Press (2022)

26. Moro, G., Ragazzi, L., Valgimigli, L., Freddi, D.: Discriminative marginalized probabilistic neural method for multi-document summarization of medical literature. In: ACL (1), pp. 180–189. Association for Computational Linguistics (2022)

27. Moro, G., Valgimigli, L.: Efficient self-supervised metric information retrieval: a bibliography based method applied to COVID literature. Sensors 21(19), 6430 (2021)

28. Palangi, H., et al.: Deep sentence embedding using long short-term memory networks: analysis and application to information retrieval. IEEE ACM Trans. Audio Speech Lang. Process. 24(4), 694–707 (2016)

29. Ramos, J., et al.: Using TF-IDF to determine word relevance in document queries. In: Proceedings of the first instructional conference on machine learning, vol. 242, pp. 29–48. Citeseer (2003)

30. Reimers, N., Gurevych, I.: Sentence-BERT: sentence embeddings using Siamese BERT-networks. In: EMNLP/IJCNLP (1), pp. 3980–3990. Association for Computational Linguistics (2019)

31. Robertson, S.E., Zaragoza, H.: The probabilistic relevance framework: BM25 and beyond. Found. Trends Inf. Retr. 3(4), 333–389 (2009)

32. Sanh, V., Debut, L., Chaumond, J., Wolf, T.: Distilbert, a distilled version of BERT: smaller, faster, cheaper and lighter. CoRR abs/1910.01108 (2019)

33. Shen, Y., He, X., Gao, J., Deng, L., Mesnil, G.: Learning semantic representations using convolutional neural networks for web search. In: WWW (Companion Volume), pp. 373–374. ACM (2014)

34. Subramanian, S., Trischler, A., Bengio, Y., Pal, C.J.: Learning general purpose distributed sentence representations via large scale multi-task learning. In: ICLR (Poster). OpenReview.net (2018)

35. Vaswani, A., et al.: Attention is all you need. In: NIPS, pp. 5998–6008 (2017)

36. Wang, X., Han, X., Huang, W., Dong, D., Scott, M.R.: Multi-similarity loss with general pair weighting for deep metric learning. In: CVPR, pp. 5022–5030. Computer Vision Foundation/IEEE (2019)

37. Xuan, H., Stylianou, A., Liu, X., Pless, R.: Hard negative examples are hard, but useful. In: Vedaldi, A., Bischof, H., Brox, T., Frahm, J.-M. (eds.) ECCV 2020. LNCS, vol. 12359, pp. 126–142. Springer, Cham (2020). https://doi.org/10.1007/978-3-030-58568-6_8

38. Yang, Z., Dai, Z., Yang, Y., Carbonell, J.G., Salakhutdinov, R., Le, Q.V.: Xlnet: generalized autoregressive pretraining for language understanding. In: NeurIPS, pp. 5754–5764 (2019)

39. Zuccon, G., Koopman, B., Bruza, P., Azzopardi, L.: Integrating and evaluating neural word embeddings in information retrieval. In: ADCS, pp. 12:1–12:8. ACM (2015)

Doctoral Symposium

Discovering Knowledge Graphs
via Attention-Driven Graph Generation

Armin Hedzic[1,2]([⊠]) [iD]

[1] Arizona State University, Tempe, AZ 85281, USA
ahedzic@asu.edu
[2] L3Harris Technologies Inc, Salt Lake City, UT 84116, USA

Abstract. Knowledge graphs are useful in many querying and knowledge management applications, and some difficult data environments have use-cases that would benefit from models that could autonomously create or modify knowledge graphs with context over multiple modalities and/or data-sets. For example, knowledge graph discovery in disconnected data with little or no existing relationship context could provide additional insights and enrich querying into the data. Additionally, a complex query itself may be best represented as a small knowledge graph in some cases. However, there are many challenges in discovering these complex relationships, especially in data-sets that cover multiple modalities. Relationship dependencies may exist at various contextual levels in the data, and some data environments have dynamic data with continuously evolving relationships and/or entities. The focus of the research is to solve challenges in this space by developing novel methods to discover or manipulate knowledge graphs to improve querying and knowledge management in difficult data environments with complex multi-modal relationships.

Keywords: Knowledge graphs · Multi-modal · Graph generation · Attention mechanisms · Neural networks

1 Introduction

Knowledge graphs are useful in many querying and knowledge management applications, and some difficult data environments have use-cases that would benefit from models that could autonomously create or modify knowledge graphs with context over multiple modalities and/or data-sets. For example, knowledge graph discovery in disconnected data with little or no existing relationship context could provide additional insights and enrich querying into the data. Knowledge management could also be improved by drawing connections between existing disconnected knowledge bases. Additionally, a complex query in a multi-modal data-set itself may be best represented as a small knowledge graph in some cases. Instead of just using keywords, consider a query consisting of an image semantically tied to keywords, or in the reverse having a query return an entity with semantically similar entities and how they may relate.

© The Author(s), under exclusive license to Springer Nature Switzerland AG 2022
T. Skopal et al. (Eds.): SISAP 2022, LNCS 13590, pp. 293–298, 2022.
https://doi.org/10.1007/978-3-031-17849-8_24

However, there are many challenges in discovering these complex relationships, especially in data-sets that cover multiple modalities. Relationship dependencies may exist at various contextual levels in the data, and some data environments have dynamic data with continuously evolving relationships and/or entities. Some relationships may be simple where only the characteristics of two entities are required to determine how they relate, but other relationships could be much more complex where nuances that define them may have a dependency on the characteristics and existing relationships over multiple neighboring entities. One focus of this research is to solve challenges in this space by developing novel methods to determine these relationships across the different possible levels of context.

Overall, the argument is that autonomous discovery and manipulation of knowledge graphs would be beneficial in a broad range of search and knowledge management use-cases and the goal of this research is to develop novel methods for creating models that would be beneficial in these data scenarios. To achieve this, a method for conditionally generating knowledge graphs is proposed that is driven by a novel hierarchical attention mechanism which intends to improve relationship discovery by attending on multiple contextual levels in the data. For the purposes of this work, a knowledge graph is defined as a heterogeneous graph with typed edges providing semantic meaning by describing entity relationships and entities of different modalities.

1.1 Problem Statement

The goal is to develop novel methods for discovering, modifying, and interpreting knowledge graphs with complex relationships that may have dependencies over multiple modalities and/or relationships for the purposes of improving similarity searches and knowledge management. Specifically, the main problem difficulty lies in discovering relationships that may be dependent on multiple contextual levels, and the goal is in finding novel mechanisms that can capture all of these contexts effectively.

2 Methodology

Given that the nature of the problem is discovering relationships between multiple data entities, the proposed methodology is to treat this as a conditional graph generation problem where the set of nodes is given, but relevant edges have to be found. To achieve this there needs to be a mechanism for constructing the graph, and a mechanism for guiding the construction conditions of the graph. The mechanism forming the construction conditions needs to be able to capture the context required to determine new relationships from existing relationships. This is where a novel hierarchical attention mechanism is proposed to attempt to capture relevant context across multiple data levels for discovering new relationships between entities. In the context of the overall problem, the following methodology describes one unit of work in graph discovery that is intended to act as a stepping stone towards a broader range of methods in discovering and manipulating knowledge graphs. However, first it is important to clarify the complexity of relationships that are intended to be discovered by going over a data set that is utilized for testing these mechanisms.

2.1 MultiModalQA Data Set

MultiModalQA (MMQA) [11] is a question answering data set generated from Wikipedia data. The questions are generated to require a joint reasoning over image, text, and table data. The data set consists of roughly 30,000 examples with diversity over dozens of domains such as science, film, sport, etc.

While the overall goal is not to perform a question answering task, the MMQA data set has some characteristics that make is suitable as a data source for the problem at hand. The MMQA data set was chosen because it has multi-modal relationships that are dependent on not only inter-entity data (ex. object in an image) but also cross-entity relationships (ex. text references a specific image). In order to utilize the data set for the problem, some pre-processing is done to convert each data entity into a feature vector to act as node features. Example graphs are then created using the relationships given in the data set to use in comparing against graphs created with the generation mechanism.

2.2 Getting Node Features

In order to utilize the previously mentioned model, node features need to obtained for each entity in the data-set. Node features are the proposed avenue for generalizing this model for different data-sets. The idea is that as long as entities in a data-set can each be converted to a single feature vector, the model could be applied. In the MMQA case pre-trained models are used to convert data entities into node features. The MMQA dataset comes with a pre-trained object detection model [1] for its image data that uses the Mask R-CNN architecture [4]. The Mask R-CNN model outputs multiple feature vectors for the objects detected in an image. To convert these feature vectors into a single vector, clustering is done on the Mask R-CNN output for the entire MMQA image corpus. Each cluster acts as a dimension in a new feature space, and for each image a single feature vector is obtained by attributing each object vector in the Mask R-CNN output to a cluster and mapping it to the new feature space. For textual data, a pre-trained FastText [5] model trained on Wikipedia data [2] is used for word embeddings, then a similar clustering approach is used to generate a single feature vector for the whole body of text.

2.3 Building Context in Iterations

Graph generation typically falls into two camps: one-shot approaches [3,6,9,10] that try to generate all the edges simultaneously, and iterative approaches [7,13] that sequentially generate edges. Approaches from the one-shot family generate graph components either independently or with weak dependency, and

while computationally efficient, can compromise the quality of the created graph
[7,8,13]. Due to complex relationships having inter-component dependencies, an
iterative approach was chosen with the idea that context can be built sequentially by first creating relatively more "obvious" edges between entities, and
on subsequent iterations leveraging the constructed context to determine more
complex relationships. As a baseline for the generation mechanism, the general
iterative method described by Li et al. [7] was used as a starting point. The
method consists of defining a set of graph operation functions, and in the conditional generation case, passing the conditional information as an input to the
functions. For the purposes of this problem, only edges need to be generated,
therefore an edge scoring model is employed to determine which two nodes are
the best candidates for a new edge. The edge scoring model uses a graph embedding of the current state of the generated graph as conditional information for
computing a score. While the scoring model consists of a simple trained linear
layer, the proposed novelty is in the generation of the graph embedding using a
hierarchical attention mechanism to guide the scoring model over the generation
loop.

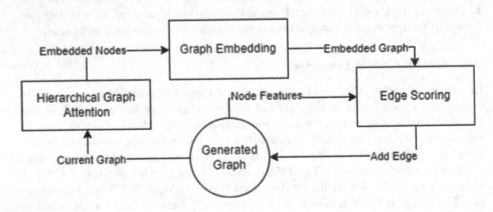

Fig. 1. The graph generation loop.

2.4   Hierarchical Graph Attention

In order to provide conditional input to the edge scoring model, the relevant
information needs to be captured. Information at different data levels is required
to determine the relationship between a question and an answer. For example,
at the relationship level an answer cannot be simply attributed to a question.
Both the question and answer must also have a relationship to a relevant piece
of context data in order to be relevant to each other. Furthermore, at the entity
level the information in a question needs to have some sort of tie to the information in a piece of data for that data to be relevant as context. With this in
mind, a hierarchical graph attention mechanism is proposed in order to capture information that would be relevant in determining new graph edges. For

the relationship level, a relational attention mechanism is utilized as described by Zhang et al. [14], supplemented by a standard graph attention layer [12] for aggregating node level data and an additional edge attention mechanism. The complete graph generation loop can be seen in Fig. 1. For training purposes the loss is determined by generating a graph embedding of the real example graph of the given nodes and the generated graph after the loop terminates. These two embeddings are used to compare how closely the generated graph matches the real graph.

3   Future Work

The current proposed approach described in previous sections is still a work in progress, and encompasses only a portion of the research goals. In the broader scheme of the research, it would be interesting to expand this work in a few ways. The proposed paths are in applying this methodology on more dynamic knowledge graphs, the discovery of knowledge graphs with latent edge relationships, and novel querying mechanisms utilizing small knowledge graphs as querying input and/or results.

In the case of dynamic knowledge graphs, the temporal aspect introduces a new set of problems. Determining which contexts are changing over time compounds the existing problem of relationship dependent context having the potential to exist at multiple data levels. Solving this problem would be very beneficial for systems that try to determine a representation of a dynamic data environment with many mobile sensors, such as in managing a fleet of autonomous vehicles.

Furthermore, the discovery of latent edges could act a method to solve the difficulties associated with combining knowledge bases constructed with different ontologies. Overcoming limitations of existing ontologies by expanding their relationships to the latent domain could provide additional insights into the data. Additionally, latent relationship discovery could lead to novel multi-modal querying methods by treating a query as relationship discovery between two knowledge graphs consisting of a small query graph and a knowledge base. The main difficulty to overcome in these approaches, in addition to previously mentioned challenges in relationship discovery, is the limitation of the discovered latent edges to only relevant relationships for the applied task.

References

1. Allenai: Allenai/multimodalqa. https://github.com/allenai/multimodalqa
2. Facebookresearch: Facebookresearch/fasttext at master. https://github.com/facebookresearch/fastText/tree/master
3. Gómez-Bombarelli, R., et al.: Automatic chemical design using a data-driven continuous representation of molecules. CoRR abs/1610.02415 (2016). http://arxiv.org/abs/1610.02415
4. He, K., Gkioxari, G., Dollár, P., Girshick, R.B.: Mask R-CNN. CoRR abs/1703.06870 (2017). http://arxiv.org/abs/1703.06870

5. Joulin, A., Grave, E., Bojanowski, P., Mikolov, T.: Bag of tricks for efficient text classification. In: Proceedings of the 15th Conference of the European Chapter of the Association for Computational Linguistics: Volume 2, Short Papers, pp. 427–431. Association for Computational Linguistics (2017)
6. Kipf, T.N., Welling, M.: Variational graph auto-encoders (2016). https://doi.org/10.48550/ARXIV.1611.07308, https://arxiv.org/abs/1611.07308
7. Li, Y., Vinyals, O., Dyer, C., Pascanu, R., Battaglia, P.W.: Learning deep generative models of graphs. CoRR abs/1803.03324 (2018). http://arxiv.org/abs/1803.03324
8. Liao, R., Li, Y., Song, Y., Wang, S., Hamilton, W.L., Duvenaud, D., Urtasun, R., Zemel, R.: Efficient Graph Generation with Graph Recurrent Attention Networks. Curran Associates Inc., Red Hook, NY, USA (2019)
9. Liu, Q., Allamanis, M., Brockschmidt, M., Gaunt, A.L.: Constrained graph variational autoencoders for molecule design. CoRR abs/1805.09076 (2018), http://arxiv.org/abs/1805.09076
10. Simonovsky, M., Komodakis, N.: Graphvae: towards generation of small graphs using variational autoencoders. CoRR abs/1802.03480 (2018). http://arxiv.org/abs/1802.03480
11. Talmor, A., et al.: Multimodalqa: complex question answering over text, tables and images. CoRR abs/2104.06039 (2021). https://arxiv.org/abs/2104.06039
12. Veličković, P., Cucurull, G., Casanova, A., Romero, A., Liò, P., Bengio, Y.: Graph attention networks (2017). https://doi.org/10.48550/ARXIV.1710.10903, https://arxiv.org/abs/1710.10903
13. You, J., Ying, R., Ren, X., Hamilton, W.L., Leskovec, J.: Graphrnn: a deep generative model for graphs. CoRR abs/1802.08773 (2018). http://arxiv.org/abs/1802.08773
14. Zhang, S., Zhang, Z., Zhuang, F., Shi, Z., Han, X.: Compressing knowledge graph embedding with relational graph auto-encoder. In: 2020 IEEE 10th International Conference on Electronics Information and Emergency Communication (ICEIEC), pp. 366–370 (2020). https://doi.org/10.1109/ICEIEC49280.2020.9152323

Visual Recommendation and Visual Search for Fashion E-Commerce

Alessandro Abluton[1,2](✉) (iD)

[1] University of Turin, 10149 Turin, TO, Italy
alessandro.abluton@unito.it
[2] Inferendo s.r.l., 15121 Alessandria, AL, Italy

Abstract. Recommender systems are historically one of the most successfull and widely known applications of AI, personalized suggestions are nowadays a valuable commercial application of such systems. Many papers have been published in this field, but it is not yet solved; these models still lack state of the art multi-modal capabilities, such as conversational or visual suggestions. In this contribution we present a novel Visual Recommendation module for fashion e-commerces capable of recommending items based on a concept of visual similarity, and a Visual Search module where users can upload a picture of some clothing and search for the most similar ones in a given e-commerce. In conclusion we discuss about the accessibility of these recommender systems for small and medium enterprises, briefly describing our idea of Recommendations-as-a-Service.

Keywords: Recommender systems · Image similarity · Deep Learning

1 Introduction

Few applications of Artificial Intelligence have seen as much commercial success as Recommender Systems; user-tailored suggestions are nowadays present in almost every aspect of our interactions with e-commerces, streaming services, newscasts, social networks and are about to enter the Web3.0 and Metaverse era. Given the astonishingly good results that such systems provided over the years it is not surprising that research on this field is flourishing and interest by both academic and industrial players is growing rapidly.

The latest trends in Recommender Systems [1] concern mostly on pushing the frontiers in several open challenges regarding conversational systems, fairness in recommendations, evaluation methods and general domain-specific enhancements. In this last context a new clear trend is the development of Visual Recommenders based on modern neural models, able to take into account the visual features of an item to make suggestions; the need for new kinds of interactions mechanism between users and e-commerces is rising, due to both a new generation of customers and to the amazing enhancements in neural networks built to handle image data.

T. Skopal et al. (Eds.): SISAP 2022, LNCS 13590, pp. 299–304, 2022.
https://doi.org/10.1007/978-3-031-17849-8_25

Another interesting topic that has not been addressed by the research community is the accessibility of these kind of services, the focus is mostly on implementing complex and resource-hungry Deep Learning systems to further enhance the quality of the suggestions. No effort is put into allowing these kind of systems to also reach Small and Medium Entreprises (SMEs), who lack resources to implement such complex systems in terms of money and data availability.

2   Visual Recommendation and Visual Search

Even if traditional recommendation approaches have proven to be accurate, efficient and easy to implement, the need for new solutions for interactions between users and e-commerces is rising. New generation of consumers are accustomed to much more complex interactions with their devices, platforms that will implement them will be rewarded on the long run.

We built a system able to perform image similarity search on top of any kind of fashion e-commerce in order to recommend the most similar-looking products. We also built an object detection module in order to add visual search capabilities to the system.

2.1   Image Similarity

The feature representation and similarity measurement, which have been thoroughly explored by multimedia researchers for decades, are key components that determine how well a content-based image retrieval system performs, this continues to be one of the most complex issues in current content-based image retrieval (CBIR) research despite a range of solutions being suggested.

Following the ideas presented by Wan et al. [3] we chose to represent item's images with embeddings in a latent space, obtained by extracting the activations of the last layers of a Convolutional Neural Network. The idea is simple, first we train a CNN on a traditional classification task, so that the network can learn to position similar items (e.g. belonging to the same class) nearby one to another in the latent space, then K-NN based search can be used to find the most similar images to a given one.

The currently implemented search is based on the *cosine distance* metric, but we plan to take into account all the tecniques available in the literature.

2.2   EfficientNet Models

The decision on which model to use led us to search for the most modern convolutional architectures available in literature, we settled on the EfficientNet [4] family of networks and we are currently still experimenting on which particular implementation to use due to the availability of 7 different EffNets (B0 to B7) with increasing levels of complexity and image resolutions they operate on. This choice depends on the typical trade-off between representation capabilities and time required to effectively train the model on a real-case dataset and to make predictions in a production environment.

We trained two different version of the same EfficientNet model: for the tasks of visual recommendation we used a dataset made of whole products images that exploits also the context around a product (dresses of different lenghts are easily distinguished when the whole figure is visible) and for visual search a dataset made of cropped products images has been used, to reduce the model context dependency. Figure 1 shows a graphical explanation.

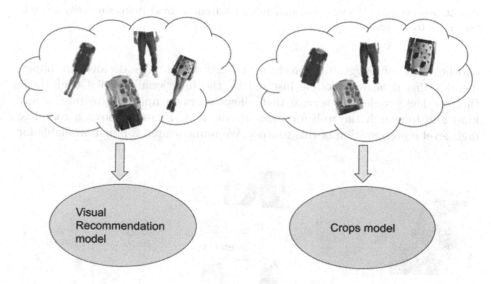

Fig. 1. Two different models are used

2.3 Visual Recommendation

In the context of fashion e-commerces *Visual Recommendation* means to be able to suggest to users the most **visually similar** items in respect to the one they are looking at. Let us consider the example situation of a user viewing the page of a Dress, in the context of visual recommendation the first image of that product (usually the most representative one) is given in input to the embedding model and an exact *K-NN* search will be performed between this and all the other images of products belonging to the same class, so for this example only dresses embeddings will be queried, Fig. 2 shows an actual example on a small e-commerce dataset.

2.4 Visual Search

Plain visual recommendations are not enough to achieve the goal of innovative interactions methods between customers and e-ecommerces, being just

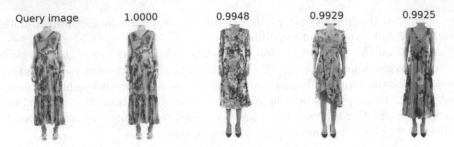

Fig. 2. An example of visual recommendations from a dress item, similarity score is shown on top of each image

another way of suggesting products to customers. We decided to implement a *Visual Search* module inspired by the functionalities of Google Lens (https://lens.google/), a service that allows users to upload a picture of any kind and to search the web for items inside of it. Figure 3 shows a complete high-level representation of this process. We implemented a plugin available for

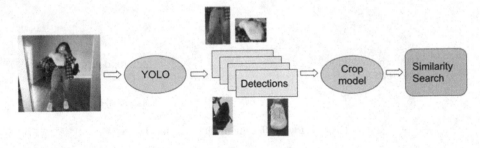

Fig. 3. High-level schema of a complete visual search process

the major e-commerce platforms in the market (Shopify, Magento, Woocommerce) that can enable this feature in any kind of fashion e-commerce. Figure 4 shows an example of the beta implementation currently available in production: users can upload a picture, items inside will be evidenced by the grey dots, when they click on one of the items the actual crop will be embedded by using the *Crop model* and the result sent to the visual recommendation module, in order to find the most similar ones in that e-commerce.

Objects inside of an image are recognized by means of the Yolo (You only look once) model [5], a well known object-detection model trained on the Open-Images dataset provided by Google [6] from which we downloaded all the images concerning the clothing categories and their relative bounding boxes.

Handling Any Fashion E-Commerce. The biggest challenge we are facing is generality with respect to all the possible categories that can be found in an e-commerce, as stated in Sect. 2.1 the convolutional network is trained on a fixed set of classes, but fashion e-commerces tend to have very different categorization of clothing with a considerable rate of errors both in terms of misplaced product classes and grammatical errors in the actual names of said categories.

To handle these problems we decided to settle on a fixed set of classes defined by us, we map each product of any e-commerce that uses our plugin on that set of classes by exploiting the classification capabilities of our CNN model. The process of training is as follows:

1. Start from a pretrained EfficientNet (on imagenet dataset).
2. Build a training dataset with our fixed set of classes, by means of manual web crawling.
3. Fine-tune the EffNet on that dataset for a classification task.

We then obtain a general model able to classify any kind of clothing picture into our set of classes, therefore able to produce embeddings with enough representative power to perform visual recommendation on any fashion e-commerce, without the need of additional fine-tuning steps for each new client.

Fig. 4. The visual search module, users can upload a picture and select items to search

3   Conclusions and Future Work

We presented a novel method for implementing visual search and recommendation on any kind of fashion e-commerce without the need of fine tuning steps and through the idea of Recommendations-as-a-Service. We built a cloud infrastructure that serves as backend for the plugins we developed, enabling virtually any kind of e-commerce on major platforms to adopt these new interactions by just installing a plugin, thus enabling SMEs with low economic budget and development resources to access these new technologies.

As future work, we plan to further develop the RaaS infrastructure in a scalable and modular way, in order to address the problem of SMEs not having enough resources to actually use these new technologies; we believe there is a niche of market yet to be filled in this regard.

Further and extensive experimentation is also still needed to enhance the quality of the visual recommenders we presented, by building better training datasets and via the implementation of some sort of continuos learning mechanism, taking into account users feedbacks on our suggestions. Finally, we would like to address some of the latest trends in recommender systems, with a particular focus on conversational and multi-modal algorithms.

References

1. Jannach, D., Pu, P., Ricci, F., Zanker, M.: Recommender systems: trends and frontiers. AI Mag. **43**, 145–50 (2022). https://doi.org/10.1002/aaai.12050
2. Koren, Y., Bell, R.: Advances in collaborative filtering. In: Ricci, F., Rokach, L., Shapira, B. (Eds.), Recommender Systems Handbook, 2nd edn., pp. 77–118 (2015)
3. Wan, J., et al: Deep learning for content-based image retrieval: a comprehensive study. In: Proceedings of the 22nd ACM International Conference on Multimedia, pp. 157–166 (2014)
4. Tan, M., Le, Q.: EfficientNet: rethinking model scaling for convolutional neural networks. In: Proceedings of the 36th International Conference on Machine Learning, pp. 6105–6114 (2019)
5. Redmon, J., Divvala, S., Girshick, R., Farhadi, A.: You only look once: unified, real-time object detection (2015). CoRR. http://arxiv.org/abs/1506.02640
6. Kuznetsova, A., et al.: The open images dataset V4. Int. J. Comput. Vision **128**(7), 1956–1981 (2020). https://doi.org/10.1007/s11263-020-01316-z

Author Index

Printed in the United States
by Baker & Taylor Publishing Services

Printed in the United States
by Baker & Taylor Publisher Services